The Book
of One

The Ancient Wisdom of Advaita

T0302996

First published by O-Books, 2010
O-Books is an imprint of John Hunt Publishing Ltd., Laurel House, Station Approach,
Alresford, Hants, SO24 9JH, UK
office1@o-books.net
www.o-books.com

For distributor details and how to order please visit the 'Ordering' section on our website.

Text copyright: Dennis Waite 2009

ISBN: 978 1 84694 347 8

A CIP catalogue record for this book is available from the British Library.

Design: Stuart Davies

Printed in the UK by CPI Antony Rowe
Printed in the USA by Offset Paperback Mfrs, Inc

The Book of One

The Ancient Wisdom of Advaita

Dennis Waite

BOOKS

Winchester, UK
Washington, USA

Contents

Angels and Demons

If you are wondering about the cover of the book, it utilizes the 'ambigram'
– a word that reads the same from a different direction or orientation. The
ambigram is a particularly potent symbol for this book for three reasons:

. it presents the appearance of duality but, on investigation is found to be
only one. In this sense, it is a metaphor for the non-dual reality in which
are resolved all seeming opposites –both good and bad, angels and
demons.

. the recognition that the symbol is an ambigram does not usually occur
immediately. It is only after a period of study and contemplation that the
realization suddenly occurs. In this sense, it is a metaphor for the enlight-
enment that takes place in the mind on the dawning of Self-knowledge.

. appearances should not be taken at face value. If we look beyond the
name and form, we may discover the unity behind the outward show.

May the reader find in this book the resolution of seeming opposites and
the dawn of enlightenment. May the seeming duality resolve into the non-
duality of Advaita.

(Special thanks go to John Langdon, the designer, who popularized the
ambigram in the book 'Angels and Demons' by Dan Brown, and to Hari
Kiran Vadlamani, who commissioned the original 'advaita' ambigram for
his own company and subsequently the triple ambigram for the book
cover.)

Endorsements

(for the first edition of the book)

Dennis Waite has written a masterful and profoundly insightful survey of the Advaita Vedanta Teaching and the Contemporary Scene. This book will greatly contribute to a deeper understanding of this important movement, sweeping the West, and which eventually leads to Self Realization. **Alan Jacobs**, Chairman , Ramana Maharshi Foundation UK

There are many places to find advaita teachings - in ancient texts, modern books, in satsang, and on the Internet. Dennis Waite has found them all. He writes as a friendly tour guide, presenting the teachings with simplicity, humor and deep understanding. The appendices alone are worth the price of admission, and contain a wealth of reference material available nowhere else. **Greg Goode, PhD (Philosophy)**, Philosophical Counselor, New York

A refreshing approach to Advaita from a Western point of view. a personal, structured approach to a very difficult topic. **Jay Lakhani**, Vivekananda Centre, London

The Book of One' is a sweeping, fresh overview of consciousness subjects shaping the path of Advaita Vedanta. Topics are handled with confidence, and their most non-dual depths are struck effortlessly. Waite offers Advaita as a resolver of the problems of life and death. The book is practical, grounded in scripture, and respectful of the reader's inclination - whether active, meditative, intellectual or devotional - and his level of familiarity. It is directed toward beginning seekers, researchers, students of philosophy or religion, those who are already familiar with Advaita and those already Self-realized who enjoy keeping up with what's being written. If you take yellow brick roads that wind through Internet fields, this book will be particularly valuable and interesting.

Unique about this book is the confident and graceful manner in which the author integrates and moves between Western, Eastern, and, if you will,

Cyber influences. It is clear that Waite himself is intimate with the terrain of the Himalayas of Cyberspace, the paths, people, and places. This book has the fluidity of the World Wide Web. He creates a swirl in which the ancient familiarity felt with sages such as Ramana or Nisargadatta, is transferred to Kant, Schopenhauer, Berkeley and Plato. This role of the internet and Western thought upon Waite's work is related to his intellectual and spiritual relationship with Dr. Gregory Goode, who is a teacher in New York, scholar in Western philosophy, and pioneer/participant in Non-duality on the internet.

'The Book of One' is framed by an exceptional Table of Contents and Appendices/Index. The TOC itself serves as an excellent introduction to the book and shows how carefully the author constructed this work. As well, there are numerous pages of recommended Websites. **Jerry Katz**, Owner of the first and largest non-dual website; author of 'One: Essential Writings on Nonduality'

'The Book of One' takes the reader step by step on an intellectual inquiry of the truth of oneself. It provides a critical examination of the meaning and purpose of one's life. This is one book that needs to be studied again and again. I must say, I thoroughly enjoyed studying this intellectually stimulating book. **Dr. Kuntimaddi Sadananda**, *AchArya* at the Washington Chinmaya Mission

An excellent understanding with many good analogies of a tricky subject to write about. Dennis invites the reader through careful examination to see through our usual sense of ourselves to what is real. **Isaac Shapiro**, Satsang teacher; author of 'Outbreak of Peace' and 'It Happens By Itself'

It is an impressive piece of work and the style is clear and has humor woven into it. It gives loads of information without feeling heavy. **Leo Hartong**, author of 'Awakening to the Dream'

I am very much enjoying your exquisite and erudite book on Advaita. I have

been savoring the thorough and razor sharp insights! A bow of gratitude for your love of truth. **Pamela Wilson**, satsang teacher

The Book of One is a masterful, comprehensive and pragmatic guide to non-duality. Dennis writes in an intimate manner, which makes it a joy to read. I especially enjoyed his skilful use of parables and metaphors. His accurate study is well documented and referenced, with excellent appendices, which serve as a fine resource for readers. I highly recommend The Book of One to those who are open to the Unknown. **Katie Davis**, satsang teacher; author of 'Awake Living Joy'

Congratulations on your book: 'The Book Of One' which is an interesting and erudite overview of the whole subject of Advaita. **Roy Whenary**, author of 'The Texture of Being'

Dennis Waite is Advaita, "not two." First and foremost, Dennis is an extremely talented writer, who is clearly devoted to his subject – the Truth of Being and its realization. If, up until now, you have missed the profound meaning and import of this cornerstone of Eastern Philosophy, The Book Of One will serve as your One needed teaching and reference guide. Dennis literally brings together a world of existing wisdom in this incisive and eloquently crafted writing, that offers every reader the supreme opportunity of an authentic life. **Sundance Burke**, satsang teacher; author of 'Simply Being Free'

His book is the most masterful and all-inclusive source that I have found to date for those studying Non-Duality. **Floyd Henderson**, author of numerous books on self-help and non-duality

A common element of Western society in recent times has been the tendency to adopt trends, and in order for these trends to become accessible for a culture dominated by materialism and rampant distractions, the direction has usually been toward the superficial, that is, presenting these trends in an increasingly superficial light. This applies in most areas and certainly in the field of spiritual teachings. Zen Buddhism made inroads in the West in the mid-20th century, and was popular in the 60s and 70s, much as Tibetan Buddhism became in the 80s and 90s. But in both cases the tendency to reduce these teachings into very simple elements has been a double-edged sword. The problem with simplifying is that a failure to understand the philosophic basis of the teachings easily happens, resulting in a "feel-good" mysticism that conveniently glosses over the one quality essential for bona fide spiritual deepening— commitment. Without being committed to awakening, without prioritizing it in one's life, there is little hope in realizing it.

In more recent decades Advaita Vedanta has joined Zen and Tibetan Buddhism in the Western market place, and the field is now busy with many teachers of Advaita and books on Advaita. Many of these are good but few — almost none of those written in a popular manner for Westerners—has bothered to delve deeply and fully into the philosophic foundation of Advaita. Dennis Waite's book "The Book of One" does exactly this. In covering the teachings in such an exhaustive fashion he prevents a super-ficial view of non-dualism from seeping in. In contrasting Advaita with some of the teachings of the Western philosophic tradition, Dennis also helps us to avoid simply "reinventing the wheel" by illustrating the universal nature of intelligence and how, ultimately, there are no original thoughts anywhere, precisely because the individual is an illusion, which is itself the very core of non-dualism anyway.

I recommend "The Book Of One" for all serious students of the great tradition of Non-dual spirituality, as an essential roadmap into the infinite realm of Consciousness, and the realization of our identity as that. **Philip T. Mistlberger**, author of 'A Natural Awakening'

There are many books on the market that focus on the theme of advaita (non-duality). However, what separates Waite's book from the others is his meticulous and yet practical approach to its theory and practice. Many modern schools of advaita advocate the 'nothing to do, nowhere to go' approach - this is fine in itself but can be greatly misunderstood to be a form of hedonistic fatalism. Whilst acknowledging that, ultimately, the ego is a non entity, Waite offers useful techniques and delineated steps along the path to freedom. Written in an elegant and accessible style, 'The Book of One' is, in my opinion, the standard 'text book' for modern-day advaita. Highly recommended. **Paula Marvelly**, author of 'The Teachers of One' and 'Women of Wisdom'

I would like to thank you very much for the 'Book of One'. I stumbled upon it at some point after 'the jungle', and coming from nothing with no background in all this, it was actually extremely helpful in supplying concepts with which to parse what came unasked. I particularly liked the discussion of the difference between reality and appearance in terms of sublation - helping to fill in the questions to the answer as it were. Your writing is sound and good, finding a way through the chaos of teachings and hand-me-downs. **David Carse**, author of 'Perfect Brilliant Stillness'

Advaita Vedanta has been examined and explained by numerous sages and philosophers over the past three thousand years; and each writer on this theme does so with his own style and signature. Dennis Waite has written 'The Book of One' in an admirably reasoned and contemporary style, producing one of the most cogent and methodical expositions of Advaita Vedanta yet written.

Understanding and Self-realization are not the same. However, there is an indelible link between the two. Intellectual understanding opens wide the consciousness of a new and wondrous perspective, and sets the stage for direct apperception, for clarity of awareness, for re-cognition of eternal Truth. It is understanding which awakens the subtler faculties of awe and intuitive knowing. As Mr. Waite points out, hearing or reading the words of the enlightened is essential for an awakening of consciousness, and Mr. Waite's 'The Book of One' is carefully crafted to provide one of the most excellent sources of understanding available. I highly recommend it to the contemporary student requiring a thorough introductory guide to the philosophy of Advaita (Non-Dualistic) Vedanta.

Postscript: I am struck by both the similarities and the dissimilarities of this book with my own book on the same subject (The Wisdom of Vedanta, first published in 1991 and to be re-released by O Books in July, 2006). The similarities appear in our common understanding of the basic principles of Vedanta, and the dissimilarities appear in our temperaments: his being predominantly that of a j~nAnI (or knower); and mine being predominantly that of a bhakta (or lover). In nearly all of my writings, I have discussed the fact that, while it is necessary to develop both sides of one's nature, everyone is predisposed to a predominant temperamental inclination toward one approach to Reality or the other; either j~nAna or bhakti. One of the best examples of this difference in temperaments is found in Sri Ramakrishna (a bhakta*) and his esteemed disciple, Swami Vivekananda (who was a j~nAnI). One may cite also as exemplars of this temperamental opposition Paramahamsa Yogananda (a* bhakta*) and Sri Ramana Maharshi (a* j~nAnI*).*

Mr. Waite acknowledges these two 'paths' as dependent on temperament, but seems to relegate the bhakti *'path' to a position inferior to his own 'path' of* j~nAna, *and gives it very short shrift. From my observations, it is usually the* bhakta *who acknowledges both 'paths' as valid, and the* j~nAnI-s *who maintain their own path as superior. I suppose that is only to be expected. Whether love or knowledge is viewed as superior, again, seems to be linked to one's own temperamental preference, neither having that status in any absolute sense. My thought is that, in the most perfect circumstance, the two blend together to form a sweet but unnamable state of being.* **S. Abhayananda**, author of 'History of Mysticism', 'The Supreme Self', 'The Wisdom of Vedanta'

FOREWORD

Why should not we also enjoy an original relation to the universe? Why should not we have a poetry and philosophy of insight and not of tradition, and a religion by revelation to us, and not the history of theirs? (Emerson, 'Nature')

It is likely that some essential curiosity about yourself or life's purpose has led you to this work on Advaita. Why might you find this book helpful? Within these pages is a clear explanation of something of great benefit to any inquiring person: a systematic approach to experiencing the connectedness of all things and the wholeness of oneself.

Most of us are driven by the mechanics and bustle of daily existence, putting one foot in front of the other, reacting to events as we tumble through them. Moments of introspection or self-examination are infrequent or ineffective. We sense the possibility of a certain deep satisfaction, of self-understanding, of a fuller life, and yet find these goals elusive amidst the pressures of ordinary living.

And yet for some there is a quiet urge to find a deeper meaning, often working subconsciously. Maybe that's why you hold this book. If so, you will find described herein one of the best systems of thought and practice ever formulated for directly understanding the essential nature of yourself.

The Self is not known through discourse, splitting of hairs, learning however great. He comes to the man He loves; takes that man's body as His own... He who has found Him, seeks no more; the riddle is solved; desire gone, he is at peace. Having approached from everywhere that which is everywhere, whole, he passes into the Whole... As rivers lose name and shape in the sea, wise men lose name and shape in God, glittering beyond all distance.
(Mundaka Upanishad, Book III, Chapter 2)

What is Advaita? Simply put, it is a philosophical and practical system aimed at self knowledge. The word has many meanings, which may be conceptualized initially as unity, truth, awareness, joy, but which are ultimately realized in self experience beyond concepts. At that point, Advaita is an indescribable knowledge of one's own being, beyond constraint, form or history, simply present in all things. It is freedom, peace, joy, everything and nothing. It is the experience of the world as oneself and oneself as all things. It cannot be taught, demonstrated, claimed or even captured in a book such as this one – it can only be indicated. You must then find it for yourself.

This inability to convey deep experience by words or thoughts is a common enough phenomenon. Consider love or joy – who could convey the experience to another? It can be described, and then when you experience it you realize what was being indicated. So it is with Advaita, a term used to refer to both the ineffable conscious reality of the 'world as self' as well as to the system of thought and practice that can help you find this experience on your own. This dual reference inherent in the term Advaita— both to the indescribable and to the description, goal and path —is a constant source of confusion, amusement and online disputations. Thus Lao Tzu opens the Tao Te Ching with the statement *"The Tao that can be spoken of is not the Tao."*

In the tradition of Advaita, this is known as a 'leading error', or *saMvAdi bhrama* (see *vidyAraNya's pa~nchadashI*, Chapter 9 for details). A leading error is something that's not quite right, but which ultimately leads you to that which is right. So the system of Advaita, including this work, is not the actual Advaita, but nonetheless can lead you to the experience of your true being and unity with all things. Remembering this is very helpful, as it prevents attachment to the system and its proponents and adherents, and keeps you free to move on. A boat may be used to cross a river, but who would carry the boat thereafter on their backs?

Nonetheless, a few compassionate sorts look after the boats out of the joy of seeing some travelers find freedom. Hence this able book, a gift of insight for the wayfarer seeking to cross the confusions of existence. Do approach it with an open mind and heart, for the study and practice of the Advaita tradition can lead you beyond any such system to experience directly for yourself the truth echoed in the world's many spiritual traditions. This book and its companion works *How to Meet Yourself* and *Back to the Truth* form one of the most approachable and clear expressions of the Advaita tradition available in English, and studying them is almost as useful as finding yourself in the presence of an affable and accomplished sage.

What is not in this book, in addition to direct experience? What will you have to find or do on your own? Firstly, some study of the tradition itself, from traditional sources as well as such helpful sites as www.advaita.org.uk (soon to be replaced by www.advaita-academy.org). Secondly, the will to do some work, for Advaita is not a magic answer but a system of practice—which means you *do* have to practice! Thirdly, clarity in self examination: introspection, both intellectual and emotional, is what clarifies self knowledge and allows it to deepen. This takes time, application and occasionally some assistance. Finally, some assistance with meditation, a variety of specific practices that are used extensively in the tradition, and which cannot really be conveyed by the written word. It is quite helpful to find a teacher who can provide you the grace of initiation into the various forms of meditation, instruct you in the related disciplines and provide support and insight until you feel confident in your practice.

I wish you great fortune in these endeavors.

We shall not cease from exploration
And the end of all our exploring
Will be to arrive where we started
And know the place for the first time.
... A condition of complete simplicity
(Costing not less than everything)...   (T.S. Eliot, Little Gidding)

John Lehmann, Advaita Meditation Center
(www.advaitameditation.org), Boston, Massachusetts, USA

Preface to Second Edition

There is nothing so good that it cannot be improved upon, apart from the absolute truth. Me

I welcomed the opportunity to produce a new edition of 'Book of One' because it gave me the opportunity to read it afresh. And it is a novel experience, reading one's own material over six years after having written it, so that it seems almost as though it had been written by someone else. It is especially satisfying because I discovered that it is actually rather good – and it seems that I can say that without immodesty because of the time lapse. I have read very many books on Advaita and reviewed quite a number of these. I know how rarely it is possible, unreservedly to endorse a book. There are always niggles and queries and the thought 'I could have explained that much better'. But this book was relatively niggle-free! And there is a very good reason why that should have been so. Up until a few years prior to writing it, I had been a member of the School of Economic Science (School of Practical Philosophy in the US), where I had been studying and teaching for many years. And, for a large part of that time, I had not known exactly what it was I was studying. The word 'Advaita' was not used in the early days and I had searched through Western philosophical texts, looking for the source without success. More significantly however, when I did eventually discover Advaita and begin to read about it for myself, I found numerous mismatches and aspects of the School's teaching that did not seem reasonable.

For example, the classes at the School were separated into 'Gentlemen' and 'Ladies' groups after a number of years because, it was explained, gentlemen were of the nature of *puruSha* (spirit), while ladies nature was that of *prakRRiti* (primary matter). It was only very much later that I discovered that this strange idea belongs to the dualistic *sAMkhya* philosophy and has nothing to do with Advaita. Also, they made much of 'sound', putting considerable emphasis on this as a motive power in the universe (which was literally 'spoken into creation'). Again, I discovered that this belongs to another alien philosophy called *sphoTa vAda*. The terminology used by the School often did not seem to tally with that used in the books that I read. Eventually I realized that, although Advaita might be the central teaching, this was mixed to a considerable degree with concepts and terms from *sAMkhya, yoga, sphoTa vAda* and others so that the net result was confusion. I left in 1998. (It should be noted that the school has continued to develop, now being guided by a different source in India and many or all of these problems may now have been rectified. I freely admit that I do not know and certainly would not wish to criticize them unfairly. After all, they were the principal impetus for my truth-finding mission and for this I will always be grateful.)

Accordingly, my primary purpose in writing this book was to set down clearly, for my own benefit, the key aspects of Advaita according to the traditional sources, endeavoring to avoid as far as possible introducing any alien teachings. I wanted to supplement those ideas by borrowing from any sources that I had encountered, which I had found particularly illuminating. And I wanted to make the presentation as readable as possible, using the best of all of the stories, metaphors and even jokes that I had come across so that a reader unfamiliar with Advaita would find the book entertaining but also be encouraged to pursue the subject further. And I like to think that this succeeded.

But all of this is not to say that something that is 'rather good' cannot be improved upon. It was bound to be the case that I was sometimes mistaken and put forward a topic as being Advaita when it wasn't really. Also, although I had learned a great deal, there were still aspects about which I was unsure. I now have the benefit of more than six years more reading and study, several more books written, and several hundred 'difficult' questions answered at my website. I now felt confident that I could correct any errors, clarify any aspects that were previously insufficiently well explained and add new topics where they might have been unintentionally omitted. So, given the opportunity by my publisher, that is exactly what I have done!

Briefly, the categories of changes that have been made are as follows:

. New chapters on *Ishvara* and Neo-advaita.

. New topics: Sheaths, Behavioral Tendencies, *dharma*, dream metaphor, gold – ring metaphor, *mithyA*, What is Enlightenment, *jIvanmukti*. Other topics have been rewritten or much expanded.

. Any parts that I thought confusing, misleading or superfluous have been deleted or re-written.

. New stories, metaphors and quotations have been added.

. Many topics have been expanded where this enhances the overall presentation.

. A number of new extracts have been added (from books read since the first edition) to provide additional interest, clarity and reinforcing argument.

.The Sanskrit Glossary has been considerably expanded and also now shows the actual Sanskrit script (Devanagari), which was not possible in the first edition.

. The Appendix of Internet Links has been revised, updated and considerably expanded – there are now many more websites than existed when the first edition was written.

. The Appendix of Recommended Reading has been revised, updated and expanded.

. Italicized ITRANS spellings of Sanskrit words have been used throughout (i.e. the Anglicized versions that were used in the First Edition have been removed), apart from a few exceptions such as proper names and the word 'Advaita'.

. The spelling has been changed to US English (apologies to UK readers but this is to suit the majority of readers).

. The text has been reworded throughout wherever there was potential confusion or poor sentence structure.

. Corrections to grammar etc. have been made as appropriate.

. Overall, the word count has increased from around 115,000 to over 150,000 and the Bibliography from 69 books to 144.

Preface to First Edition

Life is a moderately good play with a badly written third act. Truman
Capote

It might seem strange, when you think that people have been asking
questions about the meaning of life ever since they were able to ask
questions, that they do not seem to have been able to find any clear
answers. Western philosophy can be traced back to ancient Greece well
over 2000 years ago but it is almost as though, as time has progressed,
consensus about the answers has diminished rather than increased. In the
last century, mainstream science seems to have dictated the way that we
think and has led many to believe that all of human experience will
ultimately be understandable in purely material terms – even consciousness
is only 'an epiphenomenon of matter'. Deep down, most of us are less than
happy with this! (Note for second edition: This 'epiphenomenon of matter'
idea was actually a belief of the materialists or *chArvAka-s* in Shankara's
time and he refuted the idea convincingly in his Brahma Sutra *bhAShya*
III.iii.54.)

Once, people turned towards religions to provide them with answers. It
is almost certainly true that the founders of those religions did have direct
knowledge of universal truths. Unfortunately, after they died, knowledge
was often communicated only via litany and 'holy books' to priests and
committees, who then passed on only such information as they themselves
understood, or deemed acceptable, to the devotees.

It seems logical to assume that only someone who is alive *now* and has
discovered the answers for themselves can genuinely be in a position to
guide others. Are there such people out there? If it is possible to discover
universal truths and if some have done so from time to time throughout
history, then surely there must be some alive today who have also done so
– after all, there are more people, education is better and so on. If you
peruse the shelves of the 'New Age' bookshops, you will quickly come
across many books that claim to have the answers and their notice boards

7

will announce talks and meetings with various people who declare that they have 'found the truth'. How are we to differentiate and find those books and teachers who are able to help?

Even the richest Western traditions seem to lose their way for periods – and people may consequently become disillusioned. The past fifty years or so seems to be one such period and many have turned to the East in search of firm foundations for investigation and for some sort of 'spiritual path' that has been validated actually to lead somewhere. One of the most ancient of these, which, once understood, could also be found at the heart of all of the others, is called Advaita. It is this tradition that is used in this book to provide the answers to the questions of 'life, the universe and everything'.

In essence it is a breathtakingly simple approach and has the immediate, intuitive ring of truth. It is very practical, yet offers explanations satisfying to the intellect. Because it does originate deep in India's past, however, when the language of philosophy was Sanskrit, there are a few, unfamiliar concepts and a number of words that are not easily expressed in English. In order fully to benefit from this teaching, it is necessary therefore to make a little effort to learn these new terms. They are fully explained, as they are introduced, and there is a comprehensive glossary at the back of the book. Where appropriate, the relevant Sanskrit word may be given even when the English equivalent is quite acceptable. Here, the reason is that, if you read other books on the subject, especially those translated from Sanskrit or more recent Indian languages, you are quite likely to encounter *only* the Sanskrit term and you will be expected to understand it. Also, if you decide to join one of the email groups on the Internet, you will find that many writers use these words automatically.

It is often said of religions and philosophies that there are many paths up the mountain but all lead to the same place. Some are also more arduous than others! Advaita provides a simple and elegant framework within which all of the problems of life and death may be understood and resolved. The answers are ultimately surprising and a great relief. So, put aside your prejudices, open up your mind to new possibilities, and enjoy! Life, above all, should be happy – and the meaning of this will be addressed later.

A word of warning to the unwary, however: You are about to embark upon a journey from which you, the ego, can never return...

1. Introduction

There is a prayer in one of the most ancient of documents – the Brihadaranyaka Upanishad:

Lead me from the unreal to the real,
Lead me from darkness into light,
Lead me from death to immortality.

Its implication is clear. In our present state, we are ignorant of our true nature. We believe ourselves to be limited individuals, with vulnerable bodies and uninformed minds, condemned to a relatively short and frequently miserable existence in a largely inhospitable world. In virtually every generation however, there are a few people who see beyond this and discover how things really are. Though they may express this knowledge in slightly different ways, what they tell us is essentially the same, namely that we are completely mistaken in our current understanding. It is the purpose of this book to present these findings and to describe the disciplines that are open to enable us to discover the truth for ourselves.

The material is split into three sections. The first, 'The Unreal', describes how things appear to be to us now: who we think we are, what we typically want out of life and the means by which we try to achieve this. The second, 'The Spiritual Path', details the techniques and disciplines described by the scriptures and Sages within the Advaitic tradition, which are available to help us understand who we really are. The third section, 'The Real', explains how it is that we are unable to see reality now and why we are so mistaken in our present view of the world. The process by which we may realize the truth is looked at more closely, along with concepts such as cause and effect, and free will. Finally, our true nature is revealed and the nature of Consciousness itself investigated, as far as this is possible. Appendices look at the many sources available for finding more information and at the scheme used for representing Sanskrit in an Anglicized version (there is also a full glossary of all of the terms used in this book).

Why Advaita?

You may not have heard of Advaita before. It is pronounced 'Ad-wighta' in the UK or 'Ad-vighta' in the US, with the second syllable rhyming with 'might' in both cases. You will naturally wish to know what it is and why you should pay attention to what it can tell us. All religions and many philosophers have offered explanations for life and prescriptions for how to lead it. Why should we pay any more attention to this version?

Advaita is one of the branches of Hindu philosophy. Very similar ideas are expressed in Sufism, the intellectual branch of Islam, in Taoism, Madhyamika and Zen Buddhism and in the more esoteric of Christian doctrines, e.g. the Gospel according to St. Thomas discovered amongst the Dead Sea scrolls. The writings of many philosophers show that they, too, reached similar conclusions, e.g. early Greek Philosophers such as Parmenides, the Romantic Idealists Hegel, Schelling and F. H. Bradley, and mystics such as Master Eckhart. Quotations from the key texts of most religions can easily be found, which suggest that this truth was known to them but that it was surrounded by ritual or deliberately hidden by the priests for their own purposes.

In fact, I should point out now (and this is one of the numerous clarifications/ additions made to this second edition) that Advaita is not, strictly speaking, a 'philosophy', although it is often referred to as this. A better noun would be 'teaching'. Swami Paramarthananda who, together with his guru Swami Dayananda, I now regard as the person who has contributed most to my understanding of the subtler aspects, speaks of it as a *pramANa*, which can be translated as a 'means of obtaining knowledge'. Advaita effectively provides a proven methodology for bringing about Self-knowledge. We begin with the firm belief that there is a separate world, containing separate people. Through successive stages of deconstruction, Advaita questions our experience and explains in a reasoned manner what is the true nature of reality.

An analogy might be that of a child seeing a magic illusion, for example the 'sawing in half' of a lady. He sees the lady climb into an empty box; he sees her head and feet protruding from the ends and he watches as the magician saws through the box and moves the two halves apart. What he sees is indubitable and, in his naivety, he is forced to believe it to be true. If the child is intelligent, however, we may then draw diagrams showing the construction of the cabinet, and explain how there is a second lady already in the box behind a panel that is not visible because of the use of mirrors.

We are in the position of that child, seeing the world of objects and believing them to have a separate reality; seeing people being born and dying and believing them to have a separate and limited existence. Advaita explains how this is an appearance only, similar to that of the sun rising and setting. Despite the appearance, it is not actually like that at all.

The full title of the teaching is 'Advaita Vedanta'. 'Vedanta' simply means that it derives from the scriptures that form the last part (*anta* means 'end') of the Vedas, the four sacred texts of the Hindu religion. (It should also be noted that this really means the 'final conclusion' – *siddhAnta* – of the Vedas, since Upanishads may occur in the physical middle of a Veda rather than the end.) It is not itself a religion, however – there are no churches or priests. The first parts of the Vedas does contain rituals and so on but Advaita does not itself rely on these. They may, nevertheless provide a valuable source of 'preparation' for the mind. These aspects will be explained in Section 2.

If, after reading this book, you decide that the philosophy appeals to you, you may wish actively to pursue it. This is because, although you may relatively easily gain an intellectual appreciation of what is said, the full import is most unlikely to become immediately apparent. There are various ways in which practical 'research' may be done and some of these are described in more detail. Appendix 1 contains a comprehensive list of pointers to further avenues – organizations that may be joined, E-Group discussions on the Internet, sources of information on all aspects – and Appendix 2 suggests some recommended reading.

Advaita is an extremely simple philosophy. Its complete essence is summed up in its Sanskrit name: *a* – not, *dvaita* – duality. In a very real sense, there is no need for a book to try to explain it. It can all be summed up in a single sentence: "There are not two things." A well-known teacher of Advaita, Robert Adams, summed it up like this:

"Everything is Consciousness – everything. When you ask what is Consciousness, there is no valid answer. When someone asks me to write a book or give a lecture, then I have to explain Consciousness in about fifty different words, and each word has another fifty words to explain that, then those words have another fifty words. So your volume of the book is written. What does it say? 'Everything is Consciousness.' I could have written one page. And in the middle of that page I would say: 'Everything is Consciousness,' and the rest would be blank." (Ref. 70)

What do we want from life?

Everyone wants something, usually many things, most of the time. Picking up this book now, even if it is not at the forefront of your mind, you will have some idea of what it is that might bring you satisfaction. It is interesting that, when we use the word 'satisfaction', we often qualify it by the phrase 'short-term' or 'long-term'. It is as though we know that it is not possible to obtain 'permanent' satisfaction, only something which lasts a finite time before it is replaced by the more usual status quo. "I can't get no satisfaction" was the cry of the nineteen sixties' Rolling Stones' hit and it seems that youth ever since then has been trying desperately to prove that sentiment wrong.

There are several categories of people in respect of answering the question 'What do you really want?' There are the younger ones, with their whole lives in front of them; a potentially infinite vista of possibilities stretching before them: 'What should I go for to make the most of my life?' Then there are the older ones, with most of a lifetime of experience behind them; some ambitions achieved and some cherished dreams abandoned: 'What must I do to avoid the danger of regret for lost hopes?' In between these two extremes, there are the people who, perhaps, have committed themselves to some degree but may still change direction to find fulfillment. Perhaps you have, once or twice, actually succeeded in achieving your aim! But, despair, you found that it did not bring quite the expected level of happiness that you had imagined. Disappointed once or several times, you may have begun to consider the possibility that the desire of the moment is possibly not what you really want at all.

People seem to want to 'make a name for themselves'. They want to 'live on in posterity' with their name on a book in the library. They want to be able to say 'I am one of the few people who have climbed Everest, run 100 meters in under 10 seconds' or whatever. Or they want to say 'I am the most beautiful woman in the country' or have the most expensive car and so on. We seek status, admiration, and respect; want to feel more important, be more intelligent, and be able to 'drink everyone under the table' or 'take on all comers'. Just look at a copy of the 'Guinness Book of Records' to see some of the ludicrous things that people do in order to get their name in that book and be recognized as someone who has achieved dubious notoriety. Why?

Two things are infinite: the universe and human stupidity; and I'm not sure about the universe. Albert Einstein

Most people, at any given time in their life, usually have a pretty good idea of what it is that they want. If only they could have x or reach y, that would be *it*. They would have achieved fulfillment, at last be contented and able to relax. They might spend large portions of the day, dreaming about these desired objects or states and devote much of their efforts working towards them by whatever means are available or likely to bear fruit. In many cases, no doubt, people live their entire lives in pursuit of their elusive aims only to die frustrated. Perhaps these are the lucky ones – at least they still have their hope! Sometimes, objectives are achieved… and then what?

[My book 'How to Meet Yourself (and find true happiness)' (Ref. 71), looks at the topics of meaning, purpose and fulfillment in life. It uses the findings of sociological surveys, evolutionary psychology and western philosophy to point towards the truth and to introduce the philosophy of Advaita. For details and extracts, see:

http://www.Advaita.org.uk/discourses/meet_yourself/meet_yourself.htm]

There are not so many areas into which these most valued desires, ambitions or aims fall. Here are some general categories (some of which may overlap – and you may not always agree with the section into which I place them but it doesn't really matter very much):

- **Body** – I want to be healthy, thin etc; I want to run a mile in under four minutes; be beautiful – whatever that means; I don't want to get/be old (not much we can do about that one).
- **Material** – I want a Porsche; a big house in the country, with a swimming pool and a tennis court and a wood behind and at least two bathrooms and...
- **Mind/Intellect** – I want to get a degree; be able to understand quantum mechanics / Picasso / Wittgenstein / The Simpsons; I want to be self-confident.
- **Emotional/Self-esteem** – I want people to like me; find my soul-mate (and live happily ever after); I don't want to be afraid of _____ (fill in your least-favorite thing); I want to write a best-selling book on Advaita philosophy and become famous.
- **Spiritual** – I want to go to heaven; be a better person; see God.

You will probably think that many of these, in whichever category, can be summed up by the simple sentiment 'I want to be happy'. And this is so, though what exactly we mean by the word 'happy' merits some later discussion. Many people however, come to realize that most of our wants are either beyond the possibility of attainment or that, even if they *are* satisfied, the resulting 'happiness' will be short-lived. Eventually, such a seeker recognizes that all but the desires of a spiritual nature are ultimately of no consequence. It is the 'big questions' that really matter: Who am I? Why am I here and what should I do? What will happen to me after death? It is questions such as these that form the subject of this book. It will aim to tell you just what it is that you *really* want. And, if you are one of those strange individuals that wants to know the end of a book before you have even started it, it will also attempt to convince you that you already have this mysterious 'something' now!

We do not really understand the true meaning of many of the words that we commonly use. In fact, we are often *mis-taken* – we take them amiss. We are *ignor-ant* – we are ignoring or turning away from the truth. We need to *re-cognize,* or know again, the situation for what it really is. We have to *re-member* who we really are, i.e. put together the seemingly separate bits into the unity from which they originated. You see how it is that most of us have even forgotten the true meaning of our own language.

We'll begin by looking at who or what we think we are. By showing up our mistaken views we will be able quickly to dispense with some of the more basic of the wants in the list above. Some of the others are more tenacious and, in order to throw those off as well, we will have to delve more deeply into the nature of the world around us and our place in it. Along the way, we will see what (if anything) can be understood about reality itself and find out what is meant by lots of interesting things such as ignorance, truth, consciousness and action. Some deeply entrenched ideas will be challenged by questions such as: 'can we actually choose to do anything at all?' and 'does it make any difference anyway?'

The journey is full of interest and mental stimulation; is hopefully entertaining; may shatter a few sub-consciously cherished illusions; is the only worthwhile thing doing; is life. And the end may be both surprising and a tremendous relief.

SECTION 1 – The Unreal

2. What I am not

Talk to a man about himself and he will listen for hours.
Benjamin Disraeli

When we say 'I want...', we think we know something about this. But who is the 'I' that supposedly wants them? Although you may have thought 'of course I know who I am', this book aims to rectify that. As you read more about the philosophy of Advaita, you will discover that things are rarely as they first appear and our true nature is very much more profound than most of us appreciate.

You will have difficulty accepting some of the following. Some of the reasons for this are opinion, belief and habit. Your parents will have told you much; schools and universities will have added to and revised this. You may have read lots of books, containing other people's ideas, and the media try to tell you all sorts of rubbish every day. You need to try to drop this. Do not accept anyone's ideas or opinions – especially your own, and including mine – until you have consciously and dispassionately exercised reason and discrimination with a still mind. Do not trust your thoughts – thinking is a most dangerous pastime and should be avoided if at all possible. Remember that you have this in-built tendency to believe things without ever really having investigated them. Equally, however, you are asked not simply to take as true what is going to be said but to see for yourself what is actually the case and apply reason.

We can never really understand our nature. A gas can dissolve in liquid but not vice versa. Similarly, the mind can understand matter and the intellect can differentiate between concepts but what I am going to call our 'Self' is higher than these. Though this Self can (and does) penetrate all of them, it is itself inaccessible to them. What we *can* do, however, is try to find out what we are not. A good policy to adopt in this study is that of Sherlock Holmes – when all has been investigated and rejected, whatever remains, however improbable, must be the truth.

Just think for a moment how it feels to be you. There you are, reading this book, conscious of these words, this body and this mind. This is now and seems to be real. This feeling of being 'you' is something that you live with from moment to moment and its quality is the most familiar sensation you have. How it felt yesterday and the day before is easily recalled. How it felt in your childhood, though less well remembered, will still be known. Of course, you were a child then but it was *you* who were the child, not someone else. The point to note is that this feeling, ignoring the day to day changes in physical or mental well-being and the fact of ageing, is *always the same.*

Not the body

The most common belief is that we are a *body* and this body harbors a separate 'I'. We conclude that 'I' am born with the body and die when it dies. Yet our actual feeling is rather that we *have* a body than that we *are* a body. We know that the body is only a mass of water and chemicals and, if you think about it, it is simply irrational to believe that this is what *we* are. Our body is, ultimately, nothing but food (and water).

Everything you see I owe to spaghetti. Sophia Loren

How big/heavy is our body at birth? How big/heavy is it now? From where has that substance come? All our cells are completely replaced, so we are told, every seven years or less. Materially speaking, there can be no argument but that our bodies are what we eat. There is nowhere else from which all of this added weight can have come. So how are we able to make such a clearly unreasonable conclusion as that we *are* these bodies?

The answer lies in the way we think and feel. We observe a pain in the head – we say 'I' have a headache. We have not learnt how to control the body in the water – we say 'I' cannot swim. As soon as we are able to talk, we say 'my' name is Tom or Sarah; 'I' am a boy, a girl, a man; 'I' am clever or stupid and so on... and on.

Alan Watts put forward an interesting theory (Ref. 51). He recognized that most of us, if asked to say where that which we thought of as 'ourselves' was located, would point to the head, i.e. the brain. We tend to have the idea that we are essentially a brain, with various supporting organs and appendages such as legs to move the brain from A to B, a stomach to provide food, and so on. But suppose that our original form was a stomach. Without this, the rest would not survive very long. After eons of evolution, the stomach would eventually develop limbs so that it could move on, once the source of food was exhausted. It would develop senses, so that it could detect food more effectively, and the brain would be needed to control these additional functions.

In the east, most people claim that their 'seat of consciousness' is located in the centre of the chest. But this is not to say that one *is* the heart, in the way we might claim to be the brain. [In fact, this is almost certainly a legacy from the past, when Indian philosophers believed that the mind was located in the heart.] Common sense seems to tell us that whatever we essentially 'are', this is unaffected by minor parts of the body. When we cut our nails or go to the hairdressers, we do not feel we are removing part of ourselves. Someone who loses a finger or a limb still feels herself to be the same person, even if their mobility has been restricted. Beethoven was still himself – perhaps more so – after he went deaf.

At what point did you come into existence, at the moment of emergence from the birth canal of your mother? Or were you already 'you' in the womb? How early in the womb? When the fertilized egg first separated? Before then? Were you yourself even in the sperm or egg which began the development of your body? But are not all of these things simply food as well? All of the material aspects of our body, including sperm and eggs that will produce new bodies, all grow into existence as a result of food we eat. There is nothing else at this material level. Clearly we cannot be that.

Nor should we think that what we are really is in some way connected to our genes. Our DNA is nothing more than a set of instructions for converting the food that we eat into forms of more immediate value to the body. Once the body has no further use for these, there are other sets of instructions held by bacteria and worms for converting them into other forms, which are later acted upon by plant and animal DNA – and so on…

Though there is an enormous amount of intelligence invested in all these processes, there is nothing there that we can call 'I'.

When I say I live in a house and the house is leaking, I don't mean that I am leaking. Swamini Pramananda (Ref. 81)

Not the mind

Once we have seen through the initial illusion that we are our body, the next likely port of call is to think we are the mind. Pamela Wilson, a spiritual teacher and disciple of Sri Poonja (affectionately known as Papaji and a direct pupil of Ramana Maharshi) has this to say about the mind:

"What mind? Can you find it? It's like what they say about the Mafia. You know, they call it 'organized crime'. Everybody says 'Well, it's not that organized!'. So we see this grand title to a bundle of thoughts; we call it mind. We make it an object, and then we think it's a big deal, because there's a universal agreement that we all have them." (Ref. 72)

How often do you change your mind? As a child it is normal to have quite naïve ideas about the world. As we are educated, our outlook matures. An intelligent person can change his opinion on a given topic within a moment if a reasoned argument is presented. Even beliefs are only strongly held opinions. After all, didn't people once genuinely believe that the earth was the center of the universe?

And what about feelings and emotions? I am tired, and all I want to do is go to bed. Then I get a phone call from an attractive member of the opposite sex asking if I want to go to a party. Suddenly I am wide-awake and raring to go! Clearly I cannot 'be' these either. Anything that changes from one minute to the next cannot be this unchanging Self which we acknowledged earlier.

Perhaps the most enduring aspect of ourselves is what we commonly call our 'personality'. Thus some people are extraverted, others introverted. For many people, these seem to be fixed and we might be excused for thinking that this might in some way be our 'real' self. But it is possible to change this too. Someone who is very shy can overcome this with the help of reason, discussion and, above all, practice. Phobias can be conquered with counseling and discipline.

We have already discounted the possibility that we could be the material of the brain. We cannot be the thoughts or ideas occurring within it either, assuming for the moment that the mind is a part of the brain. There is the process of thinking, whereby thoughts are presented to consciousness and there is an intellect or reasoning function that we could say discriminates between these thoughts and assigns relative values to them. But we feel somehow that 'I' think and 'I' discriminate by using these thinking and intellectual tools, which themselves seem to be part of the brain. It does not appear to be reasonable that we could actually *be* them. So what is this 'I' if not any of those things?

Note that nothing has been said here about simply 'observing'. If we just watch what is happening without thinking about it or commenting on it and without discriminating between aspects that are observed, is the mind then involved? And if not, what is the 'I' that is observing? Can we observe what is going on in the mind? More about this later!

Not the ego

When a man is wrapped up in himself he makes a pretty small package.
John Ruskin

Our 'real self', whatever it is, becomes associated with something very limited in various ways. This process is one of attachment or identification. In Sanskrit, it is called *ahaMkAra*. (These strangely spelt words, which you will see increasingly frequently throughout this book represent the Sanskrit. Sanskrit itself uses a non-Roman script that is totally unintelligible without some serious study and is also only just starting to become usable on the internet – browsers are able to display them providing that the computer has the corresponding font. However, a 'Romanized' equivalent representation, called ITRANS, has been around for a number of years and is widely used on the Internet, especially in email List groups etc. ITRANS allows you to show the correct spelling and pronunciation of Sanskrit words using only those letters on the keyboard that can be transmitted by the most basic software. More details about this are contained in Appendix 3. This also provides some guidance to pronunciation; e.g. the 'M' in ahaMkAra is actually pronounced as a guttural 'n'.)

ahaMkAra means the making – *kAra* – of the utterance 'I' – *aham* – but, in practical terms, it describes the process by which the real Self is identified with something in creation. In order to communicate meaningfully with others, we *have* to use the word 'I' but most of us do not think that we use it merely as a convenience. We believe that it refers to something unique about us as an individual; something concrete that could be pointed to or picked up, except that, if asked exactly where or what this 'thing' is, we begin to find it difficult to define. Moreover, we believe that we are separate, autonomous entities that do and think things in our own right. Effectively, we mis-take ourselves for something limited. It is this single act that is the root of all of our problems. As soon as we attach the basic feeling of 'I am' to anything at all, we create duality because if 'I am something' (e.g. a woman), I have simultaneously defined something that I am not – a man.

It is as though an actor becomes so identified with the role that he is acting in a play that he goes around in his day to day life thinking the thoughts and feeling the emotions that might be felt by that role and entirely forgetting that he is an actor, merely pretending to be the role in the play. There is no reason why he should not play the part of a murderer in the matinee performance and a lover in the evening; who-he-really-is has nothing to do with either.

In an analogous manner, Advaita says that the Self actually has 'nothing to do with' the world – is totally unaffected by it. What happens is that the process of *ahaMkAra* identifies the Self with something in creation and that 'something' *is* bound by the laws of creation. Thus, whilst it seems as if our real Self is bound, subject to misery and death, it is not really so. It is only the body that dies.

Don't worry if these ideas appear to be rather far-fetched. Just let them rest for the time being, rather than throwing the book out of the window. We'll return to them in more convincing detail later... and the window will still be there.

Not a 'person'

In the West, we refer to our sense of self as the 'ego'. This word simply means 'I' in Latin. We don't think that what it actually refers to changes from moment to moment. And yet: 'I' have a toothache refers to the body; 'I' think that this is all a bit far-fetched merely refers to an opinion; 'I' am going to read this book from cover to cover may imply a reasoned discrimination. It is not at all clear, precisely what it is to which we refer when we use the word 'I'. In fact, as I hope to convince you in this book, the 'ego' does not really exist; I, as an individual 'person', do not exist.

The word 'person' stems from the Latin *'per sona'* and refers to the megaphone mask worn by actors in the Greek-Roman theatre. Since the performances were in the open air, without amplification equipment, the mask was a device through (*per*) which the sound (*sona*) was projected. Thus the word 'person' was never meant to refer to our true self but only to the mask that we present to others on the stage of life. It is interesting that the word has come to mean the exact opposite of what was originally meant; so that we now commonly think that we really are the mask.

There is no such thing as a person. What we call the person is only the summation of all of the limitations with which we have identified. If you think of a pot and the space within it, we tend to think that there is a pot-shaped space occupying the pot itself. In reality, the space is totally unaffected by the pot. If the pot breaks, the space previously 'contained in' the pot is still there. In the same way, the Self does not occupy the person. The person is an artificial construct relating to a bundle of thoughts and feelings and some matter in a particular shape and form. Furthermore, the ego relates to all of the memories and experiences of the past and the hopes and fears for the future; it has no existence in the present moment.

There is no such thing as a healthy ego any more than there is a thing called a healthy disease. Sri Poonja (Ref. 73)

Recent developments in medical science, particularly in the sphere of transplant surgery and genetic cloning, suggest that, at some time in the not too distant future, a bizarre experiment might be possible:

Suppose that, in x years time (where x = your personal prediction), becoming rather old and contemplating the prospect of dying, you decide instead to replace all of the old bits with new ones. You have become very rich and the vast expense of this process poses no obstacle. You arrange to have a series of operations over several years, during which all of your organs will be replaced by spares, specially grown for this purpose in medically farmed pigs. Some of the more personalized aspects, such as the brain, for example, you will grow from your own cells. DNA will be extracted and persuaded to produce 'stem cells' from which the required organs will then be grown. And so, when all of this has been completed, you feel, and look, like a new man. Or, to be strictly accurate, like a new woman, since you decided, having spent seventy years as a man, that it was time for a change.

Now, it so happens that you earned all of your wealth by being a pop star and, as such, you had the usual following of mad groupies. Most of these, of course, tended to lose interest as you and they entered their later decades. One, however, who was also very rich, had been so obsessed with you that she had literally wanted to *be* you, and she did not lose interest. When she learned of your intended transformation, she saw her opportunity and arranged, by suitable financial incentives with the team of surgeons and scientists, to have all of the discarded organs, limbs and even the brain for her own use. Whenever you had new parts grafted on to the rest of your (?) body, she took the old bits and had them replace her own original parts.

Thus it was that, at the end of many months stay in hospital, two people emerge into the sunshine one early summer's day. The assembled media have never before seen the first person to appear – you. After all, some of the bits are seeing daylight for the first time, while the rest have not been in quite this particular configuration before. It appears to be an attractive young woman in her late twenties. The second figure is immediately recognizable as the ageing pop star, albeit somewhat the worse for wear who was seen first entering the hospital three years earlier.

2. What I am not

Now everyone is aware of what has happened. The first of such complete makeovers to actually take place, it has been the centre of media attention ever since it was first announced. The world has been waiting to see the results with eager anticipation. The interviewer who has been awarded the prestigious job of being the first to speak to the two transformed individuals suddenly has a profound attack of philosophical angst.

How does he address you? How does he address the person who appears to be you? Who the hell are you anyway? If your name was Gary Baldy, does he now call you *Miss* Baldy? And what about the person who was a woman but now not only looks like you but whose body and brain are literally those that used to be yours? Is she still Miss Gloria Love or is she now Mr. Love or is she now *Mister* Baldy?

If such a procedure ever does take place, what will happen to your perception of who you are? Obviously you will start out being you and, as odd organs or limbs are replaced, there is no reason to suspect that you will start to feel alien in any way. After all, many people have had some degree of transplant surgery without any such identity crisis. Many people suppose that a change would happen if the brain were replaced. You would enter the unconsciousness of anesthesia being 'you' and wake up being – what: the identity of the donor? But what if the brain were replaced in parts, with tissue grown from your own DNA?

When stem cells are grown and injected into the damaged area of the brain, healthy brain tissue begins to grow back to replace the dead. Thus, in a progressive way, one assumes that 'old', imperfectly functioning parts of the brain could be deliberately burnt out by a well-aimed laser beam and new stem cells injected to grow back into brand new cells. These could be quickly trained to perform their required function with the full vitality of the original young cells. In this way, at no time would you be without a brain at all and your full identity could be retained. Or would it?

And what of Gloria, who is now the proud possessor of your cast-off brain, not to mention all of the other parts. What of her identity? If she has your brain, will she in fact *be* you, in some real sense?

Here you are, looking into a mirror after your transformation, and saying to yourself: "What does it mean to be me? Here I am looking at this hand. It is my hand. Is it a part of 'me'? Clearly not. I have now had it replaced by a spare part but I am still 'I'. Similarly as regards every other part of this body, including the brain, which is completely new, even though grown from my own DNA. Am I then only my memory? Do I still have a full set of memories after these operations? Let's suppose I do. We'll suppose that they reside in particular molecular configurations of proteins in parts of the brain. Let's allow that, because the brain was replaced a bit at a time, anything lost from one part was regenerated in one of the new bits before an old bit, containing the last legitimate traces, was taken out. So, although they are not 'original' memories, they are a bona fide reconstruction of them.

"But if this is all that I am, then Gloria must be even more 'me' than I am, since she now has the 'original' memories, in the complete, original brain. And, if that is how it works, Gloria is actually now dead, since her brain was scrapped when mine was substituted."

With this line of reasoning, though, what happens when someone suffers amnesia? Do they effectively cease to exist? And so we could go on; this sort of speculation throws up no end of seemingly strange questions about what it means to be 'me'; about who in actuality 'I' am.

Attachment in general

Before looking in more detail at what it is that we actually *are* talking about when we refer to 'I', let's have a closer look at this process of 'attachment' or 'identification'. This question of who we are has been of interest to philosophers, east and west, probably ever since man was able to think about anything other than where his next meal was coming from. The French philosopher Descartes, notorious for his seriously introspective cogitations, attempted to discover something about which we could be absolutely sure and concluded that 'I think, therefore I exist'.

The Scottish philosopher David Hume also considered the problem a century later. He was skeptical of Descartes' findings and made his own attempts to find some irreducible 'self' of which he could be certain. He decided that he could find no such thing. He wrote that mankind *"is nothing but a bundle or collection of different perceptions, which succeed each other with an inconceivable rapidity, and are in a perpetual flux and movement"*. (In this, he would probably have felt accord with the *yogachAra* Buddhist philosophers who said much the same thing over a thousand years before this.)

In effect, he was saying that, whenever he attempted to look for 'himself' he could only find thoughts, feelings and perceptions; never a 'self' that is the perceiver, feeler and thinker. And so he concluded that there was no such thing. A contemporary of Hume, Thomas Reid, hit the nail on the head when he wrote: *"A person is something indivisible... My thoughts, and actions, and feelings, change every moment; they have no continued, but a successive existence; but that self or I, to which they belong, is permanent, and has the same relation to all the succeeding thoughts, actions and feelings which I call mine"*.

But Hume would have none of this and persisted in his skeptical view. One feels one wants to get hold of him and shake him and say: "Yes, when you look, all that you find *are* thoughts, feelings and perceptions but *who is it* who finds this? What is the 'who' that is doing the looking?"

In fact, one way of considering this entire problem is to ask yourself: "Who or what is it that says 'I' when I make all these statements?" Clearly it is not the body speaking – the larynx does not originate the speech of its own volition. The mind is a tool that I use to work things out. The senses are instruments that I use. And so on. I can negate all of these things – what am I then left with?

What normally happens to us all of the time is that we 'latch on to' some object, role or idea and believe that it, or some combination of these things, somehow defines us as a separate entity. We actually come to accept that we *are* this body because it feels pain when it is injured or satisfaction when it has had a good meal and we identify with those feelings. It seems alien even to talk about it in this way – we prefer to think that 'I' have had a good meal, not that 'the body' has. We would never say 'this body has a toothache', for example, and most listeners would look at us very strangely if we did. Similarly, we say 'I *am* a teacher', not that our professional role is that of a teacher. We might concede that the latter is the true situation, since we would accept that we could leave that job and change to a less frustrating career. If the role in question is that of a father however, we might insist that ' I am *actually* a father' and that this is not something that I am able to change. But, here, it is quite likely that you are also a 'son', if your own father is still alive. So that you can see that the role is a relative one only (no pun intended).

It is fundamental to the practical side of this philosophy that *we cannot be that which we observe.* We see an object across the room. It is clearly separated from us by space; therefore we cannot be it. If we can see our body, we are in one place as it were, looking at a material thing in another place; we cannot be it. We see thoughts arising and the mind playing with these, if we are in a still, meditative state; therefore we cannot be those thoughts or that mind.

A role, too, is only an idea in mind. Consider what we mean by the word 'teacher'. We associate groups of ideas, such as taking responsibility for a child *in loco parentis*; working in a building with lots of other children; transmitting information on a particular subject to a group of children of similar academic standards and so on. These ideas, together with many others, are associated with the single word 'teacher', for the sake of convenience. I may indeed perform such activities and it is true that it is much easier to use this single word than to attempt to describe all of the various tasks that I routinely carry out. But though I may say colloquially that 'I *am* a teacher', I should also be aware that this is quite untrue.

Whatever we can see objectively, we cannot be that. This applies just as much to the idea of a role, that is actually a group of concepts in the mind, as to a physical object that we believe to exist on the other side of the room. Indeed, this is another argument to explain how it is that our real Self must forever elude the mind. We can never know it as an object simply because it is always the subject.

It is total misconception to think that 'we' are inside our bodies or inside a mind in the brain – this is another one of those examples of the usual way of thinking being the exact opposite of the way things really are. The related objects, feelings and thoughts arise in our consciousness, not the other way round.

Confusion of Self with ego

Francis Lucille, a present-day enlightened teacher, uses the analogy of the eye to help see the problem more clearly. The eye can never see itself, even though it is the organ of sight. It can see a reflection in a mirror or an image in a photograph but never directly perceive itself. But this is not to say it doesn't exist, for without it we would see nothing at all. Similarly, the 'I' is responsible for all awareness but can never be directly aware of itself as an object of awareness. This is not to say it does not exist – I would have to exist in order to deny this existence! Without it there would be no consciousness and, if there is one thing of which you are absolutely certain, without reference to any past experience or knowledge, it is that you exist; that you are conscious.

On those probably very rare occasions when everything is totally silent; when your eyes are closed so you can see nothing; when there is complete peace outside and not a sound to be heard; when your mind is still, disturbed by not a flicker of a thought; who is the witness of this silence?

But how can it be that we could possibly 'overlook' something so fundamental as our real Self? Listen to the story of the tenth man. On the face of it, it is a very silly and obvious story with nothing useful to tell us. And so I thought for a long time – I understood it but somehow the full import hadn't clicked. When it does, it is really quite profound and sobering.

There is a party of ten men travelling together to a distant village in a remote and rugged area. They encounter a swollen river, which they are obliged to cross. They join hands and begin the perilous crossing but inevitably they lose their footing in the strong current and have to swim. Much later and wetter, they reassemble on the opposite bank. As each counts the number of men who have arrived, they can only find nine and conclude that one of their number has drowned.

As they are bemoaning their loss, a monk passes by and asks them what the matter is. They explain and, quickly assessing the situation, he recognizes their mistake. He asks them to line up and, taking a stick, he hits the first man once, the second twice and so on down the line, counting out the number aloud each time. Reaching the end, he hits the last man ten times and calls out 'ten'. What had happened, of course, is that each man had counted the others but forgotten to count himself, and so had only reached nine.

The reason for the total number is significant, each standing for an element in the 'makeup' of Man. Note that this is as it was understood in ancient times – don't let any modern scientific hang-up about this distract you from the fundamental profundity of the story. (The first nine are made up of the five elements of gross matter – earth, water, air, fire and ether – together with the four subtle elements of mind: the part responsible for discursive thought, called (*manas*); the part responsible for memory amongst other things, called *chitta*; the intellectual, discriminating part, called *buddhi* and the ego (*ahaMkAra*).). The whole point of the story, however, is that we always forget the tenth, which is, of course, the true Self, known in Sanskrit as *Atman* (when we are speaking about it in a 'personal' sense) or *brahman* (in a general or 'universal' sense). Who is the one who witnesses the silence?

Wei Wu Wei has added an amusing extra part to this story – see http://sentient.org/past/wei-wu-wei.html. (Contrary to any impression given by the name, Wei Wu Wei was an *Irish* Sage, real name Terence Grey, who died in 1987. He took his name from the Taoist term 'wu wei', which means 'non-action'. There is a web site devoted to him and his works – 'The Wei Wu Wei Archives' – at http://www.weiwuwei.8k.com/). His version says that, even after hitting them all on the head and getting them to call out the number, they still did not understand how it was that each of them had only counted up to nine. When, after the monk had gone on his way they re-counted, they still only found nine and still believed one had died. Sometime later, one of them went to the river to get some water to drink. Bending down he saw his reflection and called out to the others saying he had found the drowned man.

Each of them came in turn and, looking into the water, saw the drowned tenth man, though it was too dangerous to try to pull him out. Later, the monk, returning from his journey, found the men holding a funeral for their lost friend. The bemused monk then told them then that, since each had seen his own dead face in the river and they had each mourned the death of all of the others, they were all now well and truly dead. Upon hearing this they were all instantly enlightened!

Rudyard Kipling wrote a story explaining how it was that the Gods, fearing man's imminent realization of his own divinity, hid man's godhead somewhere where he would never find it – inside himself. One of the Upanishads, called the Katha (*kaThopaniShad*), somewhat older than this, says the same thing (Ch. 4, Vs 1 - 4):

God created the senses pointing outward. Therefore one sees the outside world, not into one's own nature. A wise man, wishing to be immortal, turns his eyes within and sees the real Self.

The ignorant follow their desires and fall into the outspread trap of Death. Instead the wise, knowing the imperishable Self, do not look for satisfaction in this world of impermanence.

Only through this Self does one know form, taste, smells, sounds, sensations and sensual pleasures. What else is there in this world that remains unknown? This is truly that Self.

The wise man grieves no more, having realized the great, all-pervading Self, by which he discovers both the end of dreaming and the end of waking.

(The Upanishads are books that were mostly written a long time ago, up to several thousand years BC. There are around 108 of them today, though there was once many more, and each forms part of one of the four 'Vedas' – huge tomes containing stories, hymns, instructions on how to behave and some of the most profound philosophy ever written. More will be said on them later but expect to see quite a few references to them as we proceed.)

It is incredible how rarely we actually consider our real Self. In practically all that we do and think, when we speak of 'I' we are really referring to the ego, that illusory aspect of our true nature. It can only speak from habit and stale opinion, from memory, from the past. The Self is alive and fresh in every moment, if only this could be recognized.

In fact, there are just a few moments when most of us will have had direct access to this. The most common, perhaps, is upon awakening from deep sleep in the morning. Occasionally we may experience what might be called a 'pure feeling of existence', containing none of the limitations normally associated with our consciousness. Unfortunately, this is usually superseded immediately by a sense of panic, as the ego fights to re-establish its hold: "Where am I? What day is it?"

Other than this, the moments when we reconnect with our true nature seem to be very few and far between. They are short-lived and cannot be generated at will, being triggered by something quite outside the ego and its domain. Suddenly, the attention opens right out; everything is vibrantly alive as if an old black and white film is transformed into three dimensional color and Dolby surround sound. The small, insignificant prison of the ego dissolves into a universe and there is a certainty that this is the true reality. And then it is gone, leaving only a memory which, however, stays with us forever.

The Self exists; the ego doesn't *in reality*. We shouldn't think of ourselves as a 'thinker', 'feeler', 'doer' or 'enjoyer'. All of these things 'happen' on the stage of this play of life but the Self is not any of them. (In fact, it would be better thought of as the stage itself, on which they appear.) Without it there could be none of these, yet it neither *does* nor *is* any of them itself. It is rather like electricity, which can power a refrigerator without getting cold, a heater without getting warm or a fan without moving. But this is only a very poor metaphor! The mind will try to grasp the Self as a concept and fail. Just don't let this bother you. In fact, if you notice this frustration, that is good. It is the ego that is getting frustrated and you have spotted it in action. It is precisely through learning more about its games that some understanding can be gained and, in theory at least, its dominion reduced.

The above has been a 'taster' for what follows. It is almost certain that, if this is the first time you have encountered such ideas, you will be feeling a bit overwhelmed and not a little skeptical. It will be a general policy to introduce these radical concepts gradually, so we'll take a break now and continue to look at who we *really* are in chapter 17 'The Nature of the Self'.

3. Nature of man

Hierarchy – minerals, plants, animals, man

What exactly do we mean by the 'nature' of man and what is his place in the apparent scheme of things? We have ridiculed the concept of a 'person' and stated flatly that the ego does not really exist, yet have implied that there is something else defining us. Well, for the moment we are talking about how things appear to be, rather than how they actually are. This distinction is crucial and will be discussed in depth in the third section of the book. As far as our practical experience is concerned, the so-called 'relative' or 'empirical' level of existence, it *appears* that there are lots of things on this earth and they *appear* to differ from one another in very clear ways. So let's pursue this for a while and humor ourselves.

There seems to be a progression of awareness and intelligence in the world around us. The hierarchy could be defined as: – minerals – plants – animals – man. E. F. Schumacher describes this excellently in his 'A Guide for the Perplexed' (Ref. 52). He says that stones seem to have no awareness and no control over their environment; in fact scientists might well say that they have no *life*.

Plants grow and reproduce; they have acquired this characteristic of *life*, whatever it is. They take in nutrients from their surroundings; they grow and eventually *die*, after which they take on the characteristics of minerals. They have limited awareness in that they can respond to some outside stimuli such as light but they do this in an automatic, preconditioned manner.

Animals seem to have a new property, called *consciousness*, which plants did not have. They are able to 'lose' this, for example under an anesthetic, in which situation they revert to the plant-like behavior. They appear to exercise limited choice – e.g. whether to eat, move or sleep. But their overall behavior is well defined and they cannot act in a manner that transcends that boundary. Thus a lion will never become a vegetarian; a deer will be timid and a tiger aggressive – they are driven by their instincts. They are clearly aware of others and of their environment but only to the

33

extent that it impinges on basic aspects of their existence, such as survival and reproduction.

We talk of wild animals, but the wildest animal is man. G. K. Chesterton

The behavior of man is vastly more complex and much more difficult to generalize. There are aggressive men and timid ones and they sometimes revert to the category of animals, as far as their behavior is concerned. The key difference, however, seems to be that man has acquired yet another new characteristic – that of *self-awareness*. He is conscious of being conscious and can examine and investigate this in an objective way. He is also able to change his nature to some degree, given the right conditions, incentives and so on. He appears to be able to choose to behave in ways contrary to those that might be thought instinctual. He is aware of (or postulates) aspects far beyond the capability of the animal, such as beauty and truth and can choose to follow these even though to do so might conflict with survival. It is this 'self-awareness' which is both his supreme achievement and his downfall. On the one hand, it enables him to realize his true nature; on the other hand it causes him to judge himself, to perceive limitations and strive mistakenly all his life to overcome them. His humanity can lead to ultimate freedom but all too often brings him misery and apparent bondage.

Science, complex and sophisticated though it has become, successfully addresses only the first of these essentially discontinuous levels of existence. There have certainly been attempts to investigated the nature of consciousness but none have been (nor could ever be) successful. The reason for this is simply that there would always be a subject investigating an object. The subject is never accessible to objective investigation, by definition. Some scientists even try to explain away life and consciousness as mere side effects of evolution of the material. It is left to philosophy to try to make sense of it all.

Also, science is only concerned with trying to discover 'causes' for the various 'effects' that we see in the entire universe. But it will be seen later that the nature of reality is beyond cause and effect, time and space and so could never be amenable to investigation in this way.

The three 'Qualities' of nature

There is a scheme in Indian philosophies that is helpful in looking at the different 'levels' of existence, though it is quite alien to Western systems of thought. It applies to the entire universe, living or inanimate. In its most extreme form, this method says that everything in Nature is made up of three constituents called *guNa-s* (*guNa*). Everything contains these three *guNa-s* but in varying proportions and the relative proportions determine the nature of the thing. They are what the system calls *subtle* elements in that the senses (or science) are unable to perceive them yet they are nevertheless 'responsible for' the behavior in the gross world. This extreme form of the idea, in which matter is believed literally to be constituted of these *guNa-s*, is held by the philosophy called Sankhya (*sAMkhya*). This is a dualistic philosophy, separating reality into spirit (*puruSha*) and matter (*prakRRiti* or *pradhAna*). Advaita does not support this belief but instead holds that the *guNa-s* are 'attributes' or 'qualities' only; matter is only a form of the non-dual Brahman.

As you read on, you will realize that there is nothing mystical about them, even though they clearly cannot fit into a modern, scientific ethos. Indeed, we can make use of the principle very quickly, after first hearing about it. Even should you remain skeptical about whether there is any 'truth' in it, you will find the concept useful. This is especially so when talking about such things as how you feel, what the atmosphere in a room is like and so on – as long as the person to whom you are speaking has also met the terms.

The 'lowest' of the three *guNa-s* is called *tamas*. Minerals exhibit almost only this property. It has the characteristics of dullness, ignorance and inaction. When it predominates in a person, he is lazy, careless and stupid with a very narrow outlook on life, dogmatic and egocentric, often dwelling in the dead past.

rajas is the *guNa* that is related to activity. Thus plants have a little of this but to nowhere near the extent of animals. In a person, *rajas* is associated with emotional behavior, desire-driven activity and passion, deriving pleasure from money and material gains. Successful businessmen are driven by *rajas*, constantly seeking new goals and worrying about future outcomes.

sattva is the highest of the *guNa-s*. Only in man can it be exhibited to a large degree. It is associated with knowledge, peace, wisdom and spirituality. A man whose nature is predominantly sattvic (*sAttvika*) is free from attachments to the world and its concomitant miseries and excitements. He seeks out truth and knowledge and allows these, rather than his own selfish motives, to dictate the way in which he lives his life, in harmony with the rest of nature. Only when this *guNa* predominates is there a chance of seeing how things really are.

Note that all three *guNa-s* play an essential role in creation and should not be regarded as 'good' or 'bad' in that sense. What is being said is that it is necessary to cultivate *sattva* and suppress *tamas* in one's own nature if one is to progress on a spiritual path and reach the truth.

Animals tend to be naturally tamasic (*tAmasika*), only becoming active in order to acquire food or to mate. They are driven by instinct. In order to overcome *tamas* in ourselves, we need to get up and do something – *rajas* can eliminate *tamas*. Over a period, *sattva* can be cultivated through stillness, meditation, study and reflection and so on. This sequence is the evolution of man from animal towards God, the highest state being attained when he realizes his true nature as being beyond the *guNa*.

The 'covering' of our true nature

If our true nature is not apparent on the surface, then it follows that this must somehow be covered over. The first chapter looked at some of the ways in which we might do this. For example, we see our bodies and think that we are them. The body-idea is effectively a covering of our real nature. Thus, someone who is born with an inherited disease will very likely believe that 'they' are limited in a particular way and this belief will predispose them to behave in a particular way. Genetic traits are regarded as 'nature' as opposed to the cultural/parental/educational influences, which are treated as 'nurture' influences but the latter, too, can effectively obscure our real nature. As an example of the second type, someone brought up by parents who steal for a living may tend to act similarly and justify it to themselves as acceptable behavior.

(Note that the idea of 'covering' is only a metaphor. It will be seen in the final section of the book that who-we-really-are is not covered over by anything.)

Sheaths or layers of identification

It has been noted above that 'I', the real Self, identifies with the body for example, with the end result that I think I *am* the body. There is a system in Vedantic literature that describes these various layers of identification. They are referred to as 'sheaths' (Sanskrit *kosha*) which cover over our true essence. But, although the literal meaning of the term may be the scabbard that covers a dagger or sword, this is not a good metaphor. A better one is the famous rope-snake metaphor, in which we mistake a rope for a snake.

The first of these layers – the grossest and the one with which we first tend to identify – is the body. This is referred to as the sheath made of food (*annamayakosha*). The body is born, grows old, dies and decays back into the food from which it originally came (well, food for worms anyway) but this has nothing to do with the real Self, which is much closer than hand or skin.

The second layer is called the 'vital sheath' or sheath made of breath (*prANamayakosha*). Hindu mythology refers to the air as breathing life into the body. We might call it the vital force by means of which the body is animated and actions are performed. Although this force derives from the Self, as indeed everything does, it is *not* the Self. We each of us tend to believe that we are somehow immortal. Although we acknowledge that the body must eventually die we feel that there is this animating force which will survive that death. This is the identification with the vital sheath.

The next layer is the mental sheath consisting of the thinking mind and the organs of perception (*manomayakosha*). This is the part of the mental makeup responsible for transmitting information from the 'outside world' but which usually gets up to mischief that is really none of its business, i.e. thinking and trying to understand everything. The Sanskrit word for this 'organ' of mind is *manas*, as we have already seen. This is probably the sheath with which most of us identify.

Beyond this, however, there is the higher faculty of mind, responsible for discrimination, recognizing truth or falsehood, real or unreal, without recourse to mundane things like thought and memory. In silence, it *knows* without needing to think. We might call this the intellect; Sanskrit calls it *buddhi*. It is responsible for such judgments as Solomon's in respect of the two mothers claiming the same child. He suggested sawing the baby in two and giving half to each woman. Supposedly the false mother agreed to this while the real mother said that the other woman could have the child. This is the intellectual sheath, (*vij~nAnamayakosha*).

Some readers who meditate may have been fortunate enough to experience moments of the most profound peace and silence, when the mind is completely absent and a feeling of deep contentment can be felt. It might be thought that this is the state of realization for which we are aiming, if only it could be maintained. Instead it lasts mere minutes or, very rarely hours for a few dedicated ascetics. But no, this is just another state, albeit perhaps a desirable and blissful one. We are still observing it and therefore cannot be it. It is the final sheath, called appropriately enough the 'Bliss' sheath (*Anandamayakosha*). Because of its supremely blissful nature, it is the most difficult of the sheaths to transcend.

What we truly are, then, is the 'Real Self' or simply 'Self' with a capital 'S' as it will be called in this book. But, through identification with these various layers or sheaths, this Self is obscured. It is like water contained in a colored glass bottle. The water itself seems to take on the color of the glass, though it is itself colorless.

Behavioral tendencies

These are called *vAsanA-s* in Sanskrit, literally meaning 'wishing' or 'desiring' but used in Advaita in the sense of the sub-conscious or latent tendencies in one's nature that will have their way eventually, like it or not. (Note that we tend to add '-s' to an ITRANS representation of a Sanskrit word when we want it to be in the plural. Obviously the actual plural in Sanskrit does not end in an 's'.) Edward de Bono, of 'lateral thinking' fame describes a model that is helpful in thinking about this (Ref. 53). If you take some jello (jelly), solidified and turned out onto a plate, and you trickle very hot water onto the top, it will run off onto the plate and leave behind a faint channel where the hot water melted the jello. If you now pour more hot water, it will tend to run into the same channels as before, since these offer the line of least resistance, and deepen the channels. If this is done repeatedly, very deep channels will form and it will become difficult, if not impossible, to get the water to run anywhere else. The equivalent of an entrenched habit has been formed.

This tendency to act in a certain way, in a given situation, is called a *vAsanA*. The less aware we are at the moment of action, the more likely it is that we will act in that way. If we are alert in the moment, with our intellect able to discriminate between alternative courses of action, then it is possible that the innate tendency may be overcome. Just as the channels in the jello have been formed by the earlier pouring on of water, so our *vAsanA-s* are formed by our past actions.

4. What We Think We Can Know

Ignorance

If you think that education is expensive, try ignorance. Derek Bok

What do we know about ourselves now and how do we go about acquiring more knowledge? What does it mean to have knowledge or experience of something and do we, as the observer or knower of things, fall into the category of something we could know? If we 'knew' ourselves objectively, who would be the subject? We also need to be clear about the distinction between knowledge and belief (or mere opinion) and to understand when knowledge constitutes wisdom or truth. The Mundaka Upanishad says (2.8): *"Existing in ignorance, though thinking themselves knowledgeable and wise, the egotistical ones wander aimlessly, jostled about like the blind led by the blind."*

We are largely ignorant when it comes to spiritual matters. We go to school, listen to our elders and peers, watch television, and so on, supposedly learning the things that we need in order to function in the world. Increasingly we find however that, though these may prepare us for a career of making money and operating DVD recorders, they tell us nothing about how to find meaning and fulfillment in our lives. They do *not* take away the essential ignorance about the things that 'really matter'. In fact, they often seem to add to it.

Practically the whole of our so-called education is nothing of the sort. It is no 'leading out' (Latin: *educere*) but rather a 'stuffing in' of largely useless, so-called facts. And most of it is engineered to entrench in us the belief that *this is it*; this world is real and it is all that there is. In the west, education, of which the media and advertising are perhaps the most influential, increasingly promotes the value systems of materialism and individualism. Put more simply, this means that our entire upbringing is geared to bring about the belief: "I need money in order to make myself happy".

There can be no question but that we (i.e. science) know far more about every*thing* that there is to know than the last generation. Knowledge, in the sense of information, seems to grow exponentially. There are now entire subjects that were unknown only a hundred years ago. Yet, if we consider the nature of ourselves – who we are, what we ought to be doing with our lives, what the purpose might be, and so on, there is nothing more known now than was known several thousand years ago. Philosophies and religions vie to provide the answers but those few who make the effort to enquire are likely to remain bewildered by often-conflicting claims.

To be truly ignorant, be content with your own knowledge. Chuang Tzu (c.360 BC - c. 275 BC)

Normally, whenever we speak of knowledge, what we are talking about is knowledge *of things* – their attributes, properties and their relations to other things. We rarely try to think of what the essence of anything might be, beyond these qualities. We will discover later that such attempts quickly run into problems and that, in fact, they must ultimately fail but it remains necessary to make the clear distinction. Advaita is concerned with *essential* knowledge. In a reversal of this usual way of thinking, we could almost regard objects as being the attributes of some absolute essence (and, later, we *will*). The objects themselves, in which we must include ourselves, are always changing, whereas that which is the essential nature of all things is always the same.

Swami Chinmayananda has a useful metaphor to help us to think about this (Ref. 8). He says that when we pour water into a variety of differently shaped and colored bottles and vessels, the apparent attributes of those vessels will all be different. We will have 'short' water and 'curiously shaped' water, 'pink' water and 'yellow' water. But all of these character-istics, that we might believe to constitute knowledge of the water, are in fact nothing of the sort. They are only properties of the objects with which the water is associated . Similarly, all of our studies of the physiology of the human body and the psychology of the mind will tell us nothing about the essential nature of our Self, that is only *associated* with these bodies and minds.

On matters that *really* matter, we remain ignorant. What is worse, we do not know where to look for a reliable source that might provide the answers. Fortunately, Advaita is such a source and its revelations may be validated in this lifetime. Science provides objective knowledge, of the sort that we are normally concerned with; Advaita helps us to an intuitive understanding of the essential nature of all things – knowledge of the absolute reality.

Thinking

Many people would sooner die than think; in fact, they do so. Bertrand Russell

Thinking is an essential tool with which to tackle this problem of ignorance. It is, however, *only* a tool and it must be treated with respect if we are not to injure ourselves. A simple thought, planted in our mind by parent, peer or professor can wreak havoc with our lives. Once a thought has arisen, it becomes 'my' thought. If I like the look of it, it is very probable that I will become attached to it and it will grow into an opinion. Of course, whether or not we like the look of it depends mostly upon the thoughts that have *already* wormed their way into our minds and attached themselves to our esteem.

It is worth asking whether you ever actually *do* anything to bring about a thought. Obviously, people do have 'original' thoughts e.g. people like Einstein are usually credited with having had one or two. Where do these thoughts come from? Do such people generate them; use their exceptional minds to bring them into existence from nothing? Well no, actually. Truly original ideas seem to arise of their own accord when the usual sense of 'I' as the thinker is absent, and often in dreams or dreamlike states.

There are two famous examples. Kekulé had a vision of a snake biting its own tail and this led to his understanding of the molecular structure of benzene. And Coleridge supposedly formulated the complete poem of Kubla Khan in a dream, though this might just have been facilitated by some now-illegal substances. Thoughts such as these 'arise' without the presence of the ego to claim them as its own – pure creativity.

Note that these are quite distinct from the type of thought associated with more traditional 'day dreaming'. We would probably agree that that activity is largely a wasteful one and we often refer to the thoughts that we have as 'idle' to acknowledge this. All other types of thinking that relate to 'me' – what I want, am afraid of, worried about and so on – belong to this 'useless' category; they do not really serve any useful function at all. We may think that we can 'make sense of' the way we feel, 'sort things out' etc. but all that we succeed in doing is becoming more identified with the ideas of which these thoughts consist.

In between these two extremes lie the ordinary, day to day practical thoughts that relate to what we are doing or should be doing. Thus the thought that you have an appointment in an hour's time is probably quite useful. It ought not to be regarded as idle, though it is certainly not particularly creative. *Practical* thoughts are purely functional. They arise from we know not where; we recognize them and their value, take the appropriate action and that's the end of them – no problem!

Creative thoughts wake us up, alert us to new possibilities, solve problems etc. We can take the necessary action and, again, forget about them. Not only are they no problem, they positively enhance our lives. Of course, we cannot do anything to increase their frequency. A special case of this type of thought is one that alerts us to our true nature such as the sudden intuition that we are one with everything around us. This class of thought is rare indeed and, when it occurs, can change our lives completely, causing us actively to search for the truth, embark on a spiritual path etc.

Idle thoughts unfortunately often consume a large part of our energy. They seem to be self-sustaining; often triggering related thoughts and spreading the cloud of negativity. 'You will worry yourself to death!' people sometimes say, and this may not be entirely untrue. It all results from the power of identification – the process of *ahaMkAra*. We latch on to particular ideas and imagine all sorts of related scenarios. Then this breeds 'what if' and 'if only' questions and so on and on… The ego knows no limitations to its egoism! These are really the only type of thoughts to be avoided and the only type that causes problems as such.

Opinions

Opinion is that exercise of the human will, which helps us to make a decision without information. John Erskine

It is this category of thought that grows into 'belief. If we particularly like an idea we may very well attach ourselves to it. In the extreme we may even say this is *my* opinion but at least we will acknowledge that we share it with others. It is opinions, and their stronger brothers, beliefs, which cause most of the conflict in the world today. People pick up ideas from books, parents, teachers etc. – usually they forget where, by the time the ideas have become entrenched, and imagine that they have themselves originated them. They then go out and kill people who have merely read different books or had other parents, thus foolishly forming different opinions.

On the day I wrote this, I saw a girl in her late teens, with shaven head and ring through her nose, sporting a tee shirt proclaiming 'I ♥ my Attitude Problem'. It seemed to sum up the sort of situation that all of us get into through identification with a particular set of ideas and opinions – it's just that some seem to be more attached than most. It is a sign of immaturity that, feeling a fundamental sense of inadequacy, some need to shout very loudly 'I believe in X – so there! What are you going to do about it?'

Most people, if they ever think about such things, seem to reach the conclusion that who they are is insignificant. To the question 'who am I?' his or her response is: 'nobody'. Their views count for nothing, they have nothing to look forward to, they achieve nothing; many may not even have the recognition of family or friends. Is it surprising that some turn to strong identification with a particular set of ideas in order to feel some unity with a group holding similar views? It may then only be a short step from funda-mentalism to terrorism. In an environment that does not provide opportu-nities to mature in our outlook to life and to educate ourselves in the true meaning of the word, it seems inevitable that such problems will occur.

Beliefs

Opinions, then, if supported by others or reinforced by society etc. can easily grow into beliefs. When sailors first disappeared over the horizon, they should by rights have fallen over the edge. Even though they returned unharmed and reported nothing untoward, perfectly reasonable people might still have been convinced that the world was flat. (That this was a prevalent belief is apparently false but the principle still applied.) Vast numbers of people believe in the precepts of Catholicism, others in those of Islam. Had these people been born into each other's countries and been brought up in the opposite traditions, would their beliefs still be the same? Are beliefs not largely an accident of birth and nurture?

A belief is not merely an idea the mind possesses; it is an idea that possesses the mind. Robert Bolton

Krishnamurti suggested (Ref. 45) that beliefs come about through fear – the obverse of desire (see later). Basically we are afraid of others, of the future, death etc, and we feel the need for beliefs to cushion us against the perceived threats. Without something to believe in, many people would feel truly lost. Unfortunately, though beliefs may give a sense of belonging and unity, they can cause dissension or even wars against others holding different views. Furthermore, a mind clogged up with beliefs is not free to respond to new ideas; nor is it able to be fully in the present since all beliefs necessarily belong to the past.

We usually reckon that thinking is good and that an absence of it causes problems. If we are performing a task and something goes wrong, we might well say that we were 'not thinking'. What we actually mean is that we were not attending, probably thinking about something else! Similarly, when someone tells us to 'think what you are doing', they usually mean 'give your attention to the job' i.e. *don't* think! Or if I do something stupid, I might say, "Sorry, I wasn't thinking". Again, what I really mean is that I wasn't paying attention. I was probably miles away (or wishing that I was) and actually thinking in the 'idle' sense about something else altogether.

In all those situations where concentration is required to perform optimally, thinking is counter-productive. Using the Sanskrit terms introduced earlier, what we want is for *manas* to be working properly, just passing data from the senses to *buddhi* without comment. It is *buddhi* that then makes the decision *in stillness* as to what, if any, action to take. It is impossible to make clean, appropriate decisions while the mind is working overtime with thinking – my choices are a, b, or c; what would my father say? what did I read in the newspaper last week? And so on. *ahaMkAra* will certainly argue that it is not possible to make most decisions *without* thinking, that we have to refer to memory, consider possibilities and 'work things out'. *This is not true!* It may be the case that it is necessary to go and look up some information in an encyclopedia but the knowledge to do that will be there in the moment if there is no thinking going on to obstruct the correct working of *buddhi*.

Another term for 'idle' thinking, often used when talking about *manas*, is 'discursive' thought – going round and round! Isn't this often what we can see happening when worrying about something, for example? You quickly find that you are going over the same material again and again, getting nowhere. You have had these thoughts before – they belong to the past. They contrast quite markedly with 'creative' thoughts – new, original, and very much in the present.

When you see these thoughts re-presenting themselves from memory, see them in the present moment. Don't allow yourself to get caught up with them and carried away into day dreaming, worry or discursive thinking. If you stay in the present, the thoughts will be seen to be of no value and will simply go away. Without the power given to them by identification, they have no alternative. This is not to say that memory serves no useful purpose; obviously this could not be true. But thoughts from the memory can only arise in the present moment – there is *only* the present. See them in the present and, if the data are relevant, *buddhi* will respond appropriately in the present. All too often, what happens is that the attention is caught and *manas* goes off into reminiscences of an imaginary past or into speculation about an imaginary future – a total waste of time!

A great many people think they are thinking when they are merely rearranging their prejudices. William James

Memory

The memory is frequently over-valued. What is in there is essentially dead information, never living knowledge. Someone with a good memory can learn volumes and regurgitate them at will. In the extreme, in the context of the topic of this book, no amount of learned information will help you to understand yourself. It will only make you what Indians call a 'pandit', someone who can recite the scriptures verbatim but who has no direct experience of what he is talking about. This comes from the Sanskrit word *paNDita*, which originally meant 'wise' or 'clever'. We use the word 'pundit' in our language – the word 'sophist' would probably be a good synonym – someone who knows a lot of theory but does very little practice. The knowledge itself can become a burden, an obstacle to further development instead of an aid. The Sage, who has direct experience of the Truth, needs no information and need resort to no memories. His access to that Truth is here and now.

It is useful incidentally to make clear the distinction between information and knowledge. The Sage who realizes the truth about the Self and Reality, has direct knowledge of that immediately. This does *not* mean that he knows how to make an atom bomb or spotted dick (in the UK, this is a suet pudding containing currants). How 'things' *really* are has, in fact, nothing at all to do with the phenomenal world of objects, as we shall discover in Section 3. Factual information, which can be looked up in a reference book, is not instantly available to him and he is no better able to answer questions about such things than anyone else. (He actually knows them to be unreal, in any case.) Initially, all that we learn from books such as this is at the level of information. Once understood, it must be reflected upon and meditated upon before it is transformed into knowledge. (Note that the words 'Sage', 'teacher' and 'guru' are used almost interchangeably throughout this book to refer to one who has realized the truth, become 'Self-realized' or 'enlightened'. Strictly speaking, a teacher or guru can teach or inform others without being enlightened, whereas the Sage has direct experience of that of which he speaks.)

Experience

Bryan Magee states (Ref. 65) that *"Most of the greatest philosophers of the last three hundred years have held that all of our knowledge about the world, about what actually exists, must ultimately derive from experience"*. We will learn in Section 3 that our experience of reality is limited by the nature of our perceptual equipment so that this statement would suggest that any hope of realizing 'the truth' must be doomed.

Experience seems to be the process by which we transform information into knowledge. When we read something in a book for the first time, or are informed by a teacher, we appreciate it only at the level of theory or hearsay. We may be prepared to believe it but it is missing that vital element of personal witnessing. We do not actually 'know' it to be so. As soon as we experience it for ourselves, there is that element of 'Ah! That's what it meant.'

And yet there is more to it than this. We often say 'I know this to be true' only later to be shown to have been wrong. Is this just misuse of the language? Did I really mean 'I *believe* this to be true'? Modern Western Philosophy uses a definition along the following lines (explained by Dr. Greg Goode in a personal email): Knowledge is justified true belief, i.e. you can be said to 'know' something if – a) you believe it, b) it is true, c) you are justified in believing it. If it turns out to be false then you didn't in fact *know* it, you only *believed* it.

> *Human beings, who are almost unique in having the ability to learn from the experience of others, are also remarkable for their apparent disinclination to do so.* Douglas Adams

However, experience and knowledge can be dangerous and misleading. What might have been valid last time may now be inappropriate. By all means take note of what memory tells you but see it now, in the context of the present moment. Past experience is not itself of any value. It is not the memory of it or the thoughts about it, which are of any value but the knowledge that has been distilled from it.

Experience may not always lead to knowledge. If you observe a pencil partly immersed in water, it appears to be bent. Most people probably know that this is caused by the refraction of the light in the liquid, which has a higher refractive index than that of air. If we did not know this, however, withdrawing the pencil from the water and observing that it was now straight would not necessarily bring us this knowledge. In fact, if we then slowly push the pencil back under, you can actually see the 'bending' taking place. A child might well conclude that the water was actually bending the pencil.

Thus it is that, in order correctly to interpret experience in this field of understanding the Self, where the possibility of misinterpreting the results is extremely high, we need the guidance of someone who already has the knowledge – i.e. a guru. Failing that, we must rely on documents such as the Vedas, where this knowledge has been passed down, and repeatedly re-validated, over thousands of years. Once the knowledge that the pencil is not really bending has been attained, we are no longer taken in by the appearance, even though our eyes still pass the same messages to the brain.

Knowledge, wisdom and truth

We refer to something as known when it has been metaphorically 'pinned down'. It refers to facts – pieces of information objectified and dead, laid out on a slab for all to see. Knowledge necessarily relates to the past and is dualistic – 'I know *this*'. Knowledge often simply bolsters the ego. It is traditionally something that is earned through long years of study. A student earns knowledge in the same way that a businessman earns money. It is a comfortable relationship between a subject (the knower) and an object (the known). Knowledge might be power but it is not wisdom; nor is it truth. We would probably regard it as self-evident that someone who is knowledgeable about a given topic is in a far better position (with respect to that topic) than someone who is ignorant. But the Isha Upanishad tells us: *"Those who worship ignorance enter into blinding darkness but those who worship knowledge enter into still greater darkness"*. (Note that the 'Self-knowledge' that will be described later in the book is a truth intuited or 'realized' in the present, not an objective piece of information acquired by a subjective ego.)

The more I read, the more I meditate, and the more I acquire, the more certain I am that I know nothing. Voltaire

Someone acting from knowledge may just be relating to the past, to memories of events that might bear some similarity to those of the present but will most likely not. It is not possible to be fully aware, and therefore totally responsive to present events unless the attention is on the here and now and there are no discursive thoughts. If the mind is partly considering the body of knowledge, available in memory and relating to the matters in hand, then that part of the mind will not be available to give attention to what is in front of us. And there is no guarantee that the past information will be relevant or appropriate. Only by attending fully can the response be optimal.

Osho, a notorious Sage of recent history, uses the metaphors of a photograph and a mirror (Ref. 43). When we act through reference to the past, our mind is functioning like a photograph album, looking up information to see how something once was in the past. The picture is frozen and unreal; it cannot continue to change as the world does. Past experience and conclusions can blind us to what is happening now. On the other hand, when we act totally in the present, the mind is functioning like a mirror, reflecting what is here and now; then, spontaneity and creativity become possible.

In Indian systems of philosophy, the methods by which knowledge can be attained are called *pramANa-s*. There are six of these but the three major ones referred to by Shankara (*shaMkara*) are as follows (Shankara was an Indian philosopher in the 8th Century AD who, more than anyone else, clearly formulated and systematized the principles of Advaita):

- The most obvious is *perception* – I see a chair; I sit down in it and don't fall through it to the floor; therefore I genuinely believe it to be a chair.

- Particularly important, when much of what the philosophy says is counter-intuitive, is what we are told by the scriptures or by realized men of today i.e. from sources that we regard as expert. This is called *testimony*, with writings such as the Upanishads providing particularly valuable sources. They tell us that we are not our bodies. We reflect on this and eventually see it to be so through our own experience.

• Thirdly, there is *inference*; for example we inferred the earth to be spherical, because we saw ships gradually 'disappearing' over the horizon, before space travel actually showed it to be so.

Men occasionally stumble over the truth, but most of them pick themselves up and hurry off as if nothing ever happened. Winston Churchill

Wisdom comes through experience and from seeing clearly how things actually are. It is not to do with having lots of knowledge. The knowledge may have been gained as a result of an experience in the past but it has then been let go, not held on to. Knowledge to which one remains attached can prove an obstacle to behaving appropriately in a new situation. Every moment is new and has to be seen without prejudice. And the most profound wisdom is knowledge of Self. All false conceptions of what this is must be renounced before the Truth can be discovered.

Truth is not about acquiring more and more knowledge until some sort of critical mass is attained and the Self is realized – quite the opposite. It is about discarding more and more of the material and immaterial aspects to which the ego has become attached until nothing more is left – the Self is none of these. Ramakrishna, another early twentieth century Sage, compared it to an onion. You keep removing layers of the onion (ego) and when the last layer is removed you find nothing there.

Truth itself is simply what it *is*, here and now. You just have to accept it and not try to 'understand' it, or worse still try to describe it or otherwise pin it down. It is beyond thought, opinion, belief, knowledge or wisdom and, most importantly of all, it is beyond the ego. 'I' (the ego) cannot lay claim to it. 'I' (the Self), the ultimate subject, am it. And the Self is beyond time, space and causation. The meaning of statements such as these will become clear in Section 3. The Mundaka Upanishad (3.1.6) states: *"Truth alone triumphs, not untruth. The route of the spiritual path is opened by truth so that, free from desire, the Sages reach the highest abode of that truth."*

To return to the beginning then, we say, or think, that we are ignorant. But who is it that is ignorant? Not the Self, whose nature is still to be established, but the illusory ego. We have all experienced moments when the ego is absent, though may not have acknowledged them in this way. They are characterized by a transparent clarity, in which the truth of the situation is clearly seen without any doubt. We *know*, even though we may not appreciate from where this knowledge arises. We commonly call it *intuition*. And the 'Self-knowledge' that we are seeking is not what we normally refer to as 'knowledge' since the Self would then somehow have to be able to stand outside of itSelf in order to observe it objectively. Ramana Maharshi tells us that there is neither knowledge nor ignorance; the Self is itself true knowledge with nothing else that could be known. He says "the Sage also is ignorant, because there is nothing for him to know".

Alan Watts observed, in his early book based on Advaita:

There was a young man who said 'though
It seems that I know that I know,
What I would like to see
Is the I that sees me
When I know that I know that I know'. The Book Ref. 39

Some knowledge we are absolutely certain of and could never be convinced otherwise. Supposing, for example, that you are not Chinese and have never learned the Chinese language. If I ask you whether or not you are able to speak Chinese fluently, you will answer 'no'. Clearly, you do not have knowledge of the Chinese language. And, if I ask you if you know that to be the case, you will be able to answer with absolute certainty: 'I *know* that I do not know Chinese'.

It is with this same degree of certainty, that you can also say: 'I exist', 'I am conscious'. This may seem obvious but is worthy of reflection in any investigation into your true nature! Although it can be demonstrated that you are not a body, mind, ego, person or role, it is incontrovertible that you exist.

Self-knowledge

He who knows others is learned; he who knows himself is wise. Lao Tse

This is, of course, the real subject of this book but, though much more will be said about it, you should be aware right now of a very severe limitation. This is that all that will be said is ultimately only words, relating to ideas, all of which is just mind-stuff. And the Self is not the mind. No amount of thinking and reasoning can take you outside of the mind. Even in moments of silence, any observation or reflection will be from the standpoint of the mind and you are beyond this. Even the perception that your mind is 'still', is still only an idea *in* the mind, relating *to* the mind. Any observation of anything maintains the illusion of duality and is likely to obstruct Self-knowledge, because there must necessarily be an observer and something observed.

Unfortunately, reading and learning cannot itself give you Self-knowledge. At the end of this book, you will be in possession of lots of relevant information but you must not expect that you will 'know yourself'. Sri Ramakrishna said of the process: *Only two kinds of people can attain self-knowledge: those who are not encumbered at all with learning, that is to say, whose minds are not overcrowded with thoughts borrowed from others; and those who, after studying all the scriptures and sciences, have come to realize that they know nothing.* (Ref. 63)

But to come back to thoughts, it would be also be a mistake to feel that we have, somehow, to 'get rid of' thoughts. Thoughts are intrinsic to mind and minds are part of what it means to be a person. The thing that has to be remembered is that we, the real Self, are neither a person nor the thoughts. Once that is truly known, the thoughts can simply be enjoyed along with the rest of the apparent creation, without any problem of identification. It is only the identification that carries us away and causes problems. We exist in silence, thoughts arise, we see the thoughts and then they dissolve back into silence. We are there before, during and after this process.

Also, regardless of the fact that we may not *know* the Self, we necessarily already *are* the Self. This may seem too obvious to mention but spiritual seekers often feel that they have to 'reach' somewhere by dint of effort. This is not the case – we already *are* that which we seek. It is just that the mind needs to come to this realization.

Language

Ramesh Balsekar said: *"The limitations of words are clearly seen when they try to remind the Absolute of its true nature. Being merely the expression of thought, they can neither expose ignorance, which is non-existent, nor reveal the Absolute to which they owe their existence. For this purpose words are as useless as a lamp at midday, which can neither dispel the darkness that is not there nor reveal the light of the sun."* (From the periodical newsletter obtained by email from http://www.advaita.org/)

Much of our problems in trying to understand any of this arise through language. And we not only *speak* in language – many of us think in words for much of the time as well. So much a part of our lives has it become, that it can be difficult to realize that these words are only symbols for the things, concepts, feelings etc. to which they refer. They began as convenient fictions so that we might communicate intelligibly with one another but they have become mind-manacles, making us believe that we are talking about realities.

What do we mean, for example, by the word 'mountain', when we say 'I see a mountain'? Our own particular nature and mind filter what enters through the senses. My nature is a result of my past actions etc; yours is a result of your past actions. My thoughts and ideas, opinions and beliefs, are just one particular set of all the possible ideas and thoughts and the chance of that set corresponding with your particular set is vanishingly small. Accordingly, there is effectively zero possibility that what reaches my awareness when I look at a mountain is the same as what reaches your awareness.

Imagine the way several different people would see this hypothetical mountain e.g. a rock climber, a landscape photographer, someone who has lived all his life in Holland, someone whose child has been killed in a mountaineering accident. Would they all see the same 'picture of a mountain'?

Implicit in the development of language is the 'me' and the 'me-object' relationship. There is no named without a namer, and no namer without a named. As language develops, we are swallowed by the reality that language creates. Steven Harrison (Ref. 75)

Language is so fundamental to humans that our minds are easily misled into forgetting that the words we use are only a convenience, and an arbitrary one at that. We assign a name to something so that we can talk about it with someone else without the presence of the related object. But then we forget that original purpose and the name assumes far more significance. We take it for granted, for example, that the named object has a separate existence, both from other objects and from ourselves, the observer.

Here is what Leo Hartong says about it:

"By labeling the world around us, we apparently gain the power to manipulate it to a certain degree; but through this practice, we also get hypnotized into seeing the world as a collection of separate objects, facts and events, instead of as a single occurrence.

"When we see two islands, are they separated by water, connected by water, or does the water hide their connection? Is there really a wave and an ocean, a fire and its flames, the water and its wetness or, for that matter, a person and his environment?" (Ref. 74)

Once we begin to examine our named objects more closely, we begin to find that things may not be quite so clear as we thought. If we consider an 'object' such as a television or an airplane, it is obvious that these actually consist of many separate parts, each of which is an object in its own right. But what about a wooden table, a glass bottle and a gold ring? Well, if we take an axe to the table, we will soon reduce it to a state wherein it will no longer function as a table. Smashing the bottle will destroy its purpose instantly. And we will find that what we had previously (and still have) was really only wood and glass, respectively. In the case of the ring, we need a fairly high temperature to demonstrate that what 'really' exists is only gold. But, nevertheless, that is really the case.

It is the way that we use the words that causes the confusion. Swami Dayananda suggests that we should not refer to a 'wooden table' at all. What we should really call it is 'tabley wood'! It is, after all, only wood which happens to be being *used* as a table. With some skilful joinery, we could soon rearrange the bits and convert it into a chair.

So, can we say that wood and glass are fundamental, separate objects? No. Wood consists of complex organic polymers, synthesized in a living tree and glass is formed by the fusion of silica. Detailed analysis would reveal various chemicals held in more or less rigid structures. It is surely these chemicals that are the actual, separate objects. But no, again. The various chemicals are formed by combination of discrete elements such as carbon, hydrogen and oxygen. Extremes of temperature and pressure or other chemical or physical processes could split these substances into their separate elements. But even these are not the final story. Each element consists of a nucleus of protons and neutrons, surrounded at a relatively great distance by electrons. These fundamental particles are common to *all* elements, and therefore *all* objects.

Finally, of course, even these particles turn out not to be fundamental but are themselves made up of still more 'fundamental' ones. We need yet more powerful, nuclear fission processes to demonstrate this but science now has this capability. Ultimately, we have to concede that everything seems to be 'made up of' energy, for want of a better word. Advaita recognized all of this several thousand years ago. The philosophy states that all apparently separate things are only a form of one universal principle (called *brahman*). (Note that I am *not* saying that *brahman* equates to energy!) We give these separate things separate names for convenience but this does not alter the fact that they do not have any separate existence of their own. In effect they are neither real nor unreal. A cup has obvious utility – it can be used to hold your coffee (which you probably feel in great need of after this!) – but you have to concede that, actually, it is only clay, (assuming that it is made out of clay). It *was* clay, it *is* clay now and it will *return* to clay when it eventually breaks.

There is a special term for this 'dependent' existence: *mithyA*. It is necessary to use this Sanskrit term since English has no corresponding concept. There will be a reminder about it in Chapter 12.

Language and science are ultimately inadequate when it comes to many aspects of this subject. It is just not possible to talk about the Self or reality. The philosopher Ludwig Wittgenstein spent many years of his life agonizing over problems of logic until he was diverted into a more mystical vein by his experiences at the front in the First World War. When he finally completed his work 'Tractatus Logico-Philosophicus', he explained that the real subject of the book was in the second (unwritten) part because the world of ethics and metaphysics is beyond speech, it can only be 'shown' (or realized). The final sentence of the book is perhaps one of the most famous in Western philosophy: *"Whereof we cannot speak, thereof we must remain silent"*

Metaphysician: A man who goes into a dark cellar at midnight without a light looking for a black cat that is not there. Bowen of Colwood

5. The driving forces of our lives

Happiness

The Constitution only gives people the right to pursue happiness. You have to catch it yourself. Ben Franklin

If you have conceded the earlier arguments about identification and attachment, you might now be convinced that you don't really want the body of an athlete or the mind of a nuclear physicist. You don't want to live in the Bahamas or own a Rolls Royce. You don't even want to live forever or marry your favorite film star. You may well have already acknowledged the futility of such dreams but would you agree that, even if you did realize them, they would not really satisfy you anyway?

Why should this be so? Well, it is certainly not that these things are so unattainable, so big and important compared to insignificant little me. As I keep saying, things are often the opposite of how they normally appear. The reason that these things could never satisfy is that (ignoring for the minute the fact that they are all *mithyA*) they are all *insignificant* compared to the Self. And there is a popular saying that 'the large can never find satisfaction in the small'. There are lots of recorded instances of children from impoverished backgrounds growing up and becoming rich, achieving many of their dreams of material possessions and association with the famous. But they did not appear, thereby, to become happy and fulfilled.

So what are we actually looking for, when we direct our efforts into seeking these apparently significant, but actually *in*significant, objectives? Perhaps they are all just manifestations of one basic desire, which is simply to be happy. But what do we mean when we say this? When you are happy, do you know why? How long does it last and what brings it to an end?

Look back on your past life. Have there been things about which you said "I would be happy if only..."? Did you manage to achieve or obtain whatever it was? Did it make you happy? Did this last? Why not? This last question is not tongue in cheek. I predict with confidence that you answered, or at least will soon answer, 'No' to the question as to whether or not it lasted. Happiness does not last. It comes and goes. This seems to be one of the features of happiness and why this should be so is obviously an interesting question. In fact, Swami Paramarthananda says that according to Vedanta, if you try to make one list of all of the sources of happiness and another list of all of the sources of misery, you will find that you do not have to make two lists at all!

Do you think that people in general are happier than they used to be? Most people probably answer 'no' to this one. There seems to be a sort of wistful longing for the 'old days', when life was simple and peaceful; out in the clean country air far from the rush and stress of city life. But wouldn't you say that life is easier now than it used to be? Most people, in the West at least, don't have to worry about basic needs any more. They have washing machines and microwaves, refrigerators and vacuum cleaners, just to mention a few of the more basic convenience items. All of the drudgery has been taken out of domestic life, leaving us free for leisure activities. And just think of all of the ways in which we can spend that free time.

So how do we reconcile these two answers? Modern technology has taken away most of the tedium and given us tremendous variety for recreation and yet we are *less* happy.

Originally, to be happy meant having 'hap', which meant luck or good fortune, the implication being that one couldn't actually 'do' anything to become happy, it 'hap'pened by chance. What we want seems to be intimately involved with the feeling of happiness that we expect to result when we get it. Most people would accept that we are happy when we achieve or get something that we very much wanted. Conversely, we tend to be unhappy when such endeavors result in failure.

But this is not always the case, is it? Sometimes people think that a particular thing is all they need to make them happy but, once they get it, they feel if anything a loss, as though a promised prize has been taken away from them. And one person may dread what makes another happy. So, happiness is not to be found in objects. If it were we could just keep a supply of them and get a new one out of the drawer when the old one started to run low. And although a particular object might bring us happiness one time, there is no guarantee it will do so again. Nor does more of a happy thing bring proportionately more happiness – large cream cakes are an obvious example!

There is also the religious view, telling us that happiness results from giving, not taking – an unselfish love of others and desire for their wellbeing. How is that making someone else happy, possibly someone we do not even know, can simultaneously make us happy?

Happiness depends on what you can give, not on what you can get.
Swami Chinmayananda

Aristotle thought that happiness was not something that resulted from or went along with certain activities but actually *was* the activities themselves. Strictly speaking, he was referring to 'eudaimonia' rather than happiness, a Greek word that means rather more than happiness. Western Philosophers in the 18th and 19th Centuries defined happiness simply as pleasure rather than pain. But is this really saying anything? What is pleasure other than a condition that gives happiness? Others defined pleasure as a physical thing whereas happiness was mental, i.e. associated with reason as opposed to emotions.

These are really two contrasting views, the physical pleasures (hedonism) versus the more refined intellectual ones (eudaimonism), wherein man realizes his true potential. The former is represented, somewhat tongue-in-cheek, by Samuel Johnson, who said: "*There is nothing which has yet been contrived by man by which so much happiness is produced as by a good tavern*". William Lyon Phelps favored the other approach when he said: "*The happiest people are those who think the most interesting thoughts. Those who decide to use leisure as a means of mental development, who love good music, good books, good pictures, good company, good conversation, are the happiest people in the world.*"

Both of these views, however, have something in common – the wanting of something. Perhaps the more physical person (rajasic) wants sport and holidays etc. while the more intellectual (sattvic) wants books, music, art.

But both desire some object(ive). If they get it, they are happy; if they do not, they are miserable.

Desire

The key to understanding is to take a step back and look at the desires that drive us to seek the object or situation that we think will bring us happiness. If you have brought up a child, you know how it will want first one thing and then another. It begins with the initial perceiving of an object and the desire to possess it. This is accompanied by positive expressions to indicate the desire – pointing, asking, wheedling etc – and, if these do not succeed, negative expressions of frustration and anger – crying, shouting, lying on the floor kicking legs in the air etc.

As soon as the parent gives in and delivers the desired object, there is pleasure, apparent happiness and peace for a while until, inevitably, boredom sets in and the child looks around for some new distraction. The process is repeated. There are two main points to be noticed. Firstly, as soon as the desired object is obtained, the disturbed state of mind (yours as well as his!) is replaced by a calm and satisfied one. Secondly, when some new desire takes over, the first object is dropped, no longer providing the sought-for state of mind.

This pattern continues throughout our lives. Toy bricks are replaced by train sets; these in turn by roller skates, then by cycles, then computer games. Later, a teenager will start to take an interest in the opposite sex. Then *all* previous interests are forgotten. Even if an earlier desire is not dropped completely, there is a progression, from simple to increasingly sophisticated. There is an analogy with Maslow's hierarchy of human needs (Ref. 54) here, with basic requirements for food and shelter at the bottom of the ladder and self-actualization at the top of the hierarchy. For the purposes of this discourse, I am going to interpret the latter as the desire to 'realize' the Self, to understand fully what one is and what the 'purpose' of life might be.

Think also for a moment about the unhappiness associated with *not* having the desired object. It is not present all the time, is it? You might be sitting there, dreaming about the next generation computer that you cannot afford and the virtual reality games that you would be able to play on it, feeling miserable that you will have to work overtime for another two months before you will be able to afford it. Then, your partner comes into the room, wearing something revealing and suddenly your disappointment is completely forgotten. Clearly, just as happiness is not to be found in the object itself, neither is unhappiness associated with the lack of the desired object. As soon as the attention is redirected and the lack is forgotten, so too is the unhappiness.

Another way of looking at this is as identification with ideas in the mind, as already discussed. An idea occurs that some object will bring happiness. Consciousness becomes identified with this idea; i.e. its power gives force to the thought, and this process *is* desire. Just another example of *ahaMkAra*, really. And, if happiness should arise seemingly of itself, it is not long before we start to analyze it, looking for explanations and thus for ways to prolong it or repeat it. If the ideas are not there to begin with, we soon introduce them and generate desire.

This may be appreciated by looking at another emotion – grief. There is a story in one of the philosophical texts of Vedanta, called the Panchadashi (*pa~nchadashI*), Ref. 15, 4.34 – 4.35, which goes as follows. *"A liar told a man whose son had gone to a far-off country that the boy was dead, although he was still alive. The father believed him and was aggrieved. If, on the other hand, his son had really died abroad but no news had reached him, he would have felt no grief. This shows that the real cause of a man's bondage is his own mental world."*

Nothing external is, in itself, the source of happiness: not objects, relationships, money, status or anything else that might absorb your energy. At the moment of attainment, and for varying lengths of time thereafter, happiness may occur. Moreover, it can only occur *now*. Isaac Shapiro, another disciple of Sri Poonja, said: *"The only moment that you can ever be happy is this instant. That's it. You cannot know Truth in the past or in the future."*

Inevitably, however, this seems to be followed by some negative complement, be it disappointment, dissatisfaction, misery or even actual pain. Lasting happiness cannot be found in anything outside. We know this to be true if we would only admit it to ourselves and yet we persist in looking. As soon as the novelty of having obtained one thing has worn off, we want something else, vainly hoping that this will be the Holy Grail for which we are eternally seeking.

Pleasure and pain are regarded as opposite aspects of the emotions brought about through attachment. They go together like the poles of a magnet. They belong to the illusory ego and are not anything to do with real happiness.

So let's look a little more closely at the nature of the relationship between desire and happiness. We recognize that the happiness is not in the thing itself – it does not always bring happiness to the same person and may always bring unhappiness to someone else. E.g. the cream cake already mentioned would not be at all attractive if we felt ill and would never bring happiness to someone allergic to dairy products. It is attained when the objective is attained, when the desire for the object is satisfied and goes away. Perhaps, then, happiness is simply *absence* of desire. Perhaps our natural state is one of happiness and the presence of desire obscures this.

The desire itself need not cause any problem. If we see the desire arise but then immediately let it go, no harm is done. And, even when we act upon it, it is not the desire per se that causes us heartache but the expectations that we associate with it. Swami Dayananda says that, if the results are better than we expected, then we are elated; if the same, we are satisfied; if less, we are disappointed; and if the results are the opposite of what we expected, we are miserable. All of these emotions cloud our perception. He says: *"There is absolutely nothing wrong with desires. It is being controlled by them and always expecting them to be fulfilled that creates the problem. If we can accept the fact that certain desires will remain unfulfilled, the uncertainties of life will not affect us adversely."* (Ref. 76)

Desire is about feeling a lack; suffering because we believe we need something that is currently out of reach. If we did not have this feeling, we would be fulfilled. Nor can it be true that there really was a lack. Otherwise, once the desired object was obtained, that would bring an end

63

to the suffering. But we know from experience that the relief is always only temporary. All too soon, we identify another lack and start working towards that.

As long as we remain seduced by our desires, constantly striving to satisfy them, we will continue to suffer the cycle of temporary elation followed by more general dissatisfaction. According to traditional Advaita, this cycle continues not only in this life but on into innumerable future lives until such time as we discover the truth about ourselves and attain liberation. This perpetual cycle of birth and death is called *saMsAra*. Sureshvara, one of the four principal disciples of Shankara, spells this out in doom-laden tones in his *naiShkarmya siddhi* (I. 41-2):

> *"Descending into the terrible ocean of pain called transmigration (*saMsAra*) which comprehends all from brahmA (the creator) to a blade of grass, pushed upwards and downwards like a bucket at a well, and entering higher and lower wombs yielding experiences of pleasure, pain and delusion which appear and vanish like lightning in the sky, verily he floats hither and thither tossed by the winds of his good, evil and intermediate deeds like a dried pumpkin buffeted this way and that by tumultuous winds upon the sea.*

> *"Thus the man of desire perpetually revolves in a circle. He is born bound tight by the bonds of nescience, desire and his past actions. And he dies immersed in miseries."* (Ref. 77)

The conclusion from this analysis might be that, if we want to be happy, we must 'give up' desires and fears. Don't be a dried pumpkin! But, if nothing else, this would seem to require inordinate amounts of self-discipline given that today's society seems to be totally geared to instilling into us as many desires as possible! (No wonder today's society is also apparently so unhappy!) Perhaps a more attainable objective is to follow the suggestion of Swami Dayananda and simply stop expecting results. But another way of looking at it is that, if happiness is our true nature, we don't actually have to do anything at all!

All feelings, if we identify with them, are a form of bondage. The ego has latched on to some object, thought or feeling and the power of consciousness is being given to it. It might be desire, grief, fear or whatever; they are all projections of a sense of lack or limitation. We foolishly believe that our wellbeing depends upon getting, or not getting, the object. We can regard these thoughts as disturbances of our mind in the same way that ripples are disturbances on the surface of a lake. Just as we can only see down into the depths of the lake when the water is calm, so too can we only get a glimpse of our true nature when all of these disturbances have gone.

It is difficult to find happiness in oneself but it is impossible to find it anywhere else. Schopenhauer

We spend all our efforts looking outside of ourselves for that elusive object or situation which will finally give us lasting happiness. Yet it is the act of looking that takes us away from happiness. Happiness is what remains when searching ceases and we 'discover' the Self that we have always been – *this* is perfect happiness.

Nisargadatta Maharaj said: *"Only something as vast and deep as your real Self can make you truly and lastingly happy."* (Ref. 26) What you might think you want is due to an imagined lack or limitation. In reality, your true nature is without any limits. Therefore, you really need and should want nothing because you already have everything.

Though this way of looking at the situation may seem alien at first, it is not complicated. Our true nature is one of completeness, lacking nothing (although you will not believe this until you have read Section 3). The problem only begins when the consciousness of 'I am' becomes identified with firstly the body, then the mind and so on. Once this happens, we believe ourselves to be separate, in a universe of other things separate in space and time. Following on from this are such feelings as suffering – because we are separate from these other things – and desire – because we wish to be 're-joined' to them.

The Chandogya Upanishad tells us (Ref. 62, 7.23.1) that only the

65

infinite can *be* happiness; nothing finite can have this. Anything less than the infinite is necessarily limited. Thus it is that we, as humans, are forever searching, moving towards something greater, always wanting something more. Although we may find temporary satisfaction with some goal attained, this always fades, more or less quickly, and the search begins again. We will inevitably continue the search until that fullness is realized which is our true nature.

The 'person' that we think ourselves to be is inevitably subject to all that life has to throw at it. When things are going well, people will be generally happy; when the tide turns, as it always does, they may respond by being miserable. The extent to which they are prone to suffer on this reversal of fortune will depend upon upbringing, nature etc. The point is that, for the person, happiness and misery are the two poles of experience. Some may be fortunate to spend a life primarily at the favorable pole but others will not. But, as discussed earlier – *we are not the person*. As will be understood later, the Self that we really are is beyond these two poles. We are really limitless or infinite and, as such, can be truly happy beyond the trivial ups and downs of this transient life. The truth takes you beyond personal happiness and unhappiness.

If you are looking for personal happiness or an end to personal unhappiness, then Advaita is not the answer. Advaita is about the realization that there is no person, that who you really are is already limitless, full and complete. One comes to Advaita when it has been accepted that lasting happiness is never going to be found in people or things – how can anything that is transient and ever-changing bring lasting happiness?

This does not mean that you reject the world but that you determine to look elsewhere, namely *within* rather than outside for any 'truth'. If you can genuinely do this and resolve totally to pursue the truth without reservation, then you have a purpose that can overcome any obstacle.

We need to learn to differentiate between the transient and the eternal, truth and falsehood. This is the function of the discriminating intellect, which operates correctly only in stillness. The happiness that is brought to us briefly by the little day-to-day events and even the happiness realized when some major objective is achieved are all too transient. We (the ego) are never satisfied and go off searching to satisfy some new desire. We are looking in the wrong place, like the woman who had lost her necklace. She looked for it everywhere in vain, when it was round her neck the whole time. The limitlessness that we crave is the nature of our own Self.

Fear, anger and grief

I've developed a new philosophy... I only dread one day at a time.
Charlie Brown

Fear is simply the obverse of desire; instead of wanting something very much, we very much *don't* want something. Happiness arises in just the same manner when a fear goes away as when a desire goes away, though we might tend to call it 'relief' in this case. Anger is what results when a desire is frustrated. If, as a child, we want to go out to play and our mother says no, we have to do our homework, then we get angry. Grief is what we feel when an object to which we are attached is taken away or destroyed. All attachments ultimately bring sorrow and the irony is that the usual way of relieving that sorrow is to attach ourselves to something new. Teenagers are miserable when their boyfriend or girlfriend breaks off the relationship and they remain so until they meet someone new and it starts all over again.

All of these emotions are selfish. I am jealous because I have something and I don't want anyone else to share it. There is an airplane crash or other serious accident and I rejoice that my friend or relation was saved, having only minor distress over all those who were killed. Are we concerned when we see a supernova in the night sky, signaling the destruction of a star and any planets in its orbit? My attachments determine my emotions and these emotions will oscillate between happiness and misery, joy and grief, incessantly. Whatever the emotion of the moment, you know it will not last but will eventually be superseded by its opposite. All events, no matter how painful they may seem at the time, will also 'come to pass' – life itself is only a transient blip on the screen of eternity. Lasting equanimity can only come when all attachments have ceased. Misery and grief and all other negative emotions will only come to an end when it is fully realized that who-I-really-am is unaffected by any of these things. Even death only affects the body and mind.

Love

"I spend several hours every Sunday cleaning my car until I can see my face in it. If ever anyone scratches it they'd better watch out!"

"I can't stop buying cakes! Cream cakes especially, with jam and flaky pastry that just melts in your mouth."

"My favorite country to go for a holiday is Greece. I've been twice a year for the past twenty years – I never get tired of it."

"I'm obsessed with that guy. I can't stop thinking about him. I don't suppose I'll ever even speak to him but I can, at least, listen to his records over and over again."

"We've been married for fifteen years now. We get on really well and like the same things. I don't know what I'd do if anything ever happened to her. I guess we'll probably be together for the rest of our lives."

Even without the section heading, it wouldn't require a very incisive intellect to work out what word each of the above statements might have in common. The fact that this is so, however, must make us question whether the word has any special meaning. Most of the states of mind mentioned in the examples seem to bear an uncanny resemblance to the description given for *ahaMkAra*. They relate to identification or attachment to an external object or person.

Love is the answer but, while you are waiting for the answer, sex raises some pretty good questions. Woody Allen

'I love my car' really means that I gain some spurious feeling of status by being seen with it. Perhaps it is an expensive or rare model and I like to feel

(= imagine) that others are envying my owning it. I have invested it with the power of my consciousness so that I would feel personally injured if it were damaged.

'I love cakes' merely implies that the speaker desires them. Possibly she habitually overeats as a displacement activity for dissatisfaction at a more interpersonal level or perhaps she identifies with her body and denies herself the pleasure of eating cakes because she fears that the body's perceived attraction might suffer as a result. Such a person would probably continue along the lines of 'but I really mustn't!' or 'but I'm on a diet'.

'I love Greece' presumably means that the speaker enjoyed a holiday there once and now returns as often as possible in order to try to repeat the experience. They like the familiar and are reluctant to sample anything new.

'I love Gary Baldy (the pop star)' only signifies someone who spends large parts of their time day-dreaming, imagining themselves in places and situations with someone whose body they find attractive. The mind, personality and behavior of this object of their desire will almost certainly be totally unknown and will be imagined to exhibit whatever character-istics they themselves find most endearing.

'I love my wife' probably indicates a history of largely pleasant acquaintance from initial physical attraction, through discovery of shared enjoyments and aspirations and mutual support in more difficult times. There will undoubtedly have been many feelings over the years but there will be growing dependence through joint commitments such as home and children. There will be the reassuring familiarity of understanding the behavior of the partner (possibly!) and habitual shared activities. (See the jello model of mind described earlier under Behavioral Tendencies.) And there will be, as one grows older, more of an acceptance of the way things are, less of a tendency to want to change one's situation, more of a depen-dence upon each other. This, too, all sounds very much like various levels of attachment.

Love: a temporary insanity curable by marriage. Ambrose Bierce

Love has certainly inspired some of the most beautiful poetry ever written but the ways in which the word is often used suggests that much of what passes as love is ego related. In this sense, it is not dissimilar to what was discussed above in respect of desire. There is a perceived lack and a belief that the loved (= desired) object or person will somehow fill that need. Where a marriage, for example, appears to work very well, this is because the needs of the individuals concerned are well met by their partner. When the particular needs cease to be met, there is a danger that a marriage will break down and new partners be sought who will satisfy the perceived lack of the moment.

Whilst the people concerned are still convinced that they are separate entities, struggling for survival in an inhospitable world, how can things be any different? Whilst it is the ego wanting something for itself, love is bound to be selfish and therefore least like its true meaning. Love at this level is always a subject wanting an object for itself. Indeed, while love is at the level of the ego only, it is not possible to have a real 'relationship' at all because two objects cannot relate. It is only when those involved cease to see themselves as separate that a true meeting becomes possible.

To understand the real meaning of the word, it is necessary to ask oneself 'what is it that is loved above everything else?' If we are honest, the answer to this has to be 'me'! Remember that 'pure feeling of existence' that was suggested as being occasionally felt upon waking from a deep and refreshing sleep? Advaita suggests that it is that which we love the most – our own *and everyone else's* true nature. The reason I italicized the phrase in the previous sentence is that I am suggesting that love is most nearly itself when that same essence is re-cognized in another person or thing. And I put the hyphen into 're-cognize' precisely to emphasize that this means 'known again', because we already know it in ourselves.

The feeling of love does not come from outside, caused by the object or person 'loved' but from one's own nature. This is precisely as already discussed in respect of happiness. And it is just the same with beauty. We deem something beautiful because it strikes a chord *within* us; because that chord is resonating with the perceived object; sounding the unison of Self or Consciousness.

Sri Poonja said: *"Know that what appears to be Love for an 'other' is really Love of Self because 'other' doesn't exist. So this innermost Love can be given to no 'other'. Love of friends is for the sake of Self, not for body to body. True love has no Lover or Beloved because all Love is Love of Self."* (Ref. 31)

The reason that 'love of God' is considered to be the highest expression of this feeling is that it recognizes the existence of a reality that encompasses all and negates the ego. One's sense of 'I' is lost in the bigger picture. Along with this, any desire or other love for something separate, to be gained for oneself, disappears. It is the giving up of everything, ultimately to gain everything.

6. Actions and Results

Cause and effect

There is nothing that living things do that cannot be understood from the point of view that they are made of atoms acting according to the laws of physics. Richard Feynman

We should now be much clearer about where we are, what our problems are and what needs to be done. We have erroneously identified our Self with inferior ideas and things. We have desired objects and states in the mistaken belief that obtaining them will bring us happiness. Now we have recognized this, it is simply a matter of dropping the desires, remembering that we are not the body and mind, and everything will be fine. Is it not plain sailing from this point on? Well, actually, no... Before we attempt to find a suitable 'spiritual path' and set off on the road towards truth and self-realization, we need to consider what our scope for action might be and the extent to which this is affected by previous actions. And how do we qualify the results of actions? Are actions intrinsically good or bad and is there such a thing as 'sin'?

Most of us have long been converted to a scientific world-view rather than a religious one or any other. We believe in scientific laws and tend to be very skeptical of anything that appears to transgress them. One of the most obvious apparent laws is that of cause and effect. We turn the light switch and there is illumination; we eat food that has gone off and become sick. Even so-called accidents follow this law. Someone crosses a road without looking and is knocked over. You read a book while eating and drop food down your shirt. There is no mystery about these things. It is so much a part of the way we interpret events that, if there is no known cause for a given effect, we invent one. We see an apple falling to the ground – we posit a force called gravity as its cause.

This was the suggestion of Alan Watts, in his talk 'Ghosts' (Ref. 51). He said that gravity is a case where an unknown, undetectable force is used to 'explain' why, for example, a rock falls to the ground when it is dropped. We say that the rock falls 'because of' gravity. In fact, this explains nothing at all and, he suggested, is actually not necessary. It is part of the definition of 'rock' that it will act in this way; if we dropped it and it rose up into the air, we should instead call it a balloon. Often, when we put forward 'reasons' for things occurring, all that we are doing is describing the process in greater detail. In this case, Newton went on to define the process in mathematical detail, saying that the 'force' between two objects was proportional to the product of the masses and inversely proportional to the square of the distance between them. But what is happening is that, when the process of an apple falling, or a planet orbiting, is observed carefully, then the objects act in a way that can be described more accurately in that way.

Watts continued to argue that, if you describe a perceived problem clearly and unambiguously, rather than in the casual language of everyday speech, you can sometimes find that the problem has disappeared. Indeed, the dichotomy of cause and effect can be dissolved in many cases. We say that A 'causes' B but, if we describe what is happening in more detail, the need to resort to this pseudo-explanation may disappear.

The chain of (seeming) cause and effect can become very complicated. Hence the so-called 'butterfly effect' whereby a butterfly flapping its wings in one country can theoretically trigger a hurricane on the other side of the world. Even in our own lives, there are many events, each giving rise to perceptions, ideas, considerations, decisions and possible actions. When we do something, the chain of events that brought it about might be spread over many years and be very difficult to trace.

There is often a tendency to view this so-called 'effect' with skepticism. But the film 'Sliding Doors' in 1998 illustrated how, whether or not a seemingly trivial event occurred would result in quite different outcomes. A short TV series in 2009, called 'Collision' demonstrated this even more dramatically. Failure to swat a wasp in a service station resulted in a disastrous motorway pile-up that affected the lives of many people drastically.

We frequently claim 'I did such and such' and believe it to be true. "Yesterday, I made a bookcase" probably means that I took a parcel of

73

ready-made pieces and put in a few screws. In fact, many others were involved prior to this stage. Skilled workers used complex machinery to produce the parts. Others packaged them,

transported them and served me with the final parcel. Many more were involved constructing the machinery; producing the steel that went into its manufacture; operating other machines that produced the parts; mining the iron ore from which they were constructed. Woodcutters chopped down the trees; drivers transported the timber and so on. And, once we get down to the basic natural constituents, nature will have been working for many thousands of years to produce some of the materials, with sun, wind, water, fire all playing their part to bring about the final product. And yet, with all of this 'behind the scenes' activity, we have the audacity to claim 'I made it'.

> *If you want to bake an apple pie from scratch, you must first create the Universe.* Carl Sagan

O.K, I admit it – I didn't make it. But what is actually happening here? Clearly there are actions and effects. It seems that at least some actions can carry their effects some way in time and space before they manifest. Just think of an event that occurred in your early childhood, possibly something that someone said or made you do, which now, in later life, makes you tend to act in one way rather than another. It is with good reason that theories such as those of Freud became so widely accepted. (E.g. This is supposedly how deviant sexual behavior arises.)

Genetic causes, too, will have their way – a gene for green eyes will not permit us to have blue – but so too will nurture (causes) bring about tendencies for certain behavior (effects). You carry out so many trivial activities in the way that you observed your parents doing them, even though you may now appreciate that these are not the most efficient. Such things as the direction in which you put away the spoons in the cutlery drawer or the order in which you wash yourself are probably dictated by your parents. All learnt actions are initially learned according to the manner of your teacher, who would have learned from her teachers. Some actions may be modified when discrimination shows there to be a better way but many more are simply carried out habitually because you never bothered to give attention and look for optimal efficiency.

karma

This theory effectively says that our actions now will act as a 'cause' for events ('effects') in the future. (Note that all of what follows relating to *karma* is only meaningful at the level of how things *appear* to be in the world. It does not have anything to do with how things *really* are.) Again, the jello model seems appropriate. Even a single application of a stream of hot water will produce a trail and there will be a tendency, however slight, for that track to be followed next time. Every action has its effect that inexorably influences subsequent action. Many Eastern philosophies believe that actions will bring about future events in a lawful manner. The process is called *karma* from the Sanskrit meaning action. In a very general sense it relates to the 'reaction' that inevitably follows, sooner or later, upon action.

The law of *karma* does not say that our future is *dictated* by our past, only that we cannot escape its influence. We are able to act with some independence directed by our intellect and there is a possibility that we can overcome the influences in order to achieve desired results. Swami Chinmayananda used the metaphor of a power boat on a river. The boat cannot escape the influence of the current (*karma*) but the intelligent driver of the boat can use the motor and steer it against the current if necessary in order to reach the destination (this is the 'free will' element). If the current is strong, however, it will take much longer than if it is weak and similarly with the past influences. If we were very shy in our childhood, it will require much effort in order to be able to overcome those tendencies and learn to speak in public without embarrassment. But it can be done.

This theory goes much further, however, than the simple gross level. It applies too at the subtle level of motives and their mental/emotional consequences.

My karma ran over your dogma. Unknown

At the subtle level, then, *karma* says that the motive determines the nature of the act itself. If the motive is selfish, i.e. we want a particular outcome for ourselves, then the action is 'bad'. If it is unselfish, done for a beneficial outcome for someone else, irrespective of how it affects us, it is 'good'. In turn, these actions will have their consequence at some time in the future. A good action will accrue merit or comfort for us in the future, while a bad action will eventually bring us discomfort of one sort or another.

There is, however, a third type of action, called 'right' action, (Sanskrit *niShkAma*, meaning desire-less or disinterested). This is neither selfish nor unselfish but done simply because the intellect, operating in stillness without the prompting of the mind, determines that this is the natural response to the perceived need. It is acting in response to the need rather than re-acting in response to a desire or aversion. This type of action does not incur *karma*; does not bring about any consequences to the originator in later life (or lives). We should aspire to this type of action. The practice of monitoring one's actions and striving to act 'rightly' is called *karma yoga*. It is about acting in a way that does not incur *karma*. In practice, this theory says that we have the freedom to choose how to act but, unless we act 'rightly', the consequences or 'fruit' of our action, called *karmaphala*, will inevitably follow.

The purpose of *karma yoga* in the context of Advaita is to discipline the mind, sublimate the ego and cultivate attention and discrimination. All of these are pre-requisites to being able to assimilate the teaching and thereby realize the truth.

The Isha Upanishad (verse 2) says: *"If one should wish to live a hundred years, one should act 'rightly'. There is no other way to prevent the fruit of action from corrupting you."*

saMskAra

The motives behind our current actions affect our future ones by way of *saMskAra-s* (remember that the 'M' is usually pronounced as 'n' – see Appendix 3). When we perform an action with a desire for a result, this generates *saMskAra-s* that will affect future actions. They give rise to the *vAsanA-s* already mentioned. At any given moment, we will tend to act in the way that is determined by our *vAsanA-s*, which in turn depends upon our *saMskAra-s*.

(The terms *vAsanA* and *saMskAra* are, to a large degree, used almost interchangeably in this book and elsewhere. Correctly speaking, *vAsanA* refers to unconscious impressions, knowledge derived from memory, desires and longing, mistaken inclinations and so on, i.e. there is a generally negative interpretation to the term. In the case of *saMskAra*, there is a sense of cleansing or purification – the root *saM* means 'auspicious'.)

These *saMskAra-s* are the net result of all of our past actions in this and previous lives. (More on this later – do not let the idea of reincarnation make you throw the book out of the window again in disgust!) At the moment of action, if our attention is at the point where the action is taking place and our minds are not clouded by thoughts about whether or how to act, there is said to be a choice. We can act in accordance with our *saMskAra*, in an habitual way. This will reinforce the *saMskAra* for future occasions, just like pouring the water onto the jello. Alternatively, we can respond in the moment, with no thought for the result. This requires 'self-effort' (*puruShArtha*) to overcome the habitual tendencies. (In fact, the general meaning of *puruShArtha* is 'any object of human pursuit', these being traditionally divided into four, viz. gratification of desire (*kAma*), acquisition of wealth (*artha*), performing of duty (*dharma* – see below) and liberation (*mokSha*).) In this case, no new *saMskAra* is generated so that the tendency to act in a 'programmed' manner next time will be reduced.

Remember, people will judge you by your actions, not your intentions. You may have a heart of gold – but so does a hard-boiled egg. Anon

The practice of *karma yoga* is to live our lives acting 'rightly', thereby gradually diminishing our accumulation of *saMskAra*. It might be supposed that eventually, in an indeterminate number of lifetimes, this will reduce to zero, at which point we will become enlightened and no longer be subject to rebirth. But regardless of this, as a guide to how to consider the way in which we act, it has distinct merit, drawing attention, as it does, to the ego and its selfish desire.

All this depends upon two fundamental assumptions, firstly that we can choose to act in a particular way (i.e. that there is free will) and secondly that we 'do' anything at all to begin with. Both of these assumptions will be questioned in chapter 15, 'The Myth of Action'.

In Section 3, it will be seen that all of the topics that are being considered under the heading of 'The Unreal' are interim concepts only. They are used to provide an explanation for how things seem to be. Accepting them temporarily and following their guidance, enables us to prepare our minds for the later teaching. This is a fundamental aspect of the teaching of Advaita, and is called *adhyAropa-apavAda*. This means that we initially make what is in effect an erroneous statement (*adhyAropa*) but then later take this back or rescind it (*apavAda*), once our basic understanding has grown so as to be able to take on board a more subtle explanation. It is a bit like learning Newtonian mechanics before learning about relativity and quantum mechanics.

Good and evil

Tied up with selfish and unselfish actions are the ideas of good and evil. We believe not simply that it is *right* that we should help others less well off than ourselves and *wrong* to deliberately injure another without a just cause but that there is some sort of absolute truth involved here. It is interesting to ask oneself, however, whether anyone ever sets out to perform an act that they themselves believe to be evil. Is it not the case that, deluded as we might deem them to be, such a person would nevertheless think themselves to be doing good? Do not religious fanatics happily murder their perceived enemies in the name of their God? Our own actions are never seen as evil, only those of others. We need to ask ourselves 'in relation to what?' is an action perceived as good or bad.

We identify with the objects of our intentions and pursue them in the belief that we will benefit personally once they have been obtained. Those who might try to prevent or obstruct us are thought to be evil. Each person's upbringing determines whether they see things our way. What is good for one is not necessarily so for another. 'That is good' only means that I approve of it or that society has taught me that most men have deemed it to be something that one *ought* to approve of.

Good is what I feel good after and bad is what I feel bad after. Ernest Hemingway

We have a built-in function of mind that *decides* what is right and what is wrong – it is called *buddhi*. The problem is that we don't always listen to it because the noise created by *manas* drowns it out. We are so tied up with desires and fears and identifications with one thing or another that it is not possible to make the simple, quiet choice to do what we know to be right. Shakespeare's Polonius said, in Hamlet: *"To thine own self be true and it must follow, as night the day, thou can'st not then be false to any man."* If we are true to our conscience, following the directions of the discriminating *buddhi*, we cannot do any wrong to anyone.

All actions, good or bad, happen against a background of being that is unaffected. Osho uses the metaphor of clouds, sometimes white and fluffy, sometimes black and thundery, appearing against a background of sky that is totally unaffected by them. An act of injustice against an individual will affect that person and maybe others close to them, while those remote from the incident will be largely unmoved. An outrage such as the holocaust affected millions and its memory is potent even today. In another millennium, it will only be a topic in a history lesson.

Ultimately, however, a person's actions constitute his role in the play. They have nothing to do with his real Self, which is unaffected by them. As such, it is ultimately meaningless to ascribe any absolute sense of good or bad to them; they have relative meaning only at the level of the play. And it has to be said that plays tend to be pretty boring without their villains. There are no wholly good or wholly evil people. The consequences of actions ripple out across creation in ways that could never be predicted. In the extreme, a good, innocent person, seemingly callously murdered, might just have lived to father someone who would have destroyed the world. These consequences are the causes and effects that bring about the *karma* as discussed above. Thus it is that the Hindu religion would say that those people who find themselves in lives of suffering do so as a result of evil committed in previous lives. Needless to say, most Westerners find this hard to take and, as you will discover in a later chapter, this teaching does not *exactly* say that.

Religions tend to have difficulty coming to terms with the apparent fact of evil. How, they ask, can a God who cares for his creation allow evil to occur. The idea that apparently innocent people are being punished for the sins of others is not readily accepted today and it seems pointless trying to deny the existence of evil, which seems as prevalent now as it ever was. In David Hume's 'Dialogues Concerning Natural Religion', the character Philo says: *"Is he (God) willing to prevent evil, but not able? Then he is impotent. Is he able, but not willing? Then he is malevolent. Is he both able and willing? Whence then is evil?"* Why *is* there so little happiness and so much misery?

There is nothing either good or bad, but thinking makes it so. William Shakespeare (Hamlet)

Simon Blackburn, in his excellent book 'Think' (Ref. 47) gives a modern parable for the situation. Suppose, he says, you are a student who goes to live in the university's halls of residence. You find the most appalling conditions with the buildings in a poor state of repair, filth everywhere and rats roaming about. The food is practically inedible with some students actually starving to death. The people who supposedly manage the halls are never seen, living behind closed doors. Would it be reasonable to infer from the conditions that exist that the management a) is aware of those conditions b) cares very much for the welfare of the students and c) has unlimited power and resources to do whatever it wants to remedy the situation?

Any religion that believes in a separate God and a real world is bound to have difficulty answering these questions. The God of Advaita, although wielding the power of *mAyA* to manifest the world, does not do so arbitrarily. There is no sense of 'wrath' or any human failing at all. Everything is lawful, with an individual's actions reaping their just rewards (eventually). This is how it is at the empirical, world-level. From the standpoint of absolute reality, God too is *mithyA*. Ultimately, neither good nor evil has any real existence. Reality is beyond all seeming dualities.

We can, of course, talk and argue indefinitely about the world and its inhabitants; good and evil and an infinite number of other aspects. These all belong to the *appearance* of reality – what Advaita calls *vyavahAra* (this is the noun and the adjective is *vyAvahArika*.). As we will see, it is actually not possible to speak of the absolute reality at all – what is called *paramArtha* (adjective *pAramArthika*). But if we try to speak about reality, using pointers and metaphors, we cannot simultaneously talk about the world and the individual *jIva* because this will be 'mixing levels'. This is probably the greatest source of confusion in the teaching of Advaita. (The word *jIva* is used to describe the presumed entity that results from identification of the Self with a body-mind. A detailed description will be provided in Chapter 16, 'The Nature of the Self'.)

Note that these 'real' versus 'empirical' ways of looking at things does not mean that there are two 'truths'. There is only one truth, being looked at from two different perspectives. From the personal and worldly perspective, we are seduced by the forms of the non-dual reality and invent separate names to describe them, actually believing them to be separate things. And do not worry – all of this will probably not become clear until you have read the third section of the book. Then you can read it all again and understand it!

This danger of 'level mixing' must be borne in mind in the following analysis. At the empirical level, the level of the apparent world, this non-dual reality that we call 'Consciousness' supports everything, without involvement. Translating this into religious terms, we could say that God is neither good nor bad and is responsible for neither in the world. Using the metaphor of petrol in a car, one could not blame the petrol for the 'evil' caused by a tank nor for the 'good' caused by an ambulance. Similarly, fire can destroy but it can also keep us warm and cook our food. Any good or bad is as perceived by the actors in the play at the time and has no absolute meaning.

Should any of this seem unacceptable from the point of view of such concepts as justice and virtue, remember that all actions have their lawful effect within the world. Our freedom to commit evil acts or not is determined by our own nature and the law of *karma* means that everyone will eventually reap the fruits of their action.

The sense in which good and evil are best seen within the context of this philosophy is as follows. Good actions are those which point one back towards the truth, towards knowledge of the Self. Evil actions entrench one further in the depths of illusion, taking one further away from 'God'.

Sin

Connected with this idea of evil, there is the notion that those who perform evil acts are 'committing a sin'. People in the west tend to think of the Ten Commandments and the Garden of Eden whenever this word is mentioned. The sense of doing something forbidden by God was often inculcated in children of earlier generations, though the precise reasons why the particular act was forbidden were not always explained. 'Mortal' and 'venial' sins represent, respectively, deliberate and casual commission of evil acts. The so-called original sin refers in Christianity to the condition in which one finds oneself at birth, with the racial impurity inherited by everyone as a result of Adam's willful ignoring of God's instruction, in the Garden of Eden, not to eat from the tree of knowledge.

> *On a sofa upholstered in panther skin*
> *Mona did researches in original sin.* William Plomer

In the theory of *karma* discussed above, the fruit of 'good' action is called *puNya*, meaning virtue, while the result of 'bad' action is sin or *pApa*. The idea is that these fruits accumulate as a result of action and, in the form of *saMskAra*, determine our future situations in life. In fact, the literal meaning of *pApa* can be simply 'evil' or 'wicked'.

We each have our own sense of what is right and wrong, instilled in us through our own particular upbringing and through what has been learnt as a result of our past actions. E.g. if someone injures me in some way, physically or mentally, the suffering that I feel subsequently teaches me the lesson that it is 'wrong' to hurt others. Whenever we act, we do so against the background of this set of values. At the moment of action there are influences from these values (what *buddhi* now identifies as 'the right thing to do') and from our desires and fears (what *manas* wants to do). One of Swami Chinmayananda's definitions of sin is this 'divergence of mind and intellect'. If our action contravenes the learned principles, we believe that we have acted wrongly and we feel guilt subsequently.

This topic also relates to that of our intrinsic nature and duty, called *dharma* in Sanskrit – this will be discussed in chapter 8, when *karma yoga* is addressed in greater detail. Our acquired value system drives the way we ought to act, i.e. is part of our own personal duty (*svadharma*). If there should be a conflict between some of these values in a given circumstance, it is up to *buddhi* to exercise its function of discrimination. If we act according to the principles for good action that we have learned to respect, we cannot really be said to be sinful. For someone else it might be so regarded, having been exposed to a different culture with differing values. Swami Chinmayananda puts this very simply. He says that sin is not in action but in reaction. If, after a particular act, we feel guilt, then it was a sinful act – another quotation from Swami Chinmayananda is that one is punished *by* the sin and not *for* the sin. The feeling of guilt (= sin) results from acting at odds with how we know we ought to have acted.

The Hebrew word for sin means 'missing the mark'. For Osho, the ultimate sin is not to do all that we can to realize the truth. He refers to the parable of the seeds in the teachings of Christ (Ref. 44). The father, wanting to decide which of his three sons should become responsible for his estates, decided to set them a test. Before leaving on a long journey, he gave each a handful of seeds and asked them to preserve the seeds as best as they could to ensure their survival. The first put them in a safe in a cool cellar, thinking that this would best ensure that they could be returned to the father on his return, however long that might be. The second went to the market and sold them, thinking that the original seeds might not survive but that, as long as he had the money, he could return to the market at some later date and buy some new ones. The third sowed them all in the garden and allowed them to grow.

On his return the father condemned the first two. The whole purpose of seeds is that they should grow. Although, in doing so, the seed perishes, the plants that are formed grow into many more seeds, thus fulfilling the purpose of the original seed. So it is that we think that the most important things we have are our material possessions or our health or an inquiring mind. All of these things are transient and, as long as we pursue them, we are 'missing the mark'; we are sinning. The seed of Consciousness within us is the most important thing of all, the only thing that will last. This is our only true possession and we should be doing all that we can to allow it to grow and mature into full understanding – Self-realization.

> *I count religion but a childish toy,*
> *And hold there is no sin but ignorance.* Christopher Marlowe

In the end, there is no such thing as sin. It is a concept whereby an individual becomes identified with a guilt-inducing idea. It only bolsters ego identification, which as you will by now have gathered we are trying to sublimate. It very much depends upon the belief that there is someone who can act in the first place and, as we shall see later (Chapter 15, 'The Myth of Action'), there is no such thing as a 'doer'.

7. God or *Ishvara*

Some religions say there is only one God. Vedanta says there is only God. Swami Dayananda

In the first edition of this book, there was one small reference to *Ishvara*, in the section on *nirguNa* vs. *saguNa brahman*, in the chapter on 'Creation and Time'. And a number of readers queried this apparent omission. I only came to understand the reason for this much later. It is because my own grounding in advaita was provided, as I explained in the preface, by the SES organization and I eventually realized that much of that teaching was based upon *sAMkhya* philosophy rather than Advaita. *sAMkhya* is a dualistic philosophy but, whilst it does not actually deny the existence of a god, it sees no reason to posit one. Accordingly, there is no teaching regarding a creator of the universe, maintainer of the karmic database or any other aspect that might suggest the need for a governing deity. It followed, therefore, that little was said about *Ishvara* during the many years that I attended this school. And it is only in the past two or three years that I have come to appreciate that this omission may have been a significant loss.

The reader may have noticed that this chapter occurs in the section on 'The Unreal' and this is quite intentional. Just as, from the standpoint of ultimate reality (we will read in the last section of the book), there is no universe and no persons, neither is there any creator or god fulfilling any function. However, we are not presently looking from that standpoint and, moreover, *we never can*! We are 'we', to begin with; an author and a reader – this is duality. Here is this book in front of you and you are not the book. There *is* a universe. This is your undeniable experience. And so it is that we must accept the reality of duality from this empirical standpoint. And, within this context, a creator God is every bit as real as the creation itself.

The absolute truth is that there is only Brahman, Consciousness, Absolute or whatever your chosen name might be (although, of course, names cannot really be used because these apply to the dualistic world only). So, regardless of the appearance, there cannot actually be any separate existence in a world of objects and other beings. And yet, inescapably, this is where we find ourselves. We are in this peculiar state of perceiving duality yet being told that there is no duality. An explanation of this state of affairs is therefore needed.

Clearly, from the standpoint of the individual, I am an almost insignificant part of this vast universe. I am at the mercy of tremendous forces which move and shape the world in which we live. I am influenced by all of the other people with whom I come into contact. Yet all are inter-related. A butterfly flaps its wings and a hurricane is born. Newcomen develops a usable steam engine and the planet is doomed to global warming. In fact, not only is everything inter-related, Advaita tells us that everything is One.

At the empirical level, there is a single cause for all of the incredible beauty and complexity of the diverse elements in creation. Moreover this is not just an intelligent cause but a material cause also. Everything *is* this one, non-dual reality, being just name and form of a single 'substance'.

And yet, quite obviously, 'I' as an individual am not the designer and substance of this creation. 'I' am merely a minute part, subject to the creator's laws. 'I' do not control the wind and waves or the car that careers out of control and kills a passing pedestrian. I even have difficulty comprehending how such things can be explained.

So it must be, then, that from the standpoint of the empirical world, all I can do is recognize that I am a part of this magnificent creation, which manifests an obvious intelligence. *Ishvara* has created this universe out of His own material and subsequently manages everything that takes place within it. *Ishvara* **is** the creation, and this is why this teaching cannot be compared to religions which have a dualistic god. *Ishvara* does not stand outside of His creation: cannot stand outside (otherwise, there would be two things).

Whatever happens is thus effectively the result of His will. What else can I do but acknowledge that 'I' too am a part of *Ishvara*, belong to *Ishvara*, function only with and through the grace of *Ishvara*? This recognition is what is meant by 'surrender' (*tyAga*). Recognizing that everything is *Ishvara* and takes place due to *Ishvara's* laws, I relinquish the egotistical idea that 'I' am acting. I can only (seem to) act if this is in accordance with those laws (tying in with the concept of *karma*) and the fruits of those actions are also outside of my control (tying in with ideas behind *karma yoga*). This is the meeting place of *karma yoga* and *bhakti yoga*.

In *j~nAna yoga*, we learn about *mithyA* and eventually come to the realization that there are no separately existing things at all; that there is only *brahman*. And then the corollaries follow: *Ishvara* is *brahman*, with this inexplicable power of *mAyA* with its ability to obscure the truth and project the seeming duality. And the *jIva*, too, is *brahman*, confused and misled by ignorance. The world, too, is nothing but *brahman*. Enlightenment brings with it (or *is*) the realization that 'All this is Brahman' and 'I am That'. So the absolute truth is that there is only the non-dual reality. But, nevertheless, the world appearance remains and the j~nAnI reconciles this with the knowledge that the world is Ishvara, who is also Brahman.

A powerful metaphor which can help appreciate what is happening here is that of the dancer. The dancer and the dance are one and the same. The dancer provides the material of the dance, as well as being the intelligence which manifests as the very dance itself. This stems from the Yoga Vasishtha, which states: *"The Lord who is infinite consciousness is the silent but alert witness of this cosmic dance. He is not different from the dancer (the cosmic natural order) and the dance (the happenings)."* (Ref. 138)

As will be discussed in much more detail later, it is this two-fold view of things – the way they appear and the way they actually are – which causes most of the problems in trying to understand ourselves and the world. Advaita is the only system to utilize this approach and it is its most powerful tool. Rather than attempting to announce 'this is the way it is', when 'it' is clearly totally at odds with our own experience, it begins from where we are and moves us gently towards a realization of the truth. (As will be seen in the last chapter, this is why the recent development of so-called 'neo-advaita' is so sad, because it refuses to make use of this powerful teaching method and resorts to the 'this is it' pronouncement.)

Inner Controller (*antaryAmin*)

At the level of the seeming universe, then, everything is a part of *Ishvara*. In every case, man included, the outward form is what differentiates, what induces us to see separate objects. But the reality is that there is a common principle that governs or controls these forms. It is both material and efficient cause, like the spider with the web that is spun by itself out of its own substance. This metaphor is from the Mundaka Upanishad (amongst others) (I.i.7): *"As a spider spreads out and withdraws (its thread), as on the earth grow the herbs (and trees), and as from a living man issues out hair (on the head and body), so out of the Imperishable does the universe emerge here (in this phenomenal creation)."* (Ref. 139)

This 'inner controller' (*antaryAmin*) is *Ishvara*. One may think of it as the God whose body is the whole universe but it is also your own Self. As the Brihadaranyaka Upanishad puts it (III.vii.4): *"He who inhabits the earth, but is within it, whom the earth does not know, whose body is the earth, and who controls the earth from within, is the Internal Ruler, your own immortal self."* (Ref. 111) This refrain is then repeated for water, fire, sky, heaven, sun etc before it moves on to speak of all beings, their sense organs, minds and intellect. It concludes (III.vii.23): *"He is never seen, but is the Witness; He is never heard, but is the Hearer; He is never thought, but is the Thinker; He is never known, but is the Knower. There is no other witness but Him, no other hearer but Him. no other thinker but Him, no other knower but Him. He is the Internal Ruler, your own immortal self. Everything else but Him is mortal."*

Thus it is that, whichever god we happen to worship, we are ultimately worshipping the same 'controlling' entity, *Ishvara*, which is the controller of gods, being, senses and everything and which is, in the final analysis, our own (though initially unknown) Self.

(In Hinduism, there seem to be many gods or *deva-s*. There are the principal ones of Brahma, the creator; Vishnu, the preserver and Shiva, the destroyer (note that the symbology, roles and names are much more complex than this and Shiva has many other, more positive aspects). There are ones such as Surya, the god of the sun and Chandra, the god of the moon. There are gods for forces of nature – e.g. Vayu, the god of wind,

Agni, the fire god, Yama, the Lord of death; and ones for forces within society – e.g. Saraswati, goddess of knowledge, Lakshmi, goddess of wealth. But, as Swami Sunirmalananda points out in his commentary on the *tattva bodha* (Ref. 110): *"There is a wrong idea that Hindus worship millions of gods and goddesses. Hindus worship one God in millions of forms and names."*

It is said that the idea behind all of these gods – seemingly one for anything that you can think of – is that, whatever might be the object of one's current attention, there will be a god (or goddess) to whom one can pray and, hopefully, ultimately surrender. But, as with everything else, all of the gods too are ultimately Ishvara. Surrendering, to, seeking the benediction of, sacrificing to these gods etc. are just various ways of acknowledging the one Self. And such activities are conducted by those who are enlightened, too, although their levels of understanding and appreciation of these actions will differ from those of the unenlightened.

Macrocosm and microcosm

Ishvara is everywhere, in and through everything. The Isha Upanishad is effectively a meditation on *Ishvara*. It begins: *"The Lord pervades everything – whatever exists in this universe of ceaseless movement. Enjoy the external world with an attitude of (inner) renunciation. Do not covet the wealth of others."* (Ref. 112)

So everything can be regarded as a form of *Ishvara*, in the way that a wave is a form of the water constituting the ocean. *Ishvara* is the sum total of all things, in the way that the ocean is the sum total of all waves, representing the macrocosm, whereas the individual *jīva* is the microcosm.

Ishvara is the controller of *karma*. When the universal cycle comes to an end and creation is temporarily withdrawn (this is called *pralaya* – the resolution of the universe at the end of a *kalpa*), *Ishvara* is responsible for accounting for all of the accumulated *karma* and for reapportioning this appropriately at the beginning of the next creation, when the unmanifest (*avyakta*) again becomes manifest (*vyakta*).

This is one of the reasons why we worship *Ishvara* (or one of the gods of whom He is the Inner Controller). Whether or not we are, ultimately, free to act (see Chapter 15), the outcome of such acts is out of our control and may be favorable or unfavorable from our point of view. It is *Ishvara* who is responsible for awarding *karma phala* – the 'fruit' of action in the form of *puNya* or *papa*, good or bad *saMskAra*. It should be no surprise therefore, that people bow down before their god and offer sacrifice. Such actions constitute both propitiation and surrender. We may pray for a successful result to our action but also we should accept the result, whatever it may be, because it is the lawful one, 'awarded' by *Ishvara*. This is the other side, as it were, of *karma yoga*.

It is *Ishvara* who wields the power of *mAyA* to bring about the myriad wonderful and terrible appearances, which bemuse us throughout our lives. We are the ones who are controlled by *mAyA* – He himself is not affected by ignorance. But it should be reiterated that everything, altogether, **is** *Ishvara* and all functions lawfully. The working of *karma* is a part of this lawful operation – *Ishvara* is not a God outside of creation ensuring that all is operating according to His intentions and handing out punishment if we step out of line. The working of the world is a manifestation of *Ishvara's* power and intelligence. Science making new discoveries is uncovering the working of *Ishvara*. This is why He is said to be all-knowing (*sarvaj~na*) and all-powerful (*sarvashakti*). *Ishvara* is the knowledge and intelligence which manifests in the order in the universe. And all actions and events are the working of *Ishvara* and an expression of His power.

Mahatma Gandhi said about this verse: *"The mantra describes God as the Creator, the Ruler and the Lord. The seer to whom this mantra or verse was revealed was not satisfied with the very frequent statement that God was to be found everywhere. But he went further and said: 'Since God pervades everything, nothing belongs to you, not even your own body...'"* (Address at Kottayam, Hairijanm 1937. Quoted in Ref. 113)

Regarding the last part of the verse (do not covet), Shankara under-stands this as: *"Everything has been renounced through this thought of the 'Lord' – 'All this is but the Self' – so that all this belongs to the Self, and the Self is all. Therefore do not have any hankerings for things that are unreal."* (Ref. 100)

Ultimately, of course, *Ishvara* and the *jIva* are the same – both are *brahman*. The *tattva bodha* says: *"...so long as the knowledge of the difference between the* jIva *and* Ishvara *remains, worldliness in the form of birth and death will not go. Therefore one should never differentiate between* jIva *and* Ishvara.*"* (Ref. 110)

saguNa brahman

This means 'with qualities', to be differentiated from *nirguNa*, meaning 'without qualities', referring to the indescribable, non-dual reality. At this point, you might ask how it can be, if this is the teaching and philosophy of non-duality, that we can speak of 'two' types or even aspects of *brahman*. This treatment of 'levels' of reality is one of the key distinguishing features of Advaita . Our empirical experience is that there is a world of objects and people (and gods), while our ultimate realization is that reality is non-dual and that all these apparent things are *mithyA*.

It is appropriate to make a very important point here regarding the use of the word '*brahman'*. Pedantically, this word refers to the non-dual reality, i.e. is used in the absolute or *pAramArthika* sense. Unfortunately, this word is very commonly used as a synonym for *Ishvara*, i.e. in the relative, empirical or *vyAvahArika* sense. As long as you are aware of this, it need not cause any confusion. Whenever you encounter it being used in a dualistic way, e.g. as 'creating' or 'pervading' or 'controlling' or anything involving doing, desiring, enjoying etc, then you can be sure that it actually means *Ishvara*.

But, whether we are talking about the appearance or the reality, there is only ever Brahman. The only difference in this regard is that, at the empirical level, we call it *Ishvara*. *saguNa brahman* or *Ishvara* is the explanation given by Advaita for the existence of the world at the level of *vyavahAra*. *Ishvara* is the creator of the world, in both efficient and material, causal senses, using the power of *mAyA*. Brahman, having nothing to do with cause or effect, cannot be the creator of anything (see chapter 14 on 'Creation and Time'). Just as in other religions, *Ishvara* is both immanent (in its role as 'governor' or inner controller of the world) and transcendent (in its role as creator, sustainer and destroyer of the world). Unlike other religions, however, *Ishvara* actually *is* the material of the universe, too.

Brahman in its *nirguNa* sense is 'described' as *sat-chit-Ananda*, being, consciousness and limitlessness but these are not really attributes. Words such as 'Consciousness' are rather used as synonymous with Brahman. These are its 'essential' characteristics or definition. On the other hand, describing Brahman as the creator of the world, for example, is a secondary definition or pointer only, because such characteristics are only applicable in the limited use of the word *brahman* when it is spoken of within *vyavahAra*, i.e. this use refers to *Ishvara*.

In fact, in the scriptures, *saguNa brahman* is used in two different ways. The first of these is what is called *upAsya*, meaning for the purpose of meditation or *upAsana*. The function of meditation will be explained in the next section but the idea is that it serves to purify the mind and cultivate those attitudes that will be most conducive to gaining Self-knowledge. The second use is called *j~neya*, meaning 'to be known' and here the purpose is to act as a stepping stone to actual understanding or *j~nAna*.

And, once this understanding is gained, the realization is that, from the *pAramArthika* standpoint, there is only *brahman*. Our differentiation of brahman into *Ishvara*, *jIva* and world (*jagat*) was an error. This differentiation is real from the standpoint of the world but is realized to be *mithyA* on enlightenment. Another way of putting this is that, on enlightenment, one recognizes that the entire creation and every part of it, including the *jIva*, is one limitless conscious being, *Ishvara*, and the truth of *Ishvara* is *brahman*.

And it must be emphasized that, even after enlightenment, the person who is now enlightened remains part of the world, acts in the world and, significantly, still recognizes *Ishvara* as the creator, sustainer and dissolver of the world. Since the enlightened one now knows the real, non-dual nature of reality, he also know that this state of affairs prevails despite the dualistic nature of experience – everything is Brahman from the *pAramArthika* standpoint; everything is *Ishvara* from the *vyAvahArika* standpoint. So it is in no way contradictory for the Sage to continue to worship guru or god as part of his daily ritual.

SECTION 2 – The spiritual path

8. Mental Preparation

Self-discipline is when your conscience tells you to do something and you don't talk back. W. K. Hope

So far in this investigation, lots of statements have been made about how it is that we are mistaken in our present view of life, including some outrageous ones about how things really are. It is not reasonable for me to expect you to accept all of these at their face value. Indeed, at the very beginning, I emphasized that Advaita specifically did *not* require you to do this. So what do you have to do now so that you may come to appreciate for yourselves the truth of what has been said? What options are available for expanding your knowledge and gaining direct experience of this 'Self'?

Clearly, it is no use simply saying that the Self is unlimited and eternally blissful and such like sentiments. Our current conviction is that we *are* limited. It is somewhat like psychosomatic illnesses. You cannot just tell the patient that her problems are of that nature and expect all of her symptoms immediately to disappear. We can acknowledge the identification with body and mind and admit ignorance of our true nature but the identification and ignorance still remain. What we need to know is a) what are the ways by which we can investigate further and b) are there any prerequisites for embarking on such an investigation.

Our end aim in this investigation is to become what is called 'enlightened' or 'Self-realized'. We do not yet know what this might mean exactly but imagine that it will somehow bring an end to all of our problems. If we were no longer identified with body and mind, presumably we would no longer be bothered by pain, concerned about death, or worried if our wives go off with other men. Perhaps we imagine losing all interest in material things and spending a lifetime in meditation, peace and solitude. Before continuing, it would be useful to drop all of this – these are only ideas and concepts; part of the very ignorance we are endeavoring to dispel! So what is involved?

There seems to have been a trend over the years, accelerating in the past few decades, suggesting that we need do less and less to achieve enlightenment. The scriptures place much stress on the disciplines that need to be followed in order to aspire towards realization. Throughout most of history, Sages have reinforced this view. Shankara may have said that *bhakti* (worship) and *karma* (action) *yoga-s* are only preparation for the real process of *j~nAna* (knowledge) but he, too, insisted upon proper preparation with his so-called 'fourfold accomplishment' (*chatuShTaya sampatti* – see below). This seems reasonable. We can acknowledge intellectually that there is no path as such and appreciate that we must already be that which, in truth, we are. Nevertheless, identified as we are with one thing or another, that truth is covered over by ignorance and just as the scum must be removed from the pond before we can see the water, so too must we have to clear away the ignorance. But, in recent times, the traditional 'spiritual cleansing' seems to have been shunned. Ramana Maharshi says we need only keep asking ourselves who we are. Direct Path teachings suggest there is nothing we *can* do and the most recent statements from teachers of neo-Advaita (see Chapter 19) are that there is nothing that *needs* to be done.

Osho, for one, disagreed. He acknowledged that we are in a state of delusion, believing the apparent to be real, and said that, while we are in this state, help must be provided. He has a nice story to illustrate this. (Ref. 42) There was a man who, whilst asleep one day with his mouth open, swallowed a fly. This woke him up so that he was aware of what had happened. Thereafter, he became obsessed with the fly, believing that it was still alive and moving about inside his body. This worrying made him ill and he had to visit doctors. Eventually he was referred to psychiatrists since no doctor would accept that his claims were true. But they, too, failed to help him, since they insisted that there could not possibly still be a fly alive in his body. It had now been six months and it would have dissolved away and been excreted long ago.

By chance, he was introduced to Osho, who offered to help. Osho immediately reassured the man that he acknowledged the problem. Of course, he said, the fly was still alive and must be removed from the body before the man could recover. The man was told to lie down and close his eyes, keeping very still so that Osho could charm the fly to the surface and capture it. Osho then left the room and rushed around the house with a bottle looking for a fly... Needless to say, the man was persuaded that the fly had come out of his body and he was then cured.

The point is that Osho knew perfectly well that the man was deluded, just as had all the other doctors and psychiatrists. But the others had failed to provide any cure. Osho treated the man at the level of his delusion and the cure was effected. Similarly, he would say, it is no use telling us that we are already enlightened when we are still firmly entrenched in the illusion. The ignorance needs to be dealt with on its own terms before the truth can be acknowledged. Such reasoning suggests that 'spiritual paths' do, in fact, still have their place, regardless of what may be said by some modern teachers. Osho also notes that the Buddha defined truth as 'that which works'.

Another variation of this story, thought to have been originated by Swami Chinmayananda, is often told by Dr. K. Sadananda, *AchArya* of Chinmaya Mission in Washington DC. It concerns a man who, believing that he was a mouse, finally visited a psychiatrist for therapy since his life was suffering so much disruption. After many sessions, the man eventually acknowledged that he now firmly believed that he was a man and not a mouse and the doctor deemed him to be cured. Accordingly, he left the clinic to walk home on his own. Some short time later, he ran back into the clinic terrified and the doctor asked him what was wrong. "Well," said the man, "*I* know that I am not a mouse but how can I be sure that the *cat* at the end of the street knows this?"

Note that this is not to deny the ultimate truth of what the neo-Advaitins say. The point is that they are now speaking from the privileged position of knowing that truth. As I said in my book which addresses the teaching of Enlightenment (Ref. 80): *"The mere stating of the absolute truth will have no effect. Even if they can accept it intellectually, seekers still believe deep down that they are a separate body-mind."* There is much more about this in the last chapter of this book. And, if you want to know what the 'absolute truth' is, you will have to wait until Section 3!

Spiritual 'path' – sAdhana

There are no shortcuts to any place worth going. Anon

There are traditionally three stages by which we move from our current state of ignorance to one of enlightenment. These stages are well documented and seekers have been following them for thousands of years. If there was any shortcut to avoid the time and effort involved in such a discipline, that too would have been documented. Later, we will see that many of those modern Western teachers who I have called 'neo-advaitins' in my books deny the existence, let alone the value, of any 'spiritual path'. They claim that 'we are already That'; 'there is no person and nowhere to go'; 'This is IT'. Gaudapada, too, was making similar statements around 1500 years ago but he was careful to point out that these were directed only to those seekers who were already advanced students of advaita, and who had already been following such a path for many years and attained the requisite degree of mental discipline and discriminative ability.

So, these traditional stages are:

1) Hearing the truth from a qualified teacher or (very much second best) reading about it in such works as the Upanishads. This is called *shravaNa*, resulting in an intellectual understanding of the subject matter.
2) Reflecting upon what has been heard (since there is no chance of appreciating it on first hearing). This is the stage of *manana*, the purpose being to remove any doubts we may have about the teaching.
3) Meditating upon the essence of what has now been intellectually understood until there is total conviction. This is called *nididhyAsana*. It has the effect of eroding all of the bad habits we have acquired in respect of our dealings with the world, seeing

separation, having desires for objects etc.

Sadananda uses an excellent metaphor to illustrate this process (from a post on the Advaitin E-List). He says that we know that normally, when we switch on an electric light bulb, the light shines forth immediately and dispels the darkness. Suppose that, on operating the switch, the darkness remains. We might be mystified if we knew that the circuit was intact and the supply functional. However, the explanation might be that a layer of opaque material is covering the bulb. Although the bulb and everything else is functioning perfectly, the room will remain dark until the covering is removed. Thus it is with knowledge. We may receive the knowledge, from a Sage or through reading but we will remain ignorant until all doubts and habitual ways of thinking have been removed. In effect, it is light that dispels darkness and knowledge that dispels ignorance but these will not in themselves prove effective if there are other obstacles in the way. *shravaNa* is equivalent to switching on the light bulb and this alone is ultimately responsible for overcoming the ignorance but *manana* and *nididhyAsana* are needed to establish that knowledge and make it effective; these are equivalent to removing the coverings.

Most of us do not drop out of society in order to live in a cave, giving up all of our belongings and begging for our daily food. We have not chosen to become what the scriptures call a *saMnyAsin* or *saMnyAsI*. We have chosen to remain a householder, someone who pursues life in a family environment with a job and a home. We are unable to sit for the whole day, deep in meditation upon the nature of reality. In traditional Hindu life, the Brahmin begins his life as a student or *brahmacharya*, unmarried, religious and chaste. He then marries and has a family – this is called the period of the 'householder' or *gRRihastha*. He then retires from life with its pursuit of pleasure and money and becomes a so-called 'forest dweller' or *vanaprastha*. He now lives the life of a hermit and continues his religious studies. The final stage is called *saMnyAsa* and involves complete renunci-ation. He now relies entirely on charity for food and clothing and spends the remainder of his life in meditation and control of the senses.

Pre-requisites for the seeker

Even if you are on the right track, you'll get run over if you just sit there.
Will Rogers

In his work *tattva bodha* (Knowledge of the Truth), Shankara describes four qualities that the seeker must have before he is ready for liberation. These are called *sAdhana chatuShTaya sampatti*: *sAdhana* is normally translated as 'worship' but carries the meaning of 'leading straight to a goal'; *chatuShTaya* means 'fourfold'; *sampatti* means 'success' or 'accomplishment'. In fact, the description is somewhat misleading, since he then goes on to describe a total of nine qualities – perhaps he thought we would baulk at so many.

The first of the four is discrimination (*viveka*). This, the true function of *buddhi*, means the ability to differentiate between the transient and the permanent, the unreal and the real. (It is sometimes called, more accurately, *nitya-anitya-viveka. nitya* means 'eternal'; *anitya* means 'transient.) The second is detachment or dispassion (*vairAgya*), meaning non-attachment to whatever is the result of our actions; in particular, indifference to the pleasure that result from success or the disappointment that result from failure. The fourth is the desire to achieve enlightenment, to the exclusion of all other desires (*mumukShutva*). The third refers to the so-called 'six qualities', *shamAdi ShaTka sampatti*: –

- *shama* – literally tranquility, absence of passion but more usually translated as mental discipline or self-control
- *dama* – self-restraint but understood as control over the senses
- *uparati* or *uparama* – desisting from sensual enjoyment; 'reveling' in that which is 'near' i.e. one's own Self; also translated as following one's *dharma* or duty
- *titikShA* – forbearance or patience
- *shraddhA* – faith; trusting in the teachings of the scriptures and one's guru until knowledge arises
- *samAdhAna* – contemplation, profound meditation; more usually

translated as concentration

A little thought will show that these are not unreasonable. Clearly one has to want to find out about the Self. Since the ego is the main obstacle, self-restraint, ability to temper the desires and so on are obvious requirements. Since many of the aspects of the teaching are counter-intuitive, one must be able to remain detached so that discrimination may be exercised, and some initial faith in what is being said is needed until the statements can be verified for oneself. Also the need to stay with it, give full attention, have patience when things go wrong etc. are all natural requirements. William Cenkner (Ref. 79) tells us that: *"As the Sringeri AchArya (teacher at one of the centers established by Shankara) never hesitates to say, one cannot strive for knowledge or liberation without the capacity or competence for it."*

So, for example, this book might persuade you that certain qualities are a pre-requisite for attaining realization. Then, causes may be set in place to trigger effects such as practicing meditation, giving attention to what is in front of you, spending more time in the present and so on. Providing the desire for truth is already there, and the strongest desire you have, then you will be setting out on your notional spiritual path, even if there isn't really such a thing. And, once you do set out on this path, you will be committed. Ramana Maharshi says this first step is equivalent to putting your head into the tiger's mouth – the jaws close and there is no escape.

There are a lot of methods that purport to serve as paths to the truth. The best known of these are mentioned in the Bhagavad Gita and go by the name of *bhakti yoga*, *karma yoga* and *j~nAna yoga*. There are other *yoga*s too, such as *haTha*, *kuNDalinI*, and *rAja yoga* but these are not aspects of Advaita. There is an excellent short article by Dr. Gregory Goode at http://nonduality.com/ – the Home Page of the Non-Duality Salon – that discusses the common *yoga-s*.

In fact, these three paths cannot be totally separated. The *j~nAna yogi* will inevitably act in a manner commensurate with the *karma yogi* and will have an attitude of reverence for the 'Truth', 'Reality', 'Consciousness' or, if you prefer, 'God'.

bhakti yoga

bhakti is about devotion to and worship of a God and about humility. This may seem somewhat anomalous, since we have already stated that Advaita says there is no duality. There cannot be the Self *and* a God. But hopefully the previous chapter will have convinced you that there is no real paradox here at all. I can appreciate the ultimate non-duality whist simultaneously worshipping *Ishvara* who is the intelligent and material cause of the manifest universe of which I, the *jIva*, am a part. All is Brahman alone in the end.

bhakti is of the heart, not of the mind and, as such, is available to everyone. The idea is that, though this process begins in duality, the love of the devotee for his chosen deity eventually transcends this; the ego is subsumed and the 'two' merge into one. It is a technique that eliminates the negative – selfishness, fear and desire – and raises the man to the divine. Ramana Maharshi says that *bhakti* is giving up 'mine' whereas *j~nAna* is giving up 'I'. *bhakti yoga* turns outwards towards God, *j~nAna yoga* inwards to the Self. The *bhakta* longs for happiness, the *j~nAnI* for the Self.

It is said to be the easiest path, for those whose intellect will allow them to acknowledge and surrender to a God, since the belief brings all of the comfort and reassurance traditionally associated with religion. All of one's frustrations and pain can be ameliorated in the belief that God is actively assisting and ensuring ultimate success. Just as *j~nAna yoga* requires a particular type of mind – logical and enquiring – in order to be an appropriate path, so *bhakti* only appeals to a particular type of heart – one who can forget himself and give all of his attention and devotion to an external deity. Whereas the *j~nAnI* eliminates the ego through reason, the bhakta does it through love and surrender. Both involve devotion, though the 'object' of that devotion may be perceived in different ways and both involve renunciation. This latter is intrinsic to the process of purification of the mind, and also common to all methods, since the mind is the thing that tends to get in the way.

Although this process begins as 'little me' worshipping the all-powerful absolute from afar, it ends with 'me' disappearing as it is recognized that God and I are one. All paths up the mountain end at the same place as they say. In fact, dedicated worship of a god, thought of as single minded attention to a specific object, is only effectively another form of meditation, irrespective of the extent to which the practitioner initially believes in the ultimate reality of the god as something separate from himself.

Purification of the mind

As noted above, this is part of the process of all methods in one form or another. It does not mean ridding the mind of all thoughts – it is the nature of the mind to think. Not all modern teachers agree with this. In fact, some state that the mind *is* thoughts. This would mean that ridding the mind of thoughts would also relieve the *jIva* of the mind. An empty mind is very pleasant and, for example, meditators may well feel very pleased with themselves (thus bolstering the ego), if they reach a state of no thoughts. It brings about a quality of awareness that is rarely achieved in ordinary living. But lack of thoughts is still a state of mind – and the Self is not the mind; it is necessary to eliminate this identification before the truth can be realized.

Greg Goode summarized the aims of this purification very clearly in an exchange on the subject on the Advaitin E-List on the Internet:

- Reduce the quantity of thoughts, but not to a permanent zero.
- Improve the quality of thoughts; think about the Lord, scriptures, etc.
- Change the direction of thoughts: inward instead of outward.

The objective is simply to bring about the realization that I am not the mind and bring it into our service as a tool; not allow it free rein, and reign, as a master. Indeed, *j~nAna yoga* would have no utility if the aim were to eliminate the mind, since the mind is the means by which the understanding is brought about. In terms of yet another metaphor, it is using a thorn to remove a thorn. If one gets a thorn embedded in the foot, a second thorn is an invaluable tool to help remove the first but both are discarded once the first has been removed. So the mind is an essential tool in *j~nAna yoga* to remove the improper functioning of the mind and bring it under control.

(Note that, here 'mind' is understood as the complete organ of *manas, buddhi, chitta* and *ahaMkAra*. The totality is called *antaHkaraNa* in Sanskrit.)

Another way of looking at this involves the *guNa-s*. If you recall, the traditional view is that the three *guNa-s* determine the 'quality' of a thing, according to their relative proportions. In terms of the mind and thinking, the lowest level would be one ruled by *tamas*, by selfish and arrogant thinking, dogmatic or fanatical in nature. Such a person would find it very difficult to turn his mind towards thoughts of truth or even of anyone other than himself. A *rAjasika* person has a passionate and active mind, very emotional and egotistic, driven by desires for personal gain. Seeing the world as full of separate object and persons, seeking some and avoiding others, this person is also unlikely to be seeking to discover the truth. Only the *sAttvika* mind, seeing the world clearly, without thought of likes and dislikes, alert but still, and able to exercise discrimination, can hope to recognize the unity in creation.

Thus, a simple way of looking at purification is to seek to eliminate the tamasic and rajasic properties within oneself and cultivate the sattvic. Hence the recommended practices of such things as meditation, attention and good company described later.

Ramakrishna had a nice story (Ref. 22) illustrating how we are limited by the *guNa* in our actions. He tells of a man who was travelling through the forest when he was set upon by three thieves. After stealing all of his valuables, the first suggested that they now kill him, as they had no further use for him. Just as the first was about to run the man through with his sword, the second thief stopped him and said that there was no need to resort to such action; they could simply tie him up instead and leave him. They did so and left. Later, the third robber came back, untied the man, helped him to the edge of the forest and pointed out the way home. The man was very grateful and invited the thief back with him but the latter refused, saying that the police would arrest him if they caught him.

The first thief represents *tamas*, the destroyer; the second *rajas*, which entangles man in the world and ties him down with his egotistical desires. The third is *sattva*, which shows the way home to God or Truth, showing compassion and righteousness; it is the highest of the *guNa* but it, too, has to be transcended before realization can occur.

Purity of mind means a mind not free of thought per se but free of thoughts that distract one from the pursuit of the truth – desire, anger, fear, worry, anticipation etc. Basically any thought that implies that I am in any way separate or limited is necessarily taking us away from the truth. Furthermore, most thoughts relate to 'objects' in the world of appearances. The search for truth is inwards to the reality of the Self so that all such thoughts are of no value.

karma yoga

Here, the purification of the mind results from non-attachment to action. Not only does this not result in the formation of new *saMskAra*, it is said to actually reduce that which is already there. This can be understood in the sense of habit. Quite often, we will react to certain situations habitually. Something happens, is immediately recognized by the subconscious mind as having occurred before, and without any conscious decision we find ourselves reacting in the same way. If, however, we are alert to the trigger event in the moment that it occurs, there is a fleeting but real opportunity to see exactly what is there and respond appropriately. It is inevitable that such a response would circumvent the automatic reaction. Although the habit could easily occur again the next time, once the circuit has been broken several times, there is the possibility of eliminating the habit permanently. (Cynically, one might think '...and form a new habit'. But it is the automatic nature of 'reacting' that characterizes the 'habit', not being alert and responsive to any changed circumstance.)

There are really two aspects to this practice. The element to which *karma yoga* itself refers is, strictly speaking, non-attachment to the results of our actions. I.e. the intention is that when we act, we do so not because we wish for a particular outcome, either for ourselves or for someone else, but because our discriminative faculty perceives that this is the most appropriate response, given what is perceived at that moment. All depends on being fully in the present with our attention 100% where the 'action' is taking place. *buddhi* can only operate correctly when this is so, i.e. when *manas* is simply passing information to it from the senses. If *manas* is 'thinking', we cannot be fully in the present. Note that this does not mean that we cannot make use of past experience. Such information is already available to *buddhi* without the involvement of *manas*. It is held in the third element of the mind (*antaHkaraNa*), called *chitta* or memory.

Swami Parthasarathy tells an amusing story to persuade us that we really do need to become detached. A couple took their small child to the cinema for the first time. The little girl had not seen television either so had no prior experience of moving pictures on a screen. Accordingly, when a short wildlife film was shown before the main feature and lions were seen, apparently leaping out towards the viewer, the child was very frightened and began to cry. The parents were unsympathetic, telling the girl that these were only pictures on the screen and there was nothing there in reality to cause the child to become upset. The main film that was shown next was an epic, romantic film with many emotional moments and, part way through, the child couldn't help noticing that her mother was crying...

The key point here is this. If we are unable to sit through a film without becoming attached, when we are perfectly well aware that it is only a story, how can we possibly hope to remain detached from situations in life, in which we are personally involved and which we believe to be real? The Bhagavad Gita tells us (4.18): *"He who sees inaction in action, and action in inaction, he is wise among men, he is a yogi and accomplisher of every-thing."* It is possible to train the mind to operate at peak efficiency, whilst outwardly the body remains perfectly still and apparently inactive. Conversely, we might be engaged in concentrated and productive activity, yet mentally standing back from it all and watching all of this as though we were a non-participating witness, still and uninvolved. Both of these require a high sattvic state and are achieved through the practice of *karma yoga*.

In this world of appearance, everything is in a flux of perpetual change and yet, the active principle behind all, the *Atman*, is itself unmoving and unaffected by any of it. The 'wise among men', i.e. advanced along the notional path to realization, is able to see this inaction in action.

Consciousness is the enlivening force for everything. It is the pivotal point of stillness that makes movement possible, the centre around which the dance of life takes place and without which meaningful life would be impossible. Osho compares it to the essential but unmoving axle around which the rim of a wheel turns.

In order to come to this understanding, we start by observing the phenomenal world from the relative standpoint. We must see the operation of the illusory ego and the apparent 'play of creation', i.e. see the action in inaction, the changes that appear to take place against the background of the unchanging reality.

The thrust of *karma yoga* is to become a detached witness, unaffected by the transient pleasures and misfortunes of our day to day lives. We need to be like the leaf of the lotus, on whose surface water simply runs off without wetting it in the slightest. As Swami Chinmayananda said in his commentary on the Bhaja Govindam (Ref. 16), the lotus leaf is born in water, lives out its life in water and dies in water – but it has nothing to do with water.

It is worth noting here, though it will be emphasized again later, that just as with *bhakti yoga*, *karma yoga* cannot bring about enlightenment. No action can, since enlightenment is purely the result of self-knowledge, i.e. eliminating self-ignorance. Both of these yogas function as a preparation for the mind, instilling self-discipline, self-control etc. and decreasing the dominion of the ego.

More on *saMskAra*

In order to understand the theory behind *karma yoga*, it is necessary to enquire further into *saMskAra*. The basic principle is simple. Whatever we do, if we do it with the desire for a particular result, it will 'come back to us' in the future, rather like indigestion after eating too much. A 'bad' action will bring us 'bad' results; a 'good' action 'good' results. The way in which the results present themselves can be equated with destiny. If we perform many bad actions, our future will be pretty bleak and, when we suddenly find ourselves without a home or job, we could say that this was 'destined' to happen, as a result of our accumulation of bad *saMskAra*. If our life comes to an end before the *saMskAra* has been exhausted – not to worry, our next life will take up where this one left off as regards merit and demerit. In fact, the life into which we will next be born is said to be determined by all of this. It is all summed up by the proverb 'as you sow, so shall you reap'.

Straightforward so far. If we go into more detail, however, there are in fact three types of *saMskAra*. What we have at present is called *prArabdha saMskAra*. This literally means 'begun' or 'undertaken'. It is the fruit of all of our past action that is now having its effect. This includes past action in this life and in all previous lives. This *prArabdha* can be viewed as the 'cause' or coloring of everything that we are experiencing now. At the time of our birth, it determines the circumstances into which we are born. Every experience that we have, together with its associated pleasure or pain, is determined by our earlier actions via the instrument of this *prArabdha saMskAra*. These experiences cannot be avoided, just as, once the trigger has been pulled, the bullet can no longer be prevented from reaching its destination.

The total *saMskAra*, which has been accumulated from past action is called *saMchita saMskAra*, literally meaning 'collected' or 'piled up'. I.e. *prArabdha saMskAra* is a subset of *saMchita*. The third type is that which is generated in reaction to current situations and which will not bear fruit until sometime in the future. This is called *AgAmin saMskAra*, literally meaning 'impending' or 'approaching'. It is through this third type that we have the ability to influence our future lives.

The situations in which a man finds himself are determined by *prArabdha*, as is his nature. Thus, if he acts automatically, it will be *prArabdha saMskAra* that drives him. Since this sort of action only accumulates more *saMskAra*, it is not going to get him very far. Being in the present, with the attention at the point where the action is taking place, *buddhi* can operate and the choice may be made to act without any desire for results. This will result in no new *saMskAra* and the existing *prArabdha saMskAra* relating to that situation will be used up. It is in this way that *karma yoga* can, over a long period of time, (at least theoretically!) burn up all of the *saMskAra*. In this lifetime, the overall decrease in *saMskAra* will result in the reward of a next life that is more conducive to study (*j~nAna yoga*) and ultimately this will lead to self-realization.

Once realization is attained, the so-called *j~nAnI* still continues, from an outsider's viewpoint, to live out an ordinary life. Their actions no longer produce *saMskAra* however, so there is no *AgAmin saMskAra*. Also, the as-yet-unfructified *saMchita saMskAra* is dissolved. Only the remaining *prArabdha* continues to function. Thus the *j~nAnI* appears to be the same person with the same likes and dislikes as before. From the *j~nAnI*'s point of view, of course, there is no longer a person at all. It is because of this that future actions leave no trace for them.

Some writers say that *prArabdha*, too, is burnt up on realization, using the metaphor of a father who dies leaving three sons – how can we say that only two of the three are now fatherless? Ramana Maharshi tells us that the notion of the *j~nAnI* still being subject to *prArabdha saMskAra* is false, this illusion still being maintained only to explain to the rest of us how he is still able to function in life as before. But Shankara (who should always be regarded as the ultimate arbiter in matters of dispute) says that it is like the potter's wheel that carries on rotating for some time after he has stopped turning it. However – all of this is in danger of becoming an academic argument with no value, whatever the outcome, as in the debate of how many angels can dance on the head of a pin. But this does bring me to another related topic that has not yet been explained in any detail, namely *dharma*.

dharma

If you are a follower of the Vedas, you have no rights at all, only duties.
Swami Dayananda (Ref. 81)

The principal definition given in the dictionary relates to 'customary practice' or 'conduct' but then also to 'duty', 'justice' and 'morality'. It is about living and behaving in keeping with the prevailing morality and laws and performing ones 'duty' to the community and society as well as to immediate friends and family. The favored meaning of most traditional teachers is, however, 'nature, character, essential quality', which they often translate as 'essence'. It is sometimes said that *dharma* means 'essence' in the way that 'sweetness' is the essential property of sugar.

The Bhagavad Gita places much emphasis on it, particularly in respect of our performing our own *dharma* (*svadharma*) and not someone else's. Our 'own *dharma*' is that mode of behavior that will exhaust our *saMskAra*. Thus, for example, it says (III.35) that it is better to perform one's own *dharma* badly than that of another well. This was spoken by Krishna, representing the Self, instructing Arjuna, representing you and me, in the art of *karma yoga*. Arjuna had been trained as a warrior and it was now his duty to battle against the forces of unrighteousness. The fact that the enemy consisted of people to whom he was related or who had been involved in teaching him made him reluctant to do this but, as it was his duty, this was what he had to do. Much as he would have preferred to become a *saMnyAsin* and 'drop out' of the world, that was not his *dharma* and would be harmful to him. He would inevitably regret it later, having the consequences of his action on his conscience and feeling himself to have been a coward. This would be so *because* it was his *svadharma* to fight. *karma yoga* is also about acting according to one's *svadharma*.

It can be seen how this ties in with *saMskAra*. Arjuna's *prArabdha saMskAra* had led him to this battle and therefore it was his 'destiny' to fight. Only by going along with this could the *saMskAra* be dissolved and allow him to progress spiritually. To act in denial of this would create large amounts of *AgAmin saMskAra* to carry forward into future lives because he would be acting in order to obtain a particular outcome, (e.g. peace of mind, avoidance of injury), instead of responding to the need, in accordance with his own nature.

Our *svadharma* will consist of many elements, relating to the various roles that we take on in our lives. Thus, if we are employed, we will have contracted to our employer to do a particular job and part of our *dharma* will be to carry out that job to the best of our abilities. Even if the job is at odds with what we might *think* to be our nature, we have committed ourselves to that role and thus have a duty to carry it out as best we can given our limitations. It is quite likely that someone else, whose nature we feel to be better aligned with that job, would perform it more easily or produce better results but none of this is relevant. They will be in their own job and it will be their duty to perform *that* as best they can.

In addition to our working role, we may have a family and that will bring with it the duties of a father or mother. Accordingly, we should not, for example, leave our children behind and go off exploring the jungles of Borneo for several years. We know what our duties are. When we follow them to the best of our abilities, we have peace of mind, even if things go wrong. It is when we do something else – the *dharma* of someone else – that we feel guilt and worry etc.

Our ultimate essence, of course – our essential nature – is one, the *Atman*. Therefore, the scriptures also refer to what is called *sanAtana dharma*, where *sanAtana* means 'eternal' or 'permanent'. This phrase is also used to refer to the traditional (also carrying the sense of 'original' and 'unadulterated') Hindu practices or behavior that were in keeping with the wellbeing of the universe as well as the evolution of an individual towards his eventual realization. In fact, colloquially, the phrase is sometimes used interchangeably with 'Hinduism' to refer to the religion itself.

The idea behind the quotation from Swami Dayananda at the head of this section is as follows. Each person has many duties in their life. For example, as a father, I have the duty to look after the interests of my children and bring them up as best I can. I have no rights in this respect – it is my children who have the right to expect me to fulfill these functions. Reciprocally, my children have the duty to give me respect, obey me when I tell them to do something and so on. And I have the right to expect them to do precisely this. The interdependence of such things throughout all aspects of society is part of what Indians mean by *dharma*.

> *When I perform my duty, I learn to enjoy what I do, rather than trying to find what I enjoy doing.* Swami Dayananda (Ref. 76)

j~nAna yoga

Shankara explains that other 'paths' are ultimately only preparations for this, the one path that will lead to realization. Knowledge (*j~nAna*) is needed to remove ignorance, just as light is needed to dispel darkness. And, once self-knowledge is attained, understanding is instantaneous just as, when a torch is switched on in a cave, the darkness is gone immediately, no matter for how long it may have existed. We must be receptive to the knowledge however, or it will have no effect. If we challenge it with old opinions and habitual thought, it will 'fall on stony ground' as the bible says just as, if we put up shutters on the windows of our house, the sunlight will not be able to enter.

As with the other paths, there is a paradox here: since the Self or reality is not an object, it is not possible to have knowledge of it. Just as the torch can only shine light into the shadows but cannot directly illuminate itself, so knowledge can clear away the surrounding ignorance but cannot directly know itself. We know that we exist and that we are conscious; what is lacking is the knowledge that we are complete. Knowledge can take us almost all of the way but not the whole way; ultimately, knowledge is only 'of things' and has to be discarded in order to make the final leap of intuition. It is like the pole in pole vaulting. We need the pole in order to lift us up to the bar but we must let go of it before we can make the final leap to the other side.

j~nAna yoga is the *yoga* of wisdom. It is about enquiry, analysis and discrimination and about rejecting everything that will not stand up to this process – the method of negation. There is a frequently encountered Sanskrit phrase '*neti, neti*', meaning 'not this, not this' that is traditionally used to tell oneself that anything and everything that is seen or thought is not one's Self, the witness of all these things. This also applies to the so-called knowledge itself, of course; this too, ultimately, falls within the category of appearance only. As will be seen later, there can be no objective knowledge of reality. An excellent classical metaphor for *j~nAna yoga*, bringing out this aspect, comes from Shankara's *Atmabodha* (Ref. 17, V.5). The powdered form of a certain nut, called the 'clearing nut' or *kataka*, was traditionally used to precipitate dirt from muddy water. The powder was sprinkled onto the surface of the water, forming a slimy film. Suspended impurities were attracted to the film, which slowly sank down to the bottom, leaving the water clear and able to be decanted.

The dirt represents the ignorance – the thoughts of separation, desire etc.; the *kataka* represents the ostensible knowledge of Self. This knowledge is still part of ignorance (*avidyA*) but has the power to destroy that *avidyA*. Once the powder has sunk to the bottom, taking the dirt with it, both are discarded. It is important to recognize that the knowledge provided by Advaita is of value only for its ability to remove the ignorance. It is very easy for the follower of *j~nAna yoga* to become bogged down in all of the knowledge he accumulates. In order to achieve the desired result, once the knowledge has had its effect and removed the ignorance, i.e. once we genuinely believe all of the stuff presented in this book, we should throw all of it away; it will have served its purpose.

Faith

Faith is to believe what you do not see, and the reward of this faith is to see what you believe. St. Augustine

No matter which 'path' is chosen, there will be many times in the beginning when there is doubt over whether it is leading anywhere or even whether there is a destination to be reached at all. Thus it is that, as with traditional religions, there is some need for faith or, as it is called in Sanskrit, *shraddhA*. Initially, we probably do not even understand some of the things that a teacher tells us, or that we read. This is why Advaita asks us not to believe any of it out of hand. Take it on trust for the moment and discover through your own practice whether or not there is truth in it. And, if something is understood intellectually, have faith until it is confirmed through experience.

Faith is the intuition that something is so, even though there is no substantiating evidence. It 'feels' right. The intellect acknowledges this and provisionally gives approval to proceed with this qualified belief until such time as we actually discover the truth. *shraddhA* is not 'blind faith'. The latter implies something given *despite* the objections of common sense, inner feelings and intellect. *shraddhA* is perfect willingness to accept what is stated in the scriptures (*shruti*), or what is spoken by an acknowledged teacher – someone we have reason to believe is trustworthy – even though we may not be able to rationalize that acceptance. Given that reality is beyond words and concepts, this poses no problems once one accepts that the source of the information is unimpeachable.

shraddhA is also what is involved in science when we provisionally accept a working hypothesis, which we then confirm by experimentation. It would not initially be regarded as scientific to accept (or reject) the hypothesis without experiment. Once many scientists have independently confirmed it for themselves, the hypothesis may become a 'law'. Others then exercise *shraddhA* in accepting it without conducting the experiments themselves. It is in this sense that the statements in the shruti may be regarded as 'laws', since they have been validated many times by Sages.

Gods and religion

On the dogmas of religion, as distinguished from moral principles, all mankind, from the beginning of the world to this day, have been quarrelling, fighting, burning and torturing one another, for abstractions unintelligible to themselves and to all others, and absolutely beyond the comprehension of the human mind. Thomas Jefferson

The purpose of all religions is the same – to connect one back to the truth – and the essential truth of all religions is also the same –the one truth that is called variously 'God', 'Self', 'Absolute' etc. The nature of language and thought is such that this truth can never be expressed in any objective sense; it is something that must be realized for oneself. Inevitably, therefore, the teachers in these various religions have used different words and concepts to try to communicate with those who wish to learn. Unfortunately, what then happens over long periods of time, is that these attempts to explain by parable or metaphor come to be taken as literal truths by people who themselves become teachers without ever having intuited the truth directly. Distortions then become exaggerated until such time that a new Self-realized master can explain the confusions and correct the mistakes.

Thus it is that it becomes possible for vast numbers of people to believe themselves to be fundamentally different from equally vast numbers of others, simply by virtue of believing in the distorted teachings of one religion rather than those of another. And, as we know, this can lead to the ludicrous situation where wars take place and people are killed simply because they use a different name for this one truth. But it is the fallible nature of the church elders and the gullible nature of the laity that are to blame here, not the religions themselves. At their cores, the one truth remains, accessible to all who are prepared to make the effort.

Gandhi said: *"Raindrops of purest distilled water become diluted or polluted as soon as they come in contact with mother earth."* (Ref. 92) Given all that will be said in Chapter 13, 'The Limits of Knowledge', about the inability to comprehend or describe reality, it is inevitable that anyone who attempts to talk about the truth, which they claim to know, will fail. Even if they themselves have direct and certain knowledge of that truth, they will fail. So it must follow that the purpose of religions should be to help the seeker discover the truth for themselves.

That all religions are saying effectively the same thing can be seen from an initiative that aimed to catalogue quotations from key scriptural texts, for all categories of human thought, behavior, endeavor etc. This is now available in full on the Internet at http://www.unification.net/ws/ - 'World Scripture: A Comparative Anthology of Sacred Texts'. And there can be little doubt that, if you extract passages on key issues from the Holy Books of *any* of the main religions, it is usually impossible to tell from which books they derived, unless you are directly familiar with the words. They *are* all saying the same thing.

Religions prepare and purify the mind in readiness for full enlightenment. Their teachings help to remove some of the ignorance that prevents us from realizing the ultimate. But, whilst our ignorance can be partially cleared by the teachings of the various religions, it can only be fully dispelled when true enlightenment occurs.

There is a grave danger of our seeing only the superficial levels of religions, where people, through ignorance, misrepresent the essential truths. It is at this level where bigotry and extremism reign. In their fundamental assertions, the peaks of wisdom merge into one reality.

Nisargadatta Maharaj said: *"What is religion? A cloud in the sky. I live*

in the sky, not in the clouds, which are so many words held together. Remove
the verbiage and what remains? Truth remains."

As was noted earlier, although Advaita is one of the schools of *uttara*
mImAMsA, which itself is one of the six formal Hindu Philosophies, it is
better regarded as a teaching method. Worship of a god is permitted, even
encouraged via *bhakti yoga. Ishvara* is acknowledged as the Lord who
wields the power of *mAyA* to create the appearance of the universe. But the
absolute truth taught by Advaita ultimately negates all of this. Advaita
cannot be called a religion in the usually accepted sense of the word. On the
other hand, Advaita is tolerant of all other belief systems and religions, for
the simple reason that they are all concerned with *vyavahAra* – the unreal
creation, whereas Advaita is the only one that deals directly with
paramArtha – the non-dual, absolute reality.

Scriptures

I do not feel obliged to believe that the same God who has endowed us
with sense, reason, and intellect has intended us to forgo their use.
Galileo Galilei

Gods, then, do not have any ultimate reality and religions may sometimes
be misguided. Both of them have their utility, however, as a means of
mental preparation and for helping to quell the demands of the ego and
point us in the right direction, away from the material and external and
toward the truth within. These limitations need to be appreciated. But what
of the scriptures upon which religions are based? Whichever religion might
be under consideration, it has to be acknowledged that writers of major
scriptural texts have attempted to record important information for
posterity. There are many reasons why such attempts might seem to fail.
The historical context in which they were written is now often poorly
understood. Truths are often couched in obscure terms or hidden in the
depths of seeming irrelevancies (which were probably not irrelevant to the
culture which originated them). Vague or ambiguous presentation may have
been used because writers at that time were persecuted for attempting to

communicate ideas considered heretical by the prevailing society. Translations, too, inevitably lose something in the process – often their essential meaning! And stories written down only after many generations have communicated them verbally, with varying degrees of artistic license, may not be altogether factual.

The Hindu Vedas, with their philosophical Upanishads, are said not to suffer from these problems. They are supposed to have been passed on verbatim from generation to generation since their original observation by realized Sages. Strictly speaking, they are said to be unauthored – *apauruSheya* in Sanskrit, literally 'not coming from men'. The idea here is that the knowledge was given to man by God at the time of creation and passed down thereafter. But such statements need not confound us. The truths expressed in the Upanishads have been validated time and time again by successive Sages and they are there only to provide guidance and to act as an incentive for us to discover those same truths for ourselves – and in this lifetime, not the next! It is essential to know where we are trying to get to and it is always valuable to have some understanding of the processes by which we might reach that destination.

(I have to say that my preferred (reasonable) interpretation of the adjective 'unauthored' is that the words were originated by self-realized sages and subsequently passed on by word of mouth until such time as written materials became common. These sages, being self-realized, no longer identified themselves as body-minds, as named individuals, so they had no wish whatsoever to have their bodily-assigned names attached. They knew that what they were conveying was non-personal, eternal truth that has nothing to do with personality. The sole purpose was to pass on this knowledge so that other minds, initially believing in separation, might be enlightened. Such absolute truth is beyond authorship and hence is reasonably construed as 'unauthored'.)

A useful metaphor for understanding how the scriptures operate is that of a mirror. We are totally unable to see our own face without the aid of a mirror, no matter how good our eyes may be. In an analogous manner, no matter how clever and perceptive the mind might be, we can have no knowledge of our true self. We are always the witness, never the witnessed.

In order to find out about this Self, we need the equivalent of a mirror. Scriptures (and the guru who interprets them for us) provide this mirror.

> *Neither God nor Being nor any other word can define or explain the ineffable reality behind the word, so the only important question is whether the word is a help or a hindrance in enabling you to experience That toward which it points.* Eckhart Tolle (Ref. 93)

As already mentioned, in Advaita, the scriptures (mainly Upanishads, together with the Bhagavad Gita) constitute one of the six *pramANa-s* or sources of knowledge – it was referred to as 'testimony'. And we will see in the chapter on 'The Limits of Knowledge' that reality is defined as that which cannot be sublated by any new experience. (The word 'sublate' will be explained, too, if you haven't encountered it before'.) Furthermore, any cognition is said to be valid if its content can never be sublated. As we know from experience, and will be discussed in the third section of the book, perception, inference etc. are all subject to later correction or modification as additional information comes to light. John Grimes, in his excellent book 'Perspective on Language' (Ref.140) summarizes this and concludes that scriptural knowledge is the only source that does not suffer in this way:

"Perception and all the other pramANa-s, except words as knowledge, produce cognitions which ultimately suffer sublation. Brahman, which is the content of the cognition produced by religious discourse, remains unsublated. Because Brahman is eternal, there is no possibility of Its sublation at some later time. Thus, the cognition which religious discourse gives rise to is valid."

9. Meditation

This could have been included in the previous chapter since it is generally recognized as being a practice that is invaluable in helping to discipline the mind, bringing thoughts under control and aiding the stillness that is necessary for viveka. It should be noted however that along with all other practices, it cannot in itself lead one to recognition of the Self. Only Self-knowledge can bring about this.

Many books have been written on this subject. Mostly, these try to tell you what meditation is, from a scientific aspect, and how to practice it. They tend to emphasize the mental and physical benefits – effectively asking 'What's in it for *me*?' and telling you about all of the beneficial results, such as reducing stress, generating a feeling of well-being, getting an important job etc. Very few of them tell you that the true aim of meditation is to help eradicate *me* once and for all! But the claims are true. Whether or not you subscribe to the ideas being suggested in this book, you as a body-mind-person-ego will (all) benefit from meditation. But, because these aspects *are* only of concern to the ego, we're not really interested and will ignore them. As far as this book is concerned, meditation is a practical technique for helping to understand who we are.

Gangaji, another teacher of the Sri Poonja lineage, says this about 'meditators' and 'meditation':

"Stilling the mind is a great benefit of many practices of meditation. It is a kind of focusing or one-pointedness, where the fragmentation of the mind and all of its outward movement are consciously brought into one pointedness. It's good for the mind, like training the body is good for a healthy body. It makes for a healthier life. But regarding the truth of who you are, you have to see, finally, that nothing causes that, and finally, that nothing really even causes the revelation of that. Otherwise, you imagine that you 'did it,' and there is an investment and a pride in what you have done. You didn't do it, and you will never do it, because it cannot be done...

"I am not anti-meditation. I am anti the belief in the meditator. This belief in a meditator is actually the block to meditation revealing what it is designed to reveal. When this is revealed, then you will see that sitting silently is simply the body sitting silently. The mind calming is simply the mind calming. The mind agitated is the mind agitated. The body moving quickly is the body moving quickly. That which is silent, is silent in both movement and agitation. That which is free, is free. That who you are is always who you are."

(Quoted from the excerpt 'Find the Meditator' which was on her website http://www.gangaji.org/ in 2002.)

What is it?

Essentially the idea is that the attention is focused on one thing to the exclusion of all others. Normally, our senses are assaulted from all sides and our attention is constantly flitting amongst all of this input. Our senses and minds are in a permanent turmoil with perceptions and thoughts vying for attention; first one achieving dominance and then another. This is our normal state and we usually think nothing of it – we haven't got the time.

But, if you persist in attending to only one thing, bringing back the attention every time it is taken away by something else, then eventually this 'noise' begins to reduce. There comes a time, though this may take much practice and perseverance, when the chosen object of attention is the *only* thing that is really sensed. The other input is still there but simply washes over us and doesn't in any way distract. Once this state is reached, the single input that remains can gradually be dropped too. What remains then is silence, a peace and stillness the like of which few of us ever experience. Meditation really is worthwhile for everyone, seeking truth or not, for this rest from the chaos that is our usual waking existence. It is this peace which brings all of the side effects so acclaimed by most of the books. However, the value of the technique, from this perspective, is that in this state, the mind is no longer out of control. Normally it is worrying, imagining, calculating or merely distracting. All of this comes to a stop. And its absence is dramatic!

The mind

The true purpose of the mind is to pass information from the outside world, via our senses, and present this, uncluttered by memories or opinions, to the discriminative faculty. As noted earlier, these two functions – transmitting information and discriminating between information – are assigned to two quite different 'organs of mind' in Vedantic philosophy. In Sanskrit, they are called *manas* and *buddhi*. *manas* passes information in; *buddhi* sees which aspects are valid and makes choices; these choices are then interpreted back via *manas* to the hands, feet etc. to take action. Unfortunately, what almost invariably happens is that the information being passed from the senses is commented on by *manas*. It retrieves related data from memory (*chitta*); adds other considerations and arguments and generally confuses the whole issue. By the time *buddhi* gets a look in, it is difficult to make any sense of it at all. It is hardly surprising that our decisions are often unwise and our actions inappropriate.

This perpetual movement of mind clouds our perception. If we are trying to discover our true nature, *any* involvement of *manas* prevents us. So it is that, when all this activity ceases during meditation we at last have a chance to see how things really are. There is an opportunity to recognize the truths being spoken of in this book.

Osho has much to say about meditation (Ref. 41). He compares thought to time, suggesting that both are linear. We can only think one thing at a time, just as there can only be one moment followed by another. Both are horizontal. Meditation, however, is vertical, rising above both, beyond thought and out of time. In meditation, both of these stop and the mind is still. The mind is useless for apprehending the Self. In order to gain some understanding of the Self therefore, we need somehow to remove the distracting elements of the mind. Meditation is a way of doing this.

The Self is still, says Osho, as it must be if it is everywhere. You cannot reach it by running. Even the speed of the mind, which can jump to contemplate the interior of the Sun in an instant, is powerless to catch the Self. In a sense the mind *is* running. When we become completely still in deep meditation, the mind effectively ceases to exist. The mind always looks to the future, running after that which the ego desires. Once this is attained, another desire takes its place and the mind is off again, dreaming, wish-fulfilling. It is as if there are milestones, with the number of miles to the desired object marked on them. Since there is never a state without desire, the mind never encounters a milestone with 'zero' marked on. In meditation, we reach that state, the place where we find milestone zero – we reach our destination.

> *The Self is unmoving, quicker than the mind. The Gods do not catch It for It has gone before. Though Itself staying still, It overtakes others that are running. In It, the celestial wind sustains the activity of all beings.* IshopaniShad verse 4

japa and *mantra*

Classically, meditation begins with what is called *japa*, the simple repetition of a *mantra*. A *mantra* is a group of words, or sometimes only one or more syllables, traditionally having mystical significance, being in many religions an actual name of God or a short prayer. Catholics using a rosary to say their 'Hail Mary' are effectively carrying out meditation, though they may strenuously deny this. According to Swami Satchidananda, it actually means 'that which keeps the mind steady and produces the proper effect'.

There is an excellent talk on *japa* by Swami Dayananda, downloadable from the Internet (http://www.yogamalika.org/). He speaks of the way that our minds ordinarily operate with one thought following on from another non-stop, just as, when psychiatrists ask people to free-associate, one thought can take us off in many directions. He calls this sort of thinking 'spaghetti thinking' where, attempting to pick up one piece of spaghetti, we find more being dragged up with it. We scarcely ever experience the peace of no thoughts. When we go to sleep, the situation is even worse – *manas* goes off on its own without even the activity of *buddhi* to select sensible thoughts from all of those possible ones triggered by the previous thought and we end up with silly dreams. Only deep sleep brings rest for the mind and an opportunity to recuperate – but unfortunately we are not aware of that at the time.

The reason for this type of thinking, says Swami Dayananda, is that thoughts are so logical and linear. Any thought is likely to have a myriad of possible associations and, depending upon the general subject matter or the current state of our emotions and so on, a new thought is almost certain to be triggered automatically. Since no particular thought necessarily follows any given one, this mechanism will usually prevail.

When a thought is not part of a fixed sequence, this mechanical process does not take place. If, for example, we are reading or reciting a poem, the next word is predefined. When we speak one word, the option of other words to follow is not available. This is even more pronounced in the case of a single word repeated. Provided we accept the discipline, when we have sounded the word in the mind, the only option available to us subsequently is to sound the word again. That is the process that we have accepted. He calls this 'peanut thinking'. We pick up a peanut, put it in our mouth. We pick up a peanut... Each is a discrete action without others being dragged in with it. With ordinary thinking, we *never* know what is coming next; with *japa* we *always* do.

The value of the technique is this: with normal thinking, there is no peace – one thought follows another without end; with *japa*, between each repetition of the *mantra* is a gap of silence. We repeat the *mantra* mechanically, letting the pace and strength vary as it will, just observing and not trying to control anything. Eventually, the noise in the mind begins to become quiet and the sound of the *mantra* is all that is heard. This now becomes slower and quieter until even it disappears and silence reigns. In this fullness of peace, it is now possible for the Self to be directly aware of itself and to 'merge with it' as it were. This union is called *yoga*, and 'union' is what the Sanskrit word itself, means. It is this silence that is all-important. Many people never experience this silence; their lives are a never ending succession of events, governed primarily by *rajas* and *tamas* – rushing about and then collapsing. The silence provides the refreshment of *sattva* and only in *this* is there an opportunity for recognizing the truth.

Another thing that must be appreciated is that the stillness is only ever here *now*. It cannot be found in the past, in memory. Memories are actually present thoughts of what we imagine happened in the past. Nor can it be found in the future, in desires – these are present thoughts about what we imagine might happen. The stillness is found when all of these thoughts have been dropped. It is an aspect of our true nature.

There are a few practical considerations in respect of the practice of meditation. One should seek out times and places conducive to stillness. A quiet room away from distractions is very important. Classical texts suggest that the half-hour each side of dawn and sunset are special times of peace. These are times when *sattva* naturally predominates. Incidentally, *sattva* is also much more prevalent in the vicinity of running water and may be felt distinctly in a cathedral or other holy place. All that is required is to still the mind of any pre-judgmental criticism or other commentary and open out the attention. (If this is not done, of course, the experience will be missed because the mind remains busy and confused with *rajas*.) The trouble with not meditating early in the morning is that, once one has woken up and is into the rush of getting ready and leaving for work, *rajas* has taken over and finding the space for *sattva* is likely to be much more difficult. Similarly, meditating after a large meal, with *tamas* predominating, is quite likely to send you to sleep.

N.B. remember that the *guNa-s* – *sattva*, *rajas* and *tamas* – are not substantial constituents of matter; they are 'qualities' of the substance under discussion. E.g. a busy, peaceful or soporific atmosphere – *rAjasika*, *sAttvika* or *tAmasika*, respectively. It is only in *sAMkhya* philosophy that they are actual constituents of matter.

Scriptures such as the Bhagavad Gita give more specific guidance such as sitting with the back straight and the closed eyes cast down 'pointing towards the end of the nose'. (It is generally agreed that this should not be interpreted literally!) The reasoning behind this relates to the movement of energies (vital forces or *prANa*) in the body. Energy is said to concentrate at the base of the spine and can, through practice, be caused to move through *chakra-s* corresponding to various points in the body, up to the top *chakra* located in the brain, possibly associated with the pineal gland. The specific theory and practice of this is the subject of *kuNDalinI yoga* and it is not relevant to Advaita. For all practical purposes, you should find the most comfortable position for the body, in which it intrudes as little as possible upon your attention.

The problem with thoughts

There isn't actually *any* problem with thoughts – thinking is what the mind does... and we are not the mind. When we first embark upon a study and practice of Advaita, it often seems that we are most nearly our true 'Self' when the mind is still, and there is the perceptual and conceptual clarity of *sattva*.

When people first start to practice meditation, they often find that things go very well for a while. It is a novel experience and the ego-mind doesn't know quite what to make of it. It is as though it stops what it is usually doing and just looks on bewildered. So it seems as if the practice is 'working', that this meditation thing really is bringing us to some stillness. After a while, however, the honeymoon ends and the mental chattering can seem even worse than it was before, since we are now actively observing it.

What usually happens is one of three things: –

1) Since the mind in general is much quieter than usual and the attention more open and available, any thoughts which do arise are more apparent.
2) Since there is less confusion and distraction, there is more clarity in the mind. Therefore ideas and solutions to problems come more easily; the mind finds that this state is actually more conducive to doing its dirty work than is everyday consciousness.
3) The ego-mind sees the practice as a threat to its dominion and even its existence. It throws up more rubbish than usual to ward off the attack with those thoughts most effective in disturbing the tranquility of the mind being used as ammunition.

Although knowing all this doesn't necessarily help, when it is observed happening it can be treated less as a cause for concern and more as a source of amusement. There is no point in worrying about it – self-criticism of any kind is never useful. After all there is fundamentally nothing you *can* do about it. It is the ego-mind that wanted the stillness in the first place, that wanted to practice this meditation. And it is the ego-mind that is the cause of the problems, giving attention to these obstructing thoughts. So it stands to reason that the ego-mind is not going to be able to resolve it.

Sri Shantananda Saraswati, who was for many years the Shankaracharya of the North, said that the problem of thoughts could be compared to being in a room with a busy road outside. He said we wouldn't think of going outside every time we heard a car pass by and chasing it down the road. When a thought passes by, just leave it alone and don't go chasing after it either. (The Shankaracharya tradition was established by Shankara, whom I have already mentioned. He set up four positions, in the North, South, East and West of India, to be held by realized men, who would take on the role of teacher – *AchArya* – and could be consulted by anyone having problems or questions of a spiritual nature.)

He suggests one technique for dealing with thoughts but you can devise your own once the principle is understood. He tells us to imagine we are walking over a bridge. We start at one end, our normal waking consciousness full of mental agitation (thoughts, desires, fears etc.) and we are walking to the other side, where we will find peace and bliss – our true nature. While we walk across, thoughts and worries and so on will arise and come to our attention. As soon as this happens we imagine taking hold of the thought and throwing it over the edge of the bridge into an abyss. Eventually, no more thoughts come and there is silence.

All of this takes a varying length time. We are so used to using the mind constantly that unlearning this habit is a slow process. A few may connect with the technique from the outset. Many people find that they practice meditation for many months before they experience any real stillness at all and some take much longer than this. Also, it truly is necessary to meditate for half-an-hour at a time, ideally twice a day. Even when the stillness is reached more often, this may only occur during the last few minutes of a half-hour period. As the years go by, if the practice is kept up assiduously, the stillness will last much longer and occur routinely rather than only rarely. If one is serious in this search, the practice of meditation must become quite fundamental to one's life so that, although it will not be a problem if it is not convenient to meditate on a particular occasion, such occasions will seldom be tolerated.

10. Other practices

In addition to the basic 'path', i.e. *bhakti, karma, j~nAna* or one of the other systems that lead to the same mountaintop, together with the common practice of meditation, there are a number of general 'skills' that should be acquired and principles that should be instilled. Some of these have already been mentioned in the context of Shankara's pre-requisites for following a spiritual path – the *chatuShTaya sampatti*. These skills are concerned with 'tuning the instrument' of body-mind-intellect and subduing the ego, raising the level of *sattva* in our being and reducing *rajas* and *tamas*. Any mental attitude, or manner of interaction with the world outside, that is in keeping with these principles can be added to this list. Any that clearly conflicts with them should be avoided.

Note that reading the following list of practices is not the same as doing them! And it is worth mentioning here the distinction between such practices and the Self-knowledge that we are looking to attain. Gaining the knowledge about the benefits of meditation, for example, is not in itself of any value – you really do have to put this knowledge into practice if you want to cultivate a still mind. Self-knowledge does not work like this. When you have truly gained this, it is the end in itself. There is nothing that you need to do with this knowledge in order to 'gain enlightenment' for example. (Of course, if your nature is that way inclined, you may decide to teach or write books subsequently!)

Attention

Practically speaking, most of the exercises or techniques that can be applied during one's day to day life relate to being 'in the present'. The fact that there is *only* the present will be discussed in Chapter 14, 'Creation and Time'. But whether you agree with this or not, understanding it and following it are two radically different things.

The word 'now' is like a bomb through the window, and it ticks. Arthur Miller

(It is not incidental that Eckhart Tolle's now-famous book is called 'The *Power* of Now'!)

It doesn't seem to matter that we *know* that circling thoughts and daydreaming are futile; we still indulge in them! We worry about things that are either unlikely or about which we can do nothing (or both). We desire things that we can never attain and which would bring no real satisfaction if we got them anyway. These things, and many others, take us out of the present moment, away from reality, into an imagined world, away from ourselves, away from the truth. Once this has happened, there is nothing we can do about it until we see that it *has* happened.

At that precise moment when we see that it has happened, we are back in the present. There is an opportunity to stay there. But it can be all too easily lost. E.g. a certain way of losing it is to start criticizing oneself for having done it in the first place. In a very real sense, therefore, you can only be, and stay, in the present, if you are in the present to begin with – one of those 'Catch 22' situations. The act of remembering to be in the present can itself only take place in the present. At the moment when anything happens and your attention is given to it (as opposed to being taken away), you are *there*.

So, once you are there, how can you stay there? Well, the key really is attention. You can only properly give attention to something or someone if you are in the moment. This means that *manas* must be operating correctly. It must just be transmitting data through the senses, without comment i.e. the mind, as we know it, must be silent. This means *no thinking*. As soon as any thought *about* the experience arises, if your attention is caught by that thought, then you are no longer there.

The senses themselves are the means to success. The act of 'opening up' the attention and letting the senses simply transmit whatever is there is a powerful means for coming into the present. Our eyes and to a lesser degree, the ears, seem to be working all of the time anyway, though we miss much of what is there and allow the habitual parts of the mind-mechanism to recognize only those things that are essential for survival. Thus, for example, we may drive to work and, on getting there, have no recollection of anything that occurred. Autopilot will have taken care of avoiding traffic and following road signals etc. Surprisingly perhaps, the less frequently used senses are particularly valuable for bringing us back into the present. If you feel the surface of the chair on which you are sitting (do it now!), the novelty of giving full attention to something like texture, normally a very background thing, momentarily stills the mind and allows one to be fully in the present. There is no pre-programming for this sort of activity.

We have five senses and we have thinking and feeling. These constitute the instruments through which we experience the 'objects' of our consciousness. Normally, no single one of these functions to the exclusion of all others; we are potentially able to direct our attention to whatever is deemed, by *buddhi*, to be most worthy of it. Usually, this will be dictated by habit. If interested in cars, our eyes will be drawn to a rare model passing us on the road. If we are interested in models of a different kind, a short skirt passing in the street will distract us. At such moments, our normal, relatively wide attention narrows down to something much smaller. If some sudden noise or other unexpected sensation is received, the attention becomes 'single-pointed' and everything else is momentarily excluded from our awareness until we decide whether there is any danger.

You might be watching television when a squealing of tires sounds outside of the house. For a moment, you become quite unaware of what is showing on the screen as your attention is taken away and, in all probability, you wait with dread for the sound of a possible crash. While the squealing sound lasts, there are no other thoughts or sensations. Normally, although we may be supposedly concentrating on one thing, there are many other peripheral sensations that partially cloud the clarity. We rarely experience this sharpness voluntarily.

There is a story in the scriptures (Bhagavata Purana XI:IX:13) of an arrow-maker, who was so intent on sharpening the point of the arrow on which he was working that he completely failed to notice the king passing by. This extremity of attention is equivalent to the meditative mind giving full attention to a *mantra*. It is a level of consciousness without any of the distractions from irrelevant sensations and perceptions. Full attention is given to the point where the action is taking place but lightly and without effort. Consciousness is undivided and the ego is quite absent, i.e. 'I' am not 'giving' this attention.

It is very important to appreciate this last point, which will tie in with the revelation that will be made later that we are not the 'doer'. It is very probable that, if this book is your first exposure to these ideas, you do not believe such statements. And it *is* difficult for the mind to understand but, fortunately, it is easy to see in practice. Have you ever watched yourself doing something, for example making a cup of coffee? If not, get up and do it now – I know you'd like one! Don't interfere; just watch it happening. Legs walking, arm raising, hand moving etc. Incredible complexity even at this level but, below that, there are impulses moving along nerves, blood vessels contracting muscles and below that synapses triggering in the brain and below that enzymes and proteins interacting etc. Are 'you' *doing* any of this? Would you indeed have the slightest idea of where to begin?

You are the observer of all of this (well, some of it anyway!), which, in a very real sense, just 'happens'. You, the Self, *do* nothing. Without the petrol, the car can do nothing but in no sense could the petrol be said to be acting. In an analogous manner, no-*body* can act without the support of the Self – it is after all just a lump of food – but the Self does not act either. The Self will support the actions of a murderer just as much as those of a doctor in the same way as the petrol will enable both tank and ambulance to perform their respective functions. You are simply the equivalent of the petrol in the car – without it the car cannot move but the petrol is in no real sense responsible for how the car behaves. This is determined by the nature of the car – whether it is a tuned racing car or a rusty heap. (See the section on 'Apparent Contradictions in Advaita' later, for the analysis which proves that there is no such thing as a 'doer'.)

By *practicing* giving your attention to what is being done at any moment, and just watching what happens, it is possible to appreciate this non-involvement or 'witness' status for yourself. And be sure to practice – do not accept any of these ideas until you have verified them. Giving attention can actually be viewed as a subset of the one practice that is probably more important than any other – acknowledging that the present moment is the only reality and staying in it! Isaac Shapiro has this to say about it (extracted from a dialogue at his website http://www.isaacshapiro.de/):

> *"All that we can give to anybody or anything is our attention. Check for yourself and see if this is true. Where your attention is, is what you experience. If you put your attention on your toe, you experience your toe, if you put your attention on what you want, you experience longing, and if you put your attention on what is wrong, you experience wrongness or negativity. Where your attention is, is where you are giving all your energy to, in other words, what you are worshipping."*

Silence

> *He had occasional flashes of silence that made his conversation perfectly delightful.* Sydney Smith

Since the importance of stillness has already been emphasized in respect of meditation, it should come as no surprise that silence itself has value as an aid to these endeavors. In this context, of course, is meant not merely absence of external sounds but absence of internal mental babble too. Indeed, it is the latter that is important because, with practice, it is possible to meditate deeply even in the middle of the market place.

Silence is one aspect of being in the present that we are otherwise unable ever to appreciate. It is the characteristic that most strikes us when we have begun regular meditation and we start to experience occasional moments when thinking stops. Only in deep sleep does this occur naturally. In dreams, the mind is at its most active, no longer even held back by a restraining intellect. And in all of our usual waking hours, it is constantly on the go, as though, if it were to stop for an instant, we would cease to exist. Silence is not so much the absence of sound as the absence of the listener-ego. This is why noises outside of the room prove to be a distraction to someone who is just learning to meditate. He believes that silence is necessary in order to be able to meditate.

If you have ever been in the presence of a Sage, this is the characteristic that perhaps stands out above all others. They are here and now, without any doubt. They seem somehow to be surrounded by an aura of peace and alert silence, fully aware of everything around them and ready to respond to a need in an instant. At the same time, this is not the poised-to-leap awareness of power, the 'action-man' alertness of an entrepreneur or an elite soldier. It is totally unassuming – the pure humility of an absence of ego.

The mind is typically in constant agitation, like a small child badgering us for attention. One thought triggers another in endless chattering. Sometimes, when something catches our attention, there can be a momentary peace. This is one of the reasons why things of beauty can have such a profound effect. It is not that they have in themselves any property of their own; everything is only an appearance to which we attach name and form. They act as a pointer, enabling us to recognize that being-consciousness-bliss that is our true nature and, in doing so, bring us momentarily back to that nature, which is recognizable only in silence.

Being in the present has already been mentioned as being key to any 'path' back to the truth. Seeking out silence is another way of saying the same thing, for silence can only exist in the present. This is part of the appeal of such places as cathedrals. The sense of peace, stillness and silence can be almost tangible. The atmosphere has the ability to drag one back into the present without any voluntary wish on our part. And remember from the discussion on meditation, that the silence is always there, despite external noise or internal thoughts. It is an attitude of dispassionate witnessing rather than a physical absence of sound.

Sri Nisargadatta Maharaj says: *"No particular thought can be mind's natural state, only silence. Not the idea of silence, but silence itself. When the mind is in its natural state, it reverts to silence spontaneously after every experience, or, rather, every experience happens against the background of silence."* (Ref. 26)

Under all speech that is good for anything there lies a silence that is better. Silence is deep as Eternity; speech is shallow as Time. Thomas Carlyle

The power of silence is such that it is said that some sages in the past have effectively taught only through silence. Having acknowledged that reality cannot be spoken, being beyond objectification, this is not so ridiculous as it may at first sound. However, it could not be the literal truth since language is most definitely needed in order to convey the teaching of Advaita. Here is what I said about it in 'Back to the Truth' (Ref. 95):

> *"It is said that Ramana Maharshi often practised this (i.e. teaching through silence). In the mythology of Hinduism and Shaivism, Dakshinamurthy, who is the iconic guru and represents the god Shiva, is supposed to have taught in silence. There is a certain logic in this, given that it can be argued that language is the source of all of our problems. Clearly silence avoids all of the paradoxes that arise once we begin to use words.*
>
> *Swami Dayananda, however, says that this is a misunderstanding (Ref. 94). When it is said that* dakShiNAmUrti *taught by silence, the word actually used is* mudrA, *meaning a sign made by the position of the fingers and should be interpreted as 'language.' He says that if He was silent, all our Upanishads would be in the form of blank pages! Silence is the appropriate response only when it is either inconvenient or might be misleading to answer."*

Nevertheless, there is a beautiful story related by Catherine Ingram, a contemporary guru who was a student of Sri Poonja. It concerns Mrs. Gandhi while she was Prime Minister. It seems she was passing through a difficult period and decided to go to consult the Shankaracharya. A journalist who accompanied Mrs. Gandhi reported the story. The Prime Minister went in to see the Shankaracharya while the journalist waited outside. After about an hour, she emerged, looking very peaceful, in stark contrast to the anxious state of mind in which she had entered. When the journalist asked how it had gone, Mrs. Gandhi answered, "It was wonderful. I put forth all my questions, and he answered every one of them, but neither of us spoke a word." (Ref. 96)

Discrimination

The highest element of mind is *buddhi*. This is responsible for judgment and discrimination, differentiating between pairs of opposites, particularly between transient and eternal. In terms of the 'spiritual development' of a man, it is this that is the most important, since it is able effectively to exercise control over all of the rest of the body-mind instrument. Without it, we are no better than animals, driven by primitive instincts and selfish, acquisitive urges.

The metaphor of a horse-driven chariot is used to describe this in the scriptures (Katha Upanishad). The elements are a chariot containing a passenger and a charioteer who uses reins to control the horses that are pulling the chariot. If the charioteer does not keep a tight hold on the reins to direct the horses in the desired direction and instead allows them to go where they will, they will wander down whichever road takes their fancy. The chariot represents the physical body, pulled by horses representing the wayward senses, which will stray according to their own interests. The mind is represented by the reins, which keep the senses in check, providing they are controlled by the intellect, using its powers of discrimination. The passenger in the chariot is the *jIva*, the 'individual' Self, the observer of all this who does not actually take part. The ego doesn't exist of course – it results from the mistaken identification of the Self with the rest of the equipment. Finally, the destination is the *Atman*, the true self.

Buddhi can only operate optimally in the presence of *sattva guNa*, i.e. in stillness, without interference from *manas*, and in the present moment. The thinking mind, *manas*, cannot itself make decisions. *chitta*, in which memory functions, can throw up lots of information from the past – what has been heard or read etc. – and *manas* can churn over all of this, apply logic and so on. It is particularly useful in using doubt to question all of the possibilities. On its own, however, all will just become more confused as more and more is added to the equation. In order for discrimination (*viveka*) to function, *manas* needs simply to keep quiet.

Without a discriminating intellect, control of mind and restraint of senses, there can be no clarity, no discrimination of pairs of opposites, no purification of mind, no Self-realization. The *jIva* will remain trapped in *saMsAra.*

One final point here, courtesy of Dr. Sadananda in his reviewing of this material: Vedanta differentiates between what is called 'sharp' intellect (*tIkShNa buddhi*) and 'subtle' intellect (*sUkShma buddhi*). The former is the analytical mind characteristic of the scientist who, as the saying goes, finds out more and more about less and less until he knows everything about nothing. It is the latter that we need to cultivate. This is the ability to integrate rather than divide, to see the unity in diversity.

Indifference

This is known as *vairAgya* in Sanskrit and is the second of the fourfold qualifications. In chapter 5, 'The Driving Forces of our Lives', it was pointed out that we desire objects (and people) in the world because we think that they will bring us happiness. In fact, we should now have begun to realize that this is not the case. We are already whole and perfect but our ignorance of this causes us to seek outside of ourselves for fulfillment. We need to cultivate the attitude of indifference, or dispassion to these things in order to break the spell and enable us to see through the illusion.

In the same vein, we do not need the approval of others for all that we do. Many people will not do anything unless parents, family or friends support such action and provide encouragement. Look at the fashion industry. Many will not even wear a particular item of clothing unless the media give their ok to begin with. Similarly, if we perform an action, knowing it to be the appropriate response at the time (because we were in the present and did not act for any selfish or otherwise motivated reason), we should not be concerned with whether others condone it or condemn us. They are only expressing an uninformed opinion.

It is almost second nature to many people to consider appearances and status. The neighbors have just installed a high-definition TV receiver; Bob has bought a fast sports car. We must keep up, earn more money to acquire more material possessions. This is, of course, rubbish. None of it actually matters. We are deluded by the false values of society into believing that we need to upgrade as soon as some new technological improvement becomes available; that perfectly serviceable clothing must be thrown away and replaced, probably by something less suitable for purpose. We are brainwashed into this attitude and must struggle to obtain sufficient income to sustain this pace of change. And for many, this may mean that they do not even have the time to enjoy their new acquisitions.

We need to regain some objectivity, to be able to look at what we have and what we need and to see what will genuinely move us towards truth and happiness and what is merely another possession, containing nothing of intrinsic worth. This is dispassion or indifference. This is *vairAgya*.

Swami Dayananda has produced an excellent commentary on the Bhagavad Gita as part of a course that is available in English via the Internet at http://www.arshavidya.org/. He gives a beautiful example of *vairAgya* to differentiate between the true, objective worth of something and the false, subjective value that we all too often impose. Suppose, he says, that we buy an antique bronze sculpture. It is very expensive but we can see that it is old and worn and decide that it must clearly be worth the asking price. Later, someone much more knowledgeable on the subject tells us that, in fact, it is a fake. It has been artificially oxidized to give it its aged appearance, with knocks and scratches deliberately made. We are very disappointed and feel a sense of loss.

But, if the situation is analyzed, it is only our subjective overlay that has been lost. Objectively, nothing has changed. The actual appearance and utility, in so far as a sculpture has any utility, is the same as it was before. Certainly the seller has cheated us, knowing full well that we were paying a high price because we believed, falsely, that it was old. But this aspect of its value is entirely subjective. In fact, if our 'expert' is actually not an expert at all, the sculpture could turn out to be an antique after all and worth even more than we paid for it! Even then, the object itself would be the same; all that keeps changing is the subjective view of the observers.

If we could always view the sculpture simply as it is, without imposing our subjective impressions of value or age, we would be exhibiting *vairAgya*. These values have nothing at all to do with the object; they are false coverings put there by us. Unfortunately, it is not usually something that we do consciously. It is part of the ignorance that covers our true nature and we do it unconsciously. In order for it to become an established practice, we must – practice!

Shankara was emphatic about our need to differentiate between the only thing that matters, namely the unchanging Self, and things that do not matter, namely the ever-changing events of the world that is ultimately unreal. In the *aparokShAnubhUti*, he said that we should treat objects of enjoyment and so-called worldly problems with the same indifference that one treats the 'excreta of a crow' – this is true *vairAgya*!

Witness

Exercising discrimination and not imposing our subjective values upon things are steps along the way to being completely detached from what is happening in the world. Standing back and simply witnessing what is going on is called *sAkshibhAva* in Sanskrit, meaning 'being or becoming' (*bhAva*) a 'witness' (*sAkShI*). It is necessary not to be over-ambitious in this exercise, however. We are so entrenched in our belief of being the doer, the thinker and the enjoyer that 'standing back' and watching these happen can be very difficult indeed. In fact, its ultimate utility is in demonstrating to us that we are truly not those things – if we see them, we cannot be them.

The sort of exercise mentioned some time back about watching ourselves perform a simple activity such as making a cup of coffee or walking down the street *is* possible, for short times. Watching ourselves 'thinking' is something else again. Accordingly, as far as this aspect is concerned, set your targets relatively low to begin with and let its scope grow as your understanding of your true nature grows.

Don't make the mistake of thinking that being a witness is the aim of all these endeavors. It is a useful practice – a step along the way if you like – but we are not that. Ramana Maharshi says: *"Actually, the idea of the Self being the witness is only in the mind; it is not the absolute truth of the Self. Witnessing is relative to objects witnessed. Both the witness and his object are mental creations."* (Ref. 25, quoted in Ref. 69)

Keeping good company

You are together because a forest is always stronger than a solitary

tree. The forest conserves humidity, resists the hurricane and helps the soil to be fertile. But what makes a tree strong is its roots. And the roots of a plant cannot help another plant to grow. To be joined together in the same purpose is to allow each person to grow in his own fashion, and that is the path of those who wish to commune with God.
Ramakrishna Paramahamsa

We need to keep good company. There is a special term for this – *satsa~Nga*, meaning association with the good. This relates not only to spiritual rather than animalistic people but to fine literature rather than popular fiction, classical rather than rock music, art rather than graffiti etc; influences to improve and refine the mind rather than stultify and coarsen. This is one of the most valuable aspects of attending an organization such as one of those mentioned in Appendix 1A. One meets others who share the same values (love of truth, searching for knowledge etc.) and who can provide support during the inevitably difficult times that will be encountered on any spiritual path.

There is a danger of viewing such sentiments as being judgmental; that in stating that classical music is 'better' than pop music, we are merely expressing an opinion. This is not so. What is being said is not that classical music is intrinsically good, while pop is somehow 'bad' but that much (not all) of the former brings about a predominance of *sattva* in the attentive mind while most of the latter generates *rajas* or *tamas*. Similarly, 'good' literature directs the mind to serious and/or spiritual considerations while most popular fiction merely causes time to pass in a way which, whilst it may stimulate *manas*, does little to enhance the functioning of *buddhi*. These things can be seen to happen in practice by anyone open to the ideas; they are not simply matters of opinion.

Until the other aspects of the 'fourfold qualities' have been achieved, it is very difficult to remain fixed on the objective. It is all too easy to decide to stay in bed rather than get up early and meditate, watch television rather than study the Upanishads, go to a party rather than an Advaita study group. The support of like-minded individuals and a teacher are invaluable in this respect. Shankara, in the Bhaja Govindam (V. 9) said: *"Through the company of the good, there arises non-attachment; through non-attachment there arises freedom from delusion; when there is freedom from delusion, there is the Immutable Reality; on experiencing the Immutable Reality, there comes the state of 'liberated-in-life'."* Later (V. 13), he says: *"In the three worlds, it is the association with good people alone that can serve as a boat to cross the sea of change (birth and death)"* (Ref. 16)

Osho said that we usually seek out people who are less accomplished than ourselves. We will not marry someone who is more intelligent, for example and we don't like our friends to be more knowledgeable; the idea being that the ego needs to feel superior. But all of this work is trying to take us in the opposite direction, reducing the dominion of the ego and establishing us in the light of the Self. Thus it is that we should be seeking the company of those wiser than ourselves, whose light is brighter. This reference is from his book 'The Mustard Seed' (Ref. 44) and he likens the impulse that we have towards the truth as being the mustard seed that now requires the right soil in which to grow and mature. Satsang is that soil.

Sri Poonja said: *"Wicked habits and society will come back to you. They are very strong and so you must be. You are going upstream to the source, they are flowing downstream and will drag you along."*

One final point to be noted is that *satsa~Nga* needs to be a regular and prolonged activity in order to benefit the seeker in the ways that have been described. Meeting occasionally, with different group members and/or different teachers will not provide an appropriate setting. This is one of the fundamental reasons why the Western practice, whereby a teacher will travel around the world holding meetings for just a couple of hours with whomsoever happens to turn up, is of only limited value. (My book 'Enlightenment: the Path through the Jungle', Ref. 80, deals with this subject at length.)

Obstacles

This chapter has looked at some of the things that we can and must do if we are to come to a greater understanding of these ideas and ultimately realize their truth. It may sound a bit harsh and unwelcoming – discipline usually does have these connotations – but there is often a misapprehension that an 'enlightened' man is an ascetic and does not enjoy life. This is quite untrue. To the extent that enlightenment means being *totally* in the present, everything is enjoyed to the full. To the extent that there is no attachment, every enjoyment/pain is completely dropped once completed and the instrument is fully open to receive the next. N.B. being realized, he also knows that he is not the enjoyer. To be pedantic, enjoyment takes place in the body-mind complex and he is the witness of this. (Also note that I used the words 'to the extent that...' above. This is because a distinction has to be made between 'being enlightened' and 'gaining the fruits of enlightenment'. See the later Chapter on 'Enlightenment' for more details.)

Relatives and friends often raise objections once you become interested in this subject. Typical questions might be: "How can you spend so much time on something like this? It's incredibly selfish. What about me (your family)?" or, at a more altruistic level "...when there is so much suffering in the world?" Of course, there is no point in responding: "there are no others" or "the world is an illusion" or similar clever remarks – these tend not go down very well!

Obstacles are those frightful things you see when you take your eyes off your goal. Henry Ford

Sri Parthasarathy speaks of four levels of helping others. At the lowest level, one can give money to a charity. This is impersonal and, once the money is handed over, is probably instantly forgotten. The next level is to give some personal possession. For example you might hand over your coat to a beggar in the street. Again, this is a brief transaction and carries little in the way of personal effort. The third level is to give oneself in the sense of personally assisting in a positive way. One might, for example, give up several hours a week to help with a local charity. Here there is actual involvement, interacting with others, directly giving of oneself. The highest level, however, is to seek enlightenment. This is total renunciation of one's ego, giving *everything* 'in service' to the truth and ultimately benefiting all.

He uses the metaphor of the water supply to help explain this. When we want a drink of water, most of us think that we just need to go and turn on the tap. It doesn't occur to us that this is not actually the source of the water at all. Ultimately, all of this water comes from a distant lake or reservoir up in the mountains. When new towns are constructed, men must travel to the reservoir and tap into its resources, bringing the water down to the houses so that we may benefit. The lake itself does nothing. It simply sits there and collects the rainwater from the heavens. When people discover that they need it, they have to come and connect into it. The realized man, he says, is like the reservoir. He sits there (in his cave), holding the knowledge of life, the universe and everything, and people who wish to learn go to him to discover the truth. He does nothing, yet makes available the most valuable knowledge there is – to those who seek it.

Possibly the most common reason given by people as an excuse for why they are unable to follow a teaching such as this is "I haven't got any time." This is a pathetic excuse! Firstly, when anyone says this, what they really mean is that they have things to do that they deem to be more important. So what they are actually saying is that this work is not of a sufficiently high priority. And what this means ultimately is that they are happy to continue living in ignorance of the truth; happy to continue in a dream where all of the things that they value are illusory; happy to continue alternating between enjoyment and misery and trying not to think too much about death and what might happen then. The second reason why this excuse is so poor is that living this philosophy is not inimical to normal life – quite the contrary, in fact. Being in the present, giving attention to the immediate task, not daydreaming, listening to others (and not thinking of them as 'other') and so on are all practices that *enhance* one's daily life.

Probably the most important thing that we can do is to put ourselves under the discipline of a teacher or school. Indeed, although some teachers have said that this is not absolutely necessary, it is 'well-nigh' essential. Without the unquestioning submission to a teacher in whom we have trust, it is going to be very difficult to get rid of the ego, which wants to question and authorize everything. Apart from which, understanding the Upanishads without the help of a *shrotriya* – someone who has been taught the methodology and understands the presentation (and Sanskrit!) – is fraught with difficulty. The next chapter looks more closely at this question.

11. Gurus

What is a guru?

A guru is only a guru to a person who sees himself as that individual's disciple. Swamini Pramananda (Ref. 81)

Spiritual teachers are often called 'gurus', a term that became popular in the West in the nineteen sixties but has been traditional in the East for thousands of years. Anyone can, in theory, fulfill this role as long as they have some knowledge of spiritual truths that they are willing to transmit to others. More recently, the word has come to mean in general usage someone with specialist knowledge of *any* kind, so that we have 'business gurus' and 'pop music gurus'. Traditionally, however, we probably tend to think of an ascetic eastern gentleman in a loincloth sitting cross-legged with a serene expression on his face, dispensing laconic and ambiguous words of 'wisdom'.

The word itself is Sanskrit and literally means 'heavy'. It was also used in reference to one's parents or elders, to whom one should exhibit reverence. In the pronunciation of Sanskrit words, it refers to that part of the word that is stressed, as opposed to *laghu*, which means 'light' or unstressed. Some have suggested we should interpret it as 'heavy with knowledge'.

So long as one thinks of himself as little – laghu *– he must take hold of the great – the Guru; He must not however look upon the Guru as a person; the Sage is never other than the real Self of the disciple. When the Self is realized then there is neither Guru nor disciple.* Ramana Maharshi

Some books will tell you that the word means 'remover of darkness', where the darkness stands for ignorance (but the Sanskrit dictionary recognizes no such meaning). The guru, if 'enlightened', brings the torch of wisdom to bear on the darkness of the disciple, enabling him to see what was there all along. This sounds quite good, even if not necessarily true. (It may be true but my knowledge of Sanskrit root words, called *dhAtu-s* is non-existent.)

Osho has a beautiful metaphor for this (Ref. 42). He compares the guru to a lit candle and the disciple to an unlit one. If and when enlightenment occurs, the flame jumps from the guru to the disciple. The guru loses nothing – one candle can light a thousand others at no expense to itself; the disciple gains everything. The student, on the other hand, gives up his ego to the teacher. At the time he thinks he is giving everything but the teacher, accepting the gift, gains nothing. Furthermore, for the transformation to proceed to completion, the 'fire' of the teacher must consume the persona of the student completely. The person, the ego, will be no more; not that it was ever there in the first place of course, in reality.

Some teachers claim that it is possible to attain enlightenment without a guru. After all, some unarguably realized men such as Ramana Maharshi did not themselves have a guru (although traditional teachers might claim that he must have been almost fully prepared in his previous life). Nevertheless, it is also widely accepted that having a guru is a tremendous advantage. Simply reading and studying is likely to result in the acquisition of information rather than the transformative effect of 'Self knowledge'. What is ideally needed is the specialized knowledge of the teaching 'methodology' that is traditionally passed on from guru to disciple in the formalized *sampradAya* teaching. This is the knowledge of the *shrotriya* – someone who understands and is able to utilize the knowledge contained in the *prasthAna traya* (the Upanishads, Brahma Sutras and Bhagavad Gita).

Learning about Advaita for oneself, simply by reading books, is dangerous. If this is the only option, then at least you must read lots, from different sources, and ideally be guided by someone who knows the truth and has read those books. This is expressed succinctly: "*Swami Chinmayananda was asked why we can't simply study Vedanta ourselves in the library. He answered: 'Ask that question to the library.'*" (Ref. 97)

The physical presence of the guru is said by some teachers to be, if not essential, at least highly advantageous to a seeker. At least once, one should know from direct experience what it is like to be present in this unique peace and awareness. It is, of course, only the peace and awareness of one's own Self but this is normally covered up and the actual presence of a realized man has the 'light' capable of penetrating that darkness for a short while. Once one has actually had this experience, it is possible to remember or to be reminded of it later, when the guru is no longer present.

Francis Lucille likens this to the taste of a strange fruit. If, for example, you have not tasted a mango, I could attempt to describe it to you. I could probably describe the color, shape and texture fairly well but would have great difficulty when it came to the taste and smell. The best you would get out of it would be a hazy impression. This is analogous to the descriptions of enlightenment and so on that you might read about in a book. Someone who is very good with words and extremely perceptive – a pandit – would make a better job of it and your impression might be quite detailed. However, once you taste the fruit for yourself, there is no longer any doubt and the memory will remain strong for a long time – it will no longer be in the realm of theory or surmise, it will be a directly known and remembered experience. So it is having met the guru 'in person' for yourself. (This is the difference between what Western philosophy calls knowledge by description or conceptual knowledge and knowledge by acquaintance or perceptual knowledge.)

But one has to remind oneself here that enlightenment is not an experience and it cannot be 'transmitted' by being in the presence of someone who is enlightened. (This is extremely important to note because there are people calling themselves teachers who make precisely this claim.) What is happening is that the Self 'in the seeker', as it were, is recognizing the Self 'in the teacher' because it is not obscured there by the usual layers of masking personality. It is essentially the same effect as has already been discussed in connection with 'silence'.

You cannot teach a man anything; you can only help him find it within himself. Galileo

The method of teaching varies from one guru to another. In the West, so-called 'satsang' teaching has become popular, as already mentioned, with the teacher travelling around the world and/or holding week-long 'intensives' being held at exotic locations. Some residential meetings are advertised as 'silent retreats' but the value of silence has already been discussed. Most of such teachers simply sit and, whilst being happy to do so in silence, are equally happy to respond to any questions that are asked. Superficially they may appear to give contradictory answers to similar questions from different enquirers. In the case of a good teacher, such words are always appropriate to the hearer and their mental and emotional state, giving an explanation aimed at providing some understanding.

However, as noted, this style of teaching is inevitably of limited value. What is needed is a prolonged course of systematic undermining of our false beliefs and exposure to those concepts that point us towards the truth. It could even be called 'brain washing', since this is truly what has to be done. Our minds are full of wrong ideas about the world and the position of 'little me' within it. *sampradAya* teaching has been using proven methods from the scriptures to achieve this for thousands of years.

Gurus may or may not be enlightened. Shankara has said that their ability to teach is more important from the perspective of the seeker (and this means that they should understand and be able to unfold the scriptures). Their value is always in relation to the disciple and it is not really meaningful to talk of one without the other. Since the guru is teaching, she must always be spiritually more 'advanced' than the student but, for a disciple just starting out, as it were, there is no need for the teacher to be fully realized in order to be able to impart useful knowledge. Thus, even a parent or schoolteacher may be a guru, if transmitting information that is useful in this respect. But they cannot take one 'all the way'. The Katha Upanishad says (II.8): *"This (Atman) cannot be understood by thinking about it, nor by listening to 'men of low ability'. The only way is to be taught by one of 'unparalleled understanding'. It transcends argument and is subtler than the subtlest."* It is said that the true seeker will always find a true guru but this usually seems to take many years. This is in line with the principle of *prArabdha saMskAra* discussed earlier.

Gurus have a physical body and a personality. Even in the case of those who are enlightened, these bodies continue to 'act' for the remainder of their lives and do so in accordance with what was their personality, even though this has now been transcended. It is not their body-mind that is important but the extent to which they are aware of the truth and able to transmit it. Thus it is that some gurus may be taciturn or eccentric or exhibit any other trait, without detracting in any way from their worth as a teacher. It is not usual, certainly in the West, for a disciple to revere the Sage as if he were a living god. Occasionally, this might happen with one such as Ramana Maharshi, treating him in this way as an object of devotion in the *bhakti* sense but this is rare and more usual in India, where elders and teachers are, in any case, treated reverentially. In the West, certainly, it is normally their teaching and manner of expressing it that is important and not their personality.

The value of a guru

Teacher and scripture are an integral unit, because the former embodies the latter and the latter articulates the experiences of the former.
William Cenkner (Ref. 79)

The Chandogya Upanishad says that only someone who has a teacher can come to realize the truth (Ref. 3, 6:14.1 – 2) and provides a story to help. Imagine that someone has been blindfolded and taken on a journey involving many changes of direction and modes of transport until they are finally left in the middle of a forest. Upon removing the blindfold, he can see where he is but he does not recognize the place and has not the slightest idea how to get back to his home. Fortunately, he encounters someone and explains his situation. The stranger is able to give explicit directions, telling him which paths to follow and what landmarks to look out for. Following these instructions, the man is able to return home without any problem.

The analogy is fairly obvious. We are the man, led astray by our senses and lost in the forest of life unable to see things as they really are. The stranger is the guru, who being enlightened is able to give directions as to the spiritual path we should follow to return to our true Self. Our mind and senses on their own are of no use in our ignorance, and the knowledge of the guru is our only salvation. The way back requires much effort but there are the landmarks of the scriptures to guide us on the way.

The metaphor can be extended, too, to warn against sightseeing on the way. If we do not keep the destination in mind and keep single-mindedly to the route as described, it will be very easy to get waylaid by all of the diverting sights on the way and, if we do not remain alert, become lost again. All of the diversions of the senses are transient only, like the viewpoints we pass on the way and we must not be distracted by them if we are to reach the goal.

And yet, paradoxically as always, this idea of me as an ignorant person wanting enlightenment and the guru as an all-knowing teacher, able to show me the way, is all part of the problem. It is not really like this. 'Me' as the body, mind, intellect, life force, is part of the illusion. Apparently born and existing for an insignificant moment, it is destined to die again with nothing to be realized. We have simply identified ourselves with this form and forgotten our true nature. We think that there is a separate individual – the guru –who has not forgotten, and look to him to learn something. But there can be no progress while, as Nisargadatta says, *"you continue to regard yourself as an entity and expect the Guru, as another entity, to give you some homework to do, and when that is duly completed, to award you a sort of certificate, or something, on a platter as 'liberation'."* (Ref. 27)

There is no 'change of state' for who-I-really-am on enlightenment. I am what I have always been and always will be – the unlimited reality, never bound, ever free. All that changes is the mental perspective – a paradigm shift to realize this already-existing truth. When this occurs, it is seen that the seeker and guru are one.

There is also the danger of becoming attached to one's guru. Respect and honor is appropriate, hero worship is not. A true guru will be aware of such dangers and circumvent them – any accentuation of difference will only maintain the illusion of duality.

Ramana Maharshi, as noted above, did not have a guru and has said, on more than one occasion that one is not necessary. Actually, it has been said that Mt. Arunachala was his guru since it had tremendous significance for him and he lived for most of his life in its foothills. Wayne Liquorman says that the 'guru' is not a person at all but *"arises in the resonance between the seeker and another object"* (Ref. 28). If you are not a seeker, being in the presence of a Sage will have no particular meaning for you – he will just be another person. After realization, of course, it is known that there is no such thing as disciple and guru anyway. Others have said, acknowledging this fact, that the ultimate guru is one's own Self. This is referred to as 'sadguru' (*sadguru – sat* = true, real).

You can find a guru almost anywhere. If you want a genuine Sage, you can search the Internet, make enquiries on E-groups or fly to India and trek into the Himalayas. But, unless you regard yourself as a seeker of some years standing, I would not want to encourage you to look for a guru straight away. What I would recommend, to those encountering these ideas for the first time, is to read more. As is the case with Western philosophy, it is always best to read the original material rather than someone else's commentary or interpretation. The latter is always in danger of incorporating the commentator's misunderstandings, which will then compound your own.

Ideally, if you can, read a good translation of the Bhagavad Gita and the major Upanishads, which also include Shankara's commentaries (*bhAShya-s*). (These Upanishads are called 'major' *because* of that so make sure that the commentary is included.) Avoid the Brihadaranyaka and Chandogya to begin with because they are quite long, although the commentary on the former is the most extensive. Other essential scriptures are the *tattva bodha* (for the basic concepts of advaita) and the *vivekachUDAmaNi* for elaboration of these. Both are supposed to have been written by Shankara, although this is questionable.

Only if you are unable to feel inspired by these traditional works should you resort to books by modern Sages. (There are some exceptions to this generalization. Some of the original words of Ramana Maharshi, for example, can be truly inspiring.) Appendix 2 contains more guidance on these matters.

Having acquired more information in this way, the next step is to find some like-minded people and start to discuss those aspects that you don't understand. Ideally, you would have access to an actual study group, directed by someone who knows the subject well. Best of all, if your geographical location permits, it might be worth joining one of the organizations that teach Advaita (these can be located on the Internet – see Appendix 1). Finally, if after some years, you are convinced intellectually of the truth of this philosophy, only then should you start thinking about finding and committing to a guru.

And so, eventually (though not necessarily in this lifetime!), you will reach the end of your seeking – and meet your Self. What will you actually find? What is the nature of a 'realized man'? If all that we now see around us is in some way 'unreal', only how things 'appear' to be, what is 'reality' like? All of this forms the subject of the rest of the book. Before embarking upon it, you must bear in mind that what you will read is only at the level of descriptive knowledge. It derives mainly from written material from many sources, all of them highly respected. Living Sages can vouch for the essential authenticity of what is said *but...* reality cannot ever be *known* objectively; even less can it be spoken of, with all of the limitations of language. Only once it has been realized for oneself, can it be fully appreciated. With this proviso then, read on and discover what Advaita has to say about 'The Real'.

SECTION 3 – The real

12. Appearance and reality

Only the Self – not things, body, mind etc.

In the Introduction, it was explained that the philosophy of Advaita could be summed up as 'There are not two things'. The more critical may have already wondered why we could not more simply state that there is only One, especially given the book's title. Well, this is partly due to the fact that this 'One' is ultimately indefinable, indeed unthinkable. We have to work towards it by saying what it *isn't*, rather than what it is. Secondly, to talk about 'one' or 'everything' implies the existence of a 'nothing' as its opposite or as the vantage point of something outside from which to observe this 'One' objectively. Advaita says that there are no opposites, or that the Self transcends and reconciles all opposites – there simply are not two separate things of any sort. And there is nowhere *outside* it from which to take an objective standpoint. The words 'inside', 'outside' or 'objective' simply have no meaning within the context of Advaita.

Note that Advaita is not the same as Solipsism. That is the claim that there is only my self (with a small 's'). It, too, says that everything and everybody is an illusion but also says that only I, this person writing these words, exist. Advaita says that *I* do not exist either, as a separate person. Does this then make it the same as nihilism? No. Advaita does not say that nothing at all exists but that only the Self or Absolute exists and that every-thing else is an appearance on the background of that reality. The idea is that this cannot be 'known' in any true sense because knowledge requires a knower and a known, which is (at least) two things.

Nor is Advaita the same as monism. Monists say that there is only one 'thing'. The pre-Socratic Greek philosophers, for example, suggested that this one thing might be water, fire or air. Advaita tells us that the Self is not a 'thing'; it is not any sort of object but the universal Subject. Even this is not strictly accurate because 'subject' necessarily implies the existence of at least one 'object' and Advaita denies this – ultimately, words, and concepts, are simply inadequate to comprehend reality.

Advaita is actually more 'extreme' than monism. As John Grimes points out in Ref. 140, there are three aspects of the word 'different': two things may belong to different species; they may be different members of the same class or there may be internal differences. The definition of monism still permits internal differences whereas Advaita does not. Accordingly, if we are to call Advaita 'monism', it has to be qualified as 'absolute monism'.

Nor is Advaita equivalent to any branch of Idealism. The Self is not an appearance or concept (which is actually just another object, albeit a subtle one) and it exists in the mind of no one, including that of God.

There is *only* the Self, aka the Absolute, Truth, Consciousness, to specify a few of the names used for this unity; there are no 'others'. When we think we see separate 'things' out there in 'the world'; when we see 'objects' or 'other people'; or when we see 'thoughts' in 'the mind' or sense 'feelings' in 'the body', we are making a mistake. Our ignorance is preventing us from seeing correctly. Once this ignorance is removed, we recognize that there is, in truth, only our (real) Self, that all the apparently separate 'things' are not truly separate. Indeed, all 'things' (whether apparently solid objects or insubstantial thoughts) are only name and form of the same, non-dual reality, as you will see shortly.

How can we so completely deny the evidence of our own senses and the logic of our own minds? I am obviously I, and you are you. I am not this table on which my arms are leaning. My thoughts are not your thoughts. You don't go to the dentist when I have a toothache. The first thing this philosophy does is not to try to argue with you on these points... at least not directly. It is not disputed that this is how things *appear* to be.

Appearance versus reality – metaphor of magician

What is suggested is that you draw the wrong conclusion from your percep-tions. A good analogy is that of a magician. When a child sees a magician sawing a lady in half or extracting yards of ribbon from someone's ear, he believes these things to be real. An adult, being more experienced in the ways of the world, sees the same events as the child but, whilst he may not have any idea how the tricks are done, he knows that they are an illusion. What *seems* to be happening is not what is *really* happening. Similarly, we see the creation and believe it to consist of many separate objects and other people. The equivalent of the mature adult – someone who has recognized the true nature of reality, who has become what is called 'enlightened' or 'Self-realized' – still sees the same 'objects' and 'people' but he realizes that this is an illusion. He knows that in reality there is only the one Self, that all of this apparent creation is superimposed on this Self, making it appear as though there are separate things. Note also that this is not merely an intellectual appreciation of the concept. To the Self-realized man, it is an unassailable truth.

We have to resort to analogy or metaphor, or tell amusing stories, in order to get across these concepts because, so often, no method of purely logical explanation could suffice. As has already been pointed out, ultimately the mind cannot understand the Self.

Appearance versus reality – metaphor of dream

There is another powerful example in our everyday experience of things not being the way that they seem to be. This is our nightly experience of dreaming. The topic of dreams will be addressed in more detail in the chapter on Consciousness but is worth mentioning at this juncture. At the time of dreaming, we experience a world of objects and people which seems perfectly real. After we wake up, we may laugh at how ridiculous the dream was, having no internal logic, with events succeeding others without apparent reason and so on. But this rationalization can only take place after awakening. At the time, there *seems* to be perfectly logical cause and effect; the fantastic themes and locations do not appear to be in any way outrageous and we accept them without question.

The dream is real for the dreamer. It is only seen to have been ultimately unreal by the waker. And this is a precise metaphor for the waking world – it is real for the waker but, from the standpoint of absolute consciousness (called *turIya* in Sanskrit), it is seen to have been ultimately unreal.

Gaudapada, in his commentary (*kArikA* – a set of concise philosophical statements in verse form) on the Mandukya Upanishad deals with this metaphor at length. He points out, for example, that the objections that might be raised to argue that the dream state is not a valid analogy for the waking state can all be countered. Objectors maintain, for example, that the waking world has utility – you can make coffee in a waking-world cup and drink out of it but you can't do this with a dream cup! Gaudapada counters this by pointing out that the waking-world cup is of no use whatsoever in the dream. Your bed might be surrounded by water but you might still be dying of thirst in the dream. Only a dream drink will quench the dream thirst. And so on... (My book provisionally entitled 'OM: Key to the Universe', due out in 2012-13, will explain the entire Upanishad and *kArikA-s* at length.)

Name and form – Metaphor of gold and ring

Ridiculous as this may all seem at first sight, modern physics is coming to similar conclusions. The world is not what it outwardly seems; objects are not substantial. The more you try to 'pin down' anything, the further it recedes into un-pin-down-ability! If you think about it further, with the help of some more metaphors, the seemingly outrageous claims of Advaita begin to sound at least interesting and worthy of consideration.

One of the classical metaphors used is that of a ring made of gold. We tend to look at the ring as something distinct. But is there 'really' such a thing as a ring? Is there actually a ring, or is there only gold?

Is not the ring just a *name* we give to that particular *form* of the gold? If we apply some heat to the gold, the form will disappear and we might pour the liquid into a mould to cool and become, for example, a thimble. Is the object still a ring? Clearly it isn't. It is, however, still gold, as it was before the original ring was made and will be after the thimble has been destroyed. It is only our minds that choose to assign particular importance to one shape rather than another.

The ring or thimble always was, and always will be, gold. This is its reality, if you like. Its intermediate forms are only transient and arbitrary. We choose to give a particular form a specific name but this doesn't affect its real nature at all.

Extrapolation to energy or 'Consciousness'

This metaphor is used to explain such things as why our bodies are only a transient name and form and in no way our true nature. But let's extrapolate the metaphor a bit further. Could we not consider that the gold itself is only a name and form for the true reality, which is a particular configuration of electrons around an atomic nucleus consisting of several possible combinations of protons and neutrons? After all, if we vaporized the gold, we would no longer see an amorphous, malleable yellow metal at all, so we might think that the gold had disappeared. But at the atomic level it would retain the same 'real' nature.

And we could go still further. We could say that this particular electronic configuration was just another name and form for an even more subtle reality. And so it is! Particle physics has shown that electrons and neutrons, for example, are not actually discrete particles. Bouncing between them are even smaller particles called mesons. And, still more recent theorizing and experimentation shows that all particles are made up of various combinations of several types of 'quark'.

But even that is but another name and form for energy. So is energy the ultimate reality? No. As you almost certainly know, $E = mc^2$. Energy and mass are ultimately interchangeable. They are, if you like, both a form of matter – and matter is not conscious. What Advaita says is that matter-energy is still only name and form of the ultimate reality, *brahman*.

mithyA

And this is the most suitable place to remind you of one of the most fundamental concepts in Advaita. In the first edition of this book this was hardly mentioned, and not until the next chapter. In this edition, I introduced it as part of the discussion on language and here it is again, since it is so important.

Literally, the word means 'incorrectly' or 'improperly' and this refers to our treating things as independently 'real' when they are not. The word 'independently' is important here, because we are not saying that the chair on which you are presently sitting is illusory – obviously it is not! What is being pointed out is that it is not a substance-in-itself. It is probably made of pieces of wood, connected together by special joints and adhesive. The final form is designed to be suitable for sitting upon comfortably. In theory at least, you could disassemble the chair and use the pieces to build a table. 'Chair' is simply the *name* that you give to this particular *form*. The actual substance is wood.

Or at least that is what seems to be the case at first sight. But, as was described in the example of the gold ring, wood is not actually a fundamental substance either. It is a mixture of cellulose fibers and proteins and chlorophyll (or whatever!). These, in turn, are molecules made up of atoms, which are made up of particles...

The same analysis may be applied to anything in the universe. It is more difficult to apply to subtle things such as thoughts and emotions but the same principle applies. What Advaita says is that everything in the universe, indeed the universe itself, is only name and form of one, non-dual, fundamental reality called *brahman* (or Consciousness or Self etc.) The word for reality is *satyam*. Every (seeming) thing else is *mithyA*. Another definition, therefore, for *mithyA* is 'dependent' reality. Things have no reality of their own; there are no other 'substances'. Every seemingly separate thing is actually just a name and form of *brahman*.

Metaphor of rope and snake – *adhyAsA*

Perhaps the most famous metaphor of all, which you will certainly encounter again and again as you read more, is that of the rope and the snake. Imagine that you enter a darkened room and see dimly lying in the middle of the floor, a snake, ready to strike. Remember that most of these metaphors originate in India, where such things are presumably not uncommon and should be paid due respect! Instead of calmly walking in to collect whatever you came for, you will be quite likely to close the door and run away, heart beat in mouth, so to speak. Sometime later, you might creep back carefully with a large torch and an even larger stick. Looking gingerly in and shining the torch on the floor, lo and behold, you see only a coiled up piece of rope.

What happened is obvious. You saw the shape of the rope and, because of the dark, your heightened sensitivity, snake-o-phobia or whatever, mistakenly thought it to be a snake. In the light of day or torch, you discovered it to be what it always was.

In the same way, because of our ignorance (= dark), we see what appears to be a world of discrete objects, the 'creation' (= snake). When we bring in our torch (= gain self-knowledge, become 'en-lightened'), we discover that we were mistakenly imposing these names and forms on what is in fact our own Self (= rope).

This mistaking of the apparent world as something other than our Self is called *adhyAsa* in Sanskrit and more literally means superimposing some false appearance onto the actual reality. We'll look into this in more detail later since it is another fundamental concept.

You are the 'Self'

So, how does this gargantuan error come about and what can we do about correcting it? Well, to answer the last question first, there's some good news and some bad, as they say. The bad news is that there is nothing you *can* do about it. The good news is that there is nothing you *need* do about it. Another clever way in which someone has put this is as follows. The bad news is there is no key to unlock the door to truth/reality etc.; the good news is that it was never locked. Another thing you will find in this teaching in addition to metaphor, is paradox.

> When did I realize I was God? Well, I was praying and I suddenly realized I was talking to myself. Peter O'Toole

The explanation for this is that you *are* the Self, already. Nothing you do can change this. Note that I will continue to use the word 'Self' with a capital letter for this reality we are trying to discover. If you prefer the word 'Absolute', 'Consciousness' or '*brahman*', just scan this book into a good Word Processor and use the 'Find and Replace' option. In fact, you could say – and some people do – that *any* attempt to search for the truth, to follow a spiritual path and so on, is taking you *away* from the answer instead of towards it. You are *yourself* the answer. The real search is within, not without. (Just to respond briefly to the assertion that seeking is counter-productive, lest it be taken as true, it is not so simple as this! When we cannot see what is in front of our nose, we sometimes have to be taken away and then led back to it slowly before the truth becomes apparent.)

"But if this is so (that Self is the reality), how can it be that we do not know it?", I hear you ask. The answer that some religions give to this question is that we did, in fact start out knowing the truth. We all lived in the knowledge that there is in reality only One and we enjoyed our true nature, which is described as all existence, all consciousness, all bliss – called, in Sanskrit, *sachchidAnanda*, where *sat* means existence, reality, truth etc; *chit* means consciousness; *Ananda* means bliss (these form the word *sachchidAnanda* when they are joined together). But, it came to pass that one day, someone decided that he wanted these for himself, not to share them with others. This is effectively what the Bible calls 'original sin'. It was the beginning of the slide to our present sad state of ignorance.

But this still does not explain why the Self should *want* to do any of this. After all, if our real nature is *sachchidAnanda* why go through all the relatively meager happiness and all-too-frequent pain of this existence, especially having to believe it is real and all that we are going to get?

Play and *lIlA*

Well, says one rationalization, it is all a play, put on for our enjoyment. The Self is playing all of the parts of course, since there is no one else. But, in order to make it work, it is necessary that each of the roles be unaware of this and think themselves individual. The ignorance is a prerequisite for the play to be successful. Also, villains are needed as well as heroes. This is the play to end all plays. It is *"tragedy, comedy, history, pastoral, pastoral-comical, historical-pastoral, tragical-historical, tragical-comical-historical-pastoral"*, as Polonius puts it in Shakespeare's Hamlet.

We think it is real but we are actually only actors on a stage. In the end no one gets hurt; no one dies or is born; it is just a grand illusion and gives the Self a jolly good time. This is the theory of *lIlA*, the cosmic play.

Tony Parsons, a present-day teacher of Neo-advaita, says:

"This is the eternal drama that one is playing. I am one appearing as

two including, in the appearance, the sense of separation in order to discover that I am one. Because it is wonderful to find out you're one after being two for a while. Go and bang your head on the wall and then stop. Really. It is as simple as that. It's fun. It's the game. It's the play. Actually you're not banging your head on the wall all the time really... you quite enjoy being two, don't you? Look how much you enjoy it. Obviously hardly anybody in this room wants to become one. There is a huge attachment and a fascination with being two looking for one. It's wonderful, it's divine, it's gorgeous. I love it! I go around Amsterdam seeing people really, really holding on to their separation and their identity. They are all walking around really trying hard to be separate individuals. So it is hugely fascinating." (Ref. 82)

This is, of course, not intended to be an explanation for how thing 'really' are. It provides what may be a temporary appeasement to the continually questioning mind until the time comes when a more sophisticated rationale may be taken on board. Some may accept *IIIA* as truth; it is, after all, not much different from many dualistic, deistic beliefs. But, for anyone who has understood the basic idea of Advaita, it would not be long before the inconsistency became apparent. If reality is non-dual, how can we talk about 'roles' in a 'world', even if they are all being played by the Self? It would also be contradictory to imagine a limitless being having desires or wanting to 'play' – 'limitless' means being always totally fulfilled.

Appearance

In the Science Museum in London, they once had an interesting room as part of an exhibition on perception, optical illusions and so on. Passing down a corridor, there was a window on your right, which appeared to look into a room in a house. There was a door in the opposite corner and everything seemed perfectly normal until someone entered the room through that door – they seemed disproportionately small. What was worse was that, as they moved forward into the room, they grew in size quite rapidly until, as they neared the window, their body had become enormous.

At first sight there just seemed no explanation for this at all. The mind was forced to accept what the eyes were telling it but could make no sense of it since another part of the mind told us, quite reasonably, that this could not be true. Fortunately, when you continued down the corridor and round the corner, you discovered that you were able to look into the room through the door and even walk into it so that the next visitors could experience the same illusion. In fact, the room's perspective was not normal. The floor sloped up steeply towards the window; angles that had appeared to be right angles, because corners in rooms are *always* right angles, were not. Now that we had the complete picture, we could appreciate how the illusion arose and no longer be taken in by it, even though the eyes would still transmit the same message if we returned to look through the window again.

Someone, who has witnessed an illusion such as this, will be in a position to appreciate a much older, classic scenario, namely that described by Plato in 'The Republic'. He asks us to imagine a cave, deep under-ground where slaves are tied in such a way that they are unable to move their heads; they can only look forward towards the blank, far wall of the cave. There is a road passing behind the slaves. Along the side of the road runs a wall such that only the upper parts of people and objects protrude. At the rear of the cave are flames illuminating the road and casting shadows, on the far wall of the cave, of all the people and objects moving back and forth. The prisoners are able to see only these shadows – not the objects, nor flames, nor each other nor even themselves. This is their lifetime's experience. They believe that the shadows are the reality and cannot comprehend that there might be objects that give rise to these shadows. Nor can they imagine the mechanism by which the phenomena arise. If anyone passing by on the road should speak, his or her voice echoes off the wall of the cave and the prisoner believes the shadow is speaking. If the traveler is carrying an object, the slave is unable to tell which of the shadows is the speaker and which the object. So he assumes they are all intelligent.

The slaves devise a contest whereby they each attempt to predict which shapes will appear next, based upon their accurate observation of current shapes and movement and their memory of earlier patterns. Their skill at this pastime determines their hierarchy and whoever is most successful is chosen to be their leader.

This then represents our lives, as they seem to us at present – the phenomenal or *vyavahAra*, the relative or apparent state of existence – a state of total delusion.

Plato then asks us to imagine the feelings of one of the slaves if he were suddenly released and forced to turn to look at the road. Having been fixed in one position for the whole of his life, any movement would be painful. Not having been exposed to much light, looking directly at the flames or up the tunnel toward daylight would be most uncomfortable and he would not be able to make out much detail. If he were told that the things moving along the road were the 'reality' and that the shadows he had hitherto taken for his world were an illusion, he would have great difficulty in accepting any of it and would be inclined to think his informer mad. If he were forced up the passage and out into the sunlight, it would be a long time before he could see anything and certainly before he could make any sense of it.

Eventually, however, his eyes would adjust. He would then come to see and understand the mechanism of shadow formation and be able to differentiate real objects from their shadows or reflections and ultimately come to some understanding of the sun itself, as the source of all of these phenomena. This represents the way things really are – the noumenal or *paramArtha*.

Reality – is not what you think it is. Shillitoe

And so, Plato suggests, the time would come when the man wanted to return to the cave to rescue his friends and reveal to them the truths that he has discovered. He descends back down the passage but now finds that his eyes have difficulty readjusting to the dark. He arrives back in the cave almost totally blind and, when forced to take part in their contest, performs much worse than the poorest of them. They now regard him as the lowest of their clan and what he has to tell them has less relevance to them than the ravings of a madman. They would rather murder him than let him 'rescue them' and take them up into the light to be affected in the way that he obviously has.

He may have been 'enlightened' but they would much rather remain in the dark.

This, then, is the situation in which we find ourselves. Since you are still reading this book, it is unlikely that you are entirely happy with living out your life in the depths of the cave. But then you are probably quite reasonably suspicious of some of the things this apparent lunatic is trying to tell you. You have previously had no reason to doubt that what you see around you is real. Do you want to take the risk of venturing up the passage towards that blinding light of truth?

Before doing that, however, it is necessary to learn a few more 'home truths'. It has been mentioned, for example, that we cannot actually know reality, in the way that we probably think that we can. When we look at the book in front of us, we do not normally doubt in any way the 'truth' of what our senses appear to be telling us, namely that there is a concrete object, with fixed properties in our hands. We think that we could readily describe all of these in terms of color, texture, smell etc. and that all of these properties are 'true'. Whilst we may appreciate the description of the room illusion described above, we do not feel that this might apply to *all* of our everyday experience. It is necessary, therefore, that we next question precisely that.

13. The Limits of knowledge

What can we know? (Kant & Schopenhauer)

What is eternal rather than transient? Or alternatively we might ask what is real and what only 'appears' to be? Western philosophy has been attempting to answer this since pre-Socratic times. Descartes was perhaps the first to attempt rigorously to determine what things we could actually be sure of. The English philosopher, John Locke, formalized the notions of 'primary' and 'secondary' qualities of objects. Primary qualities were those inherent in the objects themselves, like number, position and solidity. But most of the attributes we assign to objects, such as color, smell and taste were not, he said, inherent in the objects; they were 'secondary' qualities which, though brought about in some way by the object, really only existed in our minds.

The Irish philosopher, George Berkeley was not entirely happy with this. He did not see why something like solidity should be considered any differently. After all, we are only aware that an object is solid by touching it and the sense of touch is perceived in the brain in an analogous manner to the other senses. Why should it be considered to be special in any way? It is actually even worse than this because the idea of something like 'solidity' seems to depend on our having some independent concept of an object so that we can say "this object is solid". If we need solidity in order to define the object in the first place, we end up with a meaningless statement. His conclusion was that the world of objects exists completely in the mind – the belief known as 'subjective idealism'.

Immanuel Kant, born a quarter of a century before Berkeley died, made the positive, if somewhat disconcerting, statement that we cannot *ever* know how things really are. Note that for the essence of the following explanation I am indebted to Bryan Magee's excellent autobiography "Confessions of a Philosopher" (Ref. 48).

As far as the laws of mathematics refer to reality, they are not certain; and as far as they are certain, they do not refer to reality. Albert Einstein

To begin with, our senses actually cover only a very small range e.g. we cannot hear like bats, smell like dogs or see into the ultraviolet, as bees can. We cannot see infrared or x-rays. Millions of neutrinos (sub-atomic particles) pass through our bodies and on through the earth every second but we are totally unaware of them. We are able to know these things only second hand or via science. E.g. we can see the effect of x-rays on a photographic plate; we can be aware of infrared light by the fact that our skin feels warm. So we can infer that such things must exist in order to explain these secondary phenomena. Much of our 'knowledge' in science is in fact 'inference' based on seeing a subsequent effect. E.g. practically all of our understanding of sub-atomic physics has come from working backwards to imagine what sort of things must have occurred in order for the observed tracks in cloud chambers to have come about.

Secondly, we are actually only aware of things in the past, never in the present moment. As an extreme example, by the time light from the nearest star reaches us the star itself might no longer be there – the light takes over 2 years to get here. Even looking at an object in front of us we are looking into the past – light reaches us very quickly but the nerve impulses from the sense organs take time to travel to our brain and then they have to be translated before we can interpret them. When we hear a sound, it has taken a measurable time to reach us (it only travels at about 760 miles per hour), which is why thunder occurs so much later than the lightning unless the storm is overhead – it is a sound from the past.

Thirdly, what we see, hear etc. is never the reality. Light waves and sound waves are obviously not the thing itself to begin with. The 'light' that we experience does not exist in reality; it is an effect within the brain triggered by the reception of electromagnetic waves, in a particular frequency range, on the retina. (Ref. 64) All sorts of other waves – radio and TV transmission, microwaves, UV and gamma rays – also impinge on our bodies every second but we do not have the perceptual equipment to interpret them. Their existence should be ample evidence that we can never experience any 'reality' as such. But on top of this, our sense organs extract only a small part of the total information and convert this into electrical impulses, now far removed from the 'reality'. The brain then interprets these to construct a new 'reality'. The only relationship of this to the original objects is that it enables us to interact with them in a way that we can construe as meaningful.

Bryan Magee points out in Ref. 65 that people blind from birth have no experiential feeling of being deficient in their perception of 'reality'. They do not 'know' the meaning of 'darkness' other than as a concept relating to a decreased ability to perceive something owing to external conditions. All of us are deficient in a multitude of ways. If we had the sonar capability of bats, we would function much better in the dark and so on. We do not feel ourselves to be inferior because of this but, most importantly for this discussion, we do not realize that the lack of such senses must mean that there are an infinite number of ways in which we are failing to perceive other aspects of 'reality'.

We don't see things as they are; we see them as we are. Anaïs Nin

Just spend a moment thinking about this since it is so fundamental. At the ordinary day to day level of appearances, just think how much a sighted person is aware of, that is unavailable to someone who is blind. And, if they have been blind from birth, they can have little conception of the significance of this. How can they appreciate what it means to look at a Rembrandt or a Vermeer, the Grand Canyon or a spider's web on a still, damp morning in the slanting rays of sunshine? But this can be extended by analogy to all of us. There are an infinite number of senses that we might have had, e.g. radar ears, X-ray eyes and neutrino detectors. Each one would open up a totally new world of appearances to us that we are forever denied because we lack such senses. Each one would give a different perspective on what we believe to be the outside reality of the world. And we cannot even know what we are missing because there is no one with these other senses that could provide an insight of conceptual knowledge for this perceptual information. As the American philosopher Thomas Nagel noted, no matter how well we understand the mechanism of the bat's sonar, we can have no idea "What is it like to be a bat?" (This is the title of one of his books.)

All of this means that we can *never* be aware of things as they actually are, only as they appear to be or as we infer them to be and, indeed, only as they may have been, not as they might be this instant. *These* are our 'facts'. The world is filtered through our senses and understanding. If our senses had been different, the world would have appeared quite different and the 'knowledge' we have acquired about it would have been different too. Aliens, with different senses and bodily and mental constructions would inevitably 'see' the world quite differently from us. Although the world as it is 'really' is unaffected by all of this, how it 'appears' to be is determined by our particular nature or, as Kant put it, the world must "conform to our knowledge". The world of appearances can only appear as we are capable of perceiving it.

In particular, this applies also to the concepts of time and space. Because we can only perceive things that appear to be separate in time, space or both, we assume that these concepts are 'real'. The way in which our brain makes sense of the world requires that one thing is separate in space from another or that it occupies the same space but at a different time. If one or the other didn't apply, we would say it was the 'same' thing.

Fourthly, whenever we observe or experience something, we do so over a period of time, however short. It would not be possible to sense something 'instantaneously' – we would have no way of knowing that it had occurred at all if it had no duration. But when I listen to someone speaking or to a piece of music, at any given moment (the shortest duration in which we are able to register actually hearing something) there is only a fraction of what is being said or played, only a tiny part of a word or note. And yet we know we are able to perceive continuity – we can hear a whole sentence or phrase of music and recognize it. At any given moment, all the other parts of the sentence or melody have either occurred already or haven't yet happened – they are either in the past or in the future. In order for the whole experience to appear continuous, I must be holding what has gone before in memory and linking them together with that single fraction of an experience which is happening now. And this part which is only in the mind has virtually the same immediacy as that which is actually present. If this were not so, the experience would not be seamless; we would not perceive a sentence as a whole and might even be likely to forget how it began before it reached the end So, perception of anything is only possible by virtue of this imagery in the mind combined with the present experience.

Reality is that which, when you stop believing in it, doesn't go away.
Philip K. Dick

But we don't normally appreciate any of this. We take it for granted that things are actually like this in reality, that they do occupy unique and separate points in space and/or time. We don't realize that this is a concept that we impose upon the world in order that our particular perceptual instruments can make sense of it. In fact, space and time are conceptual filters through which we view the world and it is inescapable that 'reality' conforms to this way of looking at things. Our brains use them but they are not part of reality. That we cannot think of anything that doesn't occupy space or time is a reflection of *our* limitation not that of reality.

The same applies to the other categories that the mind uses in order to make sense of the world, e.g. causation. A metaphor, which is used to explain these ideas, is that of a fishing net. Suppose we go on a fishing trip, using a net that we never actually see because it is slung beneath the boat. When we haul in the catch and find no fish smaller than 2″, we might conclude quite reasonably that this particular area contains no such fish. In fact, the net has two-inch square holes and clearly any fish smaller than this will pass straight through. Our conclusion did not reflect the nature of the sea at all; it reflected the nature of the nets. By analogy, our conclusions about the nature of reality reflect the nature of our perceptual equipment and the concepts we use to interpret the data from our senses. If we always wear blue spectacles, it is inevitable that we will see the world as blue.

Reality – the 'noumenal' world, as Kant calls it, as opposed to the 'phenomenal' world as it appears to us – has neither space nor time. Things as they really are, i.e. independent of experience ('things in themselves' or 'Ding an sich' to be strictly accurate, since he was German) are not in time and space. It is 'experience' that 'makes' the world as it appears to be. If there were no one or nothing to experience, the world as it appears to be would cease to exist. Kant says in his Critique of Pure Reason (Ref. 141):

"What we have meant to say is that all our intuition is nothing but the representation of appearance; that the things which we intuit are not in themselves what we intuit them as being, nor their relations so constituted in themselves as they appear to us, and that if the subject, or even only the subjective constitution of the senses in general, be removed, the whole constitution and all the relations of objects in space and time, nay space and time themselves, would vanish. As appearances, they cannot exist in themselves, but only in us. What objects may be in themselves, and apart from all this receptivity of our sensibility, remains completely unknown to us. We know nothing but our mode of perceiving them – a mode which is peculiar to us, and not necessarily shared in by every being, though, certainly by every human being. With this alone have we any concern."

Arthur Schopenhauer took some of this reasoning further. He recognized that we can only actually differentiate between things at all through the use of the concepts of time and space. As noted above, if something were to occupy the same place as something else in the same instant, we would be obliged to perceive it as the same object. The idea of 'succession', either in time or place, is a pre-requisite for differentiating one object from another. One 'thing' must be separate from another 'thing', either in time or in space, in order for us to be aware of two 'things'. If there were not this separation, we would only be aware of one thing. We often see something in the distance but acknowledge that it is too far away for us to make out what *it* is. In fact, if we look through a pair of binoculars, we may then be able to make out that *it* is in fact two (or more) quite separate objects. Here, the separation in space perceived by increasing the magnification has 'made' the single object into more than one. (Of course, the actual concepts of 'space' and 'time' arise by virtue of wanting to differentiate and make sense of apparently separate experiences or thoughts to begin with. So the ideas of 'succession' and 'space and time' are mutually dependent.)

We can observe the transition of a caterpillar into a butterfly and verify to our own satisfaction that the latter was formed from the material of the former. Yet we call the process a 'metamorphosis', i.e. a change of one thing into another. We cannot think that the butterfly still *is* the caterpillar. (But is this essentially any different from melting down the gold ring and reforming it into a thimble?) Similarly, if not so dramatically from our particular perception of time, we ourselves supposedly change from a baby into an old man/woman. The old man is not the baby, so we would claim. (Yet it has already been argued that the essential 'I' feels no different as the body ages.)

Even something like a poem or piece of music, while, in a sense existing neither in time nor space, nevertheless depends on the notion of succession for its existence. If a symphony could be played 'all at once' it wouldn't be very musical. And the concept of succession pre-supposes the ideas of time and space. If these did not exist, there could be no succession and therefore no differentiation.

But, Kant had already shown that time and space are *our* ways of making sense of the phenomenal world; aspects of the 'nets' through which we filter our perceptions. The world is not really as we perceive it. Reality IS, as it is, but we can never know it directly. We have to make use of the concepts of space, time and causality in order to try to understand it. It is the nature of these concepts that they artificially break up the reality into mental objects, separate in space and/or time in order that we can make sense of things. The concepts have no meaning independent of experience. Apart from the concepts and our interpretations, there is simply the noumenal Reality, in which there can be no 'differentiation'. There cannot be things as they are in themselves, independent of experience. Whatever 'reality' is like, outside of experience, it must be undifferentiated. There must be 'not two (or more)' things – and this, of course, is the philosophy of Advaita.

Language is the art of concealing thoughts; thoughts are the art of concealing truth. Atmananda Krishna Menon

More recently, philosophers such as Ludwig Wittgenstein and John Searle have pointed to *language* as the 'net' through which we define the world around us. It is the language we use that defines 'things out there' as objects, separate from other objects and from ourselves. Searle says that we experience the world through the linguistic categories that we have defined and this method of 'representation' is intimately tied up with the experience itself so that the two can hardly be separated. Of course that is precisely the purpose of language – to re-present something to the mind that is not there in actuality. Unfortunately, having succeeded so well in doing this, we cannot subsequently drop it or ignore it. Just try to see a chair as an object totally devoid of any 'chair-like' appellation or concept or try to think of the word 'chair' without simultaneously being aware of some 'chair-like' function. It seems to be very difficult for us to be aware of the perception itself without the mental name and commentary that goes with it. (Though this can be re-learned, as must be done with, for example, wine tasting or in the appreciation of art or music.) We use the name to stand for this function. Perhaps it is true that the new-born baby sees the world as an undifferentiated unity (= reality) and it is the process of language acqui-sition that introduces notions of separation and the sense of subject and object.

Since the time of Kant and Schopenhauer, 18th and 19th centuries, respectively, science has come a long way. In 1927, Heisenberg put forward his famous 'Uncertainty Principle'. In this, talking about sub-atomic particles, he reasoned that we could not simultaneously know both their position and their momentum. This is tied up with the fact that the behavior of electrons, as the most studied of sub-atomic particles at that time, cannot be completely explained by thinking of them as solid lumps of matter. In many respects they behave much more like waves and their positions can be thought of as more of a probability with the most probable locations corresponding to the peaks of the waves. As soon as we try to measure one element of such a particle, our very act of measurement interferes with it and makes the simultaneous measurement of another element impossible.

We, the observer, are inextricably linked with what we are trying to observe. The very act of observation changes the 'reality' of the situation. We cannot talk meaningfully about 'things' in isolation from us. This, of course, is just a small step away from saying that we are not actually separate from those 'things' or even that we and the supposed objects are actually aspects of a single reality.

None of this is new to Eastern philosophy. The Kena Upanishad said (verse 2): *"The eye does not go there, nor speech, nor mind; we know not how this should be taught."*

The whole of nature is connected and finely balanced. Where does 'I' end and 'not I' begin? The body would not exist for an instant, were it not for the atmospheric pressure immediately at the surface of the skin. Do we find out about what we are by looking closer and closer, at ever-increasing magnification? Where am 'I' in the multiplicity of organs, inter-relating? Where am 'I' in the areas of the brain and sensory apparatus communicating in incredibly complex ways not yet fully understood by science? What is 'alive' in hearts pumping, kidneys filtering, bacteria being attacked by white corpuscles, proteins being synthesized, DNA replicated? At even greater magnification, at the level of the atom, the complexity gives way to vast spaces occupied only by the occasional electrons, be they particles or waves. Beyond that, we enter the realm of theory, where hypothetical particles exist for infinitesimal fractions of a second, yet provide the building blocks or means of destruction for this immeasurable universe which we choose to call reality.

paramArtha

When you project a dream world for yourself and live in it, you also project a God who looks after it. When you stop the projection, both the world and God disappear. Sri Poonja (Ref. 73)

So how does Advaita define reality? Nisargadatta Maharaj made many statements on this topic. Considering his complete lack of any formal education and inability to even read, some of these sound remarkably like the sorts of propositions being made by Kant and Schopenhauer. Of course, Nisargadatta was speaking from direct experience rather than theory and inference.

"Is there a world outside your knowledge? Can you go beyond what you know? You may postulate a world beyond the mind, but it will remain a concept, unproved and unprovable."

"In reality time and space exist in you; you do not exist in them. They are modes of perception, but they are not the only ones. Time and space are like words written on paper; the paper is real, the words merely a convention."

"In reality, all is here and now and all is one. Multiplicity and diversity are in the mind only."

"In reality only the Ultimate is. The rest is a matter of name and form. And as long as you cling to the idea that only what has a name and shape exists, the Supreme will appear to you non-existing. When you understand that names and shapes are hollow shells without any content whatsoever, and what is real is nameless and shapeless, pure energy of life and light of consciousness, you will be at peace – immersed in the deep silence of reality." (Ref. 26)

Vedanta differentiates three 'orders' of reality and to appreciate them you need to understand the meaning of a term *bAdha*, which is variously translated as 'cancellation', 'sublation' or 'subration'. The word 'sublation' was given without explanation in the quotation at the end of Chapter 8. If you didn't understand it, an example might be useful. Imagine that you find yourself walking in a hot desert, in which all you can see is sand, and you are very thirsty. If, through the heat haze in the distance, you suddenly see a lake surrounded by palm trees, your heart might, for a moment, make a leap of relief at the thought of the water soon to slake your thirst. Probably quite quickly, however, you will recall that this sort of thing has been reported before; that in all probability it is only a mirage. Then you hear a voice in your head, telling you not to get excited. If you make the effort to remember, you will recall that you are not actually walking anywhere; that you are in fact testing out the very latest in virtual reality simulation and isn't it incredibly realistic? Then you wake up.

At each successive stage in the above example, your mental outlook undergoes a paradigm shift. The basis from which you had formed judgments about the world in front of you underwent a radical transformation. What you had previously thought to be 'real' was now patently unreal and you had a new set of criteria for making judgments. The previous view was now 'cancelled', 'sublated' or 'subrated'. Eliot Deutsch defines subration as *"the mental process whereby one disvalues some previously appraised object or content of consciousness because of its being contradicted by a new experience"*. (Ref. 2)

This term (I prefer 'sublation') enables some clear definitions to be made.

'Reality' is that which cannot be sublated by any new experience – only the Self falls into this category; 'Self' and 'Reality' are really interchangeable. It is only experienced when subject-object duality is transcended and all is known to be One. This is what Shankara calls *paramArtha*.

'Appearance' can be sublated – all of our phenomenal experiences fall into this category. The reason that we believe many of them to be 'real' (e.g. that there are 'objects') is simply that we haven't yet had the experience (i.e. Self-realization) that sublates that belief. It is possible to define several 'levels' of appearance. The lowest level would be something like an optical illusion, hallucination etc. and Shankara differentiates this illusory level from the level of our day to day experience. The former he calls *pratibhAsa* (adjective *prAtibhAsika*) – an example would be the magician making someone disappear. The dream worlds that we create for ourselves each night are also *prAtibhAsika*. The 'empirical' order of reality – how things seem to be in our day-to-day existence – is called *vyavahAra*. We often have our illusions sublated, e.g. when we bring a torch (and a big stick) to look more closely at the snake that is really a rope. And our dream worlds are sublated as soon as we wake up. But we only rarely have our ordinary experiences sublated, even though these experiences too are ultimately illusory and are the cause of life's problems, since we believe them to be 'real'. Once we *know* that they are only appearance, they are no longer a problem. We still see them and may continue to act as though they are real – in fact this has to be so or, once a man became 'realized', he would no longer be able to function in the world – but we know they are an appearance only.

'Unreality' is anything that is neither 'real' nor 'apparent'; it is not meaningful to talk of sublation. The scriptures use such examples as 'the son of a barren woman' or 'the horns of a hare' and the relevant Sanskrit term is *tuchCham*.

So appearances can be sublated but this does not mean that the ultimate reality can be 'known' in the sense that we normally use this word. Whilst it is necessary to make these distinctions in order that we might be able to appreciate what Advaita is saying, we must be very careful when speaking about them. The dream is real *for the dreamer*. The waking world is real *for the waker*. When we, the waker, start to talk about the nature of reality, we immediately risk major confusion. Reality is non-dual; language is dualistic and 'me' talking to 'you' is definitely presupposing duality! So we have a dilemma. We have to acknowledge the seeming duality in order to be able to discuss the actual non-dual reality.

This is why Advaita posits these 'levels of reality' and why some of the modern teachers, attempting to ignore this insurmountable problem, often seem to talk such rubbish. (So-called 'neo-Advaita' teachers deny the 'levels of reality' and endeavor only to speak of how things 'really' are.) Ref. 80 addresses this problem in depth. Here is an example (point 195):

"Many of the statements by modern satsang and neo-advaitin teachers confuse paramArtha *with* vyavahAra *and these in turn give rise to considerable misunderstanding on the part of the seeker.*

Consider, for example, the claim that practice cannot make the seeker into something that they are not already. But 'the seeker' is at the level of vyavahAra while 'what he or she really is' is at the level of paramArtha. Accordingly, the statement is invalid since it is mixing levels. It is true that the seeker is already the Self but he or she does not realize this. Practice prepares the mind for this realization."

One of the most metaphysical of the ancient teachers of this philosophy was Gaudapada (*gauDapAda*) who wrote the *kArikA* on the Mandukya Upanishad. What he said was *"That which is non-existent at the beginning and in the end, is necessarily so in the middle. The objects we see are illusions, still they are regarded as if real."* (Ref. 4)

This is now sounding not unlike the sort of statement that might be made by modern physics. All time is relative. A mayfly may live for only a few hours, a man for seventy years or more. Yet the whole of mankind has been around for but an instant in the lifetime of the earth and the earth for only a short time since the big bang. And perhaps, the entire life of the universe too is merely the equivalent of a half-day in the eternal cycle of the Yugas, as described in Hindu mythology.

All of this is transient. Reality is beyond time, space and causality. It cannot change – if it did it would no longer be the same thing and thus could not have been real. It is the ever-present background against which apparent change takes place. Without this unchanging reference point, it would indeed be meaningless to talk about the apparently changing. All of the metaphors of gold and ring, clay and pot etc. are relevant. The ring is merely name and form imposed upon the gold and thus has no 'reality' – it is only the gold that is real. Similarly, the world is name and form imposed upon the Self. Of course, there is no disputing that it seems to be real and we will continue to believe that it *is* real until our ignorance is sublated. We cannot, of course, ever see the reality upon which the world is superimposed – the world will still be *seen*, even when the ignorance has been removed. The difference will be that the illusion of separateness will now be understood; it will be known to be not other than one's own Self.

Another metaphor for this can be found in the Atmabodha (Ref. 17 V. 7). Shankara says that the appearance of the world is like seeing silver in the nacre (mother of pearl) of a shell. In reality there is no silver; this was projected by our minds onto the actual nacre inside the shell. In fact, if we had no prior knowledge of silver, we would only have seen the shininess of the shells coating. Similarly, we look at Reality and believe we see a world containing separate objects. It is our *vAsanA-s* or accumulation of ignorance and habitual ways of looking at things that cause us to make this mistake.

The Sage, having exhausted his *vAsanA-s* and looking out without any fears or desires realizes that it is only the Self in all the dualistic appearances; knows 'things' as they truly are.

You will not find any unequivocal description of reality in any writings of the Sages. As has already been noted, the mind can never comprehend this; in a sense the mind and reality are mutually incompatible, just as are the world and reality. If you think about it, it is the mind that 'sees' things via the senses –the mind is thus the 'subject', while the world is 'object'. But, from the vantage point of Consciousness, the mind is now 'object', with Consciousness as the subject. What Advaita says is that *all* objects are *mithyA*; only the Self, the ultimate subject, is *satyam*. The world is the snake imposed upon the rope by virtue of our ignorance. All that gurus and scriptures can do is tell us what reality is not and provide pointers towards that ineffable reality.

The Mandukya Upanishad, in the 7th mantra, possibly comes closest to describing the nature of absolute reality:

chaturthaM manyante nAntaHpraj~naM – the fourth (*chaturtha*) is not (*na*) that which thinks itself to be (*manyante*) the internal, subtle world (*antaHpraj~na*), i.e. not the dreamer, *taijasa*;

na bahiShpraj~naM – nor the external, gross world of objects (*bahis* means 'outside'), i.e. not the waker, *vishva*;

na ubhayataHpraj~naM – nor both (*ubhaya*), i.e. not some intermediate state;

na praj~nAnaghanaM – and not that which is a mass of (*ghana*) consciousness (i.e. not the deep-sleep state, in which the mind is resolved and there is consciousness which is 'conscious of nothing');

na praj~naM – neither simply 'consciousness', awareness or sentience;

na apraj~naM – nor unconsciousness, unawareness or insentience.

adRRiShTam – (it is) unseen (by any of the senses) (*dRRiShTa* means, seen, perceived, visible, apparent); also means 'beyond the five *j~nAnendriya-s* (sense organs);

avyavahAryam – nothing to do with 'worldly' things (*vyavahArya* is to do with common practice, ordinary life, conduct, behavior etc. i.e. transactions within *vyavahAra*);

agrAhyam – beyond understanding (*grAhya* means to be perceived, recognized or understood); also means beyond the five *karmendriya-s* (organs of action) – (*grahaNa* literally means to catch, where the organs of action are involved in catching, but is used in the sense of comprehension.)

alakShaNam – without any characteristics (*lakShaNa* is a mark or sign or, more commonly in advaita, a pointer) also translated as 'un-inferable';

achintyam – inconceivable, beyond thought;

avyapadeshyam – indefinable;

ekAtmapratyayasAraM – its essence (*sAra*) is certainly (*pratyaya*) the same as (*eka*) *Atman*;

prapa~nchopashamaM – negation (*ama*) of the experience (*pash*) of all plurality of the universe (*prapa~ncha*);

shAntaM – peace, tranquility;

shivam – favorable, propitious, auspicious;

advaitaM – non-dual;

sa AtmA – that is the Self;

savij~neyaH – that is to be understood."

The upshot of this is that no word can ever describe the nature of reality and, indeed, anything that we predicate of it cannot be true. Even to speak of it as 'consciousness' or 'non-dual' or 'brahman' has to be, in the final analysis, merely an attempt to understand it with our feeble mind. (If you want a complete elucidation of the meaning of this mantra, you will have to wait for my book 'OM: Key to the Universe, to be published 2012-13.)

It is never going to be possible for the mind to move from the world that it thinks it knows to the Reality that it wants to know. The mind and the world are part of the illusion; the world is the domain of illusory objects and the mind the domain of illusory concepts and feelings. Once the Reality is realized on enlightenment, the mind and world are known not to exist as something separate from the Self. Thus it is that questions such as 'how can I (the ego) come to know reality' are actually meaningless. It is as if one of the characters in our dream were to ask how it could know what the waking state is like. All experience is of change; reality is not an event and cannot be perceived or experienced. Thus, everything that is perceived or experienced can be known to be transient and therefore unreal. Indeed, Shankara says that, if we experience something, we can be sure that it must be *mithyA*.

More on *mAyA*

A creation implies a creator. Swami Paramarthananda suggests that the very idea is an insult. Creation necessitates change and this, in turn, would mean that the eternal, changeless, limitless reality would somehow have to downgrade itself to become time bound, changing and limited in order to become the cause of a universe. And, if there is no creator-god, then there cannot be a creation either.

Furthermore, if a creator brought anything into existence then there would be something other than the creator; at least two things. Ultimately, therefore, assuming the basic contentions of Advaita are true, creation cannot exist as an entity separate from the Self. Having said that, however, no one will seriously attempt to deny that there *appears* to be a world out there. All of our experience supports this and we must be very sure of ourselves before denying the validity of our experience. Note that whilst our experience remains in the realm of *vyavahAra*, the world does *effectively* exist as a separate entity. For the realized man, the world is still seen but is known to be not other than his own Self.

So, how far can we take the idea that what we see is not actually separate but is only an appearance, 'imagined' by God, if you like? Ramesh Balsekar, a disciple of Nisargadatta Maharaj, said that the Self can only become conscious of itSelf by manifesting as a 'separate' entity inside an apparent creation (Ref. 27). The elaboration of this is, of course, immense, incorporating everything that we can and could perceive or imagine. There are apparent individuals with apparently distinct experiences and apparent potentials for change etc. All of them, from highest intellect to lowest lump of rock is imagined and maintained by the single Consciousness. Hence the idea of *lIlA*, with the creator dreaming this vast play for His enjoyment. Consciousness then identifies with each particular body and believes itself an individual. Thus Alan Watt's way of putting it – God playing Hide and Seek.

The universe seems an awful lot of trouble for a practical joke. Tibor Fischer

It is quite understandable therefore that, in an attempt to 'explain' the mechanism by which this takes place, the concept of *mAyA* should be introduced and it is a fundamental one in Advaita. The dictionary definition uses terms such as 'magic' and 'witchcraft' i.e. deception through supernatural power. A *mAyAkAra* is a 'maker of magic' i.e. a conjurer or magician. We fail to appreciate the 'trick' because of our ignorance (*avidyA*), just as the child, in her ignorance, believes that the magician really does saw the lady in half and then put her together again.

Vedanta describes two different aspects of the 'mechanism' of *mAyA*. The following are quotations from another short book attributed to Shankara, called *dRRigdRRishya viveka* – (Discriminating between the Seer and the Seen), Ref. 56.

"Two powers, undoubtedly, are predicated of mAyA viz. projecting and veiling. The projecting power creates everything from the subtle body to the gross universe." (I.e. both world and mind).

"The manifesting of all names and forms in the entity which is Existence-Consciousness-Bliss and which is the same as brahman, like the foams etc. in the ocean, is known as creation."

"The veiling power conceals the distinction between the perceiver and the perceived objects which are cognized within the body as well as the distinction between brahman and the phenomenal universe which is perceived outside. This power is the cause of the phenomenal universe."

In the rope and snake metaphor, the veiling power (*AvaraNa*) prevents us from seeing the reality of the rope and then the projecting power (*vikShepa*) superimposes the image of the snake. In the case of the universe, the veiling power prevents us from seeing the real aspects of existence-consciousness-bliss and the projecting power misleads us into thinking that the transitory names and forms are the reality. We are ignorant of our true nature – due to the veiling power of *mAyA*. We believe ourselves to be something else (body, set of memories etc.) – due to the projecting power.

The ignorance from which these powers originate is neither real nor unreal. It is experienced as real whilst we are under its influence but disappears upon realization of the truth. This paradox is often 'explained' by saying that ignorance is 'beginningless' (*anAdi*). We can rationalize this by saying that time itself is part of *mAyA*. (In the same way, we can never describe reality because language is part of *mAyA*, too.) Assuming that you do not know the Chinese language, one might ask: "when did your ignorance of Chinese begin?" And you would be unable to give a sensible answer. It seems that ignorance may come to an end but it does not make sense to speak of its having a beginning in time.

The best explanation given by Advaita is that every seeming thing is *mithyA*... including any explanations that we give about that. Essentially ignorance does not really exist.

Swami Paramarthananda, commenting upon Gaudapada's *kArikA* on the Mandukya Upanishad (IV.59) points out that the 'cause' of the tree which appears in a dream can only be stated to be a 'dream seed'. The tree cannot be said to have a real cause because it is not itself real. Similarly, trying to discover the nature of ignorance is like trying to discover the nature of darkness by searching for it with a torch.

Another 'explanation' that is encountered is the claim that ignorance is *anirvachanIya*, which means 'unutterable, indescribable'. This might seem to be a cop-out, because Advaita cannot actually provide an explanation, but a little thought will show that this is not so. Descriptions entail the use of adjectives to describe the attributes of an existent thing. If there is no existent thing there, no description can be given. It would be like asking whether the snake, mistaken for a rope in the classic metaphor, is poisonous. We cannot honestly answer yes or no because there is no snake there.

Any conception or experience of the world, or anything in it (including ourselves, our thoughts or our feelings), as in any way separate from our Self is as a result of *mAyA*. The power of concealment clouds the reality with ignorance and the projecting power superimposes limitations upon our true nature. All limitations, including concepts of space, time and causality, arise from this.

Mistaking the real for the unreal

To say that ignorance causes us to see objects as separate from ourselves is just begging the question. The reason why this happens involves memory. In the first instant that we see an object, there is no differentiation. But then memory 'comes in', so quickly that the process is not perceived. The perception is 'looked up' in memory to find the closest match and then we superimpose the found image upon the external object. This is called *adhyAsa* but colloquially we say that we 'recognize' the object. We recognize it – know it again – because we believe we have found the appropriate picture in the memory and given it a name. It is in this way that the rope is seen as a snake. Clearly if we had no prior knowledge of snakes, we could not have made this error.

This mechanism also explains the process of *ahaMkAra*. We have an awareness of our existence – the most fundamental experience, rarely acknowledged in isolation but occasionally felt upon wakening. This is the 'rope', the dimly perceived *Atman*. Upon it, however, we superimpose all of the other, false ideas of 'I am Dennis Waite', 'I am an expert on Advaita' etc. These are the limitations (limiting 'adjuncts' or *upAdhi-s*) with which we cover up our true nature. In this scenario, it could be said that the root of our problem is failing to live in the present. Every perception is referred to the past, which is what memory inevitably refers to.

Shankara also defines *adhyAsa* as a 'mixing up' of real and unreal. When we see a rope and say 'there is a snake', it is certainly true that there is *something* i.e. the 'there is' part of the statement is real. However, we then project upon it the image of the snake from memory and this part is unreal. In the same way, when we say 'I am a man' or whatever, the 'I am' part is real; it is the 'man' aspect of the statement that is unreal. It is the purpose of this philosophy to investigate into the nature of the Self and sort out the real from the unreal. Once this has been achieved, we will have attained 'real-ization' and be forever released from the sufferings that this mixing-up has brought upon us.

We know that we 'are' and we know that we are 'conscious'. Thus we are already aware of the 'existence' and 'consciousness' aspects of our true nature. It is the 'bliss' aspect of which we are still ignorant. A better word for thinking about this, since the word 'bliss' is so easily confused with our notions of happiness, is 'unlimited'. We believe ourselves to be limited in so many ways, from the basic 'I am a man, not a woman' or 'I live in the UK and not the US' to more subtle 'I am stupid and unattractive' or 'worldly and sophisticated'. All ideas such as these are limitations, whereas our true nature is without limit of any kind.

Instead of striving to uncover our real nature, we spend all of our time in search of various properties of the *mithyA* part of our selves – acquiring *mithyA* objects in an *mithyA* world, adorning our *mithyA* bodies, enhancing our *mithyA* minds and so on. It is as though, in the case of the mistaken rope, we spend all our efforts describing the fangs, imagining how poisonous the snake is and researching into anti-venom serums.

If we could accept all of this mistaken perception as unreal, there would be no problem. (In fact, this is precisely the state of the realized man.) Our problem is that we believe the world, ourselves and objects to have a separate existence and we thereby create a problem where there is not really any problem at all.

Because we believe that we are the body, we believe we can die. We are constantly insecure. We become obsessed with money, believing it can purchase those things we need to combat our mortality and satisfy our misplaced desires. Because we believe we are limited in so many ways, we are continually trying to get those things that we imagine will remove the perceived limitations. All of our suffering results from this fundamental error that we make. And this will continue until the ignorance that is the cause of *adhyAsa* is removed.

The solution is to remove the ignorance of the Self. Only this can have the required effect – studying any other subject cannot help. The error is in respect of the Self, so the Self must be enquired into in order to dissolve the ignorance.

Objects

If there is only the Self, what can we say about the world and the 'objects' that we seem to see around us? In all of our perceptions, we erroneously superimpose Name and Form onto parts of this apparent manifestation and believe them to be separate objects. As we have already learned from a consideration of Kant and his successors, we are not seeing the 'object' itself but the mental image constructed as a result of impressions from the senses together with our thoughts, ideas and memories further superimposed upon these. Because our own nature and nurture will always differ from those of anyone else, and the acuity and functionality of our senses will probably differ too, it is certain that what 'I' see will be different from what 'you' see.

So, is there an object out there? The answer depends on your definitions. There is nothing out there that is separate from the Self but there *is* some form that we have chosen separately to identify by name. How did we reach the conclusion that there was an object in the first place? This is to some degree arbitrary and in accord with social convention, language etc. We choose to call part of the landscape a 'hill' even though it is continuous with the rest of the land. This is so that, for example, we can suggest building a castle on top of it so that we can see attackers coming from a distance. Such transient forms are initially differentiated by perceiving their attributes and assigning them some importance. Subsequently, these details are consigned to memory and we give them a name for convenience.

In fact, without Consciousness, the world would not exist. Since the world is the manifestation of Consciousness, if Consciousness did not exist then there could be no manifestation. Doesn't the world cease to exist when you go to sleep? Don't you recreate it anew each time you wake up? Is it possible I am being serious?

Had I been present at the creation, I would have given some useful hints for the better ordering of the universe. Attributed to Alfonso the Wise, 13th century

All perceptions are appearances only, not 'real' but *mithyA*. The reality that gives rise to the perceptions is forever beyond our direct knowledge because we must go through the intermediaries of senses and brain. The perceptions are only name and form imposed as a result of *adhyAsa*, by the mind, upon the one reality – the snake upon the rope. Time and space, cause and effect are all concepts of mind created in order to make sense of this imposed pseudo-reality. All these concepts cease when the mind ceases to operate, as in deep sleep. Upon awakening, memory operates and all of the mechanisms of mind, together with all of the learnt concepts we use to make sense of the appearances that strike our senses spring into action. So yes, in a very real sense, we do create our *interpretation* of what is 'out there' each time we awake. (At the level of empirical reality – *vyavahAra* – the world itself is said to be the 'creation' of *Ishvara*, wielding the power of *mAyA*. This is why we each see the same world and not our own individual creation. This will be discussed in the next chapter.)

Classical Vedanta actually says that, when we see objects, it is not in fact something coming from the objects into our organs of perception, i.e. light, sound etc; it is the other way round. Our senses 'go out', as it were, and 'grab' a part of creation, thereby making it into something separate. If there were not a mind and associated sense organs to do this, therefore, there would not seem to be any objects, only the undifferentiated Self.

If this sounds ridiculous, ask yourself: if we did not have ears, would the concept of 'sound' have any meaning? Science might have established that moving objects set up wave compressions in the atmosphere and would probably have devised instruments for detecting these. But the notion of a separate sense of 'sound', and what this might be like, just wouldn't exist. Similarly with each of the other senses. But what if we had no senses at all? Then none of the 'mechanisms' by which we become aware of objects would exist. What would this mean, then, for the objects themselves?

The fact of the matter is that is the mind, and its interpretation of information coming from the various senses, that tells us that there are objects separate from us. And, if you follow this line of reasoning further, you will realize that the mind itself is another, if subtler object. And it is consciousness that tells us there is a mind, which is effectively separate from 'I' since I have to admit that I am not the mind. *All* objects are *mithyA*, only Consciousness is *satyam*.

To ask whether or not there actually are objects is an interesting intellectual diversion in our present condition but we are in no doubt that, for all practical purposes, they do exist in the *vyAvahArika* realm – our waking 'dream'. It is somewhat like asking whether the traffic lights that we are about to drive through, in a dream that we are having, are on red or green. Whilst still in the dream it might mean the difference between life and death. When we wake up, of course, it will not make the slightest difference.

A discussion some time ago (2001) on the Advaitin E-list on the Internet revolved around the question of whether there were objects present in our deep-sleep state. The question was asked as to whether, when we woke up, the objects were instantly created by the mind or whether they had been there all the time. (We solve all of the really practical problems of the world in these discussions!) My response to this was as follows:

"Isn't it effectively the same thing? The world is seen as something other than the Self only by the mind. Everything seen as something separate is only appearance, not reality. When in the deep-sleep state, the mind is inactive so there is no appearance. But the Self is still there, as it always is. When we awake, the mind becomes active and, again there is the appearance of something separate. But it is still only the Self, as it always was. Nothing has changed other than that the mind, now active again, is superimposing name and form upon the undivided reality. Whether we call this 'the mind creating the objects' or whether we say ' the mind wakes up to the objects' amounts to the same thing. There never were any objects and there still aren't any.

"There is only the Self – the background, turIya – on which the three states of consciousness, waking, dream and deep-sleep, together with objects and mind are all only appearances. The mind and objects are both absent in the deep-sleep state. In the dream and waking states, which can be regarded as equivalent for this discussion, the mind is present but is only a false identification – another subtle object. And, while objects appear to be present (thoughts, emotions, perceptions), these are only mistaken superimpositions of name and form upon the unchanging reality.

"How can it ever be meaningful to attempt to explain one illusion by another or to say that one illusion has more reality than another? All is illusion piled upon illusion, like a complex dream. It is surely beyond the abilities of the dreamer to unravel his own dream, at the time of the dream. Why should we assume that the waker could unravel his waking

dream? Perhaps to do so would, indeed, bring realization, but then the explanation would presumably be of no more interest than the unraveled dream is to the waker...

"Without the mind we could not be aware of objects. And it is only because of the mind that objects are assumed to exist in the first place, whether or not the mind actually 'creates' them."

More recently (2009), I have been making a prolonged study of the Mandukya Upanishad and Gaudapada's *kArikA-s* for my next book. In the last chapter of this, Gaudapada utilizes an excellent metaphor for explaining objects, namely that of the firebrand. This was the wooden stick, with one end wrapped in a rag, dipped in oil and set alight for use as a torch at nighttime. A more familiar modern example would be the sparkler – the hand-held firework that throws out lots of scintillating, incandescent particles of (presumably) iron as it slowly burns down.

When we play with these as children (or as adults with children), we tend to move them around and 'draw' patterns with them. In the dark, when the glowing tip of the sparkler is moved fairly quickly, the persistence of vision of the eyes means that solid patterns seem to form in the air. But what is actually the nature of these patterns? We may see what appears to be a solid circle, for example. But is there really a circle there? Where does it come from? Does it come from inside or outside the sparkler? And when the firework dies, is the circle 'reabsorbed' into the sparkler?

If you analyze what is happening here, you will find that questions such as these cannot be answered, because they implicitly assume that there actually *is* a circle. In fact, there is no circle – what there is, is simply movement of the sparkler. The circle is *mithyA*, depending for its existence on the sparkler alone.

Similarly, says Gaudapada, the world of objects and people and minds does not exist as a real, separate entity. What is there is simply movement of Consciousness. The world is *mithyA*, depending for its existence on Consciousness alone. In IV.48 of the *kArikA-s*, Gaudapada says: *"As the fire brand, when not in motion, is free from all appearances and remains changeless, similarly, Consciousness, when not in motion, is free from all appearances and remains changeless."* (Ref. 4)

Also, we must not make the mistake of thinking that the sparkler is the 'cause' of the patterns. There is no cause-effect relationship here because, in order for such a thing to be possible, there have to be two things – and the patterns do not actually exist. This will be very important in the next chapter when we look at creation – the world cannot be considered to be an effect of any cause because there is no world separate from Consciousness.

14. Creation and time

Creation

In the beginning the Universe was created. This has made a lot of people very angry and is widely regarded as a bad move. Douglas Adams

Does what was said in the previous chapter mean, then, that there is no creation? Yes! This word has the sense of 'someone' bringing something new into existence. What is 'out there' is only an ever-changing appearance of the one thing that has always been there – Consciousness, our Self. We give various forms within it separate names for convenience but this doesn't change the reality. A wave in the ocean is still the same water, even though we identify it as something in its own right.

Whilst we remain in ignorance, we will continue to believe in a separately existing world. Terrified with what we firmly believe to be a poisonous snake in the middle of our path, no amount of unlikely sounding verbal pronouncements are going to persuade us to march on unconcernedly. In our current state, we imagine the world to consist of separate objects and beings and we use our mental concepts to misinterpret the messages from our senses. This totally 'made-up' picture is what we 'see' as the world and is effectively the same as the dreams that we construct in the dream-state of consciousness.

But the world is clearly not literally the same as our personal dream – the clue is in that word 'personal'. My dream *is* personal because its 'substance' is entirely made up from my mind. All of the places and beings in the dream do not have any substantial existence apart from my mind. Also, dreams tend to be different each night. If each dream continued from where we had left off the previous night, peopled by the same characters living a continuation of the same lives, how would we know which was waking and which dream? But the waking world *does* have this continuity. The way that Advaita explains this is by saying that, whereas dreams are created by the *jIva's* mind, the waking world is created by *Ishvara's* mind.

From the standpoint of *vyavahAra*, there is a real world with lots of separate *jIva-s*, each living their separate life. The world is created by *Ishvara* in accordance with the total *prArabdha saMskAra* of all of the living beings that were present last time around. Creation, preservation and dissolution of the world (*sRRiShTi – sthiti – laya*) continues in the never ending cycle known as *saMsAra*. All of this is watched over and controlled by *Ishvara*, with His power of *mAyA*.

In fact, it is the word 'creation' that misleads us – a far better word is 'manifestation'. The former implies that something that did not previously exist is brought into existence. The latter explains that something that already exists, but is 'unmanifest', is revealed. We move from the waking world of gross objects to the subtle world of dream where all the apparent objects are 'made out of mind' and finally into deep sleep, in which all of these are in potential, or causal form.

Taking this idea to its literal limit, we would have to say that everything already exists in potential form in its substrate. Michelangelo is reported to have claimed that he did not fashion the forms of his sculptures himself but simply chipped away the rock to reveal the form that was already there beneath. This is the theory of *satkArya vAda* – the belief that the effect already pre-exists in the cause and it is a theory held by the *sAMkhya* philosophers – not Advaitins. But it is utilized by Advaita as an interim explanation (from the standpoint of *vyavahAra*) to tie in with the notion of an actual creation, *saMsAra* and *karma*.

A corollary of this theory is that, regarding the notion of creation, we would have to say that the world already exists in causal form prior to creation. Another group of Indian philosophers, called the *nyAya-vaisheShika-s* maintain the opposite view, that the world specifically does *not* exist prior to creation. (This theory, not surprisingly, is called *asatkArya vAda*.)

Gaudapada, in his *kArikA-s*, shows how the arguments of each of these philosophers negate the others viewpoint and prove that the world can neither exist nor not-exist prior to creation. Very briefly, if something already exists, it makes no sense to speak of its coming into existence.

Neither is it meaningful to talk of a 'non-existent thing' originating. Such a sentence contradicts the laws of grammar (a verb must have a subject, and 'non-existent thing' means there is no subject) and, in any case, the law of the conservation of matter tells us that matter can neither be created nor destroyed. ($E=mc^2$ complicates the issue here but does not contradict it.)

Accordingly, if the world can neither exist nor not-exist prior to creation, the only logical conclusion is that there has not been any creation at all. This is Gaudapada's contention – the theory of *ajAti vAda* (*ajAti* means 'not born'). The world has always existed because effectively there is no world – there is only name and form of the non-dual *brahman*. The origin of the concept is unclear and it is difficult to find any overt reference in the older Upanishads. Gaudapada says: *"No kind of* jIva *is ever born nor is there any cause for any such birth. The ultimate truth is that nothing whatsoever is born."* (Ref. 4, 3.48 and 4.71 – the same statement is made twice.)

There is a Buddhist saying: "Someone who does not know (reality) just sees mountains as mountains and rivers as rivers. Once he has embarked upon a spiritual path, he no longer sees mountains as mountains and rivers as rivers. When he finally knows reality, he once again sees mountains as mountains etc." The point is that, while seeking, we get intellectually tied up with theories such as the ones above and start to make statements such as 'the world does not exist'; 'there literally is nothing at all'. Although we still see the world, we deny the evidence of our own senses because we are aware of the illusory and transitory nature of creation. Once realization has been achieved, all mental agitation ceases. The wonders of the world, including those forms that we choose to call mountains and rivers, can be appreciated and known as not different from one's own Self. Ramana Maharshi said: *"The aspirant starts with the definition, that which is real exists always. Then he eliminates the world as unreal because it is changing. The seeker ultimately reaches the Self and there finds unity as the prevailing note. Then, that which was originally rejected as being unreal is found to be a part of the unity. Being absorbed in the reality, the world also is real. There is only being in Self-realization, and nothing but being."* (Ref. 24)

The 'progress' from a deluded 'individual' involved in and suffering from the world is a process of successive sublation as discussed earlier. At the most confused levels, there are daydreams and hallucinations - *prAtibhAsika*. These are sublated by our everyday experience of objects and concepts. These in turn are sublated by spiritual pursuits such as worship of a higher being. All of these things belong to the level of relative existence however – *vyAvahArika* – and are sublated upon realization by knowledge of the Self – *pAramArthika*. This is the only reality and cannot be further sublated.

Like it or not, there simply is not, in reality, any creation. The world and everything in it, including these mind-bodies, were never actually 'brought into existence'. They are only appearances.

Gaudapada also says (*kArikA* 3.32): *"There is no dissolution, no birth, none in bondage, none aspiring for wisdom, no seeker of liberation and none liberated. This is the absolute truth."* And the same message is given much later by Ramana Maharshi (Sri Guru Ramana Vachana Mala Verses 20 – 21, quoted in Ref. 25): *"There is no creation, nor destruction; there is no one that is bound; nor is there anyone that strives for Liberation, nor anyone that has attained that state. There is no mind, nor body, nor world, nor anyone called the 'soul'; One alone exists, the pure, calm, unchanging Reality which has no second, and no becoming."*

(nirguNa) brahman

In the beginning there was nothing and God said 'Let there be light', and there was still nothing but everybody could see it. Dave Thomas

The following analysis is loosely based upon Swami Paramarthananda's talks on Shankara's *bhAShya* (analytical commentary) on the Brahma Sutra.

Before we can investigate anything , two criteria must be satisfied:

1) we must know what it is we are investigating (a definition);
2) we must have an appropriate means of acquiring data (a *pramANa*).

For example, if someone asks: "Is my car outside?", in order to be able to answer (assuming we can understand the language), we must know first know what a car is! Then, it is necessary to know something distinctive about the car, such as its make, color etc. even if not its registration number. And we must be able to acquire this information, i.e. we must be able to see (i.e. not be blind) or at least be able to ask someone else and hear their reply.

So, when the Brahma Sutra announces at the outset: *athAto brahma jij~nAsA* (thereafter begins an enquiry into *brahman*), we cannot do anything unless we know what it is into which we are to enquire.

What is *brahman* anyway? Well, it helps us to understand this if we know something about grammar and Sanskrit (although not necessarily Sanskrit grammar you will probably be pleased to hear!). If you know the difference between an adjective and a noun, you will know that an adjective usually qualifies a noun – it tells you more about it so that you can differ-entiate it from other nouns. Thus, for example, I might ask you to bring me the book from next door and, when you look, you see that the room next door is actually a library. So, if I cannot give you the title or tell you its precise location, I might say that I am referring to the small, thin, red, hardback book with the coffee stain on the front cover. Now, you are almost certainly in possession of sufficient information to be able to find the book, even if it might take you some time, depending upon the size of the library. Each of the words: small, thin, red, hardback and the phrase 'with the coffee stain on the front cover' is functioning as an adjective, qualifying the noun 'book' or telling you more about it.

'Qualify' in this context means 'attribute a specified quality to something'. Although the OED says that this meaning is now archaic, it says precisely what we want to say. One of the other meanings is also relevant, in that use of adjectives in this way makes the specified object less general, tying it down to something more specific or limited.

So a noun is normally qualified by an adjective. But this is not always the case. If I ask you what you understand by a 'big' house, you will probably describe a mansion; something with many wings, bathrooms etc, such as might have been common amongst the upper classes in past centuries. If your own home happens to be in a shanty town on the outskirts of Rio or Mumbai, however, a 'two-up, two-down' terraced house might well seem to be big. If I ask you to think of a big fly, a common house fly is actually quite small compared to a hornet, say. And that is tiny compared to the goliath beetle from Costa Rica. If you know anything about particle physics, you will know that a proton is very big compared to an electron but the particle that is being sought by the Large Hadron Collider experiments in Geneva is absolutely enormous, relatively speaking.

The purpose of this discussion is to point out that the massive hadron, big though it is for a sub-atomic particle, can scarcely be called big when we are talking about houses. Thus, in this analysis of what is meant by 'big', the adjective 'big' in each case is effectively being qualified by the noun. We cannot associate any specific concept of 'bigness' without taking into account the nature of the related noun.

And so we come eventually to *brahman*. The reason for all the preliminaries is that the word derives from the *dhAtu* (a Sanskrit 'root' word) *bRRiH* and it is effectively a noun derived from the adjective 'big'. In essence it could be translated as 'the Big'. Now, in the light of the above discussion, how can we interpret this? What we are saying is that there is no noun to put this 'big' into context. In other words, the 'bigness' is not qualified – by anything. It is 'big' without qualification or limitation of any kind; in other words 'infinitely' big.

Of course, the idea has to be subsumed in the reality. *brahman* transcends all concepts, reconciles all opposites. Everything is *mithyA* only, deriving existence from *brahman*, being simply name and form of *brahman*. And so, having appreciated the thought behind the word, you should not dwell upon it. Sri Atmananda has this to say (Notes no. 1255):

"The world, posited in space, is an appearance on the Reality. The term 'world' rightly comprehends also the generic space and time in which diversity is supposed to appear. The process of visualizing the Reality in the world is by completely separating the appearance part of it from the Reality. But usually, in that endeavor, the world alone is eliminated, leaving behind unnoticed both space and time tagged on to the Reality. The consequent superimposition of the sense of time and space, on the

Reality behind, gives it the idea of bigness. This is responsible for the fallacious concept and name, 'brahman'. When this sense of bigness is also eliminated, brahman itself stands revealed as the ultimate Reality, the 'I'-principle." (Ref. 98)

We can only describe something that has attributes because the attributes are the aspects that we describe. If you are asked to describe an object, you do so by saying whether it is big or small, what color it is and so on. Swami Dayananda explains how all of this is relevant in respect of *brahman*:

"The words can describe something that has one or more of these characteristics: jAti *(species),* guNa *(attribute),* kriyA *(action) or* sambandha *(relation or connection). For example, you can understand the word 'cow' because cow is a species. If you say 'sweet orange', sweetness is the attribute of the orange. Words like driver, cook, sprinter and so on make sense in terms of action. Similarly, you can understand words describing relationships like father, son, citizen etc. So the words can only describe an object possessing any one or more of these categories. But* brahman *does not possess any of these categories. There is no second* brahman, *so there is no* jAti *for it.* brahman *does not have any attribute, so* guNa *is not possible. Again,* brahman *does not undergo any change, so it cannot perform any action.* brahman *has no connection with anything else because anything else is not there. So it cannot be revealed by any relationship. Therefore,* brahman *cannot be revealed by any word that we use in our parlance."*(Ref. 99)

We have already talked about the qualities, or *guNa-s*, so it should come as no surprise that this concept of *brahman* is called *nirguNa brahman* – 'without qualities'. So nothing can be said about *brahman*, and even *that* is saying something and therefore saying too much. Buddha had the right idea. When asked about the nature of reality, he said all that could be said – he remained silent.

The illusion of time

Time is nature's way of keeping everything from happening all at once.
Anon

We have already discussed how space is a concept that we use in order to make sense of the world, as in the metaphor of the nets used to try to catch fish that are smaller than the mesh size. Time, too, is only a useful fiction. We use these concepts in order to make sense of the 'world' and talk meaningfully about it. In fact, this is how science now views so-called space-time – as a hypothetical entity to enable us to understand the phenomenal world.

To the extent that there could be degrees of 'unreality', past and future are very unreal! Thought or perception cannot reach them. Memories are present thoughts about past events while plans, dreams etc. are present imaginings about possible future events. The present is the point at which objects, thoughts and feelings etc, are perceived, the point at which the illusions of *mAyA* are manifest.

The Self, in its aspect as 'existence' (*sat*) is said to be *trikAlAtIta*, meaning that which transcends past, present and future. This is Advaita's effective definition of reality. The present is where it all happens but, since all is illusory, it is the birthplace of *mAyA*. Only that which exists beyond all conditionings of time, space and causality is truly *sat*. That which has no existence at any time is then *asat*. In between these two lies the world of *mithyA* mentioned earlier.

At the beginning of this book, we talked about our not being the body or mind, and about how the witnessing Self that we are now is the same as it was in our most distant memory. Hence, even in our own experience, it seems that what we really believe ourselves to be is outside of time and space. Those are both ideas that are generated by the mind and have no real existence apart from the mind. Time related ideas such as 'I am getting old' result from identification with the body. Space related ideas such as 'I am here (and you are there)' stem from seeing ourselves as separate. In fact we are not separate beings existing in insignificant bodies for only a short period of time. We are that in which time and space are conceived. We are not irrelevant specks in the universe; the universe is an appearance within the Consciousness that we are.

Things, thoughts and feelings come to us, stay for a while and then disappear. This sequence of events is construed as past, present and future. Yet throughout all, our awareness remains unaffected. We, our true Self, have no past, present or future. We are the Presence in which all else 'appears'.

The quotation at the beginning of this section is more than amusing. But it is not quite accurate. It is not "nature's way" but our mind's way. Time is a concept that enables us to make sense of our perceptions and communicate with others. In the beginning, there is only Consciousness. Then there is the 'first' thought: 'I am'. (This is what Ramana Maharshi calls the 'root' thought and the purpose of his 'method' is effectively to keep asking 'Who am I?' until we work our way back to this root thought. There is then the possibility of its dissolving back into Consciousness, thus bringing Self-realization.) As soon as there is another thought – 'I am x'; the identification of the power of consciousness with a name or form in the appearance of 'creation' – this is a second 'event'. Now there can be the concept of time to differentiate between the two thoughts. In fact, Sri Parthasarathy suggests that the basic unit of time was called the 'second' because it relates to the 'second' event (though this sounds more than a little far-fetched!). It is worth noting, incidentally, that this second thought arises as a result of ignorance – this is where all of our problems begin. Because ignorance effectively *causes* this thought (I am x), ignorance must logically be present before the thought. But we have just said that time does not effectively begin until the second thought. Consequently, we have to concede that ignorance must somehow be present *before* time. Therefore, ignorance has to be described as 'beginningless'– *anAdi*.

This is really a language problem as much as anything. We postulate this 'ignorance' to act as a 'cause' for our misconception and this gives us the idea that it is an actual 'thing' that has existence. (Post-Shankara Advaitins called it *mUlAvidyA* or root ignorance, a concept that was certainly never put forward by Shankara himself.) In fact, all that is happening is that we are failing to differentiate between the Self and not-Self – the process of *adhyAsa*. As soon as we recognize the truth, the 'ignorance' disappears along with everything else and is seen never to have existed to begin with. To speak of it as 'beginningless' therefore makes us think of it as substantial, which it never really was.

It is only our (mis-)perception and subsequent attempts to make intellectual sense of things which force us to postulate discrete events out of the continuity that is Consciousness. If there are no 'events', there is no time either.

Past and memory

Memory is the corpse of an experience from which the life has vanished.
Alan Watts

Thoughts are necessarily of the past. By the time we think of something that is happening *now*, it is no longer happening. Everything we think and feel about ourselves, our lives, is already past. We are now and always in the present. So our thoughts about it are inevitably false. This is another aspect of mistaking the unreal for the real – *adhyAsa* – and brings about such emotions as boredom, dissatisfaction and depression when they fail to meet up with our expectations.

Conventionally, events occur in the present and aspects that seem of particular relevance to us are stored away in a metaphorical database, called the memory. In the present, in what we might term 'trigger' situations, thoughts that we believe to be recollections of those saved thoughts spring to mind. We call these new thoughts 'memories' and believe that they refer to a 'past'. But they are still only a particular type of thought arising *now*, in the present. The so-called 'past' is effectively conjured up by this present memory-type thought. The existence of a past is only an inference based upon the content of these present thoughts. Any attention devoted to these memories is being wasted in this imaginary past. The consciousness that is spent in this worthless pursuit is unavailable for attending to what is here and now. So much of our efforts are spent agonizing over the past: 'I should have done/said that'; 'what did he think?' Or reminiscing: 'wasn't that wonderful?'; reliving painful or joyful experiences. All of this is energy being wasted now, in the present, on present memories that, even if there were a 'real' past, probably bear little resemblance to those supposed past events or feelings. If we did not have a memory to acquaint us of them, could we even have a concept of passing 'time'?

In fact, science has recently discovered that so-called 'long-term' memories may not even be very reliable. I related the following in my book 'How to Meet Yourself' (Ref. 71) but, since very few people read that book, it is worth repeating here:

"We know that long-term memories seem to reside in the cortex of the brain. Short term ones exist for only a few seconds before beginning the process of consolidation into longer term ones, involving one of the organs within the brain (the hippocampus). A complex protein has been identified as being responsible for the translation process. What has been discovered recently, however, is that our long-term memory is not necessarily very reliable (Ref. 109). Whenever we revisit it for whatever reason, whether mentally to relive an enjoyable experience or in order to recall a specific item of data, the information is reprocessed and stored anew in our long term memory and thus will not be quite the same as the earlier version. It is hardly surprising that witnesses of crimes or accidents have been shown not to be totally reliable. We may actually rewrite the story, with modifications, each time we remember it.

"The experimental data for this was, admittedly, derived from rats rather than humans but the mechanism is believed to be the same. Rats were taught to associate being placed in a dark room with receiving an electric shock. Needless to say, after a while it could be observed that they became anxious whenever they were shown the room, irrespective of whether they received a shock. Once this pattern was observed repeatedly, even after a significant lapse of time, it could be concluded that this association was fixed in their long-term memory.

"Some of the rats now either had their hippocampus removed or

they were treated with a drug that suppressed the action of the protein responsible for laying down long-term memories. When these rats were shown the room, they reacted as before with anxiety, showing that their long-term memory in the cortex of the brain was still registering the association with electric shock.

"Some of the other rats were shown the room (but not put into it) and then had either the hippocampus removed or were treated with the drug. In all cases, when they were subsequently put into the room, they showed no anxiety whatsoever. They wandered about quite happily, indicating that the long-term memory association had completely disappeared.

"In fact, revisiting old data from electro-convulsive therapy (ECT) back in the sixties showed that this effect had already been seen with humans. If someone was asked to relive their traumatic episodes or fears and then given ECT whilst still conscious, the related memories were found to have disappeared subsequently. Of course, such experiments would no longer be allowed today!"

It is not as though memories have any life as such. There is none of the intensity that can be known in the present moment, when the attention is not partly on an imaginary past or future. At the time of an alleged past occurrence, there might indeed have been intensity – we probably all claim to remember peak experiences that we would like to relive. But the thoughts are lifeless. There is no possibility of recreating the past event. Any intensity and all reality have drained away, leaving only a husk of meaning, stale and colorless with no possibility of change.

Do not look back. And do not dream about the future, either. It will neither give you back the past, nor satisfy your other daydreams. Your duty, your reward – your destiny – are here *and* now. Dag Hammarskjold

There is an interesting account, in an excellent book by Oliver Sacks, called 'The Man Who Mistook His Wife For A Hat' (Ref. 55), of a man who, with a particular part of his brain having been damaged, has been left without any short term memory at all. The effect of this is that, for example, his wife visits him at hospital and he welcomes her lovingly with open arms, wanting to know all that has been happening since he last saw her. If she then leaves the room to visit the bathroom and returns a few minutes later, he welcomes her lovingly with open arms and... He simply cannot remember the events of a short time ago and everything is seen afresh.

Conventionally, of course this is very tragic. However, the account makes it apparent that many aspects of such a life are, in fact, quite enviable. He is able to live each moment with an intensity quite alien to most of us because he is not burdened with this baggage of thoughts constantly telling us how to respond to every event.

In most situations we react according to these memories, thoughts, opinions and impressions generated in the distant past by parents, teachers etc. in circumstances that almost certainly bear little resemblance to those here and now. These accretions were allowed because they were found reassuring in one way or another to the ego, reinforcing the ever-deepening furrows in the jello metaphor. In the present moment, which is all there is, all of the information we need is in front of us and, if the attention is given, the knowledge will be there. The memories are useless – the ego is non-existent. Stop spending so much of your energy in maintaining them and thereby giving them power over you!

Future and imagination

Future is that period of time in which our affairs prosper, our friends are true and our happiness is assured. Ambrose Bierce

The French philosopher, Blaise Pascal said the following about past, present and future (Pensées 172):

"We do not rest satisfied with the present. We anticipate the future as too slow in coming, as if in order to hasten its course; or we recall the past, to stop its too rapid flight. So imprudent are we that we wander in the

times which are not ours and do not think of the only one which belongs to us; and so idle are we that we dream of those times which are no more and thoughtlessly overlook that which alone exists. For the present is generally painful to us. We conceal it from our sight, because it troubles us; and, if it be delightful to us, we regret to see it pass away. We try to sustain it by the future and think of arranging matters which are not in our power, for a time which we have no certainty of reaching. Let each one examine his thoughts, and he will find them all occupied with the past and the future. We scarcely ever think of the present; and if we think of it, it is only to take light from it to arrange the future. The present is never our end. The past and the present are our means; the future alone is our end. So we never live, but we hope to live; and, as we are always preparing to be happy, it is inevitable we should never be so."

Now read that again! In a sense, it is the heart of all of our problems.

Where would we be without the future? All the things we want; ambitions still to be realized; desires assuaged and fears conquered. We believe that we do not have those things that we really need but that we may gain them in some future time. For many, this seems to be the only thing that keeps them going. But so much energy is wasted, projecting our thoughts into an imaginary future. "What if this were to happen?" or "if only that came to pass" or "please don't let such and such come true". We endeavor to bring about those events that our memories suggest will be enjoyable and avoid the ones that are associated with unpleasant memories. So futile! When our projected hopes fail to materialize, misery results again.

Disappointment is the result of unreasonable expectations. Me

It is also interesting to remember that many (most or all?) of those 'good' times in the past were experienced as such because they were especially notable episodes in the midst of sad or painful periods. If we seek to bring them about again and they are to have the same effect, the dark times must be brought back along with them. As has already been discussed, happiness and misery are the two extremes of a single spectrum of emotion; you cannot have one without the other; they must alternate.

The key is desire. Desire is the motivating force behind our constant striving towards the future – dissatisfaction with ourselves and what we believe we have in the present, and a wish to remedy this. When we live totally in the present, *manas* functions correctly; there is no discursive thought. Thinking only operates when we turn away from the reality of the moment into the diversions of the imaginary past and future. The past has gone and is 'unredeemable'. Desire (= thinking) is therefore necessarily equated to the future.

The future is safe – it does not yet exist. There is no limit to what we might do in the future. We can continue to avoid reality and being in the present by postponing action. Some years ago, in the organization that I used to attend, the spiritual leader died and a replacement was sought. Someone suggested that it would be ideal if one of the school members could be appointed. Unfortunately, there were no enlightened 'individuals' and thus it was not possible. For whatever reasons, half-jokingly or just out of interest, members of the senior classes were asked whether, if they were offered instant enlightenment, they would accept. There was much reflection and a realization of a different kind – most people felt that yes, of course they wanted to become Self-realized... but not just yet! There were many things to be done first, many desires to be fulfilled before they would really be prepared to give all of that up.

This is how it is that we are in chains of our own making. We choose to perpetuate the ignorance that binds us to these identifications and prevents us from realizing that we are already free. All of these desires will never be fulfilled; desires are by their nature self-perpetuating. The 'satisfaction' of a desire is only adding fuel to a fire. It is because they are ultimately insatiable that so much value is attached to the future; why we predict and plan and push towards perceived gratification. And it is why we rarely attain happiness. Happiness is in the present and we can never stay there long enough to enjoy it. Wanting to prolong it, we must continually strive to ensure that the future satisfies those conditions that we believe are required. Ironic isn't it?

Forever 'looking forward' to planned events that we naturally wish to be enjoyable or fulfilling, our imaginations fill in the blanks of the unknown future with expectations. And then, when things don't turn out quite as we had thought – surprise, surprise – we end up being disappointed. It does not seem to matter how frequently this occurs, still we insist in indulging in this dangerous fantasizing. If only we would let events happen, as they will anyway, without burdening them with these preconceived notions of how we want them to be.

Only the present

Osho uses a metaphor of a man who has always been locked in a room and who looks through a keyhole. As he moves his eye, objects that were visible 'disappear' and new ones 'come into existence'. To the man, these successive objects are past, present and future. He thinks that the past object no longer exists and the future one has not yet come into existence. In reality, to someone outside of the closed room, whose vision is not limited by the keyhole, all of these things are there all of the time. There is no movement of time, no coming into existence from a future, existing momentarily and then fading into a past. It is our mind that is moving. How could the present existence cease to exist in a moment? How could a non-existent future suddenly come into existence?

We are seeing things the wrong way round again. Just as we used to believe that the sun went around the earth. Just as, when we are sitting in a train at a station and an adjacent train begins to move, we think it is our train that is moving.

For eternally and always there is only now, one and the same now; the present is the only thing that has no end. Erwin Shrödinger

There is only the present – this cannot be repeated too many times. Understanding this totally is the most important practical aspect of this philosophy. Not only is our attention depleted when partly or wholly given to recollections or imaginings but also our view of the present moment is distorted and conditioned. No wonder we react in habitual ways when our minds are partly dwelling on how we behaved 'last time'. Everything happens now – when else could it happen? I am writing this now and you are reading it now!

The consequences of this are far reaching. If there is only 'now', then there cannot be any 'change' from one state to another. For that to be the case, there would have had to have been a state in a 'past' from the vantage point of the latter condition and a state in a 'future' from the vantage point of the former. If there is no 'change', there cannot be any 'cause' to 'effect' a change and there can be no 'action' to bring it about. All of these cherished beliefs are related and, as soon as one is undermined, the whole system comes crashing down.

Tony Parsons even dislikes the use of words such as 'now', because they entail all of the other time-related words and concepts, none of which are meaningful when considering the truth: *"As far as I'm concerned there is no such thing as now. Now implies that there is a then. You are back in time. Now is this moment...there is no moment. There is only this. It's timeless. It isn't now and it wasn't then. There is an abyss between the two concepts."*(Ref. 82)

In his book 'As It Is' (Ref. 83), he states the following, which he says 'absolutely encapsulates' his teaching:

"There is only Source appearing. All that manifests is always and only the appearance of Source – the apparent universe, the world, the life story, the body-mind, feelings, the sense of separation, and the search for enlight-enment. It is all the one appearing as two – the no-thing appearing as everything. The drama of the search is totally without meaning or purpose; it is a dream awakening. There is no deeper intelligence weaving a destiny and no choice functioning at any level. Nothing is born and nothing dies. Nothing is happening. But this, as it is, invites the apparent seeker to redis-cover its origin. When the invitation is accepted by no one, then it is seen that there is only Source – the uncaused, unchanging, impersonal stillness from which unconditional love overflows and celebrates. It is the wonderful mystery."

Sri Poonja says: *"There is no future, there are no people, there is no earth, there is no one seeking Enlightenment, and no one gaining it. This is the final and only Truth."* (Ref 73) – and you cannot make it much clearer than that! Except that this was not an original insight – Gaudapada made this statement some 1200 years before: *"There is no death, no birth. No one is in worldly bondage, no one is trying to get liberation, no one is seeking it, and no one is liberated either. This is the supreme Truth."* (Mandukya *kArikA* II.32, Ref. 116)

15. The myth of action

'I' do not act

Relax into the moment and let the universe do the driving. Jed McKenna
(Ref. 78)

At the level of understanding of most people in everyday life, we exist as
individuals, having free will, in a world of separate objects and we *know*
that we can act. For example, you could take this book now and throw it out
of the window again. At the level of reality, Advaita tells us that there are
not two things. Books and windows are names and forms of an unchanging
unity and the idea of 'action' is meaningless.

Most of us use a car from time to time to take us from A to B and the
car moves. If asked, we would say that the energy source for the car – that
without which the car would be useless – is petrol. But, in the usual sense
of the word, the petrol does not itself move. Similarly, many devices are
powered by electricity. Refrigerators are made cold but electricity is not
cold; cookers are made hot but electricity is not hot; Fans, CDs etc are
rotated but electricity does not go round and round. These metaphors, also
mentioned earlier in the book, are used extensively by teachers of Advaita.
Similarly, the body is merely a lump of food without the consciousness that
is the Self, which motivates it. The body moves but the Self does not.

Unquestionably, the world around us seems to be in constant motion,
and this includes our bodies – both internally and externally. So, yes, the
body could be said to act – but 'we' do not. Here is a useful practical
example of this: It may be that you cycle from time to time. I enjoy cycling
in the New Forest, where I live – free exercise in beautiful surroundings and
fresh air. However, there are a few hills along the routes, and sometimes
you have to go up these rather than down. Many people just get off and
walk their cycle up. Others take it as some sort of challenge and insist on
trying to cycle to the top without having to dismount. When the going
becomes hard, they make an extra mental effort, along the lines of 'I am

damn well going to get to the top, even if it kills me'! This is the hard way!

Whenever I find myself in this situation, I remember a quotation that my class at the SES organization had to learn from the Bhagavad Gita. It goes like this:

naiva ki~nchitkaromIti yukto manyeta tattvavit
pashya~nshRRiNvanspRRisha~njighrannashnangachChansvapa~nshv
asan
pralapanvisRRijangRRihNannunmiShannimiShannapi
indriyANIndriyArtheShu vartanta iti dhArayan

And, by the time I've remembered it and spoken it in my mind, I'm at the top of the hill! No – that was a joke. Actually, I never remember the complete order of words in the second and third lines, anyway. Seriously, though, the complete translation of these two verses from the Gita (V 8-9) is as follows:

"Believing that it is merely the senses surrounding the objects of sense, though seeing, hearing, touching, smelling, eating, going, sleeping, breathing, talking, mentally grabbing or letting go, even just opening or closing the eyes, the Sage, knowing the true nature of (the Self) should think 'I do nothing at all'."

Swamini Pramananda, a disciple of Swami Dayananda, explains this very clearly (Ref. 81): *"If my sense of 'I' is placed in the consciousness, not in the body-mind, then nothing that the body-mind does belongs to me, the Self. That does not mean that the body-mind will not do anything; it will do what it needs to do. But the doing is not owned by the Self; the Self remains a non-doer. Things happen, things get done. I abide in the Self; there is no doing involved here."*

Its effect, when fully appreciated, is quite remarkable. The person who, gritting his teeth with determination, sets out up the hill with the idea 'I am going to do it', is quite likely to fail. If, on the other hand, you genuinely believe that you are doing nothing at all and you simply watch the legs moving, heart pumping etc, you find that all the 'doing' disappears. The legs move as before but there is no attempted willing involved. You are almost a bystander and the results do not matter. You no longer care whether you make it to the top or not. The whole process becomes effortless and – this is the even more amazing aspect – you are far more likely to get to the top without dismounting! I have observed this for myself time and again.

What do I have to do to be able to accept totally and be absolutely certain that I am not the doer? Obviously nothing! There's nothing I can do, I'm not the doer! Ramesh Balsekar (Ref. 81)

The Self is that which is behind everything but itself does nothing. The Kena Upanishad speaks of it at length. It begins: *"By whom commanded and directed does the mind go towards its objects? Commanded by whom does the life force, the first cause move? At whose will do men utter speech? Which power directs the eye and the ear? It is the ear of the ear, the mind of the mind, the speech of the speech, the life of the life, the eye of the eye. ... There the eye does not go, nor speech, nor mind. We do not know That; we do not understand how it can be taught. It is distinct from the known and also It is beyond the unknown."* (Ref. 9, Part 1 verses 1 – 3.)

The Self is the reality behind all appearances, itself unknowable. It does nothing, but all apparent activity takes place through its power and against its background. We are the Consciousness, which, by virtue of this body-mind instrument, is capable of seeing, hearing, speaking etc. The body-mind sees, hears, speaks and acts but 'we' do not. Everything takes place within this awareness; but the awareness itself, which is what we truly are, is beyond all movement, beyond space and time.

Shankara gives a useful metaphor in his 'Atmabodha' (Ref. 17). He says it is like looking at the movement of clouds on a moonlit night. While we look at the clouds, the moon seems to be moving too. But, as soon as we look directly at the moon, we realize that it is only the clouds moving while the moon itself remains stationary. Similarly, whilst we direct our attention to the body, mind and intellect, we believe that 'we' are doing and moving. As soon as we look from the standpoint of the *Atman*, however, we realize that all of the activities belong only to the body etc. while we, the *Atman*, remain still and detached. Furthermore, just as the clouds themselves are only visible in the first place by virtue of the light from the moon, so too are we are only conscious of the body-mind equipment by virtue of the enlivening power of the Self.

All is always now. Knowledge and experience relate to the 'past'. When we think that '*we* are thinking' or '*we* are doing something', in fact there is only 'thinking' or 'doing'. It is only when memory arises later that there is the thought '*I* was thinking or doing'. At the moment of doing, there is no doer; there is no duality. This fact is the essence of the teachings of the Direct Path adherents, stemming from Nisargadatta, Krishna Menon and others. It is because we think that we are doers that we look for results from our actions in order that we can be 'enjoyers' too. It is this misconception that is behind the path of *karma yoga* as discussed earlier.

Determinism, fate and free will

A man's worst difficulties begin when he is able to do as he likes.
Thomas Huxley

We are free to do whatever we like (in theory, and providing it is legal). The entire system of justice in civilized countries depends upon this. If a murderer had no choice about whether to commit his act or not, how could we hold him responsible? But then we do not hold the tiger morally responsible for killing its victim and eating it – this is the nature of a tiger and we do not believe freedom of choice is an issue here. If you think (or look) back to the discussion on the hierarchy of minerals, plants, animals and man, you will recall that Schumacher identified the factor that differentiated man from animals was 'self-awareness'. Our experience is that, along with self-awareness, goes the ability to 'choose'.

But is it really so? I used to say that I 'had no real choice' about which profession I entered. It seemed that circumstances had always made the key decisions inevitable. Whenever there appeared to be a choice, a retrospective appraisal of the options seemed always to make one of them unavoidable, given my particular nature and outlook at that time. And my current interests were always the result of events in the past – stimulating books I had read, influential people I had met and so on. All of my past experiences at any point in time added up to give a deciding weight to one course of action rather than another and, naturally, the same applied to each of the decisions that had gone before.

Obviously my particular personality, or nature, plays a role in whether or not I 'act' in a given circumstance. Although the interest and desire to act may be present, e.g. to go and talk to an attractive girl at a bus stop, my innate shyness and fear of rejection may prevent this. Isn't this entirely mechanical – a complex but pre-determined summation of all of the 'forces' acting upon me at that moment?

You might object that you could deliberately act 'out of character' in order to refute this. It might be difficult, especially in an example such as that above where reserve might almost literally prevent someone from speaking, but surely it not impossible. But would this be an exercise of free will or would it simply be that the wish to refute the suggestion that there is no free will was another factor in the equation? This factor could be so strong that it tipped the balance in favor of acting out of character.

What about hormones? Almost from moment to moment, it seems we are potentially subject to swings of emotion as a result of hormones in the bloodstream. If a situation is encountered that is perceived as threatening, as a result of those past experiences again, the pituitary signals the adrenal gland to pump adrenaline and cortisol into the blood. This readies the muscles for immediate response, if this should prove necessary – 'fight or flight' and many other things. Hormones such as testosterone, estrogen and progesterone play havoc with our emotions at puberty and other times. Even something as simple as a flight across the Atlantic can upset our 'internal clocks' for several weeks, even though 'we' have apparently done nothing. Levels of melatonin increase in response to diminishing levels of daylight to prepare our bodies for sleep. And there is much more about which endocrinologists are still learning.

All human things are subject to decay,

15. The myth of action

And, when fate summons, monarchs must obey. John Dryden

Where is the free will in any of this? It was mentioned in the section on thinking that we do not 'think' thoughts. Thoughts arrive, as it were, 'from the ether' and we merely react to them. Alan Jacobs speaks of this in his essay written in the form of a Socratic dialogue (Ref. 38). In it, 'Socrates' makes the following statements:

> *"A thought arrives from nowhere, touches the mind which reacts according to its patterns of education and what it believes to be the right response, and some more thought weighs the matter up.*
>
> *"What happens if you watch... is that the mind or thoughts present alternatives, and according to your disposition you choose what you consider to be the most practical, pleasurable and in the best interest for you.*
>
> *"The choice happens mechanically, like an abacus, and the mind foolishly ascribes it to itself as 'a free agent', boasting arrogantly 'I choose'.*
>
> *"In fact there was never any freedom to choose anything other than that which was chosen."*

Whether or not you think this means you are not 'free' depends upon what you understand by the word. It may be true that all of your decisions are the outcome of pre-conditioning. In a given situation, however, you still have to make a choice and the outcome will depend upon which course of action is chosen. Although a computer, programmed with all of your past history and genetic makeup might be able to predict which choice you will make, this is not the same as saying that the outcome will be the same regardless of which choice you make. I.e. determinism is not the same as fatalism. What happens still depends upon what you do and, if this is how you choose to define the word, you still have freedom.

Also, if you think what it would mean if we could act in ways that were not caused by any prior events, you might find the idea less attractive than

209

it initially appears. It would mean that people could behave totally out of character. If your dear, reclusive old granny suddenly, and for no apparent reason, mortgaged her house and bought an Aston Martin, you would probably conclude that she had become senile rather than that she was exercising her free will. More seriously, what would such a mechanism mean for morality and responsibility? We rely on being able to influence people's behavior through example and education so that, when they themselves come to act, they will be able to draw on this teaching to enable them to reach a decision.

It would not, in any case, really make any sense to do something for no reason whatsoever and, if there is a motivation for doing it, i.e. in order to achieve a particular result, then this is effectively a cause. But, if that motivation is a result of our past conditioning, i.e. we have been 'brought up' to like some things rather than others, then it cannot really be thought of as entirely 'free' will.

So, do we have free will or not? It must be one or the other – or must it? It would certainly seem that, if one way of looking at things is true, the opposite way cannot also be true. But, accepting that reality is beyond the intellect, it must presumably also be beyond simple logic. Perhaps it is equivalent to thinking of a signpost in a two-dimensional world. If it is pointing North, we clearly cannot get to the desired destination by travelling South. But, if the space is three-dimensional and the surface is spherical, then we certainly *do* get to the same place, even if it takes a bit longer.

There certainly seems to be a difference between the behavior of plants and animals as opposed to humans, and that relates to predictability and limits. This 'hierarchy' was mentioned early in the book. Plants and animals cannot transgress clear boundaries. The tiger cannot choose to become a vegetarian – it does not seem to have any free will. The behavior of pets can only be changed by rigorous and continued discipline in the form of punishment and reward. But it seems that humans do have some capability for behaving contrary to their own innate desires, and we tend to construe this as 'free will'.

Someone who is often quoted on the subject of free will is Benjamin

Libet. In the first edition of this book, there was only a short paragraph on this. But it seems to provide fairly conclusive scientific evidence indicating the illusory nature of free will so I will quote here a much lengthier exposition that I gave in 'How to Meet Yourself' (Ref. 71):

Although the brain is still little understood, much has been investigated over the past century, for example during open surgery on the brain while the patient is still conscious. Probes have been inserted into different parts and stimulated electrically, while asking the patient what he feels. Conversely, electrical activity from the brain can be measured while the patient is listening to music or recognizing colors and so on. Neuroscientists have observed the behavior of people who have suffered damage in specific locations within the brain and lost the capacity for certain functions. In these ways, scientists have made crude maps showing which parts of the brain are responsible for which senses or processes. Thus, that part responsible for initiating action is known with some certainty, even if the detailed mechanism is not under-stood.

What Libet found was that there is always a clearly detectable change in electrical potential on the scalp in the area of the brain responsible for action. This occurs between half to one second before any so-called voluntary action. He called this the "Readiness Potential" or RP. The simple experiment that he carried out was to ask the subject to move a finger. One instrument detected the RP and another detected the electrical activity of the finger muscle. The third measure was to ask the subject to state the time indicated by a clock at the point when they decided to move their finger.

On the face of it, the outcome is intuitively obvious. What one would expect to happen is that the subject decides to press a button at time X, then the RP is detected at time $X + t_1$ sec and finally the muscle trigger is detected at time $X + t_1 + t_2$. Obviously we have to decide to do something before we actually do it. How can there even be anything to test here? Equally obviously, the very fact that I am describing this experiment means that the results cannot have been straightforward.

Well actually, they were straightforward, just the complete opposite of what common sense would tell us. What was found consistently was that the reported decision to move the finger occurred more than half a second after the readiness potential had been detected (allowance was, of course, made for any delay in reporting the clock time).

The implications of this are staggering, namely that our supposed free will is an illusion. We never choose to do anything at all. We merely believe that we have freely chosen to do something after it has already happened by some mechanism that excludes our choosing, conscious or otherwise.

The process that has been proposed by a subsequent researcher, Daniel Wegner, is that any action, A, is directly triggered by a subconscious event, X. The event X, however, simultaneously gives rise to another subconscious event, Y. It is Y that is the cause of the conscious thought and decision to act, D. Thus there are two separate sequences of event: $X \rightarrow A$ is the actual subconscious cause-to-action process; $X \rightarrow Y \rightarrow D$ is the subconscious origin of the conscious decision. Because D occurs before A, we imagine that D causes A; we thus have the illusion of free will.

This is perfectly reasonable. After all, as the philosopher David Hume pointed out, the very idea of cause and effect only really means that, over many observations, we consistently observe that when the cause occurs, the effect always seems to follow. It is perfectly possible that the next observation of the cause will not be followed by the same effect. Because our actions always follow the awareness of a 'deciding' thought, we erroneously think that we have free will.

Lest you begin to despair at this point, let me reassure you that from the practical point of view, nothing has changed. Libet's experiment did not throw into doubt the feeling of free-will that we have. It only demonstrated that it does not actually function in the way that we would expect. We will still continue to act as though we have choice because that is how we feel. Indeed, despite the fact that these experiments were conducted in 1985, most people are quite unaware of them and probably most of those who are aware continue with their lives as if they were not.

It is part of what we are as human beings that we behave as though we have free-will and believe that we do. It is not difficult to imagine that the process (of believing we have free will etc.) has some survival value and has developed as part of natural selection. Ultimately, of course, it is the ego that believes it has free will and, since we have already seen that the ego is an illusion, it should cause no additional concern to learn that free will is also an illusion.

This is fine, of course, from an Advaita point of view. But is it fine from the man-in-the-street's viewpoint? Well, it makes no difference of course to his life, which will almost certainly carry on as before. It is regarded as an interesting curiosity and then forgotten. Whether the experiment is actually demonstrating what it appears to be is another matter. There have been several papers claiming to refute the conclusions but his experiments are still being cited. In fact, even as I write this, there has been a recent article in Scientific American (Nov. 2009, Ref. 142) in which it was reported that brain surgeons have 'evoked the intention to act' during surgery. Electrical stimulation of parts of the brain is necessary during operations to remove, for example, cancerous tissue. The patient has to be conscious so that he may report what is felt, so as to minimize the risk of removing vital parts. The article indicates that patients have reported feeling the 'urge to move' parts of their body (whether or not they subsequently did). This would tie in with Wegner's proposed mechanism of the 'decision to act' being the result of a subconscious event prior to any 'willing'.

But irrespective of whether or not these conclusions are true, our *experience* is effectively what we mean by the term free will. If they are true, however, what it means is that the 'feeling' of having free will is only a 'side effect' arising in the brain after it has initiated some action in automatic response to a combination of stimuli.

So we do have free will in one sense and do not have it in another. These statements can both be true. It merely depends upon the context in which it is being discussed. And this is precisely equivalent to talking about the *vyAvahArika* or *pAramArthika* levels of reality. The individual feels that he has free will and, indeed can be regarded as having it. The extent to which he is able to exercise it depends upon his past actions, the habits that have formed and so on. This is the level of the relative world of appearances. In reality, there is no individual or anyone 'acting' so the question of free will does not arise. We can allow the illusory ego its illusory free will within the constraints of its illusory *karma*. Indeed, the feeling of having free will and the belief that I am a separate individual may just be related.

Note that the absence of free will does not entail absence of the feeling of responsibility, because the vast majority of people *believe* that they have free will. And, although I don't, I do not therefore indulge in irresponsible actions because that is not my nature. As Ramakrishna is reported to have said, "Don't believe in free will but act as though you do".

Since the early days of Quantum Mechanics, when Heisenberg postulated his famous 'Uncertainty Principle', the behavior of sub-atomic particles has been used to try to extricate us from the logic of the above analysis. Prior to this, it seemed that science had to back up these sorts of conclusions. After all, it was believed that every 'effect' had to have a 'cause'– things did not just happen without any rhyme or reason. Ever since Aristotle, the common belief had grown up that everything could be explained by science. If it hadn't been yet, it was only because the techniques to study the related phenomena were not yet sufficiently sophisticated.

Philosophers seized on these ideas to try to justify their feelings that our lives could not be pre-determined, that we must be capable of free will. Unfortunately, although Heisenberg's theories have been shown to have predictive capability (the next best thing to being proven), and have led to such tools as the tunneling electron microscope, they are really only applicable at the sub-atomic level. The problem is that, although we have uncertainty about *particular* particles, once we get millions of them together, as in the gross matter with which we are familiar, probability takes over and the overall behavior becomes quite predictable.

And so we are back to the position of living out a mechanical, cause and effect existence. If, at the time of our birth we could:

a) be aware of all of the situations that would be encountered;

b) understand totally our genetic make-up;
c) understand what this means in terms of the multiplicity of physical
   and mental characteristics,

then we could know the entire course of our lives from day one.

So what does Advaita have to say on the matter? When we talk about the apparent individual – the *jIva* – there is certainly the appearance of free will. Traditionally, there is a choice between continuing to pursue one's desires, and being subjected to the eternal round of birth and death (*saMsAra*), or turning towards higher things, following a spiritual path leading towards the Self (*sAdhana*). Only if this is so can we be effectively responsible for our actions and therefore add to or subtract from our future *saMskAra*. Only in this scenario does the concept of *karma* – reaping the consequences of our action – become meaningful.

Yet, in order for *karma* to operate, there has to be an inescapable chain of cause and effect, even if the effects of a given cause do not materialize until a later life. Thus, even within this view, at the level of illusory existence, there seems to be a contradiction. I.e. we are free to choose but the consequences, including those factors that will influence our future ability to choose, will inevitably follow.

In *reality* in contrast, Advaita explains that there is no free will, because there is no individual to choose in the first place (and there is no doer anyway, as will be demonstrated shortly in the section on 'Apparent Contradictions in Advaita'). There are no actions and therefore no results. All is illusory. Unfortunately, knowing that we are dreaming does not mean, per se, that we are able to wake ourselves up.

So are we not 'free' in any sense? Well, it comes back to the main question of this book – What do we mean by 'I'? In the phenomenal world of appearances, the 'person' is not free; the ego is driven by all of its desires and attachments, effectively out of control. But then there is no 'person', is there? It is literally a 'mask'. The real Self is totally unaffected by any of this. It is always totally free. We, the Self, are free to recognize this at any and all times, to stand back, as it were, and just enjoy the play. (Remember that the nature of the Self is pure bliss, not dependent upon any external object or event for its enjoyment, unlimited in any way whatsoever.) And do not most plays have a script? Their outcome is entirely pre-determined. In fact, we might not enjoy them quite so much if they were not. It would not be quite the same if Romeo married Juliet and they lived happily ever after.

Also, thinking again about the concept of *līlā* that we discussed earlier, from the point of view of the 'individual' it is necessary that we *do* act as though we had free will. If this apparent creation and its apparent inhabitants have been brought into existence so that God can enjoy Himself by pretending to be separate beings, these beings have to believe that they have free will. Otherwise this purpose would not be served. The illusion that we are separate entities is the very thing that maintains the play. And the belief that we have free will plays a large part in maintaining our illusion that we exist as independent persons.

A final way of resolving the dilemma is to think about it in terms of the extent that we are in the present and directing our attention, i.e. using *buddhi* rather than *manas*. If we are 'miles away', we have already discussed how we go onto 'automatic pilot' – *manas* is in control and we do things mechanically, in a pre-determined way. On the other hand, if we are alert, there is the opportunity for buddhi to 'choose' between various possible courses of action, according to which is perceive as most appropriate. Although this act of choosing may still be 'mechanical', in the sense that it is determined by what we have learned in the past, the nature of the action is clearly quite different. In stillness, other factors such as morality and *dharma* can influence the outcome. Discrimination, as opposed to habit, is the driving force.

Another look at cause and effect

The effective conclusion, then, is that there is no such thing as free will, even in the phenomenal realm; that all of the so-called discriminations made by *buddhi* are the result of the deterministic influences of nature and nurture. You will appreciate that this seems somewhat in conflict with the idea behind *karma yoga*. What is the point of a practice that requires us to act in one way rather than another if we have no choice in the matter?

Furthermore, I have said that cause and effect are only concepts, similar to those of time and space, by which we try to make sense of the world-appearance. How can we rationalize these apparent contradictions?

David Bohm was a theoretical physicist who also had a long relationship with J. Krishnamurti. (Krishnamurti was an Indian educated in England and explicitly groomed for the role of a spiritual teacher by Annie Besant of the Theosophical Society. He became the head of a large popular movement and taught non-dual philosophy.) Amongst other things, he devised a theory in which he refers to an 'implicate' order of things as being the unified reality of an apparently diverse 'explicate' order. I mention this in passing because of a specific experiment that he devised (Ref. 34):

He placed two cameras in front of adjacent sides of a tank containing a single fish. In another room a child, i.e. a naïve observer, sat in front of two televisions, one connected to each camera. The observer, unaware that the screens showed different views of the same fish, could see that, when one fish moved or turned so did the other. The observer concluded that there was a cause and effect relation between the two. Because the movements were simultaneous, however, he was unable to say which was cause and which effect. The apparent, observed multiple phenomena are the 'explicate order', equating to the phenomenal realm of Kant or *vyAvahArika*, and the single reality of one fish is the 'implicate order', equating to the noumenal or *pAramArthika*.

Of course, this reflects upon the comments made earlier. Once the reality is known, the need for causality to make sense of the phenomenal world disappears. We can accept that the notion of causality is simply a way of looking at the world in order to make sense of it, while we are still in a state of ignorance. Once that ignorance is removed, we no longer need to talk of our actions, including 'decisions', as effects following upon previous actions and conditionings etc. They are all simply differing viewpoints of the unified reality, which is always only *brahman*.

Does this then mean that 'free will' becomes possible again? Not really. Everything in the explicate order is a manifestation of the implicate. An analogy that Bohm draws is that the explicate or phenomenal is like part of a hologram. If you take a hologram and break it into many pieces, each piece will still show the complete picture, just at a lower resolution. The suggested analogy is that the noumenal contains the complete picture, as it were, and this is all present *now* in full detail. I.e. everything is pre-determined i.e. no choice, no free will; everything that will happen is 'destined' to happen.

One of the many lessons that one learns in prison is that things are what they are and will be what they will be. Oscar Wilde

Ramesh Balsekar, whose principal teaching was the lack of free will, used the metaphor of a painting. Wayne Liquorman (Ref. 28) calls it the 'fifty mile painting'. He says we should imagine standing in front of this enormous painting, so big that we can only see a bit at a time. We move across looking at one section at a time and, as we move to the next part, we have the sense that the earlier part, which we can no longer see, 'caused' the present part. And so we move on through time viewing 'later' sections of the painting. In fact, if we were able to step back far enough, we would be able to see that there is just one painting and it is complete *now*. All of the actions have always been there. Predetermination does not apply, other than as a concept when we view it one piece at a time.

The trouble with metaphors in general is that they are only trying to trigger an intuitive understanding based upon a very crude analogy, since the actual subject is beyond simple description. As soon as we try to take the analogy too far or use it in a slightly different way, it is in great danger of breaking down or, worse still, becoming confusing or misleading. Once the intuition has been gained, the metaphor should be discarded before this happens.

The optimum way of looking at it is probably to acknowledge the theory of *karma* and *saMskAra* etc, whilst we are in this intermediate state of not knowing quite what is true. It can serve as a useful guide as to how we should endeavor to act in this world. It is, after all, how things 'appear' to be. There appears to be a world; we appear to be a person; it seems as though there are things with which we interact and so, logically, it is useful to have such a theory to guide us in how, *practically speaking*, we should act. Having accepted this, we can then acknowledge *intellectually* that, in reality (which we do not yet know, and cannot through mind or senses), we do nothing. Things 'happen' and we are ultimately just the impartial witnesses of their happening. In this way then, we can 'play the game', following the rules of the game. I.e. act in this way, rather than that, yet know at the same time that it is *only* a game and no one is going to win or lose.

In fact, there can only ever be a conflict between *two* things. If we look at a given situation and ask whether the outcome was the result of fate or free will, we inevitably have a problem. As was seen when we discussed *saMskAra* earlier, the situations in which we find ourselves are the manifestations of the fruit of past actions, i.e. our 'fate' is of our own making – our 'past *karma*'. 'Free will' is our current response to those situations, i.e. effectively our 'present *karma*'. If they are both aspects of *karma*, they are not essentially two different things and there is no conflict. Action in the moment is driven by both, and the outcome will depend upon which is the stronger. For example, a man whose life has been spent as a pickpocket and thief may come upon someone who has fallen ill in an otherwise empty street. In that moment, he may be aware of the choice of either helping the person or of robbing him and running away. All of his past *karma* would tend to force him into the latter action and it would be very difficult to exercise free will and overcome those tendencies. Fortunately, we are unaware of the complete nature and extent of our past *karma*; otherwise we might not even attempt to act in contravention of it.

The extent to which one believes that one can exert effort (*puruShArtha*) to overcome the effects of past actions (*karmaphala*) depends upon the extent to which we are still ruled by the ego. The ego believes in choice and effort (I will get up this hill); in reality the ego does not exist and neither does choice or effort. In realizing the truth, one comes to recognize that the freedom is not *in* choice but *from* choice.

All of this can be viewed using the jello model again. Past *karma* is represented by the existing grooves; present free will is our attempt to force the new trickle of water down a chosen path. If, despite our attempts, the water follows the old grooves, this means that, in the past, those grooves were where our free will once chose to send the water. That has now accumulated considerable past *saMskAra* that will tend to send the water in the same direction again. We will need to keep trying until the past *saMskAra* has been burnt up, i.e. until the old grooves have become more faint as a result of continually trying to force the water in our newly chosen direction. Remember also Swami Chinmayananda's metaphor of the motor boat discussed in the section on *karma* – we can always steer against the current, even when that current is strong.

One final slant on this topic is that the one Self (which we are), being without limit, must be free. No 'object' could ever have free will but every 'thing' is an appearance within and an affirmation of the Self. As has already been mentioned, everything that happens does so by virtue of the 'petrol-in-the-car' of Consciousness but Consciousness has nothing to do with those actions. Consciousness powers the act of the torturer as well as that of the surgeon. This is perfectly logical, if a little difficult for the egotistic mind to accept. Complete free will implies lack of motivation and spontaneous, uncaused action. Since we have agreed above that all activity is effect from prior causes, the only action that could be completely free would be 'first-cause' action, i.e. the action of 'God' or the Absolute. The appearances can never have free will *because* they are only appearances but the Self is always without limitation of any kind.

Once we have become enlightened, we still see the illusion but now know it as such. Now we are free to enjoy the play, knowing that we are only the witness, and remain totally unaffected by any of the events, however delightful or terrible, despite the fact that this actor in the play is following his script, as every good actor should…

As Shakespeare said:

Our revels are now ended. These our actors
As I foretold you, are all of the spirit, and
Are melted into air, into thin air:
And, like the baseless fabric of this vision,

The cloud-capp'd towers, the gorgeous palaces,
The solemn temples, the great globe itself,
Yea, all which it inherit, shall dissolve,
And, like this insubstantial pageant faded,
Leave not a rack behind. We are such stuff
As dreams are made on; and our little life
Is rounded with a sleep. 'The Tempest' Act 4, Scene 1

Apparent Contradictions in Advaita

Hopefully you are beginning to feel less concerned now, when you encounter seeming contradictions in what is being said at various points in the book. I was going to include a warning at the beginning to the effect that you, the reader, should not be surprised to find this but I thought it might put you off to admit this so early. In fact, this has been pointed out with respect to many Sages, for example Ramana Maharshi and Nisargadatta Maharaj, to name two of the most prominent ones of recent history. They would often say one thing to one person in the morning and quite the opposite to another in the afternoon. The point is that they were able to discern the mental state and spiritual 'advancement' of the enquirer and know which ideas would be most useful to them at that time. In fact, they were perfectly well aware and made no secret of the fact that a) there was no person to become enlightened anyway and b) the nature of reality is beyond any sort of description. If you recall the section on *j~nAna yoga* and the metaphor of the thorn to remove a thorn, it becomes quite reasonable to supplant one theory by another, knowing that both are false, as long as the new one brings us a little closer to the actual truth.

The belief in an external God is of value to a certain type of person in *bhakti yoga*. It helps them to surrender their egotistic feelings by revering an assumed higher being. In *karma yoga*, we believe in free will and action so that we may improve the discriminatory power of *buddhi* and increase the level of *sattva* in our being. Belief in *karma*, supported by the theory of *saMskAra*, enables us notionally to progress from someone who reacts automatically, to someone who responds appropriately without selfish considerations. Again, this reduces the dominion of the ego and thereby removes some of the ignorance that is covering the Self. Once we begin to try to say how things *really* are, we come up against the impossible. *All* of the things that can be said are ultimately false and this is only compounded by the fact that language itself is so woefully inadequate. As soon as we start talking about a 'person' 'doing' 'anything', we have already mentioned three illusions.

In the ultimate, and perfectly logical analysis, there can be no such thing as 'doing', 'enjoying' or 'knowing'. (The following argument is made by Shankara in his *brahma sutra bhAShya* I.ii.12, though I am indebted to Swami Paramarthananda for the explanation in his recorded talks.) From the standpoint of the world, there are two things: *Atman*, or Consciousness, and everything else (*anAtman*). The process of doing something (or enjoying or knowing something) necessitates that some sort of change take place. We move from a state of 'not knowing' to one of 'knowing' for example. It follows, therefore, that whoever or whatever 'does', 'knows' or 'enjoys' has to be subject to modification. 'Change' in Sanskrit is called *vikAra* (transformation, modification, change of form or nature). Something that undergoes change is called *savikAra* – 'with change'; something that cannot undergo any change is called *nirvikAra* – 'without change'.

When we discuss the nature of the Self in chapter 17, we will see that it is eternal, unlimited and *ever the same* – it is *nirvikAra*. It is only the limited, finite, apparently separate things of the world that are born, grow, decay and die, i.e. undergo change – they are *savikAra*.

If you think about it you will appreciate that, in order to do, enjoy, experience, know etc, I also have to be conscious and intelligent – *chetana* in Sanskrit. So it follows that there are two conditions for the doer, enjoyer etc: firstly it has to be conscious and secondly it has to be able to change – it has to be *chetana-savikAra*. But, to go back to the beginning of this discussion, there are only two things – *Atman*, which is *chetana-nirvikAra*, and *anAtman*, which is *achetana-savikAra* (inanimate things have no consciousness of their own). Consequently, there can be no such thing as a knower, enjoyer, experiencer, thinker...

Unfortunately, language is our principal means for communication (and the only one for a writer and his reader!) so that we have to recognize the difficulties and try to explain them, using stories and metaphor to enable an intuition of the actual truth. This is also the reason why poetry can succeed where straight, logical argument may fail. Poetry can approach the subject obliquely, appeal directly to the heart and bypass the mind with its limited, linear mode of operation. This can be seen in the lines from Shakespeare and others that have been quoted, for example, and other countries have their own masters. The Sufi tradition has Jalaludin Rumi and India has its Nobel prize winning writer, Rabindranath Tagore.

Here is an extract from Rumi:

The lamps are different but the Light is the same, it comes from Beyond;
If thou keep looking at the lamp, thou art lost;
for thence arises the appearance of number and plurality;
Fix the gaze upon the Light and thou art divested from the dualism,
inherent in the finite body;
O Thou who art the kernel of existence, the disagreement between
Muslim, Zoroastrian and Jew depend upon the stand- point.

There is one final topic that needs to be considered before reaching the culmination of this teaching and looking in detail at the nature of our true Self and the process that takes place in realizing this. We must have a closer look at the 'states of consciousness' that we believe we 'experience' or 'pass through'. What does Advaita have to say about waking, dream and deep-sleep states and where does our Self stand with respect to these? And what about that most feared of 'states' – death? What exactly happens to 'us' then and thereafter?

16. Consciousness

What do we actually mean by the word 'conscious'? It derives from the Latin '*con scire*' meaning 'to know with' and it originally referred to the insights that were shared with other people, i.e. knowledge in the sense of truths, not information. Later, it came to be used when talking about knowledge that was, to some degree, secret, shared only amongst a few. Even by the first century AD it was being used for private knowledge, known only to the individual. When the Latin was absorbed into the English language, it was used to create two words. 'Conscious' was used to refer to private thoughts and emotions, which no one else could share directly and 'conscience' was used for private knowledge deliberately withheld from others and therefore likely to make one feel guilty. (This analysis is from Ref. 66.) Here again then, we have an example of a word whose current usage is now the opposite of its original meaning. Instead of sharing with others, we are keeping it to ourselves.

Nevertheless, we think we know what consciousness is. We are fully conscious when we are awake. We become *un*conscious if we are knocked out or given a general anesthetic and when we are in a deep sleep. And dreaming is somewhere in between, isn't it? We might suggest that there are some other states, such as hypnosis, meditative trance or drug-induced hallucination and we would almost certainly claim that consciousness ceases altogether when we die. If pressed, we might argue that it is something that has evolved in step with increasing complexity of the brain; that it is something that plants do not have, animals have a little and us a lot. When it comes to the crunch, we would probably concede that we really do not have any solid ideas about what it actually is, though we would be in no doubt at all that we have it.

On the face of it, you will be reassured that Advaita agrees with our experiential observation that we are usually aware of three basic states viz. waking, dreaming and deep sleep. As you will also have expected by now, however, the philosophy's description of these states is not quite how we might have described them.

The Upanishad that deals in the greatest depth with the subject is the Mandukya, with its *kArikA* by Gaudapada. We know now, or to be strictly honest with ourselves, we know that this philosophy *says* that there is only One Self, *Atman* or *brahman*. Nevertheless, this appears to manifest in various ways and the Sages and scriptures have to work backwards, through negation and inference in order to 'explain' or enable us to intuit the nature of reality. This Upanishad demonstrates how it is the same Consciousness that functions throughout and 'witnesses' all three states of waking, dream and deep sleep. It uses the states of consciousness in order to 'talk about' reality and begins by saying that the manifestation has four facets or aspects. (In fact the Upanishad itself, as distinguished from the commentary, is very short and uses the *mantra* 'OM' as a very powerful metaphor to explain all of this. However, since it would necessitate a substantial diversion into Sanskrit to benefit from this, I will ignore it here. My book 'OM: Key to the Universe' will cover all this if I ever find time to write it...)

The first of these states is called *jAgrat*. This is the waking state and the waker-ego, called *vishva*, is conscious of the gross, physical, external world of sense objects. In the waking state, the 'individual' is complete (*vishva* = whole) with all its faculties of senses and mind.

The second state is called *svapna*, meaning 'sleep', but only for the body – the mind remains active. This is the dreaming state and the dreamer is called *taijasa*. In this, the dreamer is conscious of the subtle or internal world of objects, i.e. thoughts, feelings etc. but is unaware of the external world. In the dreaming state, Consciousness effectively projects the world of the dream from its own 'light' and the dream 'consists' of this 'light' of the mind (*taijasa* = 'originating from or consisting of light').

The third aspect is *suShupti*, meaning 'excellent rest' since both body and mind are now resting in the deep-sleep state. The sleeper-ego is called *prAj~na*, literally meaning 'intelligent', 'wise' or 'intelligence'. In the deep-sleep state, the sleeper sees neither the external nor internal worlds of objects. The senses and mind are inactive and nothing is experienced, i.e. there is no perception or conception. The state is governed by ignorance (*avidyA)* but there must be some vestige of awareness since, for example, if someone calls our name, we will probably wake up. During this state there is no 'knowing' of anything nor appearances of any kind. *prAj~na* can also be translated as 'the one who is nearly ignorant'. Because Consciousness is still present, the self is not totally ignorant, but nearly ignorant. It is said to be a state of pure consciousness and bliss, precisely because there is no mental agitation but, since there is no knowledge, we are not directly aware of this. It is said that here the Self is identified with *avidyA*.

The fourth aspect is not actually a 'state' at all – it is called *turIya* – and it is characterized by neither ignorance nor error. But I will not say anything more about this for the moment; it is not something with which most of us are familiar.

The pure consciousness of deep sleep can be considered to emerge, either to illuminate the subtle world of thoughts and emotions, as we become the dreamer, or to illuminate the external world, as we become the waker. In deep sleep, there is only ignorance – we do not also misperceive the world, mistaking a rope for a snake for example, because there is no perception at all. There is thus ignorance but no error or misperception. This non-apprehension is the same as the 'veiling power' of *mAyA* – *AvaraNa*. In dreaming and waking, the ignorance is still there but, with the mind and senses now active, we additionally fall into error – we misapprehend reality. This misapprehension 'effect' follows from the ignorance 'cause' of non-apprehension. Misapprehension is *vikShepa*, described earlier as the projecting power of *mAyA*.

If we could see the rope, we would not mistake it for a snake. The misapprehension occurs under the conditions in which there is partial ignorance – we can see that there is *something* there but not sufficiently clearly to make out that it is a rope. Thus, the (partial) ignorance is the effective *cause* for the error. (Note that, if there is total ignorance – i.e. we cannot see anything at all – there is no error either. We cannot see the rope in order to mistake it for a snake. Hence the expression 'ignorance is bliss'!) This explains why the deep-sleep state is known as the 'causal' state. In that ignorance is the potentiality for all manifestation in the dream and waking states.

Consciousness is that in which all else appears. It is there when there appears to be nothing. It can be thought of as the silence between thoughts or as the screen, upon which the movie of life is projected, unaffected by all, yet without which there would be nothing. Sri Poonja asked what we would see if he put up a blackboard the size of the wall and marked a small white spot in the middle of it. Ninety nine percent of people, he said, would say that they saw a white spot. Almost invisible, this is what draws our attention such that we do not even see the big blackboard. It is in our nature to look for objects against the background and ignore the background itself. In just the same way, we see a cloud in the sky and miss the sky. And we see the thought arising in Consciousness and know nothing about Consciousness itself.

It is inevitable that our minds will search for an understanding of what consciousness is, as though it were an object that we could observe, rather than that which enables observation to occur in the first place. All theories that we may come up with are going to fail and, worse, may delude us into thinking that we know something when we do not.

Ultimately, the scriptures summarize the matter very simply in one of the four great sayings or *mahAvAkya-s* from the Upanishads: *praj~nAnam brahma* – Consciousness is *brahman*. Consciousness equates to *brahman*, which is the one reality, all that there is. (The four 'great sayings' from the Vedas are: – *'Consciousness is brahman'* from the Aitareya Upanishad, *'That thou art'* from the Chandogya Upanishad, *'This Self is brahman'* from the Mandukya Upanishad and *'I am brahman'* from the Brihadaranyaka Upanishad.)

Before looking in more detail at the three states of consciousness, it is important to note that all of these explanations are made from the vantage point of the waking mind. Strictly speaking, it can only speak *from experience* about the waking state, since it is, by definition, not present in the other states. The true situation is summed up in the Katha Upanishad (IV.4): *"Having realized that it is the great, all-pervading Atman that sees the objects in the dream and the waking state, the wise man does not grieve."*

Dream state

In the dream-state, we are aware of many things but all of these are manufactured by our own mind. Whole worlds are created with their own space, time and causal rules. We may be 'ourselves', by the standards of waking consciousness, or someone else whose behavior and capabilities bear no relationship to our waking abilities or inhibitions. Apart from the relatively rare occurrence of a lucid dream, when one realizes that one is dreaming and is able to consciously direct events, most dreams, however ridiculous to waking analysis, seem perfectly real at the time. Our dream-ego will have its own life history, as will other characters in the dream. All appears solid and real and is understood and responded to in a way that seems perfectly normal. Even the most improbable situations are accepted without question. Only a couple of nights ago at the time of writing this, I was quite unsurprised to encounter a frozen, baby hippopotamus upside down in the kitchen sink. Goodness knows where that image came from!

The higher functions of mind – the logical delivery of *manas* and the discriminative faculties of *buddhi* – are resting, or at a low level of activity, so that events and thoughts that would be questioned in waking life are accepted without challenge. Desires that would be subdued are allowed to blossom. Thus it is that Freud and others were able to form their theories to understand the workings of the 'subconscious' mind etc, and thereby better understand the repressions and behavior of the waking mind.

The dream experience is perfectly self-consistent to the dreamer. It is only when we wake up that we are able to say 'how ridiculous'. But then it is the waker-ego that is making that judgment, not the dreamer-ego. Each state is consistent in its own sphere – *jAgrat* is acceptable to *vishva* and *svapna* to *taijasa*. This view differs from that of Descartes, who argues that the waking experience is more consistent than the dream. What he clearly meant is that, *from the vantage point of the waking state*, the waking experience is more consistent. And there is no argument with the latter statement.

Different authors have made use of a number of what could be considered to be separate theories of dreaming, as pointed out by Indich (Ref. 1). The 'presentative' theory says the mind produces the dream images in response to *saMskAra-s*, based on past experiences. The 'representative' theory says it is the recollection of previously perceived objects or impressions i.e. from memory. The 'wish-fulfillment' theory says that dreams are motivated by desires or *vAsanA-s*. 'Prophetic' dreams stem from good or bad deeds performed in the past by the individual. These last two tie in with the karmic theory whereby actions in the past determine events in the future.

The key point to note is that, when we wake up from a dream, we know immediately that the dream was false – it is sublated by the waking experience.

Waking state

There are several stories, essentially the same but from various traditions, which question the relative realities of the waking and dreaming states. In the Chinese Tao philosophy, the Emperor dreamed that he was a butterfly and then, awakening, wonders whether he is in fact a butterfly dreaming he is the Emperor. The Indian version concerns King Janaka, who had a very realistic and frightening dream that he was a starving beggar. When he awoke, he had doubts about whether he was the king who had just dreamt he was a beggar or whether he really was a beggar, now dreaming he was the king. This story goes on to describe how he summoned his advisors to clarify his quandary but to no avail. It required the Sage Astavakra, the eponymous teacher of the Astavakra Gita, to explain that he was neither the king nor the beggar but the one Self.

However, for the purposes of this section, the reason for quoting the story is to get you to ask yourselves exactly what the differences are between the waking and the dream state that you are able to call the former real and the latter unreal. You will be forced to concede that, whilst you are dreaming (lucid dreams apart), you firmly believe that the dream is real. Or at least you do not question the reality of the dream – it is accepted at its face value. The images of the dream present themselves to consciousness and you, the dreamer ego, play out a role with the other characters in the dream as if they were real. You, the dreamer ego, believe yourself to be the only 'subject', with all of the other dream characters and things being separate objects in that world which, at the time, is the only world you know. At no time does it occur to you that all of the characters and objects, including your dream self, are imaginations of your mind. It is only when you awake that the dream, seen from the vantage point of waking consciousness, is known to have been unreal – only an appearance in the consciousness of your dreaming mind, and with the entire dream world fashioned from your own mind-stuff.

This sort of analysis, incidentally, makes it easier to appreciate how your ordinary sense of self – your waker ego – can be illusory. You know that this sense of yourself in your dreams – the dream ego, *taijasa* – is every bit as real *at the time*, as your waker ego, *vishva*, seems to you now. And yet, you are perfectly happy to discard it instantly when you awake.

So what is special about the waking state? Objects and people, thoughts and feelings appear to your waking consciousness in exactly the same manner. Here you, the waker ego, play out a similar role with other waking-state characters and objects and you believe yourself to be the subject, separate from all of the other characters and objects in this world, the only one you are aware of. Can you think of any difference that would justify your calling these appearances 'real'? Remember that this is now your waker-ego in the waking state. Obviously *it* can condemn the dreams as unreal but, at the time of the dreams, it was the dreamer-ego that believed them to be true. How can you know that a further stage of awakening is not possible that will sublate the appearances of waking consciousness? If a character in your dream asked you whether you were actually asleep or not, what do you think you, the dreamer would answer? You might even pinch yourself in the dream, thereby proving to yourself and your questioner that you are awake.

The sort of response this is likely to trigger is that dreams are often of impossible things, such as flying or lifting a house or that, for example, the objects in the dream have no utility – a dream meal will not satisfy our hunger. But these are arguments from the vantage point of the waker. The activities in the dream clearly are *not* impossible to the dreamer. He really does lift up the house. The dream meal is perfectly satisfying to the dreamer. And we could equally well argue that waking objects have no utility in the dream world. E.g. we cannot use our waking car to travel to a dream destination. In order to be able to arbitrate justly on these matters, the judge would have to stand outside of both waking and dreaming states. Since we cannot be simultaneously aware of both states, we cannot draw any independent conclusions.

It often seems to happen that the things we dream about can be rationalized from recent experiences. Thus we might have a dream about headless chickens for example and, after waking, might argue that we had chicken for dinner and later watched a film about the French Revolution so this must be the explanation. And so it may be. This is a generally accepted theory and Advaita has no objections to it. However, much the same could be said about waking experiences. The dream seemed perfectly real and self-justifying while we were in the dream. And we gave no thought to such a thing as a 'waking world'. It was not until we awoke that the perspective changed. We see all of these snakes in our day to day waking life; we fear them and fight them; sometimes they bite us and sometimes we overcome them. But who is to say that they are not ropes all of the time? How could we know unless we wake up and sublate those experiences?

Ramana Maharshi says: *"Waking is long and a dream short; other than this there is no difference. Just as waking happenings seem real while awake, so do those in a dream while dreaming. In dream the mind takes on another body. In both waking and dream states, thoughts, names and forms occur simultaneously."*(Ref. 85)

and

"All that we see is a dream, whether we see it in the dream state or in the waking state. On account of some arbitrary standards about the duration of experience and so on, we call one experience dream experience and another waking experience. With reference to Reality, both the experiences are unreal." (Ref. 84)

We claim that we are awake now but we also frequently dream. We say we are both wakers and dreamers, just not at the same time. If we can be both, then presumably our true nature must be neither. And this is what Advaita tells us. The people and objects that occupy our waking lives are also appearances, with no more independent reality than the manufactured worlds of our dreams. The dream world is nothing but our own self, fabricated by the mind. Similarly, the waking world is nothing but the cosmic self, *Ishvara*, and it is manifest or fabricated using the power of *mAyA*. (And the bottom-line is that, whilst your body, mind and world are part of *Ishvara*, both you, your Self, and *Ishvara* are none other than the non-dual *brahman*.)

Deep-sleep state

In deep sleep, we are not aware of anything. All of the functions of the mind are closed down so that neither external objects nor internal percepts are cognized. Because there are no external objects, there is nothing to reflect the light of Consciousness, just as space appears black when facing away from the sun because there are no objects to reflect the light. There is no sense of 'I', nor are there any thoughts, perceptions or desires. Effectively therefore, deep sleep is closest to our true nature. It is the most blissful experience and one that we cannot do without – the expression of peace and happiness on the face of someone deeply asleep is not coincidental. Unfortunately we are not aware of it. All that we know is that, upon awakening from deep sleep, there is refreshment, energy and peace – where did all this come from? We were not feeding in our sleep. It was our essential nature, shining forth as it were without obstruction.

In deep sleep, you are ignorant of the nature of reality but you do not, as a result of this, erroneously project a separate universe (as happens in waking and dream). Nevertheless, you are still present as consciousness. When you wake up, you are able to say that, 'during the deep sleep, I was not aware of anything'. How could you say this if there was no conscious entity to know this? Some people have a problem with this explanation (I know that I did!). But consider: if I ask you 'did you know anything?', you will answer 'No'. If I now ask you: 'How do you know that you did not know anything?', you can say 'I know' with absolute certainty.

One of the questions that I was asked via my website (www.advaita.org.uk) went as follows: *"In deep sleep there is no sense of 'I'. Waking up, the sense of 'I' comes out with everything else (like in a dream). So my question is: Is it true that the sense of 'I' is perceived by that entity (our true nature) which is 'I-less' and is alone present in deep sleep? Is that the entity which is perceiving knowledge, ignorance and, at the end, the sense of 'I' too?"*

And I answered as follows: *"When we (the jIva) are in deep sleep, the mind is resolved so that we do not 'know' anything. But the Atman is not affected, is 'state-less'. In deep-sleep, we directly experience our true nature of sat-chit-Ananda but all that we know, when we wake up and the mind functions once more is that 'I slept well'.*

"I think the problem you are having is in your use of the word 'I'. Do you see that you are in danger of an 'ad infinitum' problem? Who is it who has 'the sense of I'? If you say that 'I' have the sense of 'I', then who is it that has the sense of that 'I'? The 'real I' is self-evident (you do not need a light in order to see another light).

"The point is that all of this perceiving and thinking is in vyavahAra, *and 'I = brahman' is the ultimate truth. Consciousness (turIya) is the only reality; waking, dream and deep-sleep are apparent states that 'take place' within that. You cannot say that the 'true I' is only present in deep sleep. It is* always *present (since that is all there is). But the mind is reactivated in dream and waking and the apparently separate world appears once again."*

Francis Lucille uses the metaphor of faces carved in stone. The faces, which capture our attention, are the states, but behind them, and actually the very substance out of which they are formed, is the stone itself, *turIya* – Consciousness. Krishna Menon (Ref. 60) uses the same metaphor in respect of all *objects*. We believe the objects to be separate because we only see the faces, not appreciating that these are all really formed out of the one stone, which is Consciousness.

turIya

It has been suggested that our waking experiences are comparable to those of the dreamer. If it is possible somehow to 'wake up' from this waking state and realize that the world out there, with all of its objects and life-forms is ultimately no more real than the dream, perhaps we might think that we don't want to wake up. What would it be like? We would lose everything that we know, all of the enjoyment as well as the pain. And we would not be able to achieve those ambitions that we have worked towards all of our lives.

You are a newly qualified barrister and have just finished the summing up of the defense for your first client. You now have to wait for an unknown length of time while the jury retires to consider the evidence. You go off to get some coffee out of the machine and sit down to drink it. You can barely restrain your impatience to know the outcome but, with fingernails already bitten down, you are forced to go over all of the events that have brought you here, including the years of study at university and the years of practicing as a lawyer. And... then you wake up.

You will now never know what the verdict would have been. How much does this matter to you? I rest my case!

Vijai R. Subramaniyam, in his book 'Ellam Ondre (Ref. 86), summarizes this as follows (2.6):

"If you ask what that is, it is called turIya, which means the fourth state. Why is this name used? This name is proper because it seems to say the three states of your experience – waking, dream and deep sleep – are foreign to you and your true state is the fourth, which is different from these three. Should the three states, waking, dream and deep sleep, be taken to form one long dream, the fourth state represents the waking from this dream. Thus it is more withdrawn than deep sleep, also more wakeful than the waking state.

"Therefore your true state is that fourth one which is distinguished from the waking, dream and deep sleep states. You are that only. What is this fourth state? It is knowledge, which does not particularize anything. It is not unaware of itself. That is to say, the fourth state is Pure Knowledge, which is not conscious of any object, but not unconscious itself. Only he, who has realized it even for a trice, has realized

the Truth. You are that only."

Ramana Maharshi actually describes a nominal 'fifth' state, called *turIyatIta*. The idea here is that *turIya* itself is still a 'state' and can be attained for short periods by spiritual seekers through deep meditation, for example. Once the truth is fully realized, however, the 'state' becomes permanent; there is no more return to the identifications of the other states. Though the Sage still sleeps and dreams and interacts with us on the normal plane of waking consciousness, he is always fully aware that these are appearances on the eternal background of reality. *turIya* is the detached witnessing of the apparent waking, dream and sleep states. *turIyatIta* is the Self alone with nothing separate from itSelf to witness; all apparently separate things differ only in name and form and are in reality One.

Atmananda Krishna Menon (Ref. 60) also differentiates these. His name for the state wherein there is only the detached witness, is 'Conditioned Consciousness'. The 'natural state' (*sahaja samAdhi* – see Chapter 17 on the subject of *samAdhi*), our ultimate Self, he calls 'Unconditioned Consciousness'. This is equivalent to Ramana Maharshi's '*turIyatIta*'. There is only the Self, with nothing to witness simply because there is nothing other than the Self.

But these extensions are an unnecessary complication. The straight-forward distinction in the Mandukya Upanishad between the three states of waking, dream and deep sleep, and the unchanging reality of *turIya* which underlies them, is perfectly adequate and less likely to cause confusion.

As a waker, I see myself as limited in so many ways – I am restricted to this body in this particular country and century. And I am doomed to grow old and die. Similarly, as a dreamer, I also perceive myself to be limited. Usually, I find myself afflicted by the same desires and fears that I find in waking life. As a sleeper, I do not say or think that I am limited – there is no time or space. But still there is ignorance of the 'limitless I' that I really am. Only *turIya* is free from all limitations.

Death

Every body dies, nobody dies. Swami Chinmayananda

Imagine a cupboard containing shelves filled with various jars and bottles. If the space inside one of these jars could think, it might well look at the other jars on the shelf and conclude: 'Here am I, quite separate from all other jars, having to look after this fragile glass body which defines my nature, forever unable to really communicate with other bottles.' It might well feel very isolated and vulnerable. But when, one day, the jar falls off the shelf and breaks, suddenly the space finds, not just that it is still there but that it always was there, before, as well as after the glass was formed. Moreover it is continuous with and in no way separate from the entire universal space, which is, was, and always will be single and undifferentiated.

If a wave, on the sea were able to look around and think, it would see all of the other waves and might well conclude: 'Here am I, one insignificant little wave amongst all of these thousands of waves; doomed to a perilously short existence fraught with danger. Even if I should grow to a giant tidal wave, though my life might be dramatic and go down in history, it will be over all too quickly and my existence will be no more.' And inevitably the wave *will* die but when it does so it finds that it is nothing less than a part of the vast ocean; that its imagined separate existence was only an illusion; that its apparent birth and death was just a play on the surface of the deep.

(Note, in respect of the two metaphors above, that they apply to the empirical view of existence – *vyavahAra*. At that level 'I' am a part of the totality – *Ishvara*. From the absolute perspective – *paramArtha* – I would have to say that I am not a *part* of the totality; there are no 'parts'; I *am* the non-dual reality, *brahman*.)

Jesus said, "Before Abraham was, I am" and 'I and my father are One'. The St. James version of the Old Testament translated Jehovah as saying "I am that I am". You may have wondered what could possibly have been meant by these words and most Christians will try to interpret them in a dualistic way. But I believe these examples are obvious expressions of the simple truth of Advaita.

'Ashes to ashes; dust to dust.' I don't know whether you have ever thought about the meaning of those words. Note that they do not say something like 'Thinking brain to ashes; living body to dust'. The reason is simple – the body was never alive to begin with. It is nothing more or less than the food we eat; dead matter transformed by very clever chemical and physical processes into more complex matter capable of performing all of those things with which we are familiar, providing that the body is enlivened by the spirit within. We do not live in the walls of our houses; we live in the space enclosed by them. If the house is knocked down, it no longer functions as a house but only because the walls no longer define the space. The space itself is totally unaffected. Similarly, when the body is destroyed, it no longer functions as a person but the Self is totally unaffected.

Once you have completely acknowledged that you are not any of the sheaths of identification, there is no further problem. In the silence, I can step back and see the body, with its aches and pains; see the mind with its trivial thoughts; see the intellect trying to make sense of it all. I am not any of these things, persisting as I do, unchanged throughout the never-ending changefulness of all of them. They are forms only, imposed by the mind. In reality there is only the Self.

The Katha Upanishad says (II.18): *"The Self is neither born nor dies. It did not come from anything, nor has anything come from it. It is birthless, eternal and constant. It is not destroyed when the body is destroyed."*

Arthur Schopenhauer said the following in his dialogue "The Indestructibility of Our True Being by Death":

"As an individual, with your death there will be an end of you. But your individuality is not your true and final being, indeed it is rather the mere expression of it; it is not the thing-in-itself, but only the phenomenon presented in the form of time, and accordingly has both a beginning and an end. Your being in itself, on the contrary, knows neither time, nor beginning, nor end, nor the limits of a given individ-

uality; hence no individuality can be without it, but it is there in each and all. So that, in the first sense, after death you become nothing; in the second, you are and remain everything ...here we have undoubtedly another contradiction; this is because your life is in time and your immortality in eternity."

What has been said about action and *lIlA* provides another reason for no longer fearing death. According to Osho, the reason we are so afraid of death is because it means the end of our pretence. We continually kid ourselves that we will do this or that tomorrow, those things that will justify our existence to ourselves. But at the moment of death there is the realization that there *is* no more tomorrow, that what we have achieved to date is all that we will achieve and there is the feeling of having wasted our opportunity and achieved nothing. It is because we do not want to face up to this that we fear death. But once it has been accepted that we do nothing anyway, that there is never any choice in what happens, that it is all a play, an appearance, then there is nothing to regret and consequently nothing to fear.

Reincarnation

This is one of those topics where there is a very real danger of confusing levels. And I have to confess that the first edition material must have confused the reader in exactly that way! I will endeavor to reword what follows so as to avoid the trap!

Reincarnation is intimately tied up with *karma*, for which the same danger applies. Whenever these topics are discussed, we must be very clear that they apply strictly to the *vyAvahArika* viewpoint. They relate to the *mithyA* person and not to the *satyam* Self. Although the same applies to most of the topics in this book, those such as 'creation' and '*Ishvara*' are less problematic. We can relate creation to the metaphor of the sun rising and setting and accept that the creation will continue to appear, regardless of the fact that there is no creation in the absolute sense. But, in the case of who-we-think-we-are, we are understandably concerned about what will happen to 'us' when we 'die'.

So the short summary of this topic would say something along the lines of: In reality, there never was a person who was born. Consequently, there can be no question of reincarnation. From the vantage point of the person in the world, however, the cause and effect laws of *karma* apply. If, as is usually the case, there is an accumulation of (*saMchita*) *saMskAra* at the time of death, then the subtle and causal bodies will undergo a further birth in order to 'process' that *saMskAra*. You choose your viewpoint and accept the appropriate explanation.

Consequently, in a very real sense, the topic of reincarnation is irrelevant. It is a topic about which people are often curious; after all, you might say, what happens to me when I die is a very important question. But ask yourself these questions: – to whom, exactly, is it important? Who is interested in previous or future lives? All of these questions are actually only of interest to the ego, which has a vested interest in bolstering its importance and feeling sure of its continued existence. The subject itself only has any meaning on the relative plane of existence. In reality, the Self was never born in the first place and can never die, so the question has no meaning in the noumenal sense.

At the empirical level then, the theory behind reincarnation is that of *karma*. Our past actions are the causes that must have their effects at a later time. Our *vAsanA-s* or latent desires must surface and be resolved. In deep sleep, where the mind, intellect, and ego are all effectively 'switched off', the Self is in its natural state of bliss, albeit this fact is covered by ignorance or *avidyA*. When the recuperation process is over, we inevitably return to the waking state. It could be said that the latent desires or *vAsanA-s* drag us back to the waking state. Similarly, the unfructified *saMskAra* at the time of death will drag us into another body when this one dies.

Sri Parthasarathy has a nice story about this (Ref. 23). It is about an apparently mad hermit who lives outside of a village. Each day at sunrise he emerges from his cave and begins to push a huge boulder up the adjacent hillside. Heavy though it is, he struggles in the growing heat of the day until eventually he manages to reach the top. As soon as this has been achieved, he turns around, pushes the boulder over the edge and watches as it rolls all the way back down to the bottom. He laughs out loud at this and then returns to his cave for the day. He becomes so notorious that people come from miles around to watch this insane activity and shake their heads in bewilderment. One day, several strangers come to the village explaining that they are disciples of a famous Sage who deserted them several years ago. They are told about the hermit but that this cannot be their master since he is clearly quite mad. Nevertheless they go to watch the next day and after the exhibition, fall on their knees before him – it is their master. Asked about his strange behavior they explain that all of the hermit's efforts are to try to illustrate to us our own ludicrous situation. We have spent probably millions of lives, working our way up from plants and insects to the pinnacle of evolution where we now stand on the brink of realizing our divine nature. And, for the sake of a few transient worldly pleasures, we throw all of this away and go back to the beginning.

To believe in *karma* and rebirth is also useful from moral and spiritual standpoints and to provide reassurance and motivation to those who believe themselves to be suffering. If I believe that certain types of action can lead me to the point where I will escape the cycle of rebirth (*saMsAra*) and attain everlasting bliss, then I will be better able to cope with my unsatisfactory life now. If I believe that I will come back as an insect if I turn to a life of crime, I might well be persuaded to remain law-abiding. Clearly this could be a useful idea for society to inculcate.

Sex is one of the nine reasons for reincarnation. The other eight are unimportant. Henry Miller

Sri Parthasarathy also has a useful metaphor for reincarnation. He says that we are like mirrors. The frame of the mirror represents our body, the glass our subtle body of mind/intellect and associated *vAsanA-s*. During our life, the mirror reflects the Sun, which is the metaphor for our true Self, Consciousness or *brahman*. At death, the frame is discarded and the mirror removed and put into a new frame, where it once more reflects the sun. This represents the body dying and the *jIva* being reborn in a new body. Throughout all of this, the real Self (the Sun) is totally unaffected.

That subtle aspects such as learned skills and so-called 'innate tendencies' should carry forward is something that would explain child prodigies, for example. How else do we account for children such as Mozart being able to compose operas at the age of five? Accordingly, there is not really any problem in accepting the notion of reincarnation from a *vyAvahArika* perspective.

Consciousness itself, however, which is what we truly are, is not an object, subtle or gross, not a body, not a thought. It is not subject to time or space. How could it be born, die or reincarnate? All of those things are ideas resulting from a mistaken identification of what we really are with a phenomenal appearance. It is this form, to which we attribute an illusory existence of its own, that is mistakenly supposed to be subject to bondage, death and rebirth. So, from the *pAramArthika* viewpoint, we are forced to deny the idea of rebirth.

To reincarnate the metaphor of the gold ring, if the ring is melted down and made into a bangle, the bangle might say, if it were conscious, 'In my last incarnation, I was a ring'. And this is true at the relative level. But, in reality, from the viewpoint of the gold, there was gold before and there is gold now; the appearance of ring or bangle was merely in name and form.

This was effectively explained in the chapter on *Ishvara*. The world, *Ishvara* and *jIva* are all real at the empirical level, which is our experience and understanding prior to the enlightened realization of the true state of affairs. (And even then the perception of duality continues.) Whilst it is actually the case that there is only *brahman*, that remains as knowledge at the level of mind for the seeming person in the seeming world.

Thus, for the *jIva* who still has *saMchita* and *AgAmin saMskAra*, the working of *karma* will ensure that the subtle body is reincarnated. Upon self-realization, these *saMskAra-s* are erased; the body continues to function for the remainder of this life, burning up the already matured *prArabdha saMskAra*. There is then no further rebirth.

Summary of Consciousness from Advaita viewpoint

According to Ramesh Balsekar, consciousness could be described in a hierarchical way as follows. The starting point is Consciousness 'at rest', without any attributes or qualities – *nirguNa brahman* or 'Unconditioned

Consciousness'. Then there is Consciousness 'in movement', functioning as the Witness or 'Conditioned Consciousness'. As soon as there is the thought 'I am', this becomes 'embodied' Consciousness. Finally, this becomes identified with the body-mind and is the 'attached' Consciousness – the *jIva*. The process of enlightenment is to remove the identification and return to the witness and ultimately the unattached 'I am'.

To quote Ramana Maharshi again (Ref. 24):

"The idea that I am the body or mind is so deep that one cannot get over it even if convinced otherwise. One experiences a dream and knows it to be unreal on waking. Waking experience is unreal in other states. So each state contradicts the others. They are therefore mere changes taking place in the seer, or phenomena appearing in the Self, which is unbroken and remains unaffected by them. Just as the waking, dream and sleep states are phenomena, so also birth, growth and death are phenomena in the Self, which continues to be unbroken and unaffected. Birth and death are only ideas. They pertain to the body or mind. The Self exists before the birth of this body and will remain after the death of this body. So it is with the series of bodies taken up in succession. The Self is immortal. The phenomena are changeful and appear mortal. The fear of death is of the body. It is not true of the Self. Such fear is due to ignorance. Realization means True Knowledge of the Perfection and Immortality of the Self. Mortality is only an idea and cause of misery. You get rid of it by realizing the Immortal nature of the Self."

There is nothing other than Consciousness. So isn't that the end of it, you might ask? Where is there to go from here? Why hasn't this book come to an end? (In fact, why did it even begin?) Well, you're not really convinced yet, are you? Intellectual arguments are one thing; personal experience or revelation is quite another. In order for the revelation to be made, there has to be quantum jump in understanding and, if you have studied any physics or chemistry, you will know that energy has to be input to the system in order for this jump to be possible. The energy in this case comes from Self-knowledge. Since it is ignorance that is the root cause of our mistaken understanding, only knowledge can remove it. This knowledge in turn comes from *shravaNa, manana and nididhyAsana* – the practices of *j~nAna yoga* outlined in Section 2.

Scriptures and *yoga-s*, practice and gurus, seeking and satsang exist in order to promote and assist this process. The Sage knows there are no others but, if his nature is such that he enjoys talking about the truth, seekers will discover him and learn from him.

17. The nature of the Self

Remember, you are a completely unique and distinct individual. Just like everyone else. Anon

Perceiving or thinking of the Self

We cannot perceive the Self in any way. One reason is Kant's recognition of the fact that we can never know the 'thing in itself'. All of our actual perception takes place in the mind. Signals – light, sound waves etc. – come from the 'real' object, are translated by a sense organ into nerve impulses, conducted along nerves to the brain and again translated by the appropriate part of the brain into something that is then perceived. There is no other way for us to perceive and we can therefore never know the real thing.

But the other reason is simply that, if the Self *could* be an object of knowledge, who would be the knower of it as a subject? The ultimate subject cannot ever be an object, otherwise it would not be the ultimate subject. Also, being non-dual, there is nothing else that could know it. The Self only knows anything as a result of functioning through a mind at the empirical level of reality. (For a readable and comprehensive explanation of epistemology in Advaita, see Ref. 119.)

Yet, the Self is not exactly 'unknown' – how could it be when we *are* the Self? But the mind cannot appreciate this, because the truth is covered over by ignorance. Once this is removed, the Self is there as it always was. You cannot go out and find it somewhere else. An analogy provided by Ramana Maharshi is that of a room full of junk. If you want some space, you cannot bring this in from outside. What you have to do is to get rid of the junk and the space will be there. Ramakrishna used the appropriate metaphor of scum or algae on a pond. The spiritual path is then equated to the process of gradually removing the scum from the surface, bit by bit. As each bucketful is removed, the remainder spreads to replace it so that, for a long time, there appears to be no effect. In fact, the layer becomes progressively thinner until the point is suddenly reached where the covering breaks up completely to reveal the clear water that was always there below the algae. This represents the moment of self-realization, when the covering of ignorance dissolves, and the truth shines through.

Our true state, what we really are, is that undifferentiated Consciousness which is all there is. From the *vyAvahArika* perspective, we are not aware of ourselves before conception and usually not whilst in the womb. At some point thereafter, we do acknowledge ourselves as an aware entity. It is at this point that the trouble begins. The mind recognizes duality in that first thought, a perceiving subject and an implied, perceived object. This 'undifferentiated consciousness', our true Self, now assumes the identity of that perceiving subject and the individual person comes into imagined existence. It is now downhill all the way. Attachment to this, that, and the other follows, together with subsequent bondage and misery.

The ridiculous thing is that it is this 'individual', which is only a concept brought about by Consciousness associating itself with this initial awareness, that is 'searching for itself'. But there is no individual. The real Self was never lost. The spectacles for which we are looking have been on our forehead all the time.

Descartes thought that thinking was fundamental to our being and that the mere fact that this happened was evidence for our existence. As noted above, however, the feeling we have on awakening is a 'raw' knowledge of our awareness, beyond any objectified thought, perception or feeling. Rather than "I think, therefore I am", "I am" would seem perfectly adequate.

But this 'I am' is not a point behind the eyes, a consciousness located somehow in this brain. In fact, it should not really be spoken, since the attempt to put this awareness into words inevitably fails and risks misleading us into thinking the mind can understand what is being said. We should not even say 'I' in this context, for that implies a 'you' that is different from I. Nor should we say 'am', since this suggests that I might not have been in the past or that I might not be at some time in the future. Better not speak of it at all – just "Be still and know that I am God".

Only when the doors of perception are cleansed will man see things as they really are – infinite. William Blake

Most of our thoughts are of objects, where this can be anything, including feelings and other thoughts. These are called *idam vRRitti*, where *idam* means 'this' and *vRRitti*, which can mean many things, in this context means a 'mood' of the mind. These thoughts are forever changing. A different category of thought, which is always the same, is the thought 'I am', which is called *aham vRRitti*. The *thought* 'I am' obviously isn't what we are; we are that in which the thought is arising – that which is aware of all thoughts and without which there could not be *any* thoughts. Just as, when we experience something, there are three aspects – experiencer, experienced and the act of experiencing – so in awareness there is that which is aware, that of which it is aware and the act of being aware. Our true Self is beyond all three. We need to be careful not to stop half way. When a thought arises, there is the danger that we will realize that 'I am aware of this thought' and identify with the 'I am' that is claiming ownership. As you will know now, any such 'claiming of ownership' is the process of *ahaMkAra*.

The 'soul'

There might be some confusion here regarding what is sometimes called the 'soul' by religions such as Christianity. If you relate to this word at all, you might still think that the soul is what we really are. You may accept the possibility that it will survive the death of the body and go elsewhere, perhaps into another body. If you gain lots of *puNya*, maybe you will go to heaven (*kailAsa* or *vaikuNTha*). You almost certainly, prior to reading this book, believed that this soul was separate, unique to you, and certainly distinct from what you might have called 'God'. If you are asked whether it is the same thing as what you call your ego, you might find the question more difficult to answer.

Part of the problem is that the word may be used in different ways by different people, who may or may not themselves have a clear idea of what it means. The sense in which it is used below is that of the essential characteristics that distinguish us as a person. In this sense, the soul does not exist. If it is used as a synonym for the Self, which has no individual aspects, then of course it does exist.

A simpler question to answer will be whether you associate your sense of self with the mind. I suggest that the answer to this will be 'yes'. If we have a sense of a 'soul' that survives death, we cannot imagine it doing so without carrying with it our mind, our unique memories and thoughts. After all, if it didn't it wouldn't be 'us', would it?

Ramana Maharshi has some interesting things to say about this. He compares the real Self, true Consciousness, with the sun, which is always shining, whether or not covered by the clouds and irrespective of the rotation of the earth. The Self, similarly, is always shining, irrespective of the rising and setting of the ego, for the ego disappears during deep sleep – there is no sense of self for the ordinary man during deep sleep or unconsciousness. He tells us that there is no distinction between soul and ego – they are the same and we are neither.

So what is the soul-ego? He explains that the Self, Reality, is eternal, omnipresent, outside of time and space – noumenal. The body is a construct of the mind – name and form imposed upon matter, very much bound to time and space – phenomenal and not real in itself. The two cannot really mix, The mind, in its confused attempt to reconcile the two, creates this illusory ego or individual soul. It appears conscious by virtue of the presence of the real Self but, at the same time, it seems to be material and earth-bound, by virtue of being associated with the body of food. The thought is the process of *ahaMkAra* already discussed – 'I am the body' or 'I am the mind'. Effectively therefore, we have the equation: -

Soul = ego = mind

Ramana Maharshi has a metaphor for this confusion of the reality of the Self and the unreality of the body. He says it is like a man having a dream in which he meets a beautiful woman and marries her. The bridegroom is real but the bride is not. When he awakes, he is still a bachelor. In our ignorance, we, the Self, meet an imagined bride, the body, and get married becoming a husband-soul, but the body and hence the marriage was unreal, the soul never existed. The corollary to this of course is that, since the mind is illusory, all of its problems – misery, fear, etc. etc. are equally illusory.

He has a similar story that takes this analysis a bit further. It concerns a marriage reception, at which a guest arrives who has not been invited. Initially, members of the bridegroom's party assume the guest is a friend of the bride, while the bride's family and friends think that the bridegroom invited him. And so everyone makes him welcome and assumes he has a right to be there. After a while however, members from each side get together, begin to ask questions and suspicions are aroused. The uninvited guest sees this happening, realizes he is about to be exposed and surreptitiously escapes.

The guest is the ego, belonging neither to the Self nor to the body. As long as we remain ignorant, the ego persists and is believed to have a real and legitimate existence. As soon as we begin to ask questions, however, and discover the nature of our real Self, the ego vanishes without trace.

In waking and dreaming sleep the ego is attached to the body or mind and believed to be the self that we feel we are, as opposed to all of the not-self things that we believe surround us. Thus it is that, during our day to day waking life we feel limited, bound to this isolated body and mind in the midst of a vast and alien universe. Yet this ego disappears during deep sleep, along with the body and the rest of the world. Note that, despite this we don't feel that 'we' have disappeared. We believe, when we awake, that we are the same entity that we were when we went to sleep. So even here we have good reason to question the reality of this ego.

That the mind is the main source of the problem can be thought of in this way. From the moment we were born, impressions – perceptions, feelings, thoughts – have been reaching us from all directions, except for the times when we were deeply asleep. The first impressions are stored in the memory and thereafter all future impressions are referred to these memories before themselves being stored. This is the source of all of our knowledge and experience – our mind. From the moment following the first impression, we filter all experiences through this accumulation from the past, as though we were wearing colored spectacles. Osho defines the ego as the force of Consciousness identified with this past memory. As an example, he takes the notion 'I am a Christian'. Where does this come from if not from all of the things we have been told or exposed to during our upbringing? Clearly we are not born a Christian; if Muslims brought up the child of Christian parents, it is most likely that child would become a Muslim.

This is why our recognition of Self comes in those moments when the mind is absent, when there is stillness, untainted by all of these memories from the past; when the ego is not present. This is why meditation is such a powerful technique for bringing us to such moments of recognition. When the continual chattering of the mind ceases, a tremendous peace is felt. This peace is the nature of the Self, temporarily freed from its identification with this or that limitation, temporarily without the masking effect of the ego.

Most people experience this feeling only rarely – it is Maslow's 'peak experience' – triggered by something out of the ordinary, perhaps a scene of great beauty, music or poetry. Something momentarily wakes us up from our sleepy, habitual mode of being, in which we only give part of our attention to anything, the rest being taken up by reliving the past or worrying about the future. But this quality is not in the *event*; it is in *us*, an aspect of our own nature. That this is so can be seen in the frequent but invariably unsuccessful attempts to recreate the experience by seeking the same stimulus. If it was a piece of music, subsequent hearings might evoke memories of the experience but the intensity that it had in the present moment will be missing. Now the mind is active, seeking to relive the past, whereas the first time it was absent and this was why it worked. It is the Self that 'contains' the bliss, the truth, not the music or the mind.

Description of the Self

The Self will always be a mystery because there can never be anything apart from it to comprehend it, analyze it or understand it. Sri Poonja (Ref. 73)

Sorry – no description is possible! As was discussed earlier in respect of Kant's noumenal and phenomenal, we can never observe the Self as an object. Therefore we cannot describe its properties. This leaves only a few options in this regard. Since there are some 'people', both in the past and now, who have realized the nature of the Self, we can read what they have written or listen to them. Through metaphor, parable, koan or whatever, they may give us some insight into its nature. Conversely, again through the help of realized men, scriptures and their interpreters, we can learn what the Self is *not*.

This latter method is one of the classical disciplines. Whatever we see or think about the Self, we can confidently state that it is 'not that'. We can use the phrase '*neti, neti*', 'not this, not this', as an exercise in this regard. Ramana Maharshi criticized this approach, pointing out that, since this was an intellectual activity, it could never take one beyond the mind. He said that the 'I' that eliminates the body and mind by such a method could never eliminate itself. Ultimately nothing can be said about the Self by using words; its language is silence. Hence the words from the Kena Upanishad: "The man, who claims that he knows, knows nothing; but he who claims nothing, knows," or as Lao Tse is reputed to have said, "He who speaks does not know. He who knows does not speak".

But although it may be true in an absolute sense that an activity of mind cannot take one beyond the mind, it is misleading. Enlightenment is an event in the mind, triggered by the gaining of Self-knowledge. It is not an experience, and sitting in *samAdhi* for days will not bring it about either – when we emerge from that we are back in the same, seeming duality. Here is an example of the technique called *bhAga tyAga lakShaNa*, which explains how realization can be triggered by imparted knowledge (taken from my book 'Back to the Truth, Ref. 95):

"Suppose that you and a friend, A, both went to school with a third person, X. Although you were not particularly friendly with X, you knew him quite well but, since leaving school you lost touch and have forgotten all about him. Today, you happen to be walking along with A and see Y, who is a famous film star, walking by on the other side of the street. You have seen films starring Y and admire him very much. A now makes some comment such as "Y has come a long way in the world since we knew him, hasn't he?" You are mystified since you have never

even spoken to Y as far as you know and you ask A to explain himself.
A then makes the revelatory statement: 'Y is that X whom we knew at
school.'

   "All of the contradictory aspects, that X is an insignificant, scruffy,
spotty oik that you once knew at school, while Y is a rich, famous and
talented actor, are all cancelled out, leaving the bare equation that X
and Y are the same person. Furthermore, the knowledge is aparokSha –
immediate. We do not have to study the reasoning or meditate upon it
for a long time."

In the same way, if we learn all about advaita with the help of a qualified
teacher who understands the scriptures, this is equivalent to getting to
know X. Then comes the time when we hear the words 'You are That' (*tat
tvam asi*) and the sudden realization may dawn that 'I' and '*Ishvara*' (X and
Y) are one and the same.

   Although notions about the nature of the Self cannot be adequately
addressed directly by language, the tangential approach of poetry may
sometimes give some insight into those truths that are beyond words. Art,
music and poetry can all convey images that, also, could never be spoken
of in literal terms.

Connect with senses and be awake! Truth is here.
Truth is within ourselves; it takes no rise
From outward things, whate'er you may believe.
There is an inmost centre in us all,
Where Truth abides in fullness, and around,
Wall upon wall, the gross flesh hems it in,
This perfect, clear perception, which is truth.
A baffling and perverting carnal mesh
Binds it, and makes all error; and to know
Rather consists in opening out a way
Whence the imprisoned splendour may escape
Than in effecting entry for a light
Supposed to be without. Robert Browning

The Self in Advaita

The Isha Upanishad says of the Self: *"He has filled all. He is resplendent, invulnerable without body or sinews, pure and untouched by sin. All seeing, all knowing, pervading all and Self-existent, He has distributed everything throughout eternity according to its nature."* (Verse 8)

According to classical Vedanta , our 'real' Self is called the *Atman*. The mistaken identification of this with a body and mind is called a *jIva*. You might equate this to what we may have called the 'soul', i.e. that part of us that survives death. When we speak of the *Atman* in this apparently embodied state, it is often referred to as the *jIvAtman*. In truth, of course, the *Atman* cannot be 'embodied' at all; it really has nothing to do with bodies or minds, which are all part of the mistaken superimposition of *adhyAsa*. The *jIva* is, in a sense, a 'combination' of the real *Atman* and the ultimately illusory body-mind entity. Within the phenomenal world, it obviously seems to be objectively real but when we realize the true nature of the *Atman*, it is known to be *mithyA*. The unmanifest, 'universal' Self, unassociated with bodies of any sort, is called *brahman*. *Atman* is of course identical to *brahman*, since there are not two, but the distinction is made in order for unenlightened people to be able to talk sensibly about the true nature of apparently separate individuals and of the non-dual reality.

Story of beggar-king

Another story told by Sri Parthasarathy in his lectures on the Bhagavad Gita explains graphically how we can live our lives as the *jIva*, in ignorance of our real Self.

It concerns the prince of a very prosperous country in the east. There was a sudden, unexpectedly severe, period of rain and it was soon recognized that floods were imminent. Having been unable to prepare for this, the palace realized that there was grave danger of them all being drowned. So, to guard against the possibility of the royal family being lost completely, the king instructed the prince's nanny to secure the baby, as he still was at this time, in something that would survive the flood.

The nanny, having been brought up with readings from the Old Testament, could only think of the story of Moses and the bull rushes and, accordingly, laid the baby in an old but solid wooden basket used for collecting firewood. So the storms continued unabated; the water level rose in the palace and, as can be guessed, most of the occupants drowned while the basket floated away on the tide and was lost.

After the floods subsided, what was left of the government reassembled and discovered the full horror of what had happened. They immediately organized extensive searches to try to locate the young prince, now the king since his parents had both died, but they could find no trace. And, though, they never stopped looking, and offered huge rewards for information, he was not found.

We now move forward some twenty years to a typical scene in the market place in the city where, as always, beggars gathered to try to eke out a living from scraps of food and coins cadged from the merchants and the visitors. In particular, there was one young beggar who came to the market most days and was well known by the regulars. He managed to survive well enough, for a beggar, adopting a polite and cheerful manner – he would thank profusely the stall owners who gave him a piece of fruit or an odd coin and he would never be rude to those who shouted at him or threw rotten mangoes. But it was a very monotonous existence with no prospect of improving himself and he could not claim to be particularly happy.

Also the local police were not very tolerant of begging, especially if there were state visitors in the city who might think that this reflected badly on the government. So the young man had been arrested more than once for vagrancy and carted off to the jail to spend a night or two. Not that he minded too much since they would always give him a good meal. On this occasion, however, one of the older officials had made the arrest and he felt he saw something familiar about the beggar's appearance. The younger members of the police had forgotten all about the disaster by now but this man had not and, instead of taking him to the jail, he drove the car to the palace.

There they recovered old documents and photographs from dusty drawers and engaged in much discussion. At one time someone came and made the beggar remove his shirt while they examined his back carefully. Eventually, they all agreed; there could be no mistaking the birthmark, the age of the man and his remarkable resemblance to the king, when he had been this age. They had finally found the prince.

And so, they took the beggar, washed him, clothed him in finest silk, gave him food the like of which he had never imagined, let alone tasted. And finally, they brought him into a huge hall, filled with dignitaries and members of the government, where they announced to all, the beggar himself also hearing it for the first time, that this man was their newly found king.

The beggar was not at all happy with the situation at first, when he found that, despite his exalted position and the fact that he was the richest man in the kingdom, he had certain official duties to perform about which, initially, he knew absolutely nothing. As time went on though, he learnt to perform these well enough with the help of his many advisors and he grew to enjoy his role and wealth.

One day, many months later, he was being driven through town in his Royal Rolls, when he noticed that they were close to the market. He called on the chauffeur to stop the car and leaning out, called over to a shabbily dressed man who happened to be nearby. He made the astonished man exchange clothes with him and, leaving the car, walked the hundred or so yards to the market, where he took up his old position and began begging.

And, to all appearances, things were just as they had been before. He cadged the odd coin off the office workers on their way to work and a slice of meat or piece of bread from one of the market stallholders. The regulars recognized him. Some asked good-naturedly where he had been for the last year. Others grumbled at him as they had always done, complaining about beggars in general and him in particular, chasing him off with curses or thrown tomatoes.

And he loved every minute of it, knowing now how he could buy the entire market and not even notice the change to his bank balance.

And that's the end of the story. No punch line I'm afraid but the question you have to consider is what exactly was different now from when he was at the market before? Obviously he is now the king and has untold wealth. He can therefore afford not to worry about how he is treated. Before he was just a beggar. But then, if you think about it, he was actually the king too, even then. So, what is the difference?

The point is that he didn't *know* that he was the king originally. And this is precisely how it is with us. We go through our lives thinking and acting like beggars, looking for scraps of pleasure from the people and events around us when we are ourselves the king, lacking nothing. We are existence-consciousness-bliss but, unhappily, we do not know it and continually look everywhere else but within ourselves.

This is really the central aspect of the philosophy of Advaita. Since there is only the Self, knowing what exactly this is, were it possible, would indeed be the answer to the question of life, the universe and everything. It would define reality, full stop. Shankara, in his *bhAShya* on the Brahma Sutras, refers to the story of the spiritual seeker Bashkali asking the guru Badhva three times to describe to him the nature of *Atman* but Badhva does not speak. Eventually Badhva says that he *has* answered but Bashkali will not understand – silence is the *Atman*. Its nature is beyond name and form and cannot be spoken of. It is the substratum of all, pure consciousness, but beyond space and time; it can never be approached by the mind, as Kant showed much later.

Story of man shot with poisoned arrow

A question that is often asked at this point, if not earlier, is why things are like this. How can it be that we are really *sachchidAnanda* etc. and yet we fumble our way around in the dark like this, believing ourselves to be the body-mind? Why do we have to live our lives vainly searching for occasional pleasures when we already have everything? You know that I am going to come back to the 'excuse' that this type of question cannot be answered. Ignorance is beginningless and so on. You might view this as a cop-out to some degree but it is all, effectively, beside the point. And there is another little story, a parable by the Sage Gautama, quoted in a footnote in the book 'Maha Yoga' (Ref. 25) already mentioned.

A man, travelling through a forest is ambushed by robbers and shot with a poisoned arrow. Fortunately, friends discover him quite quickly, before the poison has taken effect and he is able to explain what has happened. The friends are anxious to send for help quickly so that an antidote can be given. But the man insists on asking them about his assailant and telling them that they must make further enquiries and begin a search to find the robbers. His friends try in vain to convince him that these questions can all wait, that the important thing is to remove the arrow and treat the effects of the poison. But the man persists with his questions and entreaties and, ultimately, the delay costs him his life.

There is a grave danger here that we will act in a similar way. We want to find out why we are in this situation, how it came about that we are deluded by *mAyA* and are mistakenly identifying ourselves with body and mind. The intellect is voracious for explanations and rationalizations. Ultimately all is irrelevant. What matters is that we do all we can to extricate ourselves and save the questions for later. In any case, once we have realized the truth, these questions will no longer be of interest, just as, after we have awoken from a dream in which a serious fire has been discovered, we no longer have any concern about calling the fire brigade.

Individual differences

If we are all the same Self, how is it that we all seem to be different, not just in respect of our external bodies and our thoughts, feelings etc., but even with respect to our 'essential' nature?

There are effectively two theories in classical Vedanta to 'explain' this, each having its own problems. Both theories are only metaphors to point us in the direction of the truth. It should not be thought that one theory will be true and the other false – either, or both, may help to provide a way to look at the problem.

The first, called *pratibimba-vAda*, says that the *jIva* is a reflection of the *Atman*, similar to the reflection of an object in a mirror. The mirror in this case is made of ignorance (*avidyA*). The reflection is not a separate thing; we may tend to think it is separate because it appears in a different place. It does not exist without the object itself and it disappears once the mirror is removed. Its appearance is dependent upon the nature of the glass in the mirror. Thus, if the glass is red the reflection will be red, if dirty the reflection will be dirty; if, through spiritual discipline, we polish the mirror, the reflection can be made brilliant.

The second theory, called *avachCheda-vAda*, doesn't like the idea of mirrors. Since the Self is beyond worldly qualities (*nirguNa*), it cannot be reflected. Instead, it is *limited* by ignorance. Depending on the nature of the ignorance, this limitation can take many forms, called *upAdhi-s* or 'limiting adjuncts' in the scriptures. Thus, we all have different *upAdhi-s* and seem to be different from each other as a consequence. While the ignorance exists, we fail to see the unity in all things. It is like thinking of the space in a house as being separated into lots of rooms, with each space having its own characteristics. In fact, if the house is knocked down, it will be found that the space is still there, but only *one* space, undivided and quite unaffected by the house having been destroyed.

Limitations are categorized into three types: limited in space, time and qualities. The first means that an object/being cannot be in two places at the same time. The second means that it will not have existed at some point in the past and it will cease to exist at some point in the future. These are not usually thought of as limitations. We take it for granted that we are born and will die and that we actually have to make an effort to travel from one place to another. However, the fact of the matter is that 'who-we-really-are' is truly *not* born and does *not* die. Since the universe is within us, we *are* effectively in more than one place at the same time, in fact in *all* places at once! (Our bodies are limited in both of these ways of course.) The third limitation is the one that is more obvious, namely that we are limited in our properties e.g. if we are male, we are not female; we cannot fly or live under water without artificial aid. But, again, such limitations apply to body and mind etc, not to our real Self.

And remember, no matter where you go, there you are! Buckaroo Banzai

upAdhi-s are effectively another way of looking at *adhyAsa*, the mistaken super-imposition of an illusion upon the reality. An *upAdhi* is any aspect by which we limit the real Self by some aspect of the appearance. The result is that the truth is obscured by this limitation and thus we mis-perceive it. The cause is the same – ignorance or *avidyA*. Typically, when we use the word 'I', we are talking about the ego and this ego is the Self limited by all of the associations of body and mind. The 'real' I is pure unattached awareness, singular and without limiting properties.

Whichever theory you care to subscribe to, the effect is the same, namely that the *jIva* is an illusory entity, either the reflection of the *Atman* or the *Atman* seen through limitations. Realization removes the ignorance (the mirror or the *upAdhi-s*) and the *Atman* shines unobstructed – the *jIva* is no more.

The word *chidAbhAsa* also ought to be mentioned here. It refers to the reflection of Consciousness (witness or *sAkshI*) in the mind of the *jIva*. Simplistically, you can equate it with ego or *ahaMkAra*. It is a concept that is needed because we cannot accept the non-dual reality as a knower or doer, since that would involve change and the non-dual reality must be changeless. It is a bit like needing *Ishvara* in order to account for the world and *jIva-s* and *karma* etc. I.e. from the *pAramArthika* standpoint, all of these things are *mithyA* but from the *vyAvahArika* standpoint, they are necessary explanations for the way things appear to be.

The individual and the Self

If you do succeed in dis-identifying yourself with all the ideas you have about yourself, what are you left with? Well... the Self. And this Self is One and therefore the same Self that every 'one' is left with when they have finished dis-identifying themselves. This is the same Self, of course, that every 'thing' would be left with if it had the capacity to disidentify itself i.e. animals, plants and inanimate objects. As has already been said, these are only appearances of name and form superimposed, through ignorance in the mind of the perceiver, on the reality of *brahman*. So this should not be too difficult to accept, once you have got over the emotional abhorrence of equating your true nature with that of a cockroach or a pebble.

We are not a 'person'. In our ignorance, we mistakenly superimpose various concepts such as bodies, minds, roles, etc. upon the reality of the one Self just as, in the dark, we mistakenly superimpose the image of a snake on the rope. This is the process of *adhyAsa* and it explains how it is that each of us believes himself/herself to be a separate individual. The bodies and minds, thoughts and feelings, are only names and forms of the one undifferentiated reality. That which, in ignorance, is called 'I' is attachment of the Self to one set of body-mind-intellect, with its associated ideas, feelings and perceptions. That which, in ignorance, is called 'you' (by me) is identification with another set. Both are mistakes – there is, in reality, only one. Whilst 'I' believe I am this set and 'you' believe you are that set, 'we' inevitably believe ourselves to be separate.

Despite the fact that the scriptures repeatedly state that the Self is beyond description or thought, there are nevertheless some attempts to give an insight into it. Shankara's *Atmabodha* gives some descriptive terms: – without qualities (*nirguNa*); actionless; eternal; without doubts; stainless; changeless; formless; forever free; pure; unlimited; perfect; fulfilled; unattached; motionless; one; always bliss; truth; knowledge; infinite. Basically, any attempts at description have to indicate the absence of limitations of any kind so that most are effectively statements of what it is not, i.e. 'neti, neti' again.

Thus it is that we have to approach an understanding in a somewhat different way. Since the Self is not an object, treating it as such by the mind will never succeed. Language, devised for describing objects, is totally inadequate. Hence the use of stories like the ones above and the plethora of metaphors. What prevents us from knowing it, says Francis Lucille, is precisely this desire to see it or describe it as an object, when we ourselves *are* it. We are looking in the wrong direction. Even if we could look at it somehow as a 'non-object', this would still be being objective. This, too, would be doomed to failure. Once the mind has exhausted all its possibilities, so to speak, and 'given up', we become still and it is in the presence of this silence that the truth may be realized, because this silent Presence *is* the truth.

Thinking of ourselves as individuals, we nevertheless believe ourselves to be significant. When we are really happy, we may well think that life is good, that our feelings are 'full'; it would not be possible to be 'happier'. And yet, if we think that animals are capable of experiencing such emotions, we would probably argue that their feelings of happiness or whatever must be far inferior to ours. After all, their brain capacity and complexity is so much lower. If a flea were able to be happy, this must surely be a shadowy and insubstantial happiness indeed. And so with all perceptions, thoughts, concepts – all must be limited by the capacity of the instruments through which or in which these take place.

But it has been argued that we are not the instruments; those are all limitations that we impose upon our true nature as a result of false identification with them. If our true nature were allowed the freedom to experience to the full, what then? The Brihadaranyaka Upanishad tells us that *"All the joys of the entire cosmos put together would be only a small drop of the bliss of this Supreme Being. Whatever little satisfaction we have, whatever pleasures we have, whatever joys we are experiencing, whatever be the happiness of life – all this is but a reflection, a fractional distorted form, a drop, as it were, from this ocean of the Absolute."* (Ref. 7)

18. Enlightenment

Suffering just means you're having a bad dream. Happiness means you're having a good dream. Enlightenment means getting out of the dream altogether. Jed McKenna (Ref. 78)

What is Enlightenment?

If you search through the books amongst the shelves of a good spiritually oriented bookstore, you will find innumerable definitions, most of them hinting at unimaginable bliss and fulfillment of all that we could wish for. The vast majority of these definitions are misleading if not totally wrong.

To begin with, enlightenment is not an experience of any kind. If you accept that the Self is non-dual, it is a contradiction in terms to talk about 'experiencing the Self'. Who would experience what? Also, the Self is the only reality so it makes no sense to speak of this Self becoming enlightened. A large part of the confusion here is the failure to differentiate between 'becoming enlightened' and 'becoming liberated'. Many people talk about it as though, one minute we are limited, suffering individuals and the next minute we are boundless, free and blissful. It cannot be like this.

Although in reality there is no person, it is at this empirical level of reality (*vyavahAra*) where there appears to be a separate person. The reason for this mistaken view of things is ignorance at the level of the mind. Specifically, the nature of this ignorance is mixing up the real and unreal – *adhyAsa*.

Since the reality is that there is only *brahman*, then it follows that we are already That (as the neo-teachers keep telling us). There is no 'merging' into *brahman* because we were never separate. Nothing we can do will liberate us because we are already free. So what is the problem then? We don't know this fact. We know that we exist and we know that we are conscious but we don't know that we are unlimited. Ramana advocates *Atma vichAra* - investigation into the Self. An element of this is asking 'Who am I?' but simply repeating this like a mantra is not going to achieve anything. What is lacking is Self-knowledge and some external teaching is

261

required to provide this. Of all the means of knowledge available to us, the only one that can provide this knowledge is *shabda pramANa* – scriptural knowledge, ideally imparted by a teacher. It is the ideas in the mind which bind us but the mind is also where the self-knowledge takes place that brings enlightenment.

Of course, once this awakening has taken place, it is realized that the seeming person, mind and knowledge were all part of the mistaken view and that before, during and after, there was only the Self and no actual person to 'become enlightened'.

Swami Paramarthananda tells a story about a game he used to play as a child. They would take a child into a room that was entirely empty and then would place pillows about the room and stand the child up against one wall. He was told to memorize the positions of the pillows and then they blind-folded him. He was then told that he had to cross the room to the other wall without touching any of the pillows. The other children then watched as he very carefully edged his way forward. Whenever they laughed, he would retreat and move sideways before trying again. Eventually he reached the other wall and was allowed to remove the blindfold. He then discovered that all of the pillows had been removed before he began and that he had been moving across an empty floor trying to avoid non-existent objects.

And he says that *mokSha* is like this. As seekers, we make our way through life trying to avoid all the pitfalls of self-ignorance and arrive at the other wall of self-knowledge and enlightenment. But when we attain enlightenment, we realize that there never were any obstacles to begin with. In a sense, the ignorance was non-existent – *tat tvam asi* **already**.

Bondage

Liberation or freedom is the opposite of bondage. As stated above, the reality is that we are already free but the belief is that we are bound. The nature of the binding is what has previously been referred to as *saMsAra* – summed up in the Bhaja Govindam (V.21) as *punarapi jananam, punarapi maraNam* – once again birth, once again death. Round and round in a never-ending cycle until such time as we gain Self-realization. And the irony is that we are failing to see what is there all the time – that everything is *brahman*.

Swami Paramarthananda tells the story of another amusing game played by children on an unsuspecting newcomer to their group. They use saliva to press a coin onto the new child's forehead so that it sticks. And they tell him that he can hit himself on the back of the head to make the coin fall and, if he can do this with three hits, he can have the coin. So they then press the coin to his forehead for perhaps 10 -15 seconds and then, unbeknownst to the child they actually take it away. But it feels to the child as though the coin is still there and he proceeds to hit himself increasingly harder on the back of his head trying to dislodge the non-existent coin. Even when he is allowed further tries, he is doomed to continue to fail because there is no coin there to fall.

And so it is with *saMsAra*. We try to escape from the cycle but who-we-really-are was never on the cycle. The *Atman* was never born and will never die, so where is the question of rebirth? Only bodies are born and die and those are only insentient matter. Enlightenment is the realization of all of this – the understanding that there was no coin attached to begin with.

What is a 'realized' man?

There is no such thing as a Self-realized person. When there is no 'person' the Self is realized. Sri Poonja (Ref. 73)

You should have 'realized' by now that there is only the Self, and that the world, though real for the person, is actually *mithyA*. Since there are no 'persons', the term 'realized man' cannot be logically meaningful. And yet we are saying that our aim in life is to realize the truth, to become 'realized' or 'enlightened'. This is one of those places where there may easily be confusion as a result of 'mixing levels of reality'. It is only in the *pAramArthika* sense that there are no people. At the level of the world, there are people, who are largely ignorant about the nature of the Self and who therefore need to acquire Self-knowledge. It is this 'acquiring of knowledge' by the mind that constitutes enlightenment. But it is not knowledge as in 'information' or 'facts' but as in direct apprehension of the truth – 'Ah!'

We frequently refer to 'realized men'. This book has mentioned quite a few by name. What do we mean by this? What is such a one and how would we know if we bumped into him? As the Bhagavad Gita asks (II.54): *"What, O Kesava, is the description of one of steady knowledge, one who is constant in contemplation? How does one of steady knowledge speak, how sit, how move?"*

According to Osho, asking if we can tell whether or not a Sage is realized is like asking a blind man if he knows whether or not a light is switched on. However there are some general pointers. Such a one is *always* light: – light in the sense of appearing happy; light in the sense of there being no weighty concerns distracting his attention from the present; light in the sense of being able to clarify and illuminate the most pressing problems of life; light – his eyes seeming almost literally to emit awareness, able to penetrate to the depths of one's soul, yet with infinite compassion; light in the sense of a flame, able to ignite one's own desire for truth; vivacious, cheerful, enthusiastic; bringing light to bear on one's ignorance; a beacon, lighting the way towards the truth. And that's enough practice on the Thesaurus for the time being!

Finally, there was a beautiful quotation from Greg Goode recently, in answer to someone asking about how one could recognize the difference:

"The difference between a realized person and an unrealized person is that the unrealized person sees a difference". (Ref. 87)

The term used in the Gita for the realized man is *sthitapraj~na*, meaning one 'standing' (*sthita*) in 'wisdom' (*prAj~na*), a man of steadiness and calm, firm in judgment, contented. The characteristics described in the rest of chapter two of the Gita also contain within them implications as to what must be done in order to attain such a state: -

* One who has given up all desires and is satisfied by the Self alone
* One who is not distressed in adversity, doesn't long for pleasures, is free from attachment, fear and anger

- One who is unattached, who is neither overjoyed when good things happen to him nor hating it when evil occurs
- One who does not merely abstain from indulging in sense objects but in whom there is no longing at all
- Attachment to objects leads to desire, then to anger, delusion, confusion, loss of reason and... death! Therefore, the 'man of steady wisdom' keeps his senses always under control, being neither attracted nor repelled by sense objects.
- One who is ever tranquil, never miserable

The Gita emphasizes the need to keep the senses under control and abandon all desires several times in this chapter. The metaphor of a ship being blown off course by the wind is used to illustrate how discrimination and reason are lost when sense objects distract the mind. A key verse (II.69) in the entire scripture states: *"What is night to all beings, therein the self-controlled one is awake. Where all beings are awake, that is the night of the Sage who sees."* Here, what is being said is that ordinary people live amongst the illusory world of the senses, believing it all to be real – that is their 'day'. To them, reality is 'night' and their vision is totally useless here. One who has turned away from the senses and 'shaken off the sleep of *avidyA*', as Shankara puts it, is completely awake and the night time of reality is like day to him. Conversely, the world of transience and mere appearance is now like night time to him since it is a state of ignorance.

The chapter ends (II.72) with the announcement that *"attaining this state, none is deluded. Becoming established in it, even at the end of one's life, a man becomes one with* brahman.*"*

jIvanmukti or *j~nAna niShTha*

These descriptions do not actually apply simply to one who has gained Self-knowledge – such a person is correctly called a *j~nAnI*, literally 'one who is endowed with knowledge'. Advaita teaches that there is 'enlightenment', after which one may be referred to as a *j~nAnI* and then there are the 'fruits of enlightenment' – *j~nAna phalam* or *jIvanmukti* – which bring the 'benefits' of peace of mind etc. Being 'established' as a *j~nAnI* is also called *j~nAna niShTha*; *niShTha* means 'firmness'.

For someone who is fully prepared mentally prior to enlightenment (as per Shankara's *chatuShTaya sampatti*), the fruits accompany enlightenment. For those who were not fully prepared, further *nididhyAsana* is required. Note that mental preparation and practices such as meditation do not in themselves bring about enlightenment – for that, only self-knowledge is effective. But the preparation makes it more likely that knowledge will be heard and recognised when it is given. Those who have had no preparation at all cannot become a *j~nAnI*.

Almost invariably in the scriptures, as well as in other books and in spoken material, when a 'realized man' is described the description will be actually be of a *jIvanmukta* and not a *j~nAnI*. Someone may be enlightened but, because of insufficient mental preparation beforehand, still exhibit characteristics more usually associated with 'ordinary' people. This may include behaviour deemed to be 'inappropriate' as well as continuing to suffer the emotions and attitudes of the unenlightened. Such a person will know that there is only the Self, that the world is mithyA and so on but nevertheless still feel as though he or she is a suffering individual. This is all in accordance with the law of cause and effect operating at the empirical level or, in more advaitic terms, the working out of *prArabdha karma*. Providing that *nididhyAsana* continues to be performed (and this may consist of reading, listening to, writing about or teaching Advaita), the benefits of this knowledge will eventually be gained.

In the Bhaja Govindam, a realized man is said to behave like a child, a madman or a ghost. There is a complete absence of egotistical traits – there *is* no ego. Emotions such as love and hatred are still exhibited but only as they arise in the moment; the next moment, they are completely forgotten. He lives always spontaneously in the present with no regrets for the past or anxieties for the future. Because he has none of our concerns of the ego, no desires or fears, his behavior may, at times, seem strange or even mad, beyond our ability to comprehend. Still moving amongst us but unaffected by external events, remaining equanimous when others may be moved to extremes of joy or misery, he may also seem to be like a ghost, unaffected by what we still perceive as real.

The realized man has full awareness of the nature of things and no longer identifies with any aspect of the appearance, even though all is perceived as before. He still sees the apparent plurality and continues to use the naming conventions for all of the forms that are perceived. But he is no longer taken in by any of it. He is like the witness of the magical illusion to whom the trick has been explained. There is still thinking, functioning of the body, playing of roles in life and so on but he knows that he is not 'doing' any of these things and there is no associated ego. He now knows that he is the background reality upon which all of these appearances take place. Thus, for example, the mind still dreams because it is part of the functioning of mind to bring up topical concerns and ideas during sleep and sort through them all to try to put them in order. But the realized man knows this and does not identify with the process; he knows that 'he' is not dreaming and hence there is no *taijasa* – no dream 'ego', only *svapna* – the dream-state of the mind.

> *You are perfect; uncover the person who feels something is missing, and what remains is perfection. ... Leave the mind and body free to be what they are and you will no longer be their slave.* Jean Klein (Ref. 30)

Basically, the *jIvanmukta* no longer has *upAdhi-s*, perceived limitations. He knows he is not the body or mind, that he does not act or 'enjoy', that he does not die and so on. Note that this does not mean that someone who is enlightened no longer enjoys anything. On the contrary, because there is no attachment and no concern about whether or not a desire is fulfilled or how long an enjoyment lasts, the pleasure is more intense, simply being experienced for what it is. What is meant is that he realizes that 'he' as a person is not doing or enjoying, because there is no person.

The functions of what is perceived by others to be the person continue as before but he knows that he is merely the witness of all of this, happening without his involvement as part of nature or *prakRRiti*. Only the *guNa* 'act'. All appears as a play; all is perfect; nothing needs to be changed or can be. There is no ignorance, no misapprehension, and no *adhyAsa*. All his previous misunderstandings have been sublated and he now has direct knowledge of reality, not as an object, since he knows there are none, but as his own essence. There is still deep sleep but He does not sleep. Both aspects of *mAyA* have been transcended.

Nisargadatta says: *"Your world is transient, changeful. My world is perfect, changeless. You can tell me what you like about your world – I shall listen carefully, even with interest, yet not for a moment shall I forget that your world is not, that you are dreaming. In mine, the words and their contents have no being. In your world nothing stays, in mine nothing changes. My world is real, while yours is made of dreams. My world has no characteristics by which it can be identified. You can say nothing about it. My silence sings; my emptiness is full, I lack nothing. In your world I appear so (with a name and shape, displaying consciousness and activity). In mine I have being only, nothing else. I am my world. My world is myself. It is complete and perfect. I need nothing, not even myself, for myself I cannot lose. In your world I would be most miserable. To wake up, to eat, to talk, to sleep again – what a bother!"* (Ref. 26)

The fruits of enlightenment (*j~nAna phalam*) are characterized particularly by a total lack of desire or fear. Those can only exist where there is an ego to feel limited and want to fill the perceived emptiness and avoid threats. Note that this means threats to the ego, with its imaginary status and vulnerabilities, not the body. Natural in-built damage-avoidance activity will still continue automatically after enlightenment though, again there is the knowledge that 'I' cannot be hurt.

Once realized, some say, there is no going back. The ego is forever gone; it is known never to have existed. Nisargadatta again: *"Once you have awakened into reality, you stay in it. A child does not return to the womb!"* (Ref. 26). But, for the *j~nAnI* as opposed to the *jIvanmukta*, if *nididhyAsana* is not performed to 'complete' the transformation, then some apparent regression may occur. The water-on-jello metaphor is appropriate here – habitual ways of behaving can remain effective if vigilance drops and we do not remember our realization of the truth. *prArabdha karma* remains effective until the death of the body.

The fact is that, *j~nAnI* or not, a person still has to function in the world, interacting with others and probably still performing a daily job. There is the ever-present danger of getting involved in this, if not continually vigilant. This is likely to lead to attachment or aversion (*rAga – dveSha*) for whatever is happening. This means that the ego is once again raising its head and we will, for that time, think of ourselves as a waker once more, in a real world of separate entities. Not until one is firmly established in the knowledge of the truth – *j~nAna niShTha* – is this danger over.

(Note that some will vehemently object to the above claim. They will aver that, upon realization, the mind and even the world effectively cease to exist, But such arguments result from an over-literal interpretation of some scriptural statements and do not accord with reason. And, as Gaudapada argues in his *mANDUkya kArikA* (III.23), that which is stated in the *shruti* (scriptures) **and is supported by reason** is true and nothing else.)

Process of realization

Enlightenment does not happen in time. It happens when time stops. Sri Poonja

Papaji has made some wonderful 'throwaway' remarks on various subjects. He was once asked whether there was a sort of 'gestation' period for the spiritual seeker before becoming enlightened, like the nine months that a baby spends in the womb before being born. His reply was: *"You are ripe for Enlightenment when you want nothing else. In order to be born as a baby you have to spend nine months getting bigger and bigger. For Enlightenment you have to get smaller and smaller until you disappear completely."* (Ref. 73)

But these are on the verge of being 'mystical statements and are the forerunners of statements by modern teachers that cross over that boundary into the near meaningless. Realization is direct knowledge of the Self but it is still a 'condition' of the mind, as far as the enlightened 'person' is concerned. The term in Advaita is *vRRitti*, meaning a mental 'disposition'. Specifically, in the context of enlightenment, it is the *akhaNDAkAra vRRitti* that is involved. The literal meaning of this is 'taking on the form of the undivided', i.e. becoming one with the non-dual reality.

The Atmabodha (Ref. 17) uses the metaphor of a light placed in a jar. Such a light enables us to see the outside world just as Consciousness enables the senses and the mind to operate. If all of the objects are taken away, the light is left illuminating itself. Similarly, when we relinquish all attachment to the world of appearances and transient pleasures, Consciousness remains, illuminating itself in *sat-chit-Ananda*.

Another way of looking at it is that, as Nisargadatta says: *"Reality is not an event"* and *"whatever happens, whatever comes and goes, is not reality"* (Ref. 26). We cannot experience the noumenal; it is beyond perception or thought. Since freedom and completeness are, in a sense, the reality, it stands to reason that we cannot in any way *become* free from the point of view of the ego, the body-mind. Enlightenment is also not an 'experience'. This implies someone who experiences and some 'thing', separate from us and the experience, that is 'experienced', as in the threefold aspect of knower-knowing-known (*tripuTI*) . Thus, we have to be very careful in the way we think about all this, even if we are sometimes rather sloppier in how we talk (or write!) about it.

So enlightenment is an event in time in the mind of a person. It cannot be 'transmitted' like a disease. It can only take place in a mind that is 'ready' in the sense of possessing those attributes described earlier, such as stillness, self-control, discrimination and reason. What has to be done, by the person who has acquired such virtues to the requisite level, is to listen to a teacher who is able to communicate the teaching; who knows and understands those methods which have been proven to work; and, ideally, who is already realized himself. This is the process of *shravaNa*. Then the seeker should ask questions to remove doubts and misunderstandings. This is *manana*. And finally everything has to be reviewed and assimilated – *nididhyAsana*. And if enlightenment has still not dawned, go back to the listening stage and repeat as necessary!

Many modern teachers say that there is nothing the ego *can* do; that it is a classic 'Catch 22' situation. A person can never become enlightened, being only a mask. The Self is already pure light. We, the ego, may desire to become enlightened but this very desire to become the Self is a denial of the fact that we already are! Only when the desire for freedom has been lost can we appreciate that we are already free. As someone once pointed out, it is like asking, in connection with the oft-repeated metaphor, "When will the snake become a rope?"

Such ideas follow from statements such as this one made by Ramana Maharshi: *"When you speak of a path, where are you now? And where do you want to go? If these are known, then we can talk of a path. Know first where you are and what you are. There is nothing to be reached. There is no goal to be reached. There is nothing to be attained. The conception that there is a goal and a path to it is wrong. We are the goal or peace always. You are the Self. You exist always... If Self were to be reached, it would mean that the Self is not here and now and that is yet to be obtained."* (Ref. 88)

And, of course, what is said is true, pedantically speaking. But the fact remains that the obstacle to realizing that what he says is true is Self-ignorance. So *that* has to be removed before the truth of the statements can be appreciated. The teaching of Advaita removes this ignorance. When it finally goes and the mind totally recognizes the truth, that is called enlightenment.

There is an old Sufi story involving the eminent Mullah Nasrudin, the legendary Sufi figure from the Middle Ages. He has lost the key to his house and is discovered searching for it underneath a street lamp. He is asked whereabouts it was lost, and he points over into a dark part of the road. Asked why, if he lost it over there, he is searching underneath the lamp, he replies that it is lighter here. The point being that we continue looking everywhere but within ourselves for our true nature, for happiness, knowledge and truth. It may be easier to look outside but we are never going to find these things there.

So we have to be very careful when embarking upon our search for the truth and planning our spiritual path. Remember constantly that 'I' cannot do anything. If 'I' think I am actively seeking or that 'I' am meditating, nothing is going to happen. 'I' don't even have anything to do with the initial impetus that triggers this interest. This is said to be an act of 'Grace'.

This is a difficult concept, if one finds belief in an external God difficult to accept. But, if your understanding is that of *Ishvara*, as explained in the earlier chapter, rather than the more usual religious concept of a righteous God looking down from heaven, it all begins to seem lawful. Ramana Maharshi has said about it: *"Grace is the Self. You are never out of its operation. Grace is always there. You are neck-deep in it and yet you cry for grace. It is as if one neck-deep in water should feel thirsty. That which exists is grace, it is always there, it is available to all and it fills the entire universe since it is existence itself. That which eternally 'IS', is 'I am' and it is the inmost nature of all and so is available to all, at all times. This pure 'I am' in every one of us is grace. Grace is the beginning, middle and end. Grace is the Self."* (Ref. 88)

At present we are effectively asleep. We are either totally unaware of our true nature – the case for most people – or we only have an inkling or a belief. People who are asleep or dreaming do eventually wake up. We, too, will eventually awaken from this state of ignorance but, the scriptures tell us, this may take millions of lifetimes. Sometimes, something can happen in a dream that is so frightening that we are woken up instantly. An example might be being chased by a lion, which then suddenly leaps at us. The lion is only an image generated by our own mind yet this illusion has the power to take us from one level of consciousness to another. Events such as this can occur in waking life, too, where a 'dream lion' of the waking variety can catapult us into realization of the truth. In the normal scheme of things, these events are beyond our control. But exposing ourselves to the teaching of Advaita, through a suitable organization or a qualified teacher can dramatically increase the likelihood of this.

samAdhi

The experience of *samAdhi* through meditation was mentioned back in Chapter 3 whilst talking about the sheaths. There are two levels of *samAdhi* – *savikalpa* and *nirvikalpa*. *vikalpa* means alternative or option, doubt or indecision, so *savikalpa* means admitting of alternatives or distinctions and can also mean having doubts (*sa* = with, together with, accompanied by) while *nirvikalpa* means not admitting any alternative, without doubts (*nir* = beyond). Both these are still states, however, and there is a return to the normal waking state once they are over.

Once Self-realization has been attained, there is full and lasting knowledge of the Self. This is called *sahaja samAdhi*, or better, *sahaja sthiti*, so as not to think of it as any sort of meditative trance. Just to be even more confusing, *sahaja* actually means 'natural state' but this third type of *samAdhi* is not really a state – it is our true nature. Once recognized, it is permanent (*sthiti* meaning 'steady' or 'remaining'), but bear in mind the discussion under *jIvanmukti* above. The two *'kalpa' samAdhi*-s are always associated with meditation and cease when that ceases. The Sage, in *sahaja sthiti*, carries out the functions of a normal person, even thinking when necessary, but is forever resting in knowledge of his true Self.

In *savikalpa samAdhi*, the meditator, though experiencing profound stillness and peace, nevertheless knows that he is an experiencer of this stillness and is only having an experience. In *nirvikalpa samAdhi*, there is total loss of any sense of duality and the complete bliss of the Self is known directly. Expressing it inadequately in words: instead of knowing bliss, one *is* bliss. This recognition becomes permanent in *sahaja sthiti* and is then no longer limited in any way, as for example only being reached by profound meditation.

After *samAdhi*, the practitioner still has a sense of a personal identity; with *sahaja sthiti*, this has been lost – there is no longer any 'person' experiencing anything. Indeed, if *nirvikalpa samAdhi* can be brought on readily, this can have the effect of making enlightenment more difficult, by strengthening the ego that is enjoying the bliss and feeling pleased with itself at having brought it about. Also, *nirvikalpa samAdhi* is usually only achieved through considerable practice. Anyone who has meditated will know how difficult it is to rid the mind of thoughts for even a short while. Paradoxically, *no* effort is required to achieve *sahaja sthiti*. In fact, any effort must necessarily prevent it since effort means that the ego is involved.

samAdhi does not actually have any relevance in advaita – it is a practice in the *yoga* tradition, although it has been taken up as significant by many more recent proponents (especially in the neo-Vedanta of Vivekananda). The word does not even occur as such in the major

Upanishads. According to traditional advaita, our problem is one of self-ignorance and this can only be remedied by self-knowledge. No experience can bring this about.

The 'Transition'

Man is free at the moment he wishes to be. Voltaire

So what is it that happens exactly at the moment of realization, when one moves from the vantage point of an 'individual' to knowing that there is no such thing as an individual? At some stage in the study of these teaching, there comes a point, where there is a deep understanding and an intellectual acceptance of the truth of the four *mahAvAkya-s*. And yet there is still an ego to fall away; a clinging on to the sense that I am a doer, enjoyer etc. What is the nature of the event that must occur before the transition can be made from intellectual acceptance to full liberation? Is there anything useful that can be said about it at all?

Clearly the transition is not a physical event – matter is only a manifestation, names and forms attributed in ignorance to parts of the unity; nothing essential changes when the name or form changes. But as has already been explained, who-we-really-are is already the Self so it stands to reason that nothing is actually going to happen in the real sense. What is happening is a mental rearrangement as it were; suddenly seeing everything in a totally new way, even though everything remains as it always was. This is the mind 'taking on the disposition' of the non-dual truth – the *akhaNDAkAra vRRitti* described earlier. And the sort of event that brings this about is something akin to the *bhAga tyAga lakShaNa* also described earlier – the sudden realization that we have always know it to be like that.

Views from the Sages

It's always too early to quit. Norman Vincent Peale

Robert Adams was a Sage purportedly realized at an early age before he met

Ramana Maharshi. He died in 1991 but left behind a number of transcripts of his discussions. In one of these, transcribed in the Winter 1997 edition of 'Self Enquiry' (Ref. 38), he talks of a number of conditions that must be satisfied before realization is possible. We have to stop all of the mental and verbal arguing about what it all means. This also means dropping all of the mental concepts that we rely upon to support our position and bolster our ego, dropping thought and perception in *favor* of intuition. We must stop reacting to events; start *practicing karma yoga*, and become a detached witness. Most importantly, he says, we must practice humility. Whenever we become angry or depressed at something someone else does or says, the energy for those feelings comes from us and is therefore unavailable for things that are important. Finally, our search for the truth must be so important that all other desires cease (or even, as Greg Goode often puts it, so important that we would be willing to die for it). This is *mumukShutva*, the desire to achieve enlightenment to the exclusion of all other desires, and one of the key prerequisites for the seeker.

Ramana Maharshi actually said that knowledge of the Self is the easiest knowledge. All others require a knower, a known, and a process of knowing. *AtmavichAra*, literally reflecting on, or enquiring into, the nature of the Self, reveals that there is only the Self. He also points out elsewhere that 'knowing' the Self is not really correct because in order for this to be possible there would have to be two selves, the one knowing and the one known. A more correct way of putting it is simply 'being' the Self. Similarly, 'realize' is an incorrect term, meaning as it does 'to make real', since the Self is the only 'real' thing to begin with. We actually start off by regarding as real that which is unreal and it is this that has to be given up in order to 'realize' the Self – another example of the 'back-to-front' way we have of looking at things.

Most Sages imply or state that enlightenment occurs as a sudden (non-) event, bringing about this 'paradigm shift'. Before the event the world is seen as 'other', with separate objects and people and we have a distinct sense of 'I' as an entity, with a body and mind. No matter what we may have come to believe intellectually, that mode of perceiving seems inescapable. Afterwards, the view is radically different, changed forever.

As Nisargadatta says: *"Realization is sudden. The fruit ripens slowly, but falls suddenly and without return."* (Ref. 26)

Douglas Harding had the following to say about it: *"It was all, quite literally, breathtaking. I seemed to have stopped breathing altogether, absorbed in the Given. Here it was, this superb scene, brightly shining in the clear air, alone and unsupported, mysteriously suspended in the void, and (and this was the real miracle, the wonder and delight) utterly free of 'me', unstained by any observer. Its total presence was my total absence, body and soul, lighter than air, clearer than glass, altogether released from myself, I was nowhere around."* (Ref. 89)

Greg Goode describes his Enlightenment 'experience' as follows:

"Lots of what follows may seem quite heady and intellectual, but believe me, the heart and body definitely got involved. Part of it is that my education and training were as a professional philosopher. There were hundreds of books and many paths gone through.

"For about 5 years, I kept one question constantly in mind (whenever the mind wasn't engaged in what was before it), because I really wanted to know the answer: what is this choosing, willing entity? One day while I was reading a book by Ramesh Balsekur, standing on the Grand Central subway platform in rush hour, the answer came. It came by way of the world and the body imploding into light, and the doing, willing, phenomenal self thinning out, disappearing in a blaze of the same light to become it. No separate independent entity was experienced. No time or space was experienced, yet I knew myself as the seeing itself. All 'willings,' 'desirings,' 'thoughts' and other mentations were deeply experienced as spontaneous arisings in consciousness, happening around no fixed point or location. Not only the entity 'Greg' but also all supposed personal entities dissolved; were seen to have always been appearances in consciousness.

"Lightness, sweetness, brightness, and a fluidity of the world followed immediately as qualities of everything, and became one with all experiences. There were psychological after effects as well, like more resiliency, more psychological peace and happiness. At the time, it was

really a non-event. It's not something I ever noticed or thought about at the time, unless I'm asked and then try to reconstruct it.

"I do remember that people at work noticed; my friends and parents noticed. I didn't have a real good intellectual understanding of it at the time, and didn't seek one. I'd never met anyone else to talk to about this." (Downloaded from the Non-duality Salon web site at www.nonduality.com/goode.htm with permission given for quoting.)

The possibility of a more gradual coming about of realization is also implied by a metaphor used by William Indich (Ref. 1). He suggests that our seeing of the world of objects as real is like the shadow cast by an object in sunlight. When the sun is low, the shadow is large and caused by light being prevented from reaching the ground by the object. I.e. the shadow is a sort of 'negative projection' of the sun. In the same way, our ignorance of reality is a sort of negative projection (remember *vikShepa*, the projecting power of *mAyA*) of Consciousness. As the sun rises, the shadow gets smaller and smaller until, when it is directly overhead, it disappears completely. Similarly, as knowledge of the Self is gained – from a guru, reading the scriptures, reflecting and meditating etc. – the ignorance grows smaller and smaller until the moment when it is eliminated completely.

Nathan Gill is a modern teacher (no longer teaching at the time of the second edition of this book) who says exactly this. He believes that intellectual seekers, i.e. practitioners of *j~nAna yoga*, come to an understanding of what it means to be enlightened over their years of reading and listening to teachers but that they are still expecting the equivalent of the 'flash of light' that many speak of. He says: *"You see, this is it: people are around for years seeking, and in fact, they already know who they really are but they are still waiting around for some kind of event. There is no need for an event. Right now, this is it. The final realization is that there is nothing to realize."*(Ref. 90) He says that people who have reached this stage should simply 'assume' that they are the Self, which they already appreciate to be the case intellectually, and carry on with their normal lives, abandoning all further seeking as fruitless. They will then gradually relax into the full realization of their true nature (or not); nothing matters; everything is as it should be etc. Very reasonable – but frustrating if there is still an ego waiting for a revelatory experience. (As Haydon Bradshaw points out, it is also a dangerous doctrine for an ego that thinks it has arrived!)

But these views imply that Self-knowledge is analogous to knowledge in, say, the scientific field; i.e. an accumulation of information or facts until one knows everything there is to know (or is currently known) about a subject. As was described in connection with *bhAga tyAga lakShaNa*, knowing your Self is not objective knowledge and it tends to come in quantum jumps rather than gradually. One moment one has a view or a belief and the next one *knows*. And it may not be possible to explain how this sudden realization came about. Therefore, the idea of 'gradual realization' must be qualified by this understanding.

Classical viewpoint

The Sanskrit word that is used for Self-realization is *mokSha*, meaning emancipation or liberation. When *mokSha* occurs, all identification and belief in separateness ceases. All perceived limitations disappear. The Atmabodha (Ref. 17, v. 53) says that the Sage becomes one with Vishnu (the Self) as water mixes with water (i.e. referring to the gross body), as light mixes with light (referring to the subtle body of mind and intellect) and as space merges with space (referring to the causal body). But we must beware of falling into the trap of thinking that enlightenment means 'merging with' Brahman – we already *are* Brahman! Verse 54 tells us that there is no greater achievement, knowledge or bliss than that achieved upon enlightenment.

In Ref. 44, Osho says: *"The deepest urge in man is to be totally free. Freedom,* mokSha*, is the goal. Jesus calls it the kingdom of God: to be like kings, just symbolically, so that there is no fetter to your existence, no bondage, no boundary – you exist as infinity..."* This is our (the ego's) objective in this spiritual search, even though this aim can never be achieved (by and for an ego).

19. Direct Path teachings

Searching for yourself in any way is a complete waste of time. Jean
Klein (Ref. 30)

'Direct Path' teachers challenge the traditional belief that a long process of
sAdhana is needed by anyone seeking the truth, saying that we are already
'realized'. We just need to… well, realize it. Francis Lucille, in another
private communication, said:

> *"Why wait until the end of the purification process? The mind has no
> power to prevent one from recognizing his true nature, unless this one
> prefers to postpone this recognition. I feel that there is still, in you,
> some waiting for an event called 'enlightenment' at the end of a purifi-
> cation process. See the absurdity of this. It is more of the same game of
> rejecting the now. Consciousness is here and now. You are that, here
> and now and forever. Whatever may come up in the future can only be
> an illusion. That which is real doesn't come and go. It will not arise in
> the future. It is now and forever."*

The term 'Direct Path' comes from the teachings of Ramana Maharshi, the
first to proclaim that the traditional long-haul spiritual disciplines, over
many lifetimes, were not necessary in order to realize the truth. The phrase
that is used in relation to his teaching is *Arjava mArga* (*Arjava* – honest,
sincere, directness; *mArga* – track of a wild animal, any road or path) or
more usually *vichAra marga* (*vichAra* – inquiry into) and it is contrasted
with what might be termed the more traditional 'progressive' path. This
latter term covers the *yoga-s* dealt with earlier (*karma, bhakti, j~nAna* and
rAja), as well as the four-fold practice of Shankara to purify the mind in
preparation and techniques such as meditation.

Direct Path is, of course, not really a path at all. This is not to say that
this non-path is easy, however. Indeed, in a sense it is the others that are
easy, because specific tasks can be set and carried out without difficulty.

Initially these may be automatic or impeded by too much thinking or feeling but at least there is something clear to be done. In the case of Direct Path, the instructions are less obvious and, with more recent teachers, there is much emphasis on the fact that you cannot actually *do* anything and there is nothing to be achieved anyway – all potentially very confusing for the 'beginner' in these ideas.

Having presumably read what has gone before, the logic of Direct Path must now be inescapable to the reader. If the Reality is that there is only One, then this must be eternal and permanent, i.e. 'we' must already be it. Therefore, nothing needs to be done or can be done; we just need to acquire the knowledge and then have the direct experience that this is indeed the case. What seems to happen, however, is that our present state of ignorance is such that all of our conditioning and prior experience means that we are unable to come to terms with this immediately. Instead we must follow such 'paths' as have been described earlier, in order to prepare our minds and intellect for the simple acceptance that there is truly nothing to be done. In a sense it is an 'unlearning', a return to innocence, which is why paths such as *bhakti* can work. It requires a surrendering of all of our claims to be autonomous individuals, able to make decisions, to act and to enjoy the results of those actions. Not until all such notions have been given up do we become 'ripe' to acknowledge the truth and drop our mistaken notions of separate existence.

It is therefore the case that, practically speaking, Direct Path tends to be for those who have already been through much of the progressive 'stuff', acknowledged that they are not actually getting anywhere but also arrived at the intellectual conviction that there is, indeed, only the Self. When this is genuinely believed, but still not intuitively realized, there is really not much more that can be done other than to repeat the *shravaNa, manana, nididhyAsana* process all over again. In principle we simply give up trying, knowing that it could only ever be the ego that was doing this. Instead, we endeavor to live our lives fully in the knowledge we now have and allow the opportunity for the 'final truth' to be revealed through all of our experience. It is only when you have 'done' all that you can, that you realize *as a fact* that you cannot really do anything at all.

From the Direct Path point of view, no preparation is needed either. It follows, therefore, there is no real utility in religions either. In fact, they might almost be said to be maintaining us in our illusions of separateness and insignificance. Most people will not only not believe you if you say that you are God, they will think you are mad. They do not want to consider such a possibility; all of their understanding, their raison d'être comes from believing in their individuality and their need to achieve something.

Wayne Liquorman says (Ref. 28) that the key thing to get out of all of this teaching is simply to live in the present moment and accept whatever happens, including any reaction of our 'body-mind' to what is happening. When we do not do this, we get involved in thinking about it, speculating, rationalizing and so on. Worst of all, this is likely to lead to going over the 'past' or planning what we might do in the 'future'. Specifically, he says, as do practically all 'satsang' teachers today, that *you* are never going to become enlightened: *"No one in the entire history of the universe has ever been enlightened. There are no enlightened people."*

> *What if your precious sense of self*
> *Were to shrivel up and die?*
> *Where would you be then?*
> *What would happen?*
> *– Best not to risk it.* Ram Tzu

But, as was explained in the chapter on Enlightenment, this is really a confusion of the two-fold view of reality. At the level of the world, there *are* people and it *is* possible for them to become enlightened if they follow the teaching outlined in this book. But such a view is, perhaps, one of the main reasons why this philosophy is not more prevalent in the world. The various groups on the Internet, to which interested people gravitate, contain no more than around two thousand people each, and most considerably less. Basically, there is nothing in it for 'me'.

It is actually far worse for this particular 'non' path. At least the traditional methods say that you will 'progress' by following specific 'paths'. If you follow prescribed rituals, and chant mantras so many times per day, make offerings to deities etc., *bhakti* methods will get you there. If you avoid 'good' and 'bad' actions and seek to respond in the moment according to the need, *karma yoga* will eat up all of your *saMskAra-s* and lead you to the truth. If you read the scriptures, reflect and meditate on them, *j~nAna yoga* will enable you eventually to understand the truth. (Pedantically, *karma* and *bhakti* do not get you there – they bring you eventually to *j~nAna*, which is the only way). And similarly with other methods. But, according to direct path, there is nowhere to go, nothing can be done, you are already the Self – how could you be anything else? Frustrating isn't it?!

Robert Adams explains that, once we start studying Advaita, we come to understand all about such terms as *sachchidAnanda*, non-doing, reality versus appearance and so on and we posit a state wherein all this is known somehow 'in practice' as oppose to just 'in theory'. But when this happens in a person, there no longer is a person; the 'me' who might have become enlightened no longer exists. He says, to reiterate the same sort of quotes as above, *"No one can become enlightened. No one can become liberated; for the you that thinks it can be liberated, doesn't even exist. There is no you. There is no person. There is no human being who is a human being one day, and the next day becomes liberated. There is only the liberated Self, and you are That."* Nisargadatta, too, explains that the person does not get liberated; the Self is liberated *from* the person.

If you make any attempt whatsoever to 'get anywhere', 'find your true Self' or however you might phrase this, you are actually being counter-productive. You will never find yourself whilst you are looking. All you can do really is what you *are* doing. Just be present in the moment and let whatever happens happen. If you can just watch without getting caught up in it, fine but if you can't, worrying about it will not help – try watching the worries! All of our efforts are simply a ploy to maintain the ego in its pretence that it is trying to discover the truth. In fact, they have the opposite effect, of keeping the truth at bay. Swami Abhishiktananda (the Indian name of a French monk, Henri Le Saux, 1910 – 1973) asked: *"Has the sun really set, merely because I have closed the shutters? The fundamental obstacle to realization is precisely the notion that this realization is still awaited."*

Notwithstanding the ultimate truth of Direct Path statements, the practices of the traditional approaches (meditation, satsang, *chatuShTaya sampatti* etc.) should continue as a matter of course, having been established over thousands of years as being the necessary mental and spiritual preparation for realization. And the key practices of *shravaNa, manana, nididhyAsana* have been proven, too, whereas Direct Path and the satsang styles that have grown from Ramana Maharshi and Nisargadatta Maharaj have been around for less than a century. The ego would simply love to abandon discipline and do whatever it liked in the so-called knowledge that nothing made any difference. But then such an attitude could only bolster the power of the ego and render its dissolution even more remote. In addition, despite the acknowledgement that we cannot 'do' anything, there are two techniques which have been advocated by Direct Path teachers.

'Who am I?'

The method advocated by Ramana Maharshi is called *Atma vichAra*. This actually means 'Self enquiry' and, correctly understood, means the traditional path of *shravaNa, manana* and *nididhyAsana* with these practices being carried out under the guidance of a qualified teacher.

Most of those seekers who claim to be followers of Ramana, however, latch on the specific technique that he speaks of, in which we use the thought 'Who am I?' to take the mind back to the source of all thoughts, the Self. When other thoughts arise, the question 'To whom is this thought arising?' will elicit the thought 'to me', in which case the key question arises again. The idea is that the feeling of 'I', once it ceases to identify with all of the thoughts that arise, will eventually disappear itself, leaving an awareness that has no individual identity. All the thoughts, including the 'I thought', are in the mind, and the Self is not the mind. The 'I thought' could be thought of as the 'original thought' from which all others spring. With repeated exercise, the 'I' sense recurs less and less frequently and there is thought to then be the opportunity for full Self-realization. Ramana Maharshi puts it (quoted in Ref. 69): *"The thought 'Who am I?' destroying all other thoughts will itself finally be destroyed like the stick used for stirring the funeral pyre."* The thought 'I am' is the start of all of the trouble. Prior to this was the Reality; subsequent to it, there is a downhill slide further into ignorance.

But it should by now be clear to the reader that this technique, useful though it might be as one of the exercises to practice as part of one's 'mental preparation', is most unlikely *on its own* to lead to enlightenment. And any teacher that claims otherwise is doing you a disservice.

D. B. Gangolli explains it as follows (Ref. 81): *"Self-enquiry, according to the scriptures, is actually a giving up of your identification with the small self, ego and switching over to identification with the Self, which is your very essence of being that you can never lose. When you come to know this is real and the ego is just a false projection, a misconception, this is called Self-knowledge, Self-realization."*

Meditation without an object

The meditation practices described earlier were those corresponding to the traditional paths of enquiry. In the case of Direct Path, there is a technique is called 'meditation without an object'. This method, advocated by teachers such as Jean Klein and Francis Lucille, is an attempt to recognize the contradictions involved in the concept of meditation and circumvent them to some degree. Who, after all, is meditating and how can there be an 'object' of meditation if there are 'not two'? These verbal dilemmas necessarily arise when we are trying to talk about 'reality' whilst still firmly bound in the illusory existence of *mAyA* (i.e. the usual confusion of levels of reality).

The methods addressed in Chapter 9 could be called 'meditation with an object'. The use of a *mantra* was discussed but other objects might be an idol, prayer beads or a flame. In all of these cases, there is clearly a subject, (the meditator), giving his attention to (meditating on) an object of meditation (*mantra* etc.). In a very real sense, such practice is taking one away from the truth that there is only the Self, that this Self cannot act, that there are no things out there and so on. Logically, a practice that leads one to the truth ought to be pointing one back to the Self, not away to a presumed external object. (Note that the traditional methods of meditation are long established and have been proven to work. If you have been taught such a technique by a qualified practitioner and monitored to check that you are doing it correctly, this practice should be continued. Any method learnt from a book is far less likely to prove valuable.)

Furthermore, the 'blank state' of silence and peace that one achieves during such a meditation is still a state; in a sense, still an 'object'. Really, truly to be oneself (i.e. one's Self), nothing (no 'thing') should be involved. After all, by definition, one already is oneself when there is no qualification at all, when one is doing nothing. Just be – you are the silence. You could say, with a twist of the usual way in which the word is used that you *are* meditation. It is, above all, a non-doing. The reason most people find it difficult is that their entire waking life is a habitual state of doing – dropping this is totally contrary to their nature.

Meditation without an object, then, is a (non-) technique that recognizes all of this. It is necessary to qualify it in this way because, being a method of the Direct Path school, it is not really meaningful to have techniques. There is no one to do anything. There is nowhere to go. There is only the Self. Jean Klein, a major exponent of this perspective between 1960 and 1998, says that you cannot meditate intentionally. Any effort to get rid of thoughts and so on is doomed to failure because the attempt would be part of what you are trying to eliminate. All objects, thoughts etc. are creations of the mind and maintain the subject-object duality. Ramana Maharshi said: *"No meditation on any kind of object is helpful... In meditating on an object whether concrete or abstract you are destroying the sense of oneness and creating duality. Meditate on what you are in reality."* (Ref. 91)

(I have to add here, in this second edition, that I do not agree with these statements and can only presume that both had failed to understand the mechanism of traditional meditation – it *does* work! Re-read the section on 'peanut' thinking versus 'spaghetti thinking' to remind yourself of how and why.)

So what can one do? Nothing. One can only open the attention and allow all input. Everything – perceptions, thoughts, feelings, opinions, worries, aches, etc. – is welcomed and allowed to 'do' what it likes. But – and here's the catch – 'we' must not interfere. We simply let everything happen but take no part in it. If a thought arises to which we would normally react, we simply watch. If a reaction does take place, again we just watch it, avoiding any criticism or regret. If these occur, the same policy is followed.

Be who you are, as you are, right now. Nothing else is possible anyway.
Nathan Gill (Ref. 38, April 2000)

By simply being the witness of all that arises, you are eventually taken back to the ultimate observer – your true Self. To rework the quotation from Conan Doyle, you cannot be what you observe; when all that we observe has been allowed to pass, what remains, however improbable, must be the Self.

Francis Lucille uses the analogy of watching a play. Whilst we remain interested in the activities of the actors, we are unaware of the stage upon which it is all taking place. Similarly, as long as we think that our happiness is going to be derived from what he calls 'mentations' (perceptions of external objects, thoughts and emotions), we remain caught up in all of their transient play. It is only once we acknowledge that all of that is not real and is not going to provide ultimate happiness that we can suddenly become aware of the background – Consciousness, which *"reveals itself as the ultimate immortality, splendor and happiness we were looking for"*.

(Note for the second edition: Teachers such as Ramana Maharshi, Nisargadatta Maharaj and their disciples are not strictly regarded as 'Direct Path'. The primary teacher of this approach is considered to be Atmananda Krishna Menon and his successors include such teachers as Jean Klein, Francis Lucille, Greg Goode and Rupert Spira.)

20. Neo-advaita

Traditional advaita is not under threat. It has survived for well over a thousand years because it works. Neo-advaita is a flash-in-the-pan which will fade away when it is discovered that it doesn't. Me

Increasingly over the past 10 – 20 years, a new 'breed' of Advaita teaching has come to the fore in the West. Superficially it seems similar to the Direct Path teaching already mentioned but it lacks the intellectual rigor and many of its proponents do not have a solid background of understanding of the basic concepts of Advaita. Particularly worrying is the fact that its 'nothing to do' statements appeal to the modern ethos of wanting everything now, with little or no effort. Those who are dissatisfied with their lives in a social or psychological sense and are looking for something more (but still for 'me') inevitably look towards the spiritual for this. (In the past, this may have been specifically religious; today it is more likely to be 'new age'.) With the rise of the Internet, charismatic individuals with a flair for 'neo-speak' may quickly rise to prominence and attract seekers to their short satsangs.

What it 'teaches'

Here is a brief summary from my book 'Enlightenment: the Path Through the Jungle' (Ref. 80):

Effectively, it states the 'bottom-line' conclusions without having carried out any of the intervening stages. Instead of systematically undermining all of the seeker's pre-existing beliefs, it attempts to supplant them with a radical new belief. This new belief is contrary to everyday (i.e. dualistic) experience and there is no rationale given in justification.

Neo-advaita has no methodology, since its teachers explicitly reject the scriptures as a pramANa *along with everything else. This aspect is the key to the essence of traditional teaching. Just as the eyes are the*

means for acquiring knowledge of form and color, the ears the means for acquiring knowledge of sounds and so on, so are the scriptures (together with a teacher who understands the methods) the means for obtaining Self-knowledge.

It does not admit of any 'levels' of reality and does not recognize the existence of a seeker, teacher, Self-ignorance, spiritual path etc.

Despite insisting that there is no one to become enlightened and that this word itself has no meaning, neo-advaitins nevertheless admit that the way that they now perceive the world differs from how they once saw it. And many speak of the (non-)event which triggered this transformation. It is never explained why there is such a reluctance to refer to this (non-)event as 'enlightenment'.

Differences between Neo- and Traditional Advaita

If the purpose of teaching is for 'education', i.e. the 'leading out' (Latin 'educere') from ignorance into knowledge, then traditional advaita counts as teaching, neo-advaita doesn't. Neo-advaita is a belief-system without a system – i.e. no structure, no method, no practice; the 'bottom line' without any preceding text. Me (Ref. 80 again)

The difference between the two approaches is that the traditional one is self-consistent, whereas the neo-advaitin one is not. Neo-advaita is actually hypocritical in a sense, because it denies the existence of a 'person' yet still utilizes the medium of a dialog with one. Traditional Advaita positively acknowledges the person at the level at which the discussion takes place. Only the traditional view is valid because the person firmly believes that he or she *does* exist no matter what anyone says to the contrary. Education has to begin from this starting point.

It is true that we are already the Self; we are already free, unlimited and complete. The problem is that we think we are not. Ignorance of this fact leads us to yearn for 'completing ourselves' in some way and, inevitably, where we look is at the world around us. We see something that we think will make us happy and this breeds desire. Desire (*kAma*) leads to action (*karma*) and, because we fail to act 'rightly', this generates *karmaphala* in the form of *puNya* and *papa*. And this inevitably leads to rebirth in order to process the accumulated *saMskAra*. And then the same cycle begins all over again – this is *saMsAra*.

Gaudapada effectively makes the same statements as the neo-Advaitins – we are already the Self and do not really need to do anything to 'attain' this. Swami Paramarthananda tells one of the Mullah Nasrudin stories to illustrate this. The Mullah, on his travels, reached a village late at night and, passing a well, looked down into it. And he saw the moon. Jumping to the conclusion that the moon must have fallen down the well, he rushed to find a rope and hook so that he could pull it out. After many unsuccessful attempts, the hook finally caught and he began to pull with all his strength. What had happened, of course, was that the hook had lodged under a heavy rock but he firmly believed that he was now rescuing the moon.

Unfortunately, the rock was too heavy for the rope and, after a final tremendous pull, the rope snapped and the Mullah fell back onto the ground from where, looking up, he saw the moon now resting back in its usual place!

This, says Swami Paramarthananda, is a metaphor for the process of enlightenment. We believe that we are limited and struggle through years of *sAdhana* until finally, when the rope finally breaks, we 'attain' *mokSha*. So was all the effort really necessary, when we always have been the non-dual Self? The neo-Advaitins insist that no effort is required.

However, Swami Paramarthananda also tells another story which may help to remove any doubts. It is an extension of the story mentioned much earlier about the lady who is looking everywhere for her necklace but then realizes that it has been around her neck all the time. This version has the lady discovering her loss after returning from visiting a friend, to whom she had been showing the necklace. She realizes that she must have left it there and runs out into the street and all the way back to her friend's house only to have the friend point out that the necklace was around her neck the whole time. The question he now asks is: was it necessary that the lady make the effort of going round to her friend in order to find the necklace?

Clearly she already had the necklace but, equally clearly, she did not *know* that she had it. And this is the key point of the metaphor. We already are free but we do not know it. The effort of *sAdhana* and *j~nAna yoga* is to acquire the knowledge that will remove the notion that we are bound.

Enlightenment is of the mind, the self-knowledge that destroys the self-ignorance takes place in the mind. There is no frustration at all when advaita is taught correctly. On the contrary, it is a joyful process in which aspects that caused confusion are replaced by clarity. It is also the *person* that seeks enlightenment and the *person* that finds it, even though the 'finding' also includes the realization that there never was a 'person' in reality.

Levels of Reality

The key to the resolution of this seeming paradox relates to 'levels' of reality. The absolute truth is that there is no creation, there are no objects, no people, no duality of any kind. This is what the neo-advaitin teachers claim and this, too, is what traditional advaita teaches. But it does not seem like this to the 'person' who is deluded by self-ignorance into believing that they are a separate individual living in an alien world.

A useful metaphor is the dream. The dream world may be endlessly complex and totally believable to the dreamer but this is not seen until the dreamer awakens. When I wake up, the monster that was frightening me in the dream does not 'go away'; rather I understand that the monster never existed, even though it seemed totally real whilst I remained in the dream. Similarly, the seeming duality of the world will continue so long as I look out from the vantage point of a separate person. Creation can only be negated from the standpoint of *turIya*, the ultimate non-dual reality. It is pointless for the teacher to insist that 'we are only stories'; that 'nothing makes any difference'; 'there is nothing to do', 'nothing to be sought' etc.

Neo-advaita refuses to admit the validity of the empirical world of the person, whereas traditional advaita does. Traditional teaching openly acknowledges the person and aims to remove the self-ignorance via a series of well-proven, stepwise procedures, carefully gauged to the level and understanding of the seeker. Neo-advaita simply restates the bottom-line reality. No matter how many times this message is repeated, it is most unlikely to have any effect (unless to make the seeker feel hopeless and depressed). Furthermore, it is not at all helpful to deny the existence of the person since that is what the seeker believes himself to be. The belief in 'I' must not be denied, since that essential 'I' *is* the non-dual reality.

Conclusion

You should, by now, have a good *intellectual* appreciation of what Advaita is saying and therefore will understand the unequivocal truths expressed by Direct Path and neo-Advaita teachings. But simply stating how things are is not going to have much effect upon those minds that have been habituated since birth to separation and an egotistic outlook on life. Furthermore, if a seeker accepts the truth of the statement that they are already free and nothing needs to be done (or can be done), they are left in an impossible situation. They are still suffering but can do nothing to alleviate it. (After all, 'there is no one suffering'.)

It is possible that someone who has been studying for many years and understands all of the basic concepts *may* hear that key concept which triggers enlightenment for him. But this seems unlikely, since there is no method at all to neo-advaita, so that any success relies upon a chance comment rather than a disciplined progression.

Accordingly, most spiritual seekers will derive most benefit from the traditional approach. Simplistically, you should aim to follow a path that fits well with your nature. If intellectual analysis such as that given in this third section appeals to you, then *j~nAna yoga* is likely to appeal immediately. If your temperament is rajasic, *karma yoga* will be the best place to start. The more emotional person, to whom reverence of and surrender to a supreme being is attractive, should follow *bhakti yoga* initially, described as the easiest and most enjoyable of paths. As noted above, because the problem is Self-ignorance, you have to come to *j~nAna yoga* eventually. And, if you attend a good organization or find a qualified teacher, all of these aspects will be covered effectively at the same time, since they really go hand in hand.

With an organization, you will immediately come into contact with like-minded seekers and the value of satsang has already been discussed. Alternatively, if a suitable organization cannot be found locally, join an E-Group or two on the Internet; read what others have to say on the subject and ask questions. There are many books on all aspects of the subject and vast amounts of information on the World Wide Web. Appendix 1 is intended to help you to begin to narrow down your search on the Internet and Appendix 2 reviews a number of books that I can personally recommend for the relative beginner. Browse until you find something that strikes a chord; then study more assiduously. There are no shortcuts or simple answers but effort will be rewarded. Your search must become a way of life in order that it may answer your questions about life and bring the fulfillment of understanding.

Most people eventually need a teacher. Here is what Swami Dayananda says about it (Ref. 76):

*"Vedanta has always been an oral tradition, passed from teacher to student. It is a means of knowledge (*pramANa*). As an oral tradition, it requires a teacher who handles the words and unlocks the meaning behind the words. To say 'You are full, you are limitless,' is one thing, but to make the student see what that actually means is another. If that is not done, the words just evolve into another conditioning. Thus, the subject matter being so unique, being neither an object nor a concept, yet undeniably there, the communication of it requires very special handling. Words must be elaborately defined so that what is meant is what is received. Paradoxes must be juggled, illustrations handled, and contexts set up so that the implied meanings can be seen. For this a teacher is necessary, because he knows the truth as well as the method-ology for revealing it."*

ॐ तत् सत्

Glossary of Sanskrit Terms

Each word is presented in the following format:
ITRANS representation, **Devanagari Script** – meaning.

Words appear in order of the English (Roman) alphabet, not the Sanskrit alphabet.

(This section is considerably expanded from the Glossary in the first edition of the book but is nevertheless much reduced from that in Ref. 95. For the latest and most complete version, however, visit the website - http://www.advaita.org.uk/sanskrit/sanskrit.htm)

a, अ – as a prefix to another word, it changes it into the negative. E.g. *vidyA* – knowledge, *avidyA* – ignorance.

AchArya, आचार्य – a spiritual guide or teacher. See Shankaracharya.

adhikArin or *adhikArI*, अधिकारिन् or अधिकारी – a seeker who is mentally prepared (see *chatuShTaya sampatti*) and therefore ready to receive the final teaching from the guru; literally 'possessing authority, entitled to, fit for.'

adhyAsa, अध्यास – used to refer to the 'mistake' that we make when we 'superimpose' a false appearance upon the reality or mix up the real and the unreal. The classical example is when we see a snake instead of a rope, which is used as a metaphor for seeing the world of objects instead of the reality of the Self. This concept is fundamental to Advaita and Shankara devotes a separate section to it at the beginning of his commentary on the Brahmasutra.

advaita, अद्वैत) – not (*a*) duality (*dvaita*); non-dual philosophy. (Adjective – *advitIya* – unique, without a second.)

AgAmin, आगामिन् – That type of *saMskAra* which is generated in reaction to current situations and which will not bear fruit until sometime in the future. It literally means 'impending,' 'approaching' or 'coming.' See *prArabdha, saMchita, saMskAra*.

aham, अहम् – I am.

aham vRRitti, अहम् वृत्ति – the thought 'I am' as opposed to thoughts about objects, feelings etc. – *idam vRRitti*. See *vRRitti*.

ahaMkAra, अहंकार – the making, *kAra*, of the utterance 'I,' *aham* – this is the equivalent of what we would call the 'ego' but specifically refers to the identification or attachment of our true Self with something else, usually the body or mind but can be much more specific e.g. I am a teacher, I am a woman. It is one of the 'organs' of the mind in classical Advaita – see *antaHkaraNa*.

ajAti, अजाति – *a* – no or not; *jAti* – creation; the principle that the world and everything in it, including these mind-body appearances were never created or 'brought into existence'. Most clearly stated by Gaudapada in his *kArikA* on the Mandukya Upanishad. *jAta* is the adjective, meaning born, brought into existence. The theory that there has never been any creation is called either *ajAta vAda* or *ajAti vAda*.

aj~nAna, अज्ञान – (spiritual) ignorance. See *j~nAna*. An *aj~nAnI* is one who is not enlightened, i.e. still (spiritually) ignorant.

AkAsha, आकाश – space, ether or sky; one of the five elements in the Upanishads, the subtle fluid supposed to pervade the universe. Associated with sound and hearing.

anAdi, अनादि – without any beginning, often used to refer to 'ignorance'.

Ananda, आनन्द – 'true' happiness; usually called 'bliss' to differentiate it from the transient variety that always alternates with pain or misery. It is an aspect of our true nature and is often combined with the other elements of our real nature – sat and chit – into a single word, *sachchidAnanda*. See sat, chit and *sachchidAnanda*.

AnandamAyAkosha, आनन्दमयकोश – the sheath made of bliss (one of the 'five Coverings' that surround our true essence).

ananta, अनन्त – eternal, without end.

anAtman, अनात्मन् – something other than spirit or soul (not Self or *Atman*); perceptible world. See *Atman*.

anirvachanIya, अनिर्वचनीय – not able to be categorized; literally: unutterable, indescribable, not to be mentioned. Used to describe nature of reality etc.

anitya, अनित्य – transient. Noun **anityatva,** अनित्यत्व – the condition of being transient; transient or limited existence (mortality).

annamAyAkosha, अन्नमयकोश – the sheath made of food, *anna*. (One of the 'five Coverings' that surround our true essence).

anta, अन्त – end, conclusion, death etc.

antaHkaraNa, अन्तःकरण – used to refer to the overall 'organ' of mind; the seat of thought and feeling. It derives from *antar* – within, interior – and *karaNa*, which means 'instrument' or sense-organ (an alternative for *indriya*). It consists of a number of separate functions – see *manas, buddhi,* chitta and *ahaMkAra*.

apauruSheya, अपौरुषेय – literally 'not coming from men'; used to refer to the *shruti* – scriptural texts passed on verbatim from generation to generation since their original observation by realized sages. See *shruti*.

artha, अर्थ – acquisition of wealth. One of the four *puruShArtha*-s. See *puruShArtha*.

asat, असत् – non-existent. See *sat*.

asatkArya vAda, असत्कार्य वाद – the doctrine which denies that the effect pre-exists in the cause (usually in reference to the creation).

Ashrama, आश्रम – generic term for one of the four 'stages' in the life of a Hindu Brahmin, viz. *brahmacharya, gRRihastha, saMnyAsa, vanaprastha*.

aShTAvakra, अष्टावक्र – the eponymous Sage of the Astavakra Gita (or *saMhitA*). The word literally means 'twisted' (*vakra*) in 'eight' (*aShTan*) ways. Astavakra was so called because he was born severely deformed after being cursed in the womb by his father (because the unborn child had criticized him for making mistakes whilst reading the scriptures!). (Later in life, after he had secured his father's release through defeating the court philosopher in debate, his father blessed him and, after swimming in a sacred river, the boy was cured.) See *gItA, saMhitA*.

Astika, आस्तिक – literally 'there is or exists'; used to refer to one who believes in the existence of God or, more specifically, one who defers to the authority of the Vedas. See *nAstika, veda*.

atha (*atha,* अथ) – now, then therefore; often used to express the sense of an auspicious beginning e.g. spoken prior to reading a key verse of scripture.

atma (*Atma*, आत्म) – see *Atman*.

Atmabodha, आत्मबोध – knowledge of Self or supreme spirit; a book attributed to Shankara.

Atman, आत्मन् – the Self. Usually used to refer to one's true (individual) nature or consciousness but Advaita tells us that there is no such thing as an 'individual' and that this *Atman* is the same as the universal Consciousness, *brahman*. see also *jIva*.

AtmavichAra, आत्मविचार – *vichAra* in this context means reflection or examination upon the *Atman*, the Self. See *Atman*.

avachCheda-vAda, अवच्छेद वाद् – theory that the Self is limited by ignorance in the forms of *upAdhi*-s. *avachCheda* means 'cut-off.' See *upAdhi*.

AvaraNa, आवरण – the veiling power of *mAyA*. In the rope-snake metaphor, this prevents us from seeing the reality of the rope. See *mAyA*, *vikShepa*.

avasthA, अवस्था – state; literally 'to stay, abide, exist, remain or continue doing (anything).' In Advaita, it is most frequently encountered as *avasthA traya* – the three states of waking, dreaming and deep sleep.

avidyA, अविद्या – ignorance (in a spiritual sense) i.e. that which prevents us from realizing the Self. See also *mAyA*.

avyakta, अव्यक्त – unmanifest, imperceptible, invisible; the universal spirit (*paramAtman*).

bAdha, बाध – sublation or subration. This is the process by which an accepted point of view or understanding is superseded by a totally different one when some new information is received. An example is seeing a lake in the desert and then realizing that it is only a mirage. The adjective is *bAdhita*, meaning negated, contradictory, absurd, false.

bhAga tyAga lakShaNa, भाग त्याग लक्षण – a technique used by the scriptures to point to aspects that cannot be explained directly in words. The oneness that is pointed to (*lakShaNa*) is understood by 'giving up' (*tyAga*) the contradictory parts (*bhAga*). An example would be in the apparent contradiction of the *jIva* being 'created' while *Ishvara* is the 'creator.' Both are given up in order to recognize their identity as *brahman*.

bhagavat, भगवत् – holy; prosperous, happy; illustrious, divine. In the context of Bhagavad Gita, it refers to the God, Krishna and Bhagavad Gita means Krishna's Song (the *t* changes to a *d* when the words join). See below.

Bhagavad Gita (*bhagavadgItA*, भगवद्गीता) – the scriptural text forming part of the Hindu epic, the Mahabarata. It is a dialogue between Krishna, the charioteer/God, representing the Self and the warrior Arjuna, representing you and me, on the battlefield of Kurukshetra prior to the commencement of battle. The scripture is regarded as *smRRiti*. See *bhagavat*, *smRRiti*.

bhakta, भक्त – one who practices *bhakti yoga*. See *bhakti yoga*.

bhakti yoga, भक्ति योग – devotion or worship as a means to enlightenment. See also *karma* and *j~nAna*.

bhAShya, भाष्य – explanatory work, exposition or commentary on some other scriptural document. Thus Shankara, for example, has written *bhAShya-s* on a number of Upanishads, the Bhagavad Gita and the Brahmasutra.

bhoktRRi, भोक्तृ – one who enjoys, an experiencer or feeler.

brahma, ब्रह्म – God as the creator of the universe in Hindu mythology (the others are Vishnu, *viShNu*, the preserver and Shiva, *shiva*, the destroyer). N.B. Not to be confused with *brahman*!

brahmacharya, ब्रह्मचर्य – the first stage of the traditional Hindu spiritual path, beginning one's life as an unmarried, religious and chaste student. (*charya* means 'due observance of all rites and customs'.) One of the five *yama*-s in Raja *yoga*. See also *gRRihastha*, *saMnyAsa*, *vanaprastha*.

brahman, ब्रह्मन् – the universal Self, Absolute or God. There is only *brahman*. It derives from the Sanskrit root *bRRih*, meaning to grow great or strong and could be thought of as the adjective 'big' made into a noun, implying that which is greater than anything. See also *Atman*, *brahma*, *jIva*, *jIvAtman*, *paramAtman*.

Brahma Sutra (*brahmasUtra*, ब्रह्मसूत्र) – a book (in sutra form, which is terse verse!) by Vyasa. This book is the best known of the third accepted source of knowledge (*nyAya prasthAna*). Effectively, it attempts to summarize the Upanishads. It has been extensively commented on by the three main philosophical branches of Indian thought, *dvaita*, *advaita* and *vishiShTAdvaita*, and the proponents of each claim that it substantiates their beliefs. Shankara has commented on it and provided extensive arguments against any interpretation other than that of Advaita. See *bhAShya, nyAya prasthAna, shruti, smRRiti*.

brahmavidyA, ब्रह्मविद्या – knowledge of the one Self. (Also *brahmavitva*, with someone with this knowledge being called a *brahmavit*.) See *brahman*.

Brihadaranyaka (*bRRihadAraNyaka*, बृहदारण्यक) – one of the major Upanishads (and possibly the oldest). The word derives from *bRRihat* – great, large, wide, tall etc. and *Aranyaka* – produced in (or relating to) a forest. See Upanishad.

buddhi, बुद्धि – the organ of mind responsible for discrimination and judgment, perhaps nearest equated to the intellect in Western usage. See also, *ahaMkAra, antaHkaraNa, manas* and *chitta*.

chakra, चक्र – literally 'circle' or 'wheel'; one of the points in the spine through which energy is supposed to flow in *kuNDalinI yoga*, (which has nothing to do with Advaita).

Chandogya (*chhAndogya*, छान्दोग्य) – one of the major Upanishads. See Upanishad.

chatuShTaya sampatti, चतुष्टय सम्पत्ति – the fourfold pre-requisites specified by Shankara as needed by a seeker before he can achieve Self-realization. *chatuShTaya* means 'fourfold'; *sampatti* means success or accomplishment. See *sAdhana, vairAgya, viveka, mumukShutva*.

chetana, चेतन – consciousness, intelligence etc.

chit, चित् – pure thought or Consciousness. See *Ananda, sat, sachchidAnanda*.

chitta, चित्त) – the organ (part) of mind responsible for memory. See *antaHkaraNa, ahaMkAra, buddhi, manas*.

dama, दम – self-restraint but understood as control over the senses; one of the six qualities that form part of Shankara's *chatuShTaya sampatti*. See *chatuShTaya sampatti, shamAdi ShaTka sampatti*.

darshana, दर्शन – audience or meeting (with a *guru*); viewpoint; one of the six classical Indian philosophical systems (*pUrvamImAMsA, uttaramImAMsA, nyAya, vaisheShika, sAMkhya, yoga*).

deva, देव – (noun) a deity or god; the gods; (adj.) heavenly, divine.

devanAgarI, देवनागरी – the script used in Sanskrit representation. The word literally means 'city of the Gods' (*deva* – gods; *nAgara* – belonging or relating to a town or city).

dharma, धर्म – customary practice, conduct, duty, justice and morality. One of the four *puruShArtha-s*. The favored meaning of most traditional teachers is, however, 'nature, character, essential quality,' which they often translate as 'essence.' Our own *dharma* (*svadharma*) is what we ought to do with our lives in order to dissolve our accumulation of *saMskAra*. See *saMskAra, karma.*

dhyAna, ध्यान – meditation, usually in the sense of the mechanical act using a *mantra* as opposed to *nididhyAsana.*

dRRigdRRishya viveka, दृग्दृश्य विवेक – 'Discrimination between the Seer and the Seen' – a work attributed to Shankara. *dRRik* is the seer or perceiver and *dRRishya* that which is seen or which can be objectified.

dRRiShTisRRiShTivAda, दृष्टिसृष्टिवाद् – the theory that our mistaken view of the world arises from a mental image (based on memory and sense data) superimposed upon the reality. *dRRiShTi* means 'seeing'; *sRRiShTi* means 'creation'; *vAda* means 'thesis' or 'doctrine.' See also *adhyAsa, ajAti, sRRiShTidRRiShTivAda.*

duHkha, दुःख – pain, sorrow, trouble.

dvaita, द्वैत – duality, philosophy of dualism; belief that God and the *Atman* are separate entities. Madhva is the scholar most often associated with this philosophy.

dveSha, द्वेष – hatred, dislike.

Gaudapada (*gauDapAda,* गौडपाद**)** – The author of the commentary (*kArikA*) on the Mandukya Upanishad. He is said to have been the teacher of Shankara's teacher. See *kArikA,* Mandukya, Upanishad.

gIta, गीत – a sacred song or poem but more usually refers to philosophical or religious doctrines in verse form (the word also means 'sung'). The most famous are the Bhagavad Gita and Astavakra Gita. If the word is used on its own, it will be referring to the former. See Bhagavad, *aShTAvakra.*

gRRihastha, गृहस्थ – this is the second stage of the traditional Hindu spiritual path, called the period of the householder, in which the *brahman* performs the duties of master of the house and father of a family. See also *brahmacharya, gRRihastha, saMnyAsa, vanaprastha.*

guNa, गुण – According to classical Advaita, everything in creation exhibits three 'qualities,' *sattva, rajas* and *tamas* in varying degrees and it is the relative proportions that determine the nature of the thing in question. See *sattva, rajas* and *tamas* for more details.

guru, गुरु – literally 'heavy'; used to refer to one's elders or a person of reverence but more commonly in the West to indicate one's spiritual teacher.

haTha, हठ – *haTha yoga* refers to the physical aspects of *rAja yoga*, i.e. *Asana*-s and *prANayAma*. It literally means 'violence, force or obstinacy,' 'absolute necessity' and stems from the idea of 'forcing the mind' to withdraw from objects. Monier-Williams has the additional words: *'performed with much self-torture , such as standing on one leg , holding up the arms , inhaling smoke with the head inverted etc.'*

idam vRRitti, इदम् वृत्ति – thoughts of objects, concepts, feelings etc., as opposed to *aham vRRitti* – the thought 'I am.' See *vRRitti.*

indriya, इन्द्रिय – the number five symbolizing the five senses. The five sense organs are called *j~nAnendriya*-s and the five 'organs' of action are the *karmendriya-s.*

Isha Upanishad (*IshopaniShad,* ईशोपनिषद्) – also known as the *IshAvAsya* Upanishad, because its first verse begins: *OM IshA vAsyamidam{\m+} sarvaM. IshAvAsya* means 'pervaded by the Lord.'

Ishvara, ईश्वर – the Lord; creator of the phenomenal universe. See sa*guNa brahman.*

jaDa, जड – inert, lifeless.

jagat, जगत् – the world (earth), mankind etc.

jAgrat, जाग्रत् – the waking state of consciousness. The 'waker ego' is called *vishva.* See also, *suShupti, svapna, turIya.*

janma, जन्म – birth.

japa, जप – the simple repetition of a *mantra*; usually associated with the initial stage of meditation. See *mantra.*

jAti, जाति – birth, the form of existence (as man, animal etc.); genus or species.

jIva, जीव – the identification of the *Atman* with a body and mind; sometimes spoken of as 'the embodied *Atman*.' See *Atman*.

jIvanmukta, जीवन्मुक्त – a *j~nAnI* who has also acquired the fruits of Self-knowledge, *j~nAna phalam. (mukta* is the adjective – liberated; *mukti* is the noun – liberation)

jIvAtman, जीवात्मन्् – another word for *Atman*, to emphasize that we are referring to the *Atman* in this embodied state, as opposed to the *paramAtman*, the 'supreme Self.' See *Atman*.

j~nAna yoga, ज्ञान योग – *yoga* based on the acquisition of true knowledge (*j~nAna* means 'knowledge') i.e. knowledge of the Self as opposed to mere information about the world of appearances. See also *bhakti, karma*.

j~nAnendriya, ज्ञानेन्द्रिय – an organ of perception (eye, ear, nose, tongue, skin), plural *j~nAnendryAni*.

j~nAnI or *j~nAnin,* ज्ञानी खर ज्ञानिन्् – one who practices *j~nAna yoga*. (*j~nAnin* is the *pratipAdaka; j~nAnI* is the nominative singular *pada*.) See *j~nAna yoga*.

kali yuga, कलि युग– the present age (Iron age) in the cycle of creation. See *kalpa*.

kalpa, कल्प – one day in the life of Brahma, the Creator; equal to 994 cycles of ages and 4,320,000,000 years (if you're really interested).

kAma, काम – desire, longing; one of the four *puruShArtha-s*. Not to be confused with *karma*. Shankara differentiates this from *rAga*, which is attachment to something one already has whereas *kAma* is wanting something one doesn't have. See *puruShArtha*.

kArikA, कारिका – (strictly speaking) a concise philosophical statement in verse. The most well known is that by Gaudapada on the Mandukya Upanishad. (Not to be confused with *karika*, which is an elephant!). See Gaudapada, Mandukya, Upanishad.

karma, कर्म – literally 'action' but generally used to refer to the 'law' whereby actions carried out now will have their lawful effects in the future (and this may be in future lives). Note that *karma yoga* is something different – see below. See also *saMskAra*.

karmakANDa, कर्मकाण्ड – that portion of the Vedas relating to ceremonial acts, the rituals that should be followed, sacrificial rites and so on. These may be helpful in the mental preparation for enlightenment but they are certainly not necessary.

karmaphala, कर्मफल) – the fruit (*phala*) of action; i.e. the result or consequence of our actions.

karma yoga, कर्म योग – the practice of acting in such a way as not to incur *saMskAra*, by carrying out 'right' actions, not 'good' or 'bad' ones. See *bhakti, karma, j~nAna*.

karmendriya, कर्मेन्द्रिय – an organ of action, plural *karmendriyAni*. These are hand, foot, larynx, organ of generation and organ of excretion.

kataka, ktk – the 'clearing nut' plant, used for precipitating dirt from drinking water.

Katha Upanishad (*kaThopaniShad*, कठोपनिषद्) – one of the 108+ Upanishads and one of the 10 major ones. *kaTha* was a sage and founder of a branch of the Yajur Veda. See Upanishad.

Kena Upanishad (*kenopaniShad*, केनोपनिषद्) – one of the 108+ Upanishads and another one of the 10 major ones. *kena* means 'whence?' ('how?,' 'why?' etc.) and is the first word of this Upanishad. See Upanishad.

kosha, कोश – literally 'sheath' as in the scabbard of a sword; one of the five layers of identification that cover up our true nature.

krodha, क्रोध – anger, passion.

lakShaNa, लक्षण – pointer; indicating or expressing indirectly; accurate description or definition.

laya, लय – literally 'dissolution' (and the last stage in the cycle of creation, preservation and destruction of the universe). Also used to refer to the four-stage process for dissolving ignorance described in the Astavakra Gita. See Astavakra, Gita.

lIlA, लीला – literally 'play,' 'amusement' or 'pastime'; the idea that the apparent creation is a diversion for a creator – a means for Him to enjoy Himself. He plays all the parts in such a way that they are ignorant of their real nature and believe themselves separate.

loka, लोक – world, universe, sky or heaven etc. (adjective *laukika* - worldly).

mahAvAkya, महावाक्य – *maha* means 'great'; *vAkya* means 'speech, saying or statement.' The four 'great sayings' from the Vedas are: – 'Consciousness is *brahman,*' 'That thou art,' 'This Self is *brahman*' and 'I am *brahman.*'

manana, मनन)– reflecting upon what has been heard (*shravaNa*). This is the second stage of the classical spiritual path, to remove any doubts about the knowledge that has been received via *shravaNa.* See also *saMshaya, shravaNa, nididhyAsana.*

manomAyAkosha, मनोमयकोश – the mental sheath (one of the 'five Coverings' that surround our true essence).

manas, मनस्‌ – the 'organ' of mind acting as intermediary between the senses and the intellect (*buddhi*) on the way in and the intellect and the organs of action on the way out. These are its primary functions and 'thinking' ought to consist only of the processing of data on behalf of the intellect. Unfortunately, it usually tries to take on the role of the intellect itself and this is when thinking becomes a problem. See *ahaMkAra, antaHkaraNa, buddhi* and *chitta.*

Mandukya (*mANDUkya,* माण्डूक्य**)** – One of the major Upanishads and possibly the single most important, when considered in conjunction with the *kArikA* written by Gaudapada. (In many versions of this Upanishad, there is no distinction made between the original and the additions made by Gaudapada and there is some argument over which is which.) See Gaudapada, *kArikA,* Upanishad.

mantra, मन्त्र – a group of words (or sometimes only one or more syllables), traditionally having some mystical significance, being in many religions an actual 'name of God' or a short prayer. Often used in meditation (always in Transcendental Meditation). See *japa.*

mArga, मार्ग – path, track, way. *vichAra mArga* is translated as 'Direct Path,' referring to the particular method of teaching Advaita.

mAyA, माया – literally 'magic' or 'witchcraft,' often personified in Hindu mythology. The 'force' used to explain how it is that we come to be deceived into believing that there is a creation with separate objects and living creatures etc. See also *AvaraNa* and *vikShepa.*

mAyAkAra, मायाकार) – a maker of magic i.e. a conjurer or magician.

See *mAyA*.

mithyA, मिथ्या – dependent reality; literally 'incorrectly' or 'improperly,' used in the sense of 'false, untrue.' It is, however, more frequently used in the sense of 'depending upon something else for its existence.' It is ascribed to objects etc., meaning that these are not altogether unreal but not strictly real either i.e. they are our imposition of name and form upon the undifferentiated Self. See *adhyAsa*.

moha, मोह – delusion, bewilderment, infatuation, preventing the discernment of truth; 'love' in its selfish form of love of another person, where something is desired for oneself, as opposed to *prema*, 'pure unselfish love.'

mokSha, मोक्ष – liberation, enlightenment, Self-realization; one of the four *puruShArtha-s*.

mukti, मुक्ति – setting or becoming free, final liberation. (*mukta* is the adjective – liberated)

mumukShu, मुमुक्षु – one for whom the desire to achieve enlightenment is the predominant goal in life; a seeker.

mumukShutva, मुमुक्षुत्व) – the desire to achieve enlightenment, to the exclusion of all other desires. See *sAdhana, chatuShTaya sampatti*.

Mundaka Upanishad (*muNDakopaniShad*, मुण्डकोपनिषद्) – Another one of the 108+ Upanishads and also one of the 10 major ones – but not to be confused with the Mandukya. *muNDa* means 'having a shaved head' and the Upanishad is so called because everyone who comprehends its sacred doctrine is 'shorn,' i.e. liberated from all error. See Upanishad.

naimittika, नैमित्तिक – occasional, special. *naimittika karma* are those occasional duties that we have to perform, such as helping a neighbor who has helped one in the past.

nAma-rUpa, नामरूप – name and form.

nAstika, नास्तिक – atheist, unbeliever; usually refers to one who does not recognize the authority of the Vedas.

neti, नेति – not this (*na* – not; *iti* – this). From the Brihadaranyaka Upanishad (2.3.6). Used by the intellect whenever it is thought that the Self might be some 'thing' observed e.g. body, mind etc. The Self cannot be anything that is seen, thought or known. See Brihadaranyaka, Upanishad.

nididhyAsana, निदिध्यासन – meditating upon the essence of what has now been intellectually understood until there is total conviction. The third stage of the classical spiritual path. See also *shravaNa* and manana. It is to be understood as 'right apprehension' (*vij~nAna*) rather than simply mechanical as *dhyAna* might be construed.

nidrA, निद्रा – sleep.

nirguNa, निर्गुण – 'without qualities'; usually referring to *brahman* and meaning that it is beyond any description or thought. Since there is only *brahman,* any word would imply limitation or duality. See *brahman,* sa*guNa, Ishvara.*

nirvikalpa, निर्विकल्प – (referring to *samAdhi*) 'without' doubts about one's identity with the one Self. See *savikalpa, samAdhi,* vikalpa.

niShkAma, निष्काम – desireless, disinterested. *niShkAma karma* is so-called 'right action,' performed in response to the need, neither selfishly nor unselfishly – it generates no *saMskAra.*

nitya, नित्य – eternal. It also means 'ordinary, usual, necessary, obligatory.' It is used in this latter sense in connection with action. *nitya karma* are those daily duties that we have to perform, such as looking after one's children.

nyAya, न्याय – logical argument; literally, 'that into which a thing goes back,' a 'standard' or 'rule'; one of the 6 classical Indian philosophical systems, whose principal exponent was Gautama in the 3rd Century BC. So called because the system 'goes into' all physical and metaphysical subjects in a very logical manner.

nyAya prasthAna, न्याय प्रस्थान – refers to logical and inferential material based upon the Vedas, of which the most well known is the Brahmasutra of Vyasa (*vyAsa*). (*nyAya* can also mean method, axiom, logical argument etc.) See *pramANa, prasthAna-traya, smRRiti, shruti.*

pa~nchabhUta, पञ्चभूत – the five elements, viz. earth – *pRRithivI*; water – *ap*; fire – *tejas*; air – *vAyu*; space or ether – *AkAsha.*

Panchadashi (*pa~nchadashI,* पञ्चदशी**)** – literally means 'fifteen' because it has this many chapters – a book written by Vidyaranya (*vidyAraNya*), based upon the Upanishads. It discusses many Advaitic truths and uses some original metaphors to illustrate the concepts.

pa~ncha kosha, पञ्च कोश – the five sheaths.

paNDita, पण्डित – literally 'wise' as an adjective or 'scholar, teacher, philosopher' as a noun and used in this way in the scriptures. However, it has come to mean someone who knows a lot of theory but does very little practice. We sometimes use the word 'pundit' in our language – the word 'sophist' would probably be a good synonym.

pApa, पाप – literally 'bad' or 'wicked' but used in the sense of the 'sin' that accrues (according to the theory of *karma*) from performing 'bad' actions, i.e. those done with a selfish motive. See also *puNya.*

paramArtha (noun), परमार्थ); *pAramArthika* (adj.), पारमार्थिक – the highest truth or reality; the noumenal as opposed to the phenomenal world of appearances (*vyAvahArika*). See *prAtibhAsika* and *vyAvahArika.*

paramAtman, परमात्मन् – usually translated as the 'supreme Self' as opposed to the *Atman* in the embodied state, the *jIvAtman.* Swami Dayananda insists that it actually means 'limitless' in the sense of not limited by time or place and therefore changeless (Ref. 99). See *Atman.*

paramparA, परम्परा – literally 'proceeding from one to another'; *guru paramparA* refers to the tradition of guru – disciple passing on wisdom through the ages. See also *sampradAya.*

Patanjali (*pata~njali,* पतञ्जलि) – philosopher, writer of the 'Yoga Sutras' and responsible for *aShTA~Nga* or *rAja yoga.*

phala, फल – fruit; often used in the context of the consequences that necessarily follow as a result of action. See *karmaphala.* (Remember that 'ph' is pronounced as in 'uphill', not as an 'f'!)

praj~nA, प्रज्ञा – (verb) to know or understand, find out, perceive or learn; (noun) wisdom, intelligence, knowledge. Not to be confused with *prAj~na* below.

prAj~na, प्राज्ञ – the 'deep sleep ego' in the deep sleep state of consciousness, *suShupti.* Literally, 'wise, clever' (adj.) or 'a wise man' or 'intelligence dependent on individuality.' See also *vishva, taijasa.*

pralaya, प्रलय – the destruction of the world at the end of a *kalpa.* Note that this means 'making unmanifest' rather than actual destruction. All of the accumulated *saMskAra* is used to manifest the creation again in the next *kalpa.* See *kalpa.*

prakRRiti, प्रकृति – literally the original or natural form or condition of anything; generally used to refer to what we would call 'nature' or the generic concept of 'matter'. *sAMkhya* philosophy uses the word *pradhAna* for this, also.

pramA, प्रमा – true knowledge, basis or foundation.

pramANa, प्रमाण – valid means for acquiring knowledge. There are 6 of these in Vedanta: – perception (*pratyakSha*), inference (*anumAna*), scriptural or verbal testimony (*shabda* or *Agama shruti*), analogy (*upamAna*), presumption (*arthApatti*) and non-apprehension (*anupalabdhi*). The first three are the major ones referred to by Shankara.

prANa, प्राण – literally the 'breath of life'; the vital force in the body with which we identify in the 'vital sheath.'

prANamAyAkosha, प्राणमयकोश – the sheath made of breath (one of the 'five Coverings' that surround our true essence).

prANAyAma, प्राणायाम – usually understood to mean control of breathing in advanced *yoga* techniques or as a prelude to meditation. According to Swami Chinmayananda, however, it does not mean this but relates to the five 'departments' of active life as described in the chapter on Spiritual Practices.

prArabdha, प्रारब्ध – This literally means 'begun' or 'undertaken.' It is the fruit of all of our past action that is now having its effect. This is one of the three types of *saMskAra*. See *AgAmin, saMchita, saMskAra*. Also, there are three types of *prArabdha karma* – *ichChA*, *anichChA* and *parechChA* (personally desired, without desire and due to others' desire).

prasthAna traya, प्रस्थान त्रय – *prasthAna* means 'system' or 'course' in the sense of a journey; *traya* just means 'threefold.' It refers to the three sources of knowledge of the Self: *nyAya prasthAna, shruti* and *smRRiti*. See *nyAya prasthAna, shabda, shruti, smRRiti*.

pratibhAsa (noun), प्रतिभास); ***prAtibhAsika*** (adj.) , प्रातिभासिक – appearing or occurring to the mind, existing only in appearance, an illusion. See *paramArtha, vyavahAra*.

pratibimba, प्रतिबिम्ब – a reflection. In logic, *bimba* is the object itself, with the *pratibimba* being the counterpart with which it is compared.

pratibimba vAda, प्रतिबिम्ब वाद – the theory that the *jIva* is a reflection of the *Atman*, similar to a the reflection of an object in a mirror.

pratyakSha, प्रत्यक्ष – 'present before the eyes, clear, distinct etc.' but particularly 'direct perception or apprehension' as a valid source of knowledge. Opposite of *parokSha*, hidden. See *pramANa*.

preyas, प्रेयस् – the 'pleasant' as opposed to the 'good'; more agreeable, more desired.

puNya, पुण्य – literally 'good' or 'virtuous'; used to refer to the 'reward' that accrues to us (according to the theory of *karma*) through the performing of unselfish actions. See also *pApa*.

pUrNa, पूर्ण – full, complete, satisfied, perfect.

puruShArtha, पुरुषार्थ) – The general meaning of this term is 'any object of human pursuit' but it is used here in the sense of human (i.e. self) effort to overcome 'fate,' the fruit of one's past actions. The four classical pursuits are *kAma, artha, dharma* and *mokSha*. *puruShArtha-lAbha* is fulfillment of those pursuits. See *karma, saMskAra*.

rAga, राग – any feeling or passion but especially vehement desire; interest in, attachment. Shankara differentiates this from *kAma*: *rAga* is attachment to something one already has whereas *kAma* is wanting something one doesn't have. *rAga-dveSha* is love-hatred.

rAja, राज – literally 'king or sovereign,' as in *rAja yoga* (or *aShTA~Nga yoga*) of Patanjali, where it is usually translated as 'royal *yoga*.'

rajas, रजस् – the second of the three *guNa-s*. Associated with animals and activity, emotions, desire, selfishness and passion. Adjective – rajassic (Eng.); *rAjasika* (Sanskrit) See *guNa*.

RRiShi, ऋषि – author or singer of sacred Vedic hymns but now more generally used to refer to a saint or Sage.

rUpa, रूप – form, outward appearance.

sadguru, सद्गुरु – the ultimate guru – one's own Self (*sat* = true, real). See *guru*.

sAdhaka, साधक – a seeker or, more pedantically, a worshipper.

sAdhana, साधन – literally 'leading straight to a goal'; refers to the spiritual disciplines followed as part of a 'path' toward Self-realization. See also *chatuShTaya sampatti*.

sAdhu, साधु – a sage, saint, holy man; literally leading straight to the goal, hitting the mark.

saguNa, सगुण – 'with qualities.' The term is usually used to refer to *brahman* personified as the creator, *Ishvara*, to symbolize the most spiritual aspect of the world of appearances. See *brahman*, *Ishvara*, *nirguNa*.

sahaja sthiti, सहज स्थिति – Once Self-realization has been attained, there is full and lasting knowledge of the Self. '*sahaja*' means 'state' but this stage of *samAdhi* is not a state – it is our true nature. It is permanent (*sthiti* meaning 'steady' or 'remaining'), unlike the earlier stages of *samAdhi*. See *nirvikalpa*, *samAdhi*, *savikalpa*, *vikalpa*.

sAkShin, साक्षिन् – a witness, the ego or subject as opposed to the object (also *sAkshI*).

samAdhAna, समाधान – contemplation, profound meditation; more usually translated as concentration; one of the 'six qualities' that form part of Shankara's *chatuShTaya sampatti*. See *chatuShTaya sampatti*, *shamAdi ShaTka sampatti*.

samAdhi, समाधि – the state of total peace and stillness achieved during deep meditation. Several 'stages' are defined – see *vikalpa*, *savikalpa*, *samAdhi*, *nirvikalpa samAdhi* and *sahaja sthiti*.

saMhitA, संहिता – a philosophical or religious text constructed according to certain rules of sound. There are many of these in the Vedas. The reference in this book is in conjunction with the Astavakra *SaMhitA* or Gita. This book is not part of the Vedas. See *Astavakra*, *gIta*.

sAMkhya, सांख्य – one of the three main divisions of Hindu philosophy and one of the six *darshana-s*; attributed to Kapila.

sampradAya, सम्प्रदाय – the tradition or established doctrine of teaching from *guru* to disciple (*shiShya*) through the ages. See also *paramparA*.

saMsAra, संसार – the continual cycle of death and rebirth, transmigration etc. to which we are subject in the phenomenal world until we become enlightened and escape. *saMsArin* – one who is bound to the cycle of birth and death.

saMshaya, संशय – uncertainty, irresolution, hesitation or doubt. See *manana*.

sanAtana, सनातन – literally 'eternal' or 'permanent'; in conjunction with *dharma*, this refers to our essential nature. The phrase *sanAtana dharma* is also used to refer to the traditional (also carrying the sense of 'original' and 'unadulterated') Hindu practices or as a synonym for 'Hinduism.' See *dharma*.

saMchita, संचित – one of the three types of *saMskAra*, literally meaning 'collected' or 'piled up.' That *saMskAra*, which has been accumulated from past action but has still not manifest. See *AgAmin*, *prArabdha*, *saMskAra*.

sa~Nga, सङ्ग – assembly, association, company. See *satsa~Nga*.

saMskAra, संस्कार – Whenever an action is performed with the desire for a specific result (whether for oneself or another), *saMskAra* is created for that person. These accumulate and determine the situations with which we will be presented in the future and will influence the scope of future actions. There are three 'types' – *AgAmin*, *saMchita* and *prArabdha*. The accumulation of *saMskAra* (*saMchita*) dictates the tendencies that we have to act in a particular way (*vAsanA-s*). This is all part of the mechanism of *karma*. See *AgAmin*, *karma*, *prArabdha*, *saMchita* and *karma*.

saMnyAsa, संन्यास – the final stage of the traditional Hindu spiritual path; involves complete renunciation. The word literally means 'putting or throwing down, laying aside'; i.e. becoming an ascetic. One who does so is called a *saMnyAsin* (*saMnyAsin*). See also *brahmacharya*, *gRRihastha*, *vanaprastha*.

sat, सत् – existence, reality, truth (to mention a few). See also *Ananda*, *chit*, *sachchidAnanda*.

sat – chit – Ananda or **sachchidAnanda**, सच्चिदानन्द – the oft used word to describe our true nature, in so far as this can be put into words (which it can't). It translates as being-consciousness-bliss but see the separate bits for more detail.

satkArya vAda, सत्कार्य वाद – the doctrine of the effect actually pre-existing in the cause (usually in reference to the creation) This is the belief of the *sAMkhya* system of philosophy.

satsa~Nga, सत्सङ्ग – association with the good; keeping 'good company'; most commonly used now to refer to a group of people gathered together to discuss (Advaita) philosophy.

sattva, सत्त्व – the highest of the three *guNa-s*. Associated with stillness, peace, truth, wisdom, unselfishness and spirituality, representing the highest aspirations of man. Adjective – sattvic (Eng.); *sAttvika* (Sanskrit). See *guNa*.

sattvApatti, सत्त्वापत्ति – the (4th) stage on a spiritual path, after which there is no longer any need for effort to be made (so-called because there is now an abundance of *sattva*). *Apatti* means 'entering into a state or condition.'

satya, सत्य – true, real. *satyam* – truth. Also one of the *yama-s* – truthfulness, sincerity.

savikalpa, सविकल्प – (referring to *samAdhi*) still 'with' doubts about one's identity with the one Self. See *nirvikalpa*, *samAdhi*, *vikalpa*.

shabda, शब्द – scriptural or verbal testimony. See *pramANa*, *nyAya prasthAna*, *prasthAna-traya*, *shruti*, *smRRiti*.

shakti, शक्ति – power, strength (especially in connection with a deity).

shama, शम – literally tranquility, absence of passion but more usually translated as mental discipline or self-control; one of the *shamAdi ShaTka sampatti* or 'six qualities' that form part of Shankara's *chatuShTaya sampatti*. See *chatuShTaya sampatti*, *shamAdi ShaTka sampatti*.

shamAdi ShaTka sampatti, शमादि षट्क सम्पत्ति – the six qualities that form part of Shankara's *chatuShTaya sampatti*. These are *shama*, *dama*, *uparati*, *titikShA*, *samAdhAna* and *shraddhA*.

Shankara (*shaMkara*, शंकर) – 8th Century Indian philosopher responsible for firmly establishing the principles of Advaita. Though he died at an early age (32?), he commented on a number of major Upanishads, the Bhagavad Gita and the Brahmasutras, as well as being attributed as the author of a number of famous works, such as Atmabodha, Bhaja Govindam and Vivekachudamani.

Shankaracharya (*shaMkarAchArya*, शंकराचार्य) – The title given to one of the four teachers (see *AchArya*) following the tradition in India established by Shankara (see Shankara). He set up four positions, North, South, East and West, to be held by realized men, who would take on the role of teacher and could be consulted by anyone having problems or questions of a spiritual nature.

shAnti, शान्ति – peace, tranquility.

sharIra, शरीर – one's body (divided into gross, subtle and causal aspects); literally 'that which is easily destroyed or dissolved.'

shAstra, शास्त्र – order, teaching, instruction; any sacred book or composition that has divine authority.

shAstrIya anumAna, शास्त्रीय अनुमान – inference based upon the material contained in the scriptures.

shiShya, शिष्य – pupil, scholar, disciple.

shraddhA, श्रद्धा – faith, trust or belief (in the absence of direct personal experience); the student needs this initially in respect of what he is told by the guru or reads in the scriptures; one of the 'six qualities' that form part of Shankara's *chatuShTaya sampatti.* See *chatuShTaya sampatti,* s*hamAdi ShaTka sampatti.*

shravaNa, श्रवण – hearing the truth from a sage or reading about it in such works as the Upanishads; first of the three key stages in the classical spiritual path. See also *manana, nididhyAsana.*

shreyas, श्रेयस्‌ – the 'good' as opposed to the 'pleasant'; most excellent, best, auspicious.

shrI, श्री – used as a title, c.f. 'reverend,' to signify an eminent person. May also be used in a similar manner to refer to revered objects or works of scripture, for example.

shrotriya, श्रोत्रिय – someone (usually a *brAhmaNa*) who is well-versed in the scriptures.

shruti, श्रुति – refers to the Vedas, incorporating the Upanishads. Literally means 'hearing' and refers to the belief that the books contain orally transmitted, sacred wisdom from the dawn of time. See *nyAya prasthAna, pramANa, smRRiti.*

shubhechChA, शुभेच्छा – good desire; the initial impulse that start us on a spiritual search. *shubha* means 'auspicious,' 'good (in a moral sense)' and *ichChA* means 'wish,' 'desire.'

smRRiti, स्मृति – refers to material 'remembered' and subsequently written down. In practice, it refers to books of law (in the sense of guidance for living) which were written and based upon the knowledge in the Vedas, i.e. the so-called *dharma-shAstra-s* – Manu, Yajnavalkya, Parashara. In the context of *nyAya prasthAna,* it is used to refer to just one of these books –

the Bhagavad Gita. See *pramANa*, *nyAya prasthAna*, *shruti*.

sRRiShTi, सृष्टि – creation.

sRRiShTidRRiShTivAda, सृष्टिदृष्टिवाद् – the theory that the world is separate from ourselves, having been created (by God or big-bang) and evolving independently of ourselves, i.e. the 'common sense' view of things. See also *adhyAsa*, *ajAti*, *dRRiShTisRRiShTivAda*.

sthitapraj~na, स्थितप्रज्ञ – meaning one 'standing' (*sthita*) in 'wisdom' (*prAj~na*); a man of steadiness and calm, firm in judgment, contented. The name given by the Bhagavad Gita to one who is Self-realized.

sthUla, स्थूल – large, thick, coarse, dense; the gross body (*sthUla sharIra*).

sukha, सुख – comfortable, happy, prosperous etc. *sukham* – pleasure, happiness.

sUkShma, सूक्ष्म – subtle, as in the subtle body – *sUkShma sharIra*.

suShupti, सुषुप्ति – the deep-sleep state of consciousness. The 'sleeper ego' is called *prAj~na*. See also, *jAgrat*, *svapna*, *turIya*.

sva, स्व – one's own.

svabhAva, स्वभाव – one's natural disposition.

svadharma, स्वधर्म – one's own *dharma*. See *dharma*.

svapna, स्वप्न – the dream state of consciousness. The 'dreamer ego' is called *taijasa*. See also, *jAgrat*, *suShupti*, *turIya*.

svarUpa, स्वरूप – one's own character or nature and, e.g., *svarUpAnanda* – one's own Ananda (limitless bliss).

taijasa, तैजस – the 'dreamer ego' in the dream state of consciousness, *svapna*. See also *vishva*, *prAj~na*.

Taittiriya (*taittirIya*, तैत्तिरीय) – one of the principal Upanishads. (*taittirIya* was one of the schools of the Yajur Veda.)

tamas, तमस् – the 'lowest' of the three *guNa-s*. Associated with matter and carrying characteristics such as inertia, laziness, heedlessness and death. It literally means 'darkness' or 'gloom.' Adjective – tamasic (Eng.); *tAmasika* (Sanskrit). See *guNa*.

taTastha, तटस्थ – a property distinct from what is really being spoken of but that by which it is known. An example would be telling someone that the house they are referring to in the street ahead is the one with the crow

---

on the chimney. The house is what the listener is interested in but the crow is a *taTastha lakShaNa*, i.e. that by which it is known.

titikShA, तितिक्षा – forbearance or patience; one of the 'six qualities' that form part of Shankara's *chatuShTaya sampatti*. See *chatuShTaya sampatti*, *shamAdi ShaTka sampatti*.

trikAlAtIta, त्रिकालातीत – that which transcends past, present and future (describing the Self).

turIya, तुरीय – the 'fourth state' of consciousness (*turIya* means 'fourth'). The word 'facet' is better than state. A preferred description would be the background against which the other states (waking, dream and deep sleep) take place or the real 'content' of those states. It is our true nature. (When it is defined merely as the highest 'state' then our true nature is called *turIyatIta*, but this is not a traditional term.)

tyAga, त्याग – renunciation.

upAdhi, उपाधि – Literally, this means something that is put in place of another thing; a substitute, phantom or disguise. In Vedanta, it is commonly referred to as a 'limitation' or 'limiting adjunct' that prevents us from realizing the Self.

Upanishad (*upaniShad,* उपनिषद्**)** – one of the (108+) books forming part (usually the end) of one of the four Vedas. The parts of the word mean: to sit (*Shad*) near a master (*upa*) at his feet (*ni*), so that the idea is that we sit at the feet of a master to listen to his words. Monier-Williams (Ref. 5) states that, 'according to native authorities, *upaniShad* means 'setting at rest ignorance by revealing the knowledge of the supreme spirit.' See Vedanta.

uparama, उपरम – see uparati.

uparati, उपरति – desisting from sensual enjoyment; 'reveling' in that which is 'near' i.e. one's own Self; also translated as following one's *dharma* or duty; one of the 'six qualities' that form part of Shankara's *chatuShTaya sampatti*. See *chatuShTaya sampatti*, *shamAdi ShaTka sampatti*.

upAsana, उपासन – worship, homage, waiting upon; literally the act of sitting or being near to; sometimes used in the sense of 'meditation.'

upAya, उपाय – another term for 'path' (see *marga*) – that by which one reaches one's aim, a means or expedient, way.

vAda, वाद् – speech, proposition, discourse, argument, discussion, explanation or exposition (of scriptures etc.)

vairAgya, वैराग्य – detachment or dispassion; indifference to the pleasure that results from success or the disappointment that result from failure. Literally to be 'deprived of' (*vai*) 'passion or desire' (*rAga*). See *sAdhana, chatuShTaya sampatti.*

vanaprastha, वनप्रस्थ – the third stage of the traditional Hindu spiritual path, in which the *brahman* retires from life and becomes a 'forest dweller,' living as a hermit. See also *brahmacharya, gRRihastha, saMnyAsa, vanaprastha.*

vAsanA, वासना – literally 'desiring' or 'wishing' – latent behavioral tendency in one's nature brought about through past action (*karma*) and the *saMskAra* that resulted from this. See *karma, saMskAra.*

Vasishta (*vAsiShTha,* वासिष्ठ) – eponymous sage of the 'Yoga Vasishta' one of the classical works of Advaita.

veda, वेद् – knowledge, but the word is normally only used to refer to one of the four Vedas (see Vedanta) and *vidyA* is used for knowledge per se. See *vidyA.*

Vedanta (*vedAnta,* वेदान्त) – literally 'end' or 'culmination' (*anta*) of the Vedas (*veda*), referring to the four Vedas, the Hindu equivalents of the Christian bible (called *RRig veda; sama veda; atharva veda; yajur veda*). Traditionally, the last part of the *veda-s* (i.e. 'end') is devoted to the Upanishads. See *upaniShad.*

vichAra, विचार – consideration, reflection, deliberation, investigation. *vichAra mArga* is translated as 'Direct Path,'

vidyA, विद्या – knowledge, science, learning, philosophy. *Atma-vidyA* or *brahma-vidyA* is knowledge of the Self.

Vidyaranya (*vidyAraNya,* विद्यारण्य) – author of the Panchadashi.

vij~nAna, विज्ञान – discerning, understanding, comprehending; 'right apprehension' in the case of *nididhyAsana* as opposed to *dhyAna. vij~nAna vAda* is the philosophical theory of Idealism.

vij~nAnamAyAkosha, विज्ञानमयकोश – the intellectual sheath (one of the five 'coverings' that surround our true essence).

vikalpa, विकल्प – doubt, uncertainty or indecision.

vikAra, विकार – transformation, modification, change of form or nature. *savikAra* is subject to change, *nirvikAra* is changeless.

vikShepa, विक्षेप – the 'projecting' power of *mAyA*. In the rope-snake metaphor, this superimposes the image of the snake upon the rope. See *AvaraNa, mAyA*.

vishva, विश्व – the 'waker ego' in the waking state of consciousness, *jAgrat*. Also sometimes referred to as *vaishvAnara*. See also *taijasa, prAj~na*.

vivarta, विवर्त – an apparent or illusory form; unreality caused by *avidyA*.

vivarta vAda, विवर्त वाद – the theory that the world is only an apparent projection of Ishvara (i.e. an illusion).

viveka, विवेक – discrimination; the function of *buddhi,* having the ability to differentiate between the unreal and the real. See *sAdhana, chatuShTaya sampatti*.

Vivekachudamani (*vivekachUDAmaNi,* विवेकचूडामणि) – the title of a book attributed to Shankara. *chUDAmaNi* is the name given to the jewel worn on top of the head. An English version of the book is called 'The Crest Jewel of Discrimination.'

vRRitti, वृत्ति – in the context of Vedanta, this means a mental disposition. In general, it can mean a mode of conduct or behavior, character or disposition, business or profession etc. See *aham vRRitti* and *idam vRRitti*.

vyavahAra (noun), व्यवहार; *vyAvahArika* (adj.), व्यावहारिक – the 'relative,' 'practical,' or phenomenal world of appearances; the normal world in which we live and which we usually believe to be real; as opposed to *pAramArthika* (reality) and *prAtibhAsika* (illusory). See *pAramArthika* and *prAtibhAsika*.

yoga, योग – literally 'joining' or 'attaching' (our word 'yoke' derives from this). It is used generally to refer to any system whose aim is to 'join' our 'individual self' back to the 'universal Self.' The Yoga system pedantically refers to that specified by Patanjali. See *bhakti, j~nAna, karma*.

yuga, युग – one of the four ages in the cycle of creation. See *kalpa, kali yuga*.

yukti, युक्ति – reasoning, argument, induction, deduction (as opposed to intuition – anubhava).

Appendix 1 – Sources of further information

In the past fifteen years, the information relating to Advaita that is available on the Internet has multiplied dramatically. In 1995, a few discussion groups enabled interested seekers to share their understanding and discuss their experiences but there were few actual web sites. Web search technology was also in its infancy, so that it was not easy to discover the little information that might be found. In August 2006, when I was writing 'Back to the Truth', typing the keyword 'Advaita' into the most popular search engine (Google) returned 936,000 results – three times more than the previous year. (In October 2009, this has actually decreased to 655,000 but I suspect that this is because Google is more discriminating. This view is supported by the fact that my own website is first and second in the list...) More careful selection of search criteria can recover information about virtually any aspect of the subject. Even entire classical works can be downloaded for study off-line, as well as more modern works such as the unparalleled 'Talks with Sri Ramana Maharshi', made available at Sri Ramanasramam.

This appendix aims to provide a very brief introduction to the sort of material that may be found. The source is my own web site – www.advaita.org.uk – part of whose purpose is to link to those sites that I have found to be particularly good in their related classification. As editor of the Advaita category for the Open Directory Project – http://dmoz.org/Society/Religion_and_Spirituality/Advaita_Vedanta/ – the aim is that I should be aware of *all* sites dedicated to Advaita, whether about specific teachers, organizations, publications, philosophy or history.

Note that, because site owners may change their web hosts, or even cease to maintain a site altogether, the addresses given below may change and it is always best to check with site directories such as the one above to ensure that the most up-to-date address is used. You should also note that my own site is destined to be replaced sometime in 2010 by www.advaita-academy.org, to reflect the formation of the charitable trust Advaita Academy. This organization is being formed with the sole purpose of increasing awareness of the traditional teaching of Advaita throughout the world.

A. Organizations and Traditional Teaching

These are bodies which provide specific teaching on Advaita, usually in the form of regular talks or discussion groups. They may also publish their own books or at least provide a bookstore from which books on Advaita may be purchased. Some of the larger ones may operate from many locations, possibly throughout the world. Whilst their principal aim is to advertise their facilities and encourage new members, many also provide information on-line for the casual 'browser.' This may be anything from biographical information of founders to complete downloadable books (usually in PDF format for ease of reading on-line).

See also the sections below relating to Swami Dayananda and Swami Chinmayananda. Both have organizations at various locations throughout the world and their disciples are some of the best teachers to be found anywhere.

Sections on Ramakrishna and Vivekananda, Ramana Maharshi and Nisargadatta Maharaj are also included because some of their written material is extremely valuable and they are universally recognized as enlightened sages. However, it should be noted that the first three did not belong to any recognized sampradAya. Nisargadatta did, but his teaching became increasingly radical as his life progressed. None of these teachers can therefore be regarded as 'traditional Advaita' in the strict sense.

1. UK-Based

Shanti Sadan was founded by Hari Prasad Shastri in London in 1929. Free talks are organized on most Wed and Fri Evenings at W11 as well as One-Day Courses at other venues in Central London. They publish a wide range of books, both translations of Advaita classics and original works by Hari Prasad Shastri. These include the highly recommended, six-volume, Shankara Source Book, and a quarterly journal, Self-Knowledge. http://www.shanti-sadan.org/

School of Economic Science

Also known as the School of Practical Philosophy in the US, this is one of the most widespread organizations related to Advaita, with centers in a number of countries around the world, especially in the UK. There are also branches in Belgium, Canada, Cyprus, Greece, Malta, the Netherlands, Ireland, Australia, New Zealand, Spain, Trinidad, Venezuela and South Africa. The principal emphasis is on *karma yoga*.

Most of the ideas are presented in the first term of 12 lectures but students are encouraged to continue attendance indefinitely. Eventually, stable groups may form to practice and discuss the philosophy, attending regular residential courses of 2 – 10 days at a time, in addition to their 36 weekly meetings per year, to enable more concentrated practice. Transcendental Meditation is introduced after two years. It is also a world-class center for the study of Sanskrit.

The school provides a valuable introduction to Advaita and can be highly recommended. There are several shortcomings but these only become apparent after some time, namely the absence of a residential sage, an obsession with conquering the ego and the confusing of Shankara-based Advaita with teachings from other traditions.

The school is now affiliated with Shri Vasudevananda of Allahabad, and it is very likely that the last problem mentioned has improved since I left (over a decade ago). http://www.schooleconomicscience.org/

The Study Society was originally founded to continue the methods of P. D. Ouspensky but, in the sixties, became associated (along with SES above) with Sri Shantananda Saraswati. They utilize the same *mantra* technique of meditation and hold weekly group meetings but on a much more casual basis than SES. They also practice the Sufi 'Mevlevi Turning'. Talks and concerts are also held at their headquarters in London. http://www.studysociety.com/about/

The Saraswati Society has held satsang in Sutton, Surrey over 2 decades. They combine Sufi teaching with Advaita and practice Mevlevi whirling (Sema) to traditional music along with meditation and teaching from the

Bhagavad Gita. http://www.saraswati.soc.btinternet.co.uk/

School of Meditation
Another organization based in London, this also has branches in several parts of the UK as well as in Greece and Holland. Its origins are in the same tradition from which the Maharishi Mahesh Yogi's Transcendental Meditation school derives. It adheres to the tradition however, whereas the TM organization has adapted the original techniques. It is the School of Meditation that 'initiates' members of SES into meditation. The principle of this School used to be a senior member of SES and visited the same Shankaracharya for guidance. Contact is still maintained between these schools along with the Study Society. They hold weekly meetings, primarily to discuss the practice of meditation and its background. Guidance is available for life for all who have learnt meditation with the school. There is also the opportunity to attend two residential weekends each year. (Apologies are rendered for inaccuracies in these details in the first edition of this book.) http://www.schoolofmeditation.org/

Vedanta Institute UK is effectively the UK branch of the Vedanta Cultural Foundation established in 1976 in India by Swami Parthasarathy. Annual lectures, management seminars, study groups, talks, workshops and retreats are organized. Activities take place in various parts of London, Manchester, Nottingham and Birmingham. http://www.vedanta.org.uk/

2. US-Based
Arsha Vidya Gurukulam is an institute for the traditional study of Vedanta and Sanskrit, located in the Pocono Mountains, at Saylorsburg, Pennsylvania. It offers studies in the Upanishads, Bhagavad Gita, Brahmasutras, and other classical Vedic texts. It was established in 1986 by Swami Dayananda Saraswati. There is also a home study course for Bhagavad Gita ($210 in US) and for Sanskrit ($55 in US) and an excellent bookstore. http://www.arshavidya.org/

Arsha Bodha Center is a similar organization in central New Jersey founded by Swami Tadatmananda, a disciple of Swami Dayananda. There are regular classes in Vedanta and Sanskrit and numerous other events. Payment is by donation. http://www.arshabodha.org/index.htm

Transcendental Meditation
This main site provides details of what TM is, scientific research carried out to validate its benefits and where you can be initiated (you submit an online form and someone from your nearest branch then contacts you). There is information about Maharishi Mahesh Yogi, the TM program and frequently asked questions and answers. It is very much advertised as a means for achieving relaxation and as a benefit to bodily and mental health, with no obvious references to Advaita or any other philosophy. i.e. it appears to be for 'me', not for realizing the Self. You may also enroll in the Maharishi Open University, which offers Internet Video Broadcasts and courses in 'Yogic Flying' amongst other things. http://www.tm.org

Meditation Station
The Meditation Society of America has produced these pages, which look likely to contain everything you ever wanted to know about meditation, including descriptions of 108 different techniques, concepts, words of wisdom and a message board. There are also newsletters, CDs... and a tee-shirt! http://www.meditationsociety.com/

Another site that has information on many aspects of meditation is **My Meditation Garden** (N.B. This is not an 'organization' and is included here as related information only.) The articles are comprehensively catego-rized in the Site Map and include audio, and video. Note that the expressed aims are almost exclusively concerned with 'worldly' benefits, which of course are ultimately irrelevant from the point of view of Advaita. Accordingly, if looking for a technique to use, you should take care to choose one which does not divert you from the single aim of stilling the mind. (The other benefits will still be a side-effect!) http://www.mymedita-tiongarden.com/

The **Advaita Yoga Ashrama** was set up to spread the teachings of *yoga* and Advaita according to the lineage of Sri Swami Sivananda. The site introduces many aspects of Advaita and gives details of activities and retreats at affiliated centers throughout the world. http://www.yogaAdvaita.org/

The School of Practical Philosophy is affiliated to the UK SES organization above. There are classes and weekend retreats. Students are eventually initiated into *mantra* meditation. There are branches in NYC, Boston and San Francisco. www.practicalphilosophy.org

The **Advaita Meditation Center** (formerly The Philosophy Foundation) is a School of Advaita in Waltham, Massachusetts, offering classes, seminars •
and retreats in Advaita philosophy, meditation and related subjects. The faculty includes senior students have been studying and practicing together for over 30 years, and welcomes anyone who is interested in Advaita, whether beginner or experienced. The School is affiliated with the Sringeri Sharada Peetham in Sringeri, India, the Southern Seat established in 820 CE by Shankara, and is guided by His Holiness Shri Bharati Tirtha Swamigal. http://www.advaitameditation.org/

Swami Satchidananda was the founder of 'Integral Yoga,' which now has institutes throughout the world. This is a huge site which contains details of his life, work and publications with photos, audio and written extracts of his teaching. Sri Gurudev, as he was known, was the author of the excellent commentary on the Yoga Sutras of Patanjali – see Recommended Books (note that this is not Advaita, but the mental preparations are similar). http://www.swamisatchidananda.org/

Satchidananda Ashram Yogaville is the international headquarters for Integral Yoga and there are details about the ashram, courses and retreats. Publications may also be purchased here. (Note that the emphasis throughout is on practical *yoga* techniques and not primarily Advaita theory, though *j~nAna yoga* is also addressed.) http://www.yogaville.org/. Integral Yoga publications may be ordered from http://www.shakticom.org.

AHAM is the 'Association of Happiness for All Mankind' , which has a center in N. Carolina, US and one in Tiruvannamalai, South India. Some meetings are also held at Vancouver Island in Canada. Founded and directed by Arunachala Ramana (Mr. Dee W. Trammell), their purpose is to prepare students for the Self-enquiry method of Ramana Maharshi in a modern manner. The essence of the teaching is described and there are (Flash) guided meditations. There are extracts and quotations from A. Ramana and Ramana Maharshi. There is an extensive book catalogue. http://www.aham.com/

SAT, the **Society of Abidance in Truth**, has a temple in Santa Cruz, California. Teaching is given by Nome, and is particularly influenced by Ramana Maharshi. There are regular satsangs, as well as retreats and special events. A few books are published by SAT but the bookstore holds many more, as well as music, MP3 downloads, photos of Ramana, etc. http://www.satramana.org/

Vedanta Cultural Foundation United States is the USA branch of the organization established in 1976 in India by Swami Parthasarathy. The teacher there is Gautam Jain, who gives regular talks in New York and New Jersey. The site contains details about the organization, Swami Parthasarathy and his books/CDs. http://www.satramana.org/

3. India-Based
The **Official Website of the Divine Life Society** at Uttaranchal, India. This is a huge website containing well organized articles from Swami Sivananda on many aspects of spiritual practice and *yoga-s*, PDF books to download by Swamis Sivananda, Chidananda, Krishnananda, Venkatesananda and others, information about the DLS and the Sivananda Ashram, a multi-media centre, bookstore, e-magazine and much more. http://sivanandaonline.org/html/

The **Divine Life Society**, Sivananda Ashram, Rishikesh, Himalayas, India. This organization, led by Swami Krishnananda until his death in 2001, has books by Swami Krishnananda on *yoga*, meditation, spiritual practice, Gita, Upanishads, mysticism and philosophy. Many books and discourses may be downloaded free of charge. http://www.swami-krishnananda.org/

Another **Divine Life Society** site – http://www.sivanandadlshq.org/home.html – dedicated to Swamis Sivananda, Chidananda and Krishnananda has much information available for free download: teachings, 'inspiring messages,' saints and mystics, Gods and scriptures together with many discourses. A large number of the full-length books have already been made available in html or PDF format for free download. (The former are readable by any web browser, the latter by Adobe's free Acrobat Reader.)

A related organization is the **Yoga Vedanta Center**, established by Swami Vishnudevananda, a disciple of Swami Sivananda. http://www.sivananda.org/

Swami Omkarananda Ashram, Rishikesh
There are lots of articles and information to download, including a comprehensive summary of Western Philosophical thinking on the nature of reality, with definitions of all of the 'isms' etc. This is the organization that produces the excellent, free PC utility for generating Sanskrit script from ITRANS text, for copying into any word processor. http://sanskrit.bhaarat.com/Omkarananda

Yoga Malika
This is an institution in Chennai, India, guided by Swami Dayananda Saraswati and Swami Paramarthananda Saraswati. It provides classes in Vedanta, trains teachers, maintains a library of books and cassettes etc. Some talks by Swami Dayananda and Paramarthananda may be downloaded , including an excellent one on *japa*. A few are also available in Real Audio format. There is a year-long 'self-help' program that can be studied at the site for ten-minutes per day with a different practice each month. http://www.yogamalika.org/

Vedanta Life Institute
Founded by Sri Parthasarathy, who has been touring the world for the past

25+ years giving the most wonderful lectures on the Bhagavad Gita, full of profundity and humor and illustrated by many excellent metaphors and stories. The 'Vedanta Academy', near Mumbai in India, offers a three year residential course on Vedanta, based on study, contemplation and practice. It is open to those aged 16 – 30. Short-term, practical residential courses are also available for business men and professionals on topics such as stress and time management. Books may also be purchased (though not by credit card) and there are Vedantic Centers at various locations around the world. http://www.vedanta-edu.org/

Adhyatmaprakasha Karyalaya is the organization established by Swami Satchidanandendra. The headquarters are in Holenarasipura and there are four other branches around India. There are lectures and seminars, a monthly magazine (not English) and publications, some of which may be viewed on-line using a djvu plugin.

http://www.adhyatmaprakasha.org/index.php

Mathas

Shankara, the Sage who formalized classical Advaita, established four 'seats' in India in the N, E, S and W of the country, their purpose being to provide living Sages throughout history to pass on the teaching and answer questions from any seeker of the truth. These four *maTha-s* or monasteries still exist today at Puri in the East, Sringeri in the South, Dvaraka in the West and Jyotir Math at Badari in the North. There is also a fifth *maTha*, Kanchi Kamakoti Peetham, at Kanchipuram.

The **Sringeri** *maTha* is currently headed by His Holiness Shri Bharati Tirtha Swamigal. The site contains lots of information about the area, temples, branches, functions and its history and *guru paramparA*. http://www.sringeri.net/

Also see http://www.srisharada.com/welcomefinal.htm where there is an on-line book by M.K.Venkatarama Iyer (1976), entitled 'Contribution of Bharati Tirtha and Vidyaranya to Development of Advaitic Thought' with chapters on metaphysics, *jIva*, *mAyA*, knowledge, truth and error, ethics and religion, and *mokSha*. A commentary on the *vivekachUDAmaNi*, by Sri Sri Chandrasekhara Bharati Mahaswamigal, is also under construction.

The **Self Realization Fellowship** – http://www.yogananda-srf.org/ – established by Swami Paramahamsa Yogananda, maintains traditional links with the **Puri matha**.

Shri Kanchi Kamakoti Peetham – http://www.kamakoti.org/index2. html – has more than 1000 pages of information on Hinduism and Advaita. See their site map for links to everything about Hindu *dharma*, together with many articles and tributes to Shankara and his lineage.

The **Jaganath Puri** Site – http://www.jagannathpuri.com/index.html – is essentially a tourism site and contains details about such things as the architecture and the worship that takes place at the temple.

The **Jyotir matha** is briefly described at http://www.templenet. com/Tamilnadu/df067.html , one of the pages of 'TempleNet' – http://www.templenet.com/, that has information on Indian Temples in general.

bharatonline.com is another tourism site but has masses of information and photos of temples throughout India.

The **Adi Sankara Advaita Research Center** – http://Advaitacentre. org/index.htm – is related to the Kanchi Kamakoti Peetham. It is concerned, as the name suggests, with carrying out studies relating to Advaita as taught by Shankara. It publishes a newsletter and journal and organizes talks and seminars. There are several articles on-line and a number of publications may be purchased.

4. Related to Swami Chinmayananda

The **Central Chinmaya Mission Trust** (http://www.chinmayamission. com/index.php) is an International Non-profit Organization that 'helps people bring the essence of Vedanta and Upanishads into their daily lives.'

It was established by Swami Chinmayananda, a disciple of Swami Sivananda and Tapovan Maharaj. It's mission statement is 'To provide to individuals, from any background, the wisdom of Vedanta and practical means for spiritual growth and happiness, enabling them to become positive contributors to the society.' There are centers in Africa, Australia, France, Canada, Hong Kong, India, Singapore UK, USA, and many more. Chinmaya Mission West (http://www.chinmaya.org/) is the site for North America and contains links or email addresses to some of the major centers and retreats. Books and tapes, magazines etc. may also be purchased from within the organization.

One of the local centers, for example, is the **Chinmaya Mission Washington Regional Centre** at http://www.chinmayadc.org/. They organize talks, study groups, lectures on Sanskrit, dance, etc. in various locations in Maryland and Virginia. The UK branch of the organization at http://www.chinmayauk.org/ has study groups on the Bhagavad Gita, Atmabodha and on Swami Chinmayananda's own book on Self-Unfoldment, at various locations in London. There is also an excellent html-based package for studying the Bhagavad Gita, containing the complete commentaries of Swamiji. Many other local branches are listed at http://dmoz.org/Society/Religion_and_Spirituality/Hinduism/Gurus_and_Saints/Swami_Chinmayananda/

5. Related to Sri Ramakrishna and Swami Vivekananda

It should be noted here that the teaching of these Sages and their disciples diverges from that of traditional Advaita in a number of areas. (For example they claim that enlightenment may be attained through *nirvikalpa samAdhi*, which Shankara rejects.) Their teaching is actually given the name of 'neo-Vedanta' (not to be confused with neo-Advaita) in India.

There are even more organizations throughout the world established in their names. Sri Ramakrishna Math at Chennai is perhaps the root site for all of the others. It has biographies, books, news, events, audio and video and articles from the English version of the magazine 'The Vedanta Kesari.' http://www.sriramakrishnamath.org/

The **Vedanta Society of Southern California** – http://www.vedanta.org/ – has information about Vedanta in general and the Ramakrishna order in particular. There are links to other centers around the world, a calendar of events, recommended reading and pointers to bookstores, and photographs for purchase.

The **Vedanta Centre UK** at Bourne End in Buckinghamshire – http://web.onetel.net.uk/~suman11/index.htm – began its life in London in 1948 but moved to its present location in 1977. Discourses are held on Sunday by its head, Swami Dayatmananda. A wide selection of books may be purchased from this site and, being mostly published in India, these are very reasonably priced. Lectures are also held at Bharatiya Vidya Bhavan (http://www.bhavan.net/) in London.

Addresses and telephone/ fax/ email addresses for all of the centers throughout the world are obtainable from http://www.sriramakrishna. org/foreign_c.htm.

See http://www.ramakrishna.org/ and http://www.vivekananda.org/ for information specifically on Sri Ramakrishna Paramahamsa and on Swami Vivekananda, respectively.

The **Complete Works of Swami Vivekananda** are available at http://www.ramakrishnavivekananda.info.

For many more sites, see the Open Directory listings at http://dmoz.org/Society/Religion_and_Spirituality/Hinduism/Gurus_and_S aints/Sri_Ramakrishna,_Sri_Sharada_Devi,_and_Swami_Vivekananda/ .

6. Related to Bhagavan Ramana Maharshi

The main organization related to **Ramana Maharshi** is **Sri Ramanasramam**, the ashram at the foot of Mount Arunachala at Tiruvannamalai in India, where he lived for practically the whole of his life. The mountain is believed by his followers to be the oldest and holiest place on earth, itself capable of bringing about self-realization to one who stays there. http://www.sriramanamaharshi.org/

There is information relating to Ramana Maharshi and his teaching and a few of his works may be downloaded for study offline. There is extensive information about the ashram itself.

The site that previously hosted the Sri Ramanasramam material was dissolved in early 2007 when the Ashram formed its own website above. The original site was split into two new ones:

The first website is dedicated to Arunachala, Bhagavan Sri Ramana Maharshi and to helping devotees in whatever way it is possible to do so. It also has a forum for use by devotees. http://www.arunachala-ramana.org/

The second site provides a live video feed of Arunachala. http://www.arunachala-live.com/

The **Society of Abidance in Truth** (SAT) is in Santa Cruz, California. The resident Sage is Master Nome. There are events, lectures, retreats etc. based on the teaching of Ramana Maharshi. http://www.satramana.org/

The **Ramana Maharshi Foundation UK** was affiliated to Sri Ramanasramam but is now independent. There are members throughout the world but meetings are principally held at Hampstead in London on the afternoon of the second Saturday of each month. There are short readings on a particular theme, interspersed with periods of silence and followed, in the second half, by an open, moderated discussion. Topics alternate between *bhakti* and *j~nAna* emphasis. http://www.ramana-maharshi.org.uk/

The organization publishes an informal A4 newsletter two or three times per year containing general information about the group and lists of forthcoming talks and residential retreats with Sages.

The **Ramana Maharshi Center for Learning** at Bangalore publishes a monthly magazine, 'The Ramana Way,' as well as a number of other books and pamphlets on the teachings of Ramana, principally by A. R. Natarajan. http://members.tripod.com/~rmclb/index.htm

Arunachala Ashrama has centers in New York and Nova Scotia. As well as information about the ashrams with their events and satsangs, there are details of Ramana's life and teachings and about Sri Ramanasramam. Books, audio, video and photos may be purchased via Paypal. http://www.arunachala.org/

The advaita section of **luthar.com** has masses of articles relating to

Ramana. http://luthar.com/

A weekend seminar on Ramana Maharshi's *upadeSha sAra* was given by Dr. K. Sadananda at the Washington Chinmaya Mission during Summer 2003 and a tape recording of the lecture, consisting of 8 tapes, may be purchased from them. These are excellent but some Sanskrit background would be beneficial since Sri Sadananda is fond of quotations from the Gita and other sources! The contact is S. Balan (sbalan@cox.net), the secretary. The cost is $20 for anyone local but postage will vary for other locations.

David Godman is the author of possibly the best book relating to Ramana Maharshi – 'Be As You Are.' (Ref. 69) This site contains interviews, a biography of Ramana and details of David's books amongst other things. http://www.davidgodman.org/

Happiness of Being contains essays and translations etc. on Self-knowledge, exploring in depth the philosophy and practice of the spiritual teachings of Bhagavan Sri Ramana. These include a complete book, which may be downloaded in PDF format, entitled 'Happiness and the Art of Being'. The author, Michael James, has lived in Tiruvannamalai for over 20 years and studied with Sri Sadhu Om for the last 8 1/2 years of the latter's life, assisting in the translation of Guru Vachaka Kovai. There is also a Discussion Forum. http://www.happinessofbeing.com/

There are a number of pages covering Ramana's biography and extracts from his teaching at the **Gnostic and Mystical Philosophy** site. http://www.hermetic-philosophy.com/ramana_maharshi1.htm

Ramana Maharshi and Us has articles about Ramana, personal stories and a free lending library. http://www.ramanamaharshi.info/

Arunachala Samudra has all the information you could ever want about Mt. Arunachala - history, tourism, associated kings and sages, poems and prayers - and there are some wonderful photographs. http://www.arunacha-lasamudra.org/index1.html

Finally, there is a very useful page of links to Ramana related sites and Egroups, etc. at http://www.geocities.com/bhagavanramana .

For even more sites, see the Open Directory listings at http://dmoz.org/Society/Religion_and_Spirituality/Hinduism/Gurus_and_ Saints/Ramana_Maharshi/.

7. Related to Sri Nisargadatta Maharaj

The **Advaita Fellowship** of Redondo beach, California is concerned with the teaching stemming from Sri Nisargadatta Maharaj to Ramesh Balsekar and Wayne Liquorman. (Note that Ramesh died Sept. 2009.)

http://www.advaita.org/

Timothy Conway has a page containing masses of biographical and other information as well as photos and an extensive list of resources. http://www.enlightened-spirituality.org/Nisargadatta_Maharaj.html

http://www.nisargadatta.net/ is another site specifically devoted to Nisargadatta Maharaj and http://www.prahlad.org/gallery/nisargadatta _maharaj.htm contains links to still more sites.

There are four 2 1/2 hour DVDs narrated by Dr.Stephen Wolinsky (a disciple), which may be purchased from Neti Neti Films (http://www.netinetifilms.com/). These include actual footage of Nisargadatta Maharaj. The teaching certainly relates to Nisargadatta, although there is also much material that does not. Talks address Buddhist and tantric teachings as well as more modern, Western philosophies such as that of Korzybski, Derrida, Post-Deconstructionism and even quantum mechanics.

There is an article on a meeting with Nisargadatta Maharaj by Dr. Lakshyan Schanzer, complete with photos, at Dr. Harsh Luthar's site. http://luthar.com/meeting-nisargadatta-maharaj-by-dr-lakshyan-schanzer

Maharaj Nisargadatta is primarily set up to provide details of this teacher and contains a huge collection of quotations, together with biography, lineage and photos and the complete text of 'I am That'. However, there are also many more essays and books on Advaita in general, including many of the books by Ramana Maharshi, Upanishads, Gita and Brahmasutras, works by Sivananda and Krishnananda, Ramakrishna and Vivekananda, and a number from the Bhaktivedanta Trust. http://www.maharajnisargadatta.com/index.php

Nisargadatta.we.bs has concise details of Nisargadatta himself, the Navnath *sampradAya* and the principles of *nisarga yoga* (*nisarga* means 'natural state'). There are a number of key articles about his teaching, together with photos and videos. In particular, however, all of his books may be downloaded in PDF format. http://nisargadatta.we.bs/

Sri Ranjit Maharaj (died Nov. 2000) was the lesser-known disciple of Shri Siddharameshwar Maharaj, along with Nisargadatta Maharaj. Enlightened at a very early age, he lived very simply in Bombay after Siddharameshwar Maharaj died, never married, had a simple job, and, for most of his life, very few disciples. There are excerpts from talks, including two in MP3 format and a program of events.
http://www.sadguru.com/index.html

The **Way of the bird** is another site dedicated to Ranjit Maharaj by his disciple Andrew Vernon. It contains quotations and commentaries organized as 1 per day for each month of the year. The complete book is also downloadable as a PDF file (1.5Mb). http://www.wayofthebird.com/
http://www.inner-quest.org/Ranjit_Meeting.htm provides a description of a meeting with Ranjit Maharaj along with aspects of his teaching, covering reality, knowledge and ignorance, master and death.

8. Related to Swami Dayananda
Swami Dayananda, unlike the other section teachers listed above, is still living and teaching and, also unlike the others, teaches traditional Advaita according to the proven principles of Shankara. His books are the best I have found for presenting these ideas in a readable and totally reasonable way so that they are both informative and convincing. And his quality as a teacher is demonstrated by the fact that many of his disciples are also

teaching around the world in an equally effective manner. Swami Paramarthananda in particular, who is one of the most influential in my own understanding, now has a wealth of talks, available in mp3 format, on most of the key scriptural works.

Arsha Vidya Gurukulam is an institute for the traditional study of Vedanta and Sanskrit, located in the Pocono Mountains, at Saylorsburg, Pennsylvania. It offers studies in the Upanishads, Bhagavad Gita, Brahma-sutras, and other classical Vedic texts. It was established in 1986 by Swami Dayananda Saraswati. There is also a home study course for Bhagavad Gita ($210 in US) and for Sanskrit ($55 in US) and an excellent bookstore. http://www.arshavidya.org/

There is now a branch of **Arsha Vidya in the UK**. The teacher is Swamini Atmaprakashananda, a direct disciple of Swami Dayananda. Classes, on such topics as Tattva Bodha and Mundaka Upanishad, take place on most evenings in and around London and are free. Gita Home Study Centers are also scattered about the country. http://www.arshavidya.org.uk/

Swami Dayananda Ashram (http://www.arshavidhyapitam.org/) is the website of the Arsha Vidya Pitham at Rishikesh. There are details of the ashram facilities and the temple, teachers both within and outside India, together with contact emails or websites. There are classes at the ashram in Vedanta, yoga and Sanskrit and there is an on-line bookstore. The following links are provided to other related facilities (in addition to the others listed on this page):

. **Coimbatore-anaikatti ashram** - http://www.arshavidya.in/
. **Swi. Brahmaprakasananda** – Nagpur - http://www.arshavidya-nagpur.org/
. **Sw. Viditatmananda** – Ahmedabad - http://www.tattvatirtha.org/
. **Sw. Tadatmananda** in New Jersey - http://www.arshabodha.org/
. **Vijay Kapoor** – San Francisco bay area -
http://www.arshavidyacenter.org/

. **Gloria Arieira** – Brazil - http://www.vidyamandir.org.br/

There are also other teachers in the USA and Canada, who do not have websites, listed at the **AVG website** - http://www.arshavidya. org/teachers_uscan.html.

Arsha Vidya Satsangs has details of satsangs held by Arsha Vidya Gurukulam at various locations in the US as well as Australia and Canada. Also, there are many pdf files and mp3 audio files of satsang excerpts from Swamis Dayananda, Viditatmananda, Tattvavidananda and Pratyagbodhananda. These can all be downloaded and contain a wealth of material on assorted topics. http://www.avgsatsang.org/

The **shAstraprakAshikA Trust** in Chennai, India sells audio cassettes of recordings of lectures and discourses by Swami Dayananada, Swami Paramarthananda, Swami Omkarananda and Swami Guruparananda. You may also pay on line and download mp3 files. http://www. sastraprakasika.org/
    Note that Swami Paramarthananda's complete talks on the **Gita** are available on-line or for downloading. http://www.archive.org/search.php? query=creator%3A%22Swami%20Paramarthananda%22

Vedantavidyarthisangha.org is dedicated to hosting selected classes of Swami Paramarthananda (a direct disciple of Swami Dayananda), including some of the ongoing classes in Chennai. Talks either require a 'Flash Player', which may be downloaded from the site, or are in real-audio format. http://www.vedantavidyarthisangha.org/

Yoga Malika is an institution in Chennai, India, guided by Swami Dayananda Saraswati and Swami Paramarthananda Saraswati. It provides classes in Vedanta, trains teachers, maintains a library of books and cassettes etc. Some talks by Swami Dayananda and Paramarthananda may be downloaded , including an excellent one on japa. A few are also available in Real Audio format. There is a year-long 'self-help' program that can be studied at the site for ten-minutes per day with a different practice each month. http://www.yogamalika.org/

Vedanta: The Yoga of Objectivity - Neema Majmudar and Surya Tahora, disciples of Swami Dayananda, are the authors of this website. This site gives a detailed presentation of Vedanta and its teaching methodology, with pop-up quotes from relevant scriptures together with articles (in PDF format for download) and dialogs on specific aspects. There is also a schedule of talks, seminars and retreats (held in India, Bangkok, etc). http://www.discovervedanta.com/index.htm

Radha (Carol Whitfield Ph.D.) studied Advaita Vedanta and Sanskrit with Swami Dayananda Saraswati in India during the 1970's. Since returning from India, she has taught Vedanta extensively on both coasts. She is a university professor and a Jungian-oriented clinical psychologist. She now teaches Vedanta in Berkeley California. Website for online classes www.arshakulam.org.

Sri Vasudevacharya (Michael Comans) is a direct disciple of Swami Dayananda. He teaches, principally in Melbourne and Sydney, and has provided courses on the Bhagavad Gita, the principal Upanishads and Sanskrit. The site contains several articles, details of classes and related links. He is the author of the excellent book: "The Method of Early Advaita Vedanta", which discusses the teaching of Gaudapada, Shankara, Sureshvara and Padmapada. http://srivasudevacharya.org/

B. Internet-specific resources

1. General information on Advaita

http://www.advaita.org.uk/ is the website of the author of this book. (By the time that you read this, it might have changed its primary name to Advaita Academy – http://www.advaita-academy.org) It contains all of the (up to date) information contained in this Appendix. In addition, there are over 250 essays by teachers and writers, a section devoted to informative links to current satsang teachers and past sages, lineage charts for most of the modern teachers, a comprehensive Sanskrit glossary and more. Hopefully the new site will expand to host, for example, video and audio interviews and up to date news. A quarterly E-journal '*akhaNDAkAra*' is published and a fortnightly newsletter is also intended.

http://www.advaitin.net/ is the **Advaitin Home Page** for the email discussion group called the Advaitin List. There is information about Shankara and extracts from his works, general information about Advaita and Hinduism, details of history, terminology and Vedantic scriptures. The site also contains a number of related links and the opportunity to join the Advaitin E-Group (see below).

There is an excellent set of bookmarked links, available only to members of the Advaitin E-Group. http://groups.yahoo.com/group/advaitin /links is maintained by **Sunder Hattangadi,** who seems able to provide references to any Advaita related topic imaginable.

Ananta Yoga Learning Center presents essays, poetry and links which are a mixture of Kashmir Shaivism, Patanjali's Yoga and Advaita. A number of classics from the scriptures may also be viewed on-line or downloaded. http://www.upnaway.com/%7Ebindu/anantayogaweb/

Arsha Vidya Satsangs has details of satsangs held by Arsha Vidya Gurukulam at various locations in the US as well as Australia and Canada. Also, there are many PDF files and mp3 audio files of satsang excerpts from Swamis Dayananda, Viditatmananda, Tattvavidananda and Pratyagbodhananda. These can all be downloaded and contain a wealth of material on assorted topics. http://www.avgsatsang.org/

Inner Quest has articles and teachings from Ranjit Maharaj, Sri Poonja, Nisargadatta Maharaj, Ramesh Balsekar and Chandra Swami; a catalogue of videos, DVDs and books from various teachers, traditional and modern, including Ramana Maharshi and J. Krishnamurti; details of meetings in Paris (last section in French only). http://www.inner-quest.org/

Realization.org is a very professionally produced site with a wealth of information and articles on many topics with regular updates. There are biographies of sages and excerpts from books, articles on Advaita, *bhakti* and *j~nAna yoga*, meditation, Sanskrit and much more. Each page has links to associated material. The editor of the site is a Ramana Maharshi devotee. http://www.realization.org/

Sentient.org is based around Ramana Maharshi, his teaching and teachers who have been influenced by him. There are also essays on awakening and on teachers in general. http://www.sentient.org/index.html

The ***shAstraprakAshikA* Trust** in Chennai, India sells audio cassettes of recordings of lecture and discourses by Swami Dayananda, Swami Paramarthananda, Swami Omkarananda and Swami Guruparananda. You may also pay on line and download mp3 files. http://www.sastraprakasika .org/

Wikiverse – http://advaita-vedanta.wikiverse.org/ – has a number of pages of general description on aspects relating to Advaita in an encyclopaedic style.

3rd Millennium Gateway is a large site with only some of the content directly relating to Advaita. There are links to current and past teachers, resources, articles and books. In addition, there are pages on spirituality, cosmology, religion in general, new age, frontiers of science, scriptures, social issues and environment. There are articles, interviews and reviews. Everything is supported by lots of annotated links. http://www.thirdmg.com/

When I awoke – http://www.wheniawoke.com/ – contains tales of awakening in various non-dual traditions (though principally Advaita). Essays from a number of teachers describe their enlightenment experience and there is a practical exercise from Ken Wilber.

If pictures help you to understand new concepts and you have the

Shockwave plugin Flash 5.0 or later installed, you may be interested in **Who Are You?** This poses a set of visually stimulating questions on the nature of ourselves and the world of appearances. http://www.ods.nl/ikben/gb/

Dr. Harsh K. Luthar has a huge website, **Luthar.com**, connected to the Harshasatsangh EGroup and Ezine. Many sections are unrelated to advaita but one section is entitled 'Advaita, Yoga and Spirituality' and contains archives of material stretching back to August 2000. New articles on a variety of topics by various authors are continually being added. Most of these relate to Ramana Maharshi in one form or another. http://luthar.com/category/yoga-meditation-philosophy-and-spirituality

Numii Net is an attractive, professionally produced site principally devoted to providing details of teachers, past and present. But there are also articles, stories of awakenings and a question and answer section. This is an ambitious site in its early stages but should grow to become a substantial resource. http://www.numii.net/word_press/

2. Sites of Western Writers

Non-Duality Salon

This is the site maintained by Jerry Katz, possibly the best known adherent of non-duality, thorough his Internet activities. Amongst other things it has some extremely useful pages listing living teachers, alphabetically or by location. Each entry contains a few quotations, together with a pointer to the teacher's own website, if applicable. There are also many personal accounts of satsangs with various teachers. The links can keep you surfing for some considerable time!

Jerry is also the author of a new book, called 'ONE: Essential Writings on Nonduality' which explains and illustrates non-duality from a wide variety of perspectives, both practical and theoretical. See Appendix 2.

Pure Silence is the website of Mark McCloskey, who is selflessly (!) spreading the message of non-duality without thought of personal gain.

There are a large number of short articles on various aspects of life, emphasising the need to live in the present from the silence that is our true nature. There are also several audio extracts from his acclaimed 'Pure Silence' CD, profits from which are donated to Netaid.org. http://www.puresilence.org/

There are some interesting musings on aspects of Advaita as well as some autobiographical stories from **Michael Reidy** and a number of quotations. Not a high-tech website (!) but well worth a visit. http://homepage.eircom.net/%7Eombhurbhuva/

Philip Teertha Mistlberger - Teachings and Writings on the Spiritual Path. A wide selection of writings from various traditions, including Zen, Tibetan Buddhism and Tantra. A book is advertised, entitled 'A Natural Awakening: Realizing the Self in Everyday Life' with the first two chapters on-line and the first of these provides a crystal clear description of the seeker's situation and the nature of enlightenment as described by Advaita. Another short article lists the 'Nine Essential Points of Spiritual Enlightenment' - Excellent! See the recommendation of his book in Appendix 2.

http://www.geocities.com/annubis33/

Nirmala has several excellent Ebooks freely available for downloading and also audio and video extracts from satsangs. http://www.endless-satsang.com/

Jean-Pierre Gomez, a student of 'Sailor' Bob Adamson, answers a number of questions that frequently arise for the seeker of enlightenment. http://www.you-are-that.com/

shiningworld.com is the website of James Swartz. There is much to read here - and it looks very good! Many perennial questions on Advaita are addressed in 12 different categories and opinions are expressed on a number of issues. Books and essays may be read on-line or downloaded as PDF files. Some may be purchased as hard copy and the entire site is available on CD. There is also a large section on dream analysis. A tour of temples in India is organised annually. There are galleries of artwork, some of which may be purchased as cards and hi-res images. http://www.shiningworld.com/

Wide Awake Living is the website of Alice Gardner and is about enlightenment and waking up to what is already here, now. There are essays, poetry, links and details about her book 'Life Beyond Belief'. http://www.wideawakeliving.com/index.html

Advaya is the website of Philip Renard, who has been influenced by a number of teachers but principally by Nisargadatta Maharaj and Alexander Smit. He teaches in the Netherlands (Bilthoven) but his site has a parallel stream in English, where there are a number of articles, including a series on Ramana, Nisargadatta and Atmananda. http://www.advaya.nl/

Ashram Vidya Order is the site of the New York based Aurea Vidya Foundation which publishes the books of Raphael. Raphael marries the tradition of Advaita Vedanta with the teaching of Plato and the neo-Platonists and with the philosophies of Orphism (Pythagoras and Parmenides). He calls the resultant the 'Primordial Tradition'. The site has monthly readings together with short pages of material outlining the principles. http://www.vidya-ashramvidyaorder.org/

Philosophy of Oneness is the website of Jan Kersschot. There are details of his books, endorsements from Tony Parsons and Nathan Gill, two interviews and several short essays. A discussion forum is also available. http://www.kersschot.com/philosophy.html

What Never Changes is the website of Annette Nibley, a disciple of John Wheeler and Stephen Wingate. There is a large number of essays and dialogues on a wide range of topics. Regular meetings are held in Mill Valley, California and there are details of these and other, special events.

http://www.whatneverchanges.com/

Only Timeless Being is the website of Felipe Oliveira, a disciple of John Wheeler and Bob Adamson. There are numerous essays, which may be read on-line or downloaded as a PDF booklet. There is also a link to his poetry site. http://felipeoliveira.com/onlybeing/index.html

Aloha Sangha – Weekly meetings in Honolulu explore the varieties of non-dual experience and expression, with emphasis on the teachings of Nisargadatta, Sri Ramana, and Zen Buddhism. Meetings are led by Tom Davidson-Marx, who has been practicing meditation and yoga for several decades. The site contains a number of essays, articles and guidelines for practice. http://home.earthlink.net/%7ealohasatsang/index.html

An Introduction to Awareness – information on the book by philosopher James M. Corrigan along with a podcast and philosophical essays. This is the branch of western philosophy called 'Indefinite Monism' which bears many similarities with Advaita. http://www.anintroductiontoaware ness.com/

Non-Dual Spirituality or Advaita – this is one of the sections at Timothy Conway's 'Enlightened-Spirituality.org' website. A very wide-ranging selection, including short and clear expositions of advaita; a long Q&A section on non-dual awakening; an essay comparing *bhakti* and *j~nAna yoga*; papers on non-duality and psychotherapy; essays critical of neo-advaita; and loads of material on Nisargadatta Maharaj, Ramana Maharshi, Jnaneshvar, Bankei and Douglas Harding. Many other non-dual mystics (from Milarepa to Moshe Cordovero to Juan de la Cruz) are included elsewhere on Timothy's website. http://www.enlightened-spirituality.org/nondual-spirituality.html

The Integral Ego – information on the book 'Integral Therapy: Love is the Healing Principle' by Dr. D. B. Sleeth. The use of non-duality in mental health therapy. Influenced by the 'radical non-dualism' of Adi Da and the theories of Ken Wilber. http://dbsleeth.com/

Swami Abhayananda's website is principally concerned with promoting his books, two of which I have read and would recommended ('The Supreme Self' and 'The Wisdom of Vedanta'). There is also a brief biography and a number of articles and links. In particular, he is now offering a number of his earlier books as free downloads, including 'Jnaneshvar: The Life and Works of the Celebrated 13th Century Indian Mystic-Poet', 'History of Mysticism: The Unchanging Testament' and 'Dattatreya's Song of the Avadhut'. http://www.swami-abhayananda.com/

The End of Seeking – Essays on such topics as our true nature, the ego, spiritual practice etc. from Mike Graham, who has been influenced by Nisargadatta Maharaj, Ramana Maharshi and especially 'Sailor' Bob Adamson (for whom there is a separate section). http://www.theendof-seeking.net/

Know Yourself offers audio and video downloads of talks and satsangs from a number of teachers. These include Nirmala, Burt Harding, Unmani Liza Hyde, Catherine Ingram, Gina Lake, Wayne Liquorman, Om C. Parkin, Bernie Prior, Isaac Shapiro and Metta Zetty. Audios are typically £6 for a 1 - 1.5 hour talk and £12 for a 1.5 hour video.
http://www.knowyourself.org/index.php

Stillness Speaks is the website of Chris Hebard, who is aiming to introduce seekers to authentic teachers of advaita, both traditional (Swami Dayananda and James Swartz) and modern (Pamela Wilson and Francis Lucille). There are a number of free PDF downloads of James Swartz's writing, recom-mended books, a weblog and a page of links. There are also satsangs (in Texas) to watch and discuss videos of Eckhart Tolle and Adyashanti. (The site is also growing faster than I can update the description!) http://www.stillnessspeaks.com/index.php

Reflections of the One Life is the website of Scott Kiloby, who teaches in

New Harmony and Evansville, Indiana. In addition to details of his meetings and retreats, there are many essays, quotations and videos (which can be viewed free of charge). He also holds frequent, free meetings via Skype.

Living in Paradise is the website of Tan, who provides a number of short essays and questions & answers on what it means to seek... and find. There is no teaching as such, and the words have the tenor of neo-advaita but there is also the ring of authenticity. http://human-life.de/index.htm

the urban guru cafe – Not sure where to put this - it is the first 'podcast' site to which I have linked. There are frequent new 'shows' (every week to 10 days or so), consisting of music (mainly good 60's – 70's pop as far as I can make out), along with readings, voices, poems, interviews etc. The teaching appears to be principally from the 'Sailor' Bob 'school'. mp3 files may be played on-line or downloaded. As the headline says: 'entertaining - controversial - innovative – informative'.

http://urbangurucafe.com/wordpress/index.php

Seeing-Knowing is the website of Gilbert Schultz, a disciple of Nisargadatta and 'Sailor'Bob. There are (or will be) articles, audio, videos and details of his books. http://seeing-knowing.com/

Mark West - Non Duality has numerous articles from Mark West, also a disciple of Nisargadatta and 'Sailor' Bob Adamson. There are also audio talks and interviews with Mark and several videos. There are details of the book 'Gleanings from Nisargadatta' - Talks with Sri Nisargadatta Maharaj transcribed by Mark 1976-77. http://markwestsite.com/

Nondual Poetry – Words pointing beyond words. A beautifully presented site from Susan Kahn, which features poetry and other writing (not all relating to the advaita tradition) from a number of teachers and writers, including the site author. Susan also has a more specific, advaita-oriented site – Non-dual Pointing, Knowing who you really are. This includes a podcast on her work as a Non-dual Psychotherapist. http://www.nondualpoetry.com/ and http://www.nondualpointing.com/

The Awakened Eye - encounters with non-dual awareness. Artists and artisans, educators and philosophers, scientists, sages and saints, present their understanding and teachings about non-dual awareness: "the eye wideawake and the awakened 'I' are not two". http://www.theawak-enedeye.com/

Consciousness Is All is the website of Peter Dziuban, author of the book of the same title. You can read five sample chapters from the book and there are video and audio presentations. You are invited to arrange a consultation at the rate of $50 per hour, which includes an mp3 recording of your discussion. http://www.consciousnessisall.com/

3. Sites of Eastern Writers

Advaita Vedanta – This is the site created by S. Vidyasankar. Based around Shankara, it is a very authoritative site, winner of several awards and cited by the Encyclopaedia Britannica (though it does use a non-standard translit-eration scheme for the Sanskrit). There are general descriptions of Advaita with detailed information on many aspects accessible through compre-hensive hyperlinked references. There is a biography of Shankara and details of his 'lineage' with scholarly discussion of many related aspects, such as dating his birth and death. The teachings of pre- and post-Shankara philosophers are also discussed in the same rigorous, academic manner. The many schools of philosophy that cite the Upanishads as their source are discussed and their relationships explained. Overall, the site is excellent as a source of reference material and very professionally produced. It is clearly aimed primarily at the serious student. (Note that the site is no longer updated.) http://www.advaita-vedanta.org/avhp/

Ahwan – The Spiritual Approach to Life has a large number of articles based on the lectures of Sri Bimal Mohanty expounding the traditional teaching of Vedanta. Subscription requested for access to further articles.

http://www.ahwan.com/

Vedantaquest is the website of Dr. Narendra Tulli, who is seeking to unite science with the teaching of Advaita according to Shankara. There are details of his books on the Srimad Bhagavad Gita and Brahmasutra (with extracts) and of prospective projects. He also gives courses on Introductory and Advanced Vedanta covering the *prasthAna traya* with the commentaries by Shankara (in English at the Delhi branch of Kailas Ashram). http://www.vedantaquest.ind.in/

Reflections is the website of Dr. Haramohan Mishra and contains a number of articles on aspects of Advaita as well as details of his books, including Advaita Epistemology, Sadananda's Vedantasara and commentaries on the Isha and Katha Upanishads. http://www.reflectionsindia.org/

Gokulmuthu Narayanaswamy has provided '**Introduction to Vedanta**' - the series of lectures for beginners by Swami Paramarthananda, based upon Shankara's Tattva Bodha. These consist of some 90MB of files (3 - 4MB per file) in Real Audio (rm) format. http://www.esnips.com/web/IntroductionToVedanta

Inner Journey: Spiritual Activities the Easy Way is the website of Dr. N. K. Srinivasan. There are some introductions to various topics in advaita, commented extracts from the Bhagavad Gita, instructions on meditation and some book recommendations. http://www.freewebs.com/nk srinivasan/index.htm

4. Hinduism

One of the best general sites on **Hinduism** and related topics has pages on many topics with an easily accessible index to all of the pages. Both philosophical and practical aspects are covered. http://www.hinduism.co.za/

Many of the classics of Hinduism and Advaita are available as public domain downloads at the **Internet Sacred Text Archive**, including the Vedas, Upanishads, Mahabharata and Ramayana. http://www.sacredtexts.com/hin/

India Divine – has general information on Hinduism and scriptures with articles, downloads, screen-savers etc. Audio lectures on Vedanta may be heard on-line or downloaded. There are bi-monthly newsletters published by Bhaktivedanta Ashram in India and much more. http://www.indiadivine.com/

Hinduism Online is another large site specialising in all topics relating to Hinduism. http://www.himalayanacademy.com/

Gems From The Ocean Of Traditional Hindu Thought – Prof. V. Krishnamurthy had made extracts from his books available here. There are a wide range of topics relating to Hinduism in general and Vedanta in particular.

http://www.krishnamurthys.com/profvk/index.html

ProfVK (as he is known) has also now compiled and ordered the material into a single book, which is being made available in PDF format. This may be viewed (and saved locally as required) from the **Advaitin.net site**. There are a wide range of topics relating to Hinduism in general and Vedanta in particular and it can be highly recommended. http://www.advaitin.net/profvk/FinalGems.pdf

Shri Kanchi Kamakoti Peetham (also listed under Indian Organisations) – contains lots of general information on Hinduism. In particular, there is an English translation of two volumes of 'Hindu Dharma' from the Tamil, containing talks on many subjects by Sri Sri Sri Chandesekharendra Saraswati Mahaswamiji. There are also a number of articles by various people on, for example, the life and teaching of Shankara. Five hours of audio and video are also offered. http://www.kamakoti.org/

HinduWiki was begun in Sept 2006 with the ambition of containing all information relating to Hinduism, set up and maintained by users of the site in the same manner as Wikipedia. Looks very promising if it receives the necessary level of support. http://www.hinduwiki.com/

An excellent hierarchical index of a great many sites may be found at

the **Khoj India Directory**. http://www.khoj.com/Society_and_Culture/
Religion_and_Spirituality/Hinduism/

Vedic Life is a huge website for all aspects relating to the Vedas as well as
information and links relating to Spiritual Masters and Ashrams.
http://vediclife.rvishu.com/Vedic_Life_-_An_Introduction.html

For a massive site on all things to do with India, including religions and
scriptures but also history, culture, economy etc. see **bharatadesam -
everything about India**. http://www.bharatadesam.com/

A free, on-line book all about Hinduism is available at Sri Kanchi
Kamakoti Peetham: '**Hindu Dharma**' by Sri Sri Sri Chandrasekharendra
Saraswathi MahaSwamiji. This comprises two volumes of speeches from
the Tamil Book 'Deivatthin Kural'. http://kamakoti.org/newlayout
/template/hindudharma.html

5. Ezines and Ebooks

Amigo is a free Web magazine about Non Duality. There are articles by the
editor (Kees Schreuders), Wolter Keers (a disciple of Ramana Maharshi)
and others such as Douglas Harding, Krishna Menon and Tony Parsons.
Dutch teachers such as Jan van Delden and Hans Laurentius also have
essays and satsang extracts translated into English. New issues come
available several times per year. They are professionally produced and
some of the articles are excellent. See Issue 2, for example, for lucid
discussions on the topic of free will (or not!). http://www.ods.nl/am1gos
Note that at the time of writing this second edition, there have not been any
new Amigo issues since May 2006 but I understand that another is due soon
(2010).

Dancing with the Divine is an on-line magazine containing articles and
poems of non-dual wisdom. http://www.dancingwiththedivine.com/

There is an e-book '**Introduction to Advaita**' by D. Krishna Ayyar that
can be read in full on-line. Despite claiming to be 'a presentation for
beginners' this is very comprehensive, covering practically any topic that
you might think of. This is a classical treatment that uses all of the correct

Sanskrit terminology. http://www.vedantaadvaita.org/

Another e-book is partially presented at '**Garland of Advaitic Wisdom**'. This advertises the complete book by Ajati, a devotee of Ramana Maharshi. With an emphasis on *ajAtivAda*, the theory that nothing has ever been created, a number of pages are available on line. There are quotations from a number of classic Advaita scriptures as well as from Ramana Maharshi, Zen and Tao. http://www.ajati.com/

An excellent, step by step, **Introduction to Advaita**, presented in the form of a dialogue (of 1008 single lines) has been written by Professor V. Krishnamurthy (see elsewhere). The complete dialogue may be downloaded as a PDF file from the Advaitin site (see above). http://www.advaitin.net/advaitadialogue.pdf

Self Knowledge is a journal (of Adhyatma Yoga and Advaita Vedanta) produced by Shanti Sadan. There are articles on key yoga teachings and a selection from the archives. http://www.shantisadan.org/journal.php

Friends of the Heart publishes monthly e-zines with articles by Katie Davis, author of 'Awake Joy: The Essence of Enlightenment' and Sundance Burke, author of 'Free Spirit: A Guide to Enlightened Being' as well as other articles by Advaita and non-dual published authors, conscious singer/songwriters, artists, meditation or movement meditation experts, and ecstatic poets. There are also free EBooks available. http://www.katiedavis.org/friendsoftheheart.html

6. E-Groups and Weblogs (Blogs)

These are discussion groups in which the participants communicate via email. Someone will write on a specific topic or question in which they are interested and this message will be sent to all members. Anyone may then respond and these responses are similarly copied to everyone. E-Groups (E for 'Electronic' presumably) have evolved from the original 'Listservs,' 'Newsgroups' and 'Bulletin Boards' that provided a similar function in the early days of the Internet (and which still exist in some cases). It is likely that 'network' groups such as 'Facebook' will take over from these over the next few years.

A group may be organized by an individual through his or her own website but, more usually, a central facility makes many different groups available. The biggest of these is Yahoo at http://groups.yahoo.com/. There are thousands of such groups, including 144 related to Advaita (as at 30th Sep 2009). Usually anyone may join but the owner of a group is always able to exclude or ban members. Sometimes the posted messages are 'moderated,' which means that the owner of the group will read messages before allowing them to be posted to everyone else. This enables the filtering out of abusive or off-topic messages. Many groups, however, are un-moderated and this can often result in a majority of messages consisting of irrelevant chat or so-called 'flame' mail, in which two or more members are simply very rude to each other! Unfortunately, this has happened on otherwise very good, supposedly non-dual discussion groups.

Because there are so many, I have personally only sampled a few and currently belong to only four. Accordingly, my recommendations here are not based upon extensive familiarity.

Advaita-L is probably the most authoritative group available for Advaita philosophy in the tradition of Shankara. Much of the material posted can be very academically biased however and is often related to Hindu ritualistic aspects. Naïve posts or observations not strictly within the guidelines for the list are not well tolerated. http://lists.Advaita-vedanta.org/cgi-bin/listinfo/Advaita-l

Advaitin is the group that I would most recommend. It exists to discuss any Advaita-related topic, on any level. Though it takes the teachings of Shankara as its baseline, followers of Direct Path methods are not at all frowned upon! There are 2075 members as of September 2009. Many of its senior members are very knowledgeable and able to comment learnedly on all topics. There are also numbers of relative newcomers, both from traditional Indian backgrounds and from other Western traditions. Questions from newcomers to the philosophy are always treated with respect and never answered patronizingly. There are clear guidelines for behavior in the group and intervention by the moderators is very rare. Disrespectful posts, or ones that are outside of the guidelines are not tolerated, however. In the 11 years of my membership there have been many excellent discussions. There are also ongoing expositions with discussion from time to time, on topics such as the Bhagavad Gita. http://groups.yahoo.com/group/advaitin

NonDualitySalon is a long-established group. It is run by Jerry Katz, who also has one of the largest web sites on Non-duality, listed above under 'General Information on Advaita.' http://groups.yahoo.com/group/Non dualitySalon/

Million Paths – There is intentionally not a lot of discussion on this list, which exists primarily for members to post extracts and quotations from the Sages. Principal amongst the sources are Ramana Maharshi and Nisargadatta Maharaj, though any Advaita material (actual or effective) is acceptable. This list provides an excellent opportunity to discover ideas, and ways of expression, that strike a chord. 359 members at October 2009. http://groups.yahoo.com/group/millionpaths

Harsha Satsangh discusses the teachings of Ramana Maharshi and others. It is a busy group with 1262 members as at October 2009. http://groups.yahoo.com/group/HarshaSatsangh

NDhighlights provides daily posts – the editors are Jerry Katz, Gloria Lee, and Mark Otter. There are no discussions on the material. The extracts that are posted draw on other sources on the Internet, including many non-dual E-groups and websites. News articles, discourses, poetry and random infor-mation that has caught the interest of the poster – anything may appear. If you do not know where to look for inspiration, something here is likely to appeal eventually. 1852 members at October 2009. http://groups.yahoo.com /group/NDhighlights

There are 83 E-groups (Oct 2009) with reference to Ramana Maharshi at Yahoo alone. The largest one is Italian and Harsha Satsangh and Million Paths have already been mentioned. Of the remainder, the only one I have personally had any dealings with was **Ramana_Maharshi** (296 members) – http://groups.yahoo.com/group/Ramana_Maharshi/). There is a 'silent group' **SriRamana** (173 members) – http://groups.yahoo.com/group/ SriRamana), which simply emails members with a short quotation from Ramana each day.

Others – Note that there are many other E-Groups that I have not investigated, including ones that are concerned with only a single teacher, e.g. Nisargadatta, Vivekananda. A large number now operate through yahoo and the complete list of those may be searched at http://groups.yahoo.com/. Many of them are also described at http://www.nonduality.com/list.htm

7. Web Logs

Web logs, now better known as 'Blogs,' began as transient web sites on which the owner was able to change information very quickly, often on a daily basis. Typically, these allowed people with lots of opinions on current affairs and the ability to express them in amusing ways to run what amounted to their own electronic newspaper or diary. There are now sites that provide the software to allow anyone to set up such a facility very easily. Of course, only those sites belonging to people who genuinely have something interesting to say survive, since the others never attract frequent visitors.

There are now a number of such Blogs devoted to Advaita-related topics and several of these may have 'staying power.' The ones that have come to my attention are as follows:

http://Advaitavedantameditations.blogspot.com/ from **Floyd Henderson**. Floyd also has a main site (http://floydhenderson.com/), which contains details of his books and an Advaita Quotes blog (http://advaitaquotes.blogspot.com/).

http://www.atmainstitute.org/ajablog.htm from **Aja Thomas**. Aja founded the Atma Institute in Portland, Oregon, where he teaches traditional Advaita along with Sanskrit, one of the very few western teachers to offer this.

http://nondualitynotes.blogspot.com/ from **Gilbert Schultz**, a former student of 'Sailor' Bob Adamson.

Acalayoga is devoted to providing information about Ramana Maharshi with links to downloads and extracts, up-to-date information on events and other relevant thoughts. http://acalayoga.blogspot.com/

Happiness of Being is the weblog of Michael James, who has a major website devoted to Ramana Maharshi. http://happinessofbeing.blogspot.com/

Ramana Maharshi - In the Lineage of the Self aims to develop, in the words of the author, 'an Experiential Language meaning a way of conveying spirituality through a language that lends itself most directly and immediately to an experiential awareness of Self.' http://identity-whatisit.blogspot.com/

KrishnaViswaroopam is apparently a more traditionally based blog, drawing on the teachings of the Upanishads and Swami Vivekananda. http://krishnaviswaroopam.blogspot.com/

Non-duality Cartoons has a number of... well, cartoons depicting various aspects of non-duality from illustrator Bob Seal. http://advaitatoons.blogspot.com/

Self-Identity Anonymous is the blog of E J Shearn, author of the '12 Step' model of Self-Enquiry (using the model of Alcoholics Anonymous 'Twelve Step Program'). http://12stepselfinquirey.blogspot.com/

Arunachala Grace – Not specifically about Advaita philosophy, this beautifully produced blog contains stories, pictures and general information relating to Mt. Arunachala and Ramana Maharshi. http://www.arunachala-grace.blogspot.com/

Guruphiliac – is the place to go for debunking and exposure of gurus (with humor). The headline claims 'Revealing Self-Aggrandizement and Superstition in Self-Realization since 2005' - and it is still going strong! http://guruphiliac.blogspot.com/

Awaken to Nonduality contains book excerpts, extracts from other web publications, thoughts and musings on non-duality from several contributors. http://community.livejournal.com/nonduality/

The Seer is the weblog of Peter Sumner, a spiritual mentor based at Gurukula in Fremantle, Western Australia, particularly influenced by Eckhart Tolle. There are frequent updates with extracts from books, topical observations and comments and even jokes. http://www.clearsightblog.net/

Self Knowledge is the weblog of Dr. Shyam Subramanian, one of the moderators of the Advaitin Egroup. http://www.adi-shankara.org/

A practical approach to Advaita – an introduction to Advaita and how to put the philosophy to practice in everyday life. http://practicaladvaita.blogspot.com/

Tattva Bodha – an intelligent commentary on the tattva bodha, explaining many Advaitic terms from first principles. http://tattvabodha.blogspot.com/

You Are Dreaming is the blog of Randall Friend, a disciple of 'Sailor' Bob Adamson and Gilbert Schultz. http://avastu0.blogspot.com/

Absolute Freedom is the blog of Charlie Hayes, influenced by Nisargadatta Maharaj, 'Sailor' Bob, John Wheeler et al.

Awake by Katie is the interactive blog of Katie Davis (see 'Friends of the Heart' in 5. above). http://www.awakebykatie.blogspot.com/

Sundance and Katie is the interactive blog of Sundance Burke and Katie Davis. http://www.sundanceandkatie.blogspot.com/

Professor Narayana Moorty has a blog based around his notes and papers for a possible book on U. G. Krishnamurti. http://moortysblogpage. blogspot.com/

Awakening to One is the blog of Sukhbir Singh, containing clearly presented, thought provoking analysis of some of Advaita's key topics. http://awakeningtoone.blogspot.com/

Ganapati-Advaita Ashram is the blog of Nathan Spoon, who teaches at this small ashram in Charlotte, NC. His background includes other traditions such as *tantra*, Kashmir Shaivism and *kuNDalinI* but Nathan now teaches Advaita and his blog addresses such topics as practice and self-enquiry. http://ganapatiadvaitaashram.blogspot.com/

The Philosophy of Advaita Vedanta - Nonduality contains articles on numerous aspects of advaita. These take the form of short definitions or discussions on terms or discrete topics and the emphasis is on traditional interpretation according to Shankara. http://advaitaphilosophy. blogspot.com/

Arunachala and Sri Ramana Maharshi – is the weblog of David Godman, the author of possibly the best book on Ramana's teaching, 'Be As You Are'. Its purpose is to provide 'musings on any matters relating to the life and teachings of Ramana Maharshi' and there are numerous quotations and extracts from related books. http://sri-ramana-maharshi.blogspot.com/

Jerry Katz now has a **Nonduality blog**. Possibly the most 'active' nondualist on the Internet, Jerry's writing is always readable and interesting and often thought-provoking, whether reviewing books or films (he seems to read more than anyone I know!) or finding the non-dual in the most unlikely places. Read his fascinating piece on lucid dreams on April 29 '08. http://nonduality.org/

Just Rest is the blog of Vincent Flammini, influenced by 'Sailor' Bob, John

Wheeler et al. There are articles and discussions with questioners, emphasizing the need to 'just stop and rest'. http://www.tryresting.blogspot.com/

Living in the Embrace of Arunachala is the blog of Richard Clarke and is providing an extensive photographic and personal record of the environs of Arunachala, covering temples, village life, general walking and much more. It is also the most complete reference for the Inner Path *pradakShiNa*. http://richardarunachala.wordpress.com/

Yoda Sutras – In a beautifully designed and presented website, Phalachandra juxtaposes news reports on a wide range of cutting-edge science subjects with a vast number of fascinating aphorisms from Osho, whom many people consider as one of foremost proponents of Advaita Vedanta in our age. http://yoda.t-pog.com/

Radiance of Being is the blog of Rodney Stevens. Influenced principally by John Wheeler, he provides pointers, reviews, questions & answers and generally expresses observations on 'simply being' in the present. http://radianceofbeing.blogspot.com/

8. Upanishads
There are many sites specifically relating to the scriptures – *shruti*, *smRRiti*, *brahmasUtra-s* and *prakaraNa grantha*. Some of these concentrate on just one element, especially those on the Bhagavad Gita in the next section but others are more eclectic. The following are particularly useful for Upanishads.

Celextel's Online Spiritual Library has translations of more Upanishads than I have found elsewhere (108 of them!), including many that I had not even heard of before. There are also translations of the *gIta*, *brahmasUtra*, *pa~nchadashI* and a number of works by Shankara. http://www.celextel.org/

The **Sanderson Beck Foundation** has lots of background information to the Upanishads and translations of a number of them. http://www.san.beck.org/EC7-Vedas.html

You can download a PDF format file of **11 of the major Upanishads**, translated by Swami Nikhilananda at http://sanatan.intnet.mu/upanishads /upanishads.htm. Recommended (but there is no Sanskrit text).

sankaracharya.org also has Swami Nikhilananda's translations as well as translations of the Vedas and Shankara's works and *bhAShya-s* on the *gIta* and *brahma sutra-s*. http://www.sankaracharya.org/

Max Muller translations may be downloaded at http://www.sacred-texts.com/hin/upan/

Vidya Vrikshah has word-by-word translations, together with the original Sanskrit for a number of the main Upanishads and other scriptures, as well as presentations on the main concepts of Vedanta and discussions of music and poetry. (Note that these will be found in the 'Presentations' section and you may need to download and install the fonts from the 'Software' section before you can see the script correctly.) http://www.vidyavrikshah.org/

You can search eleven of the major Upanishads for **key words** (in English) at http://atomicshakespeare.com/word/

9. Bhagavad Gita

The complete set of lectures by Swami Paramarthananda may be streamed or downloaded from **Internet Archive**. All talks are available in MP3 format (64kbs or 128kbs for 1st chapter; later chapters are only 24kbs). Some are available in Ogg Vorbis format. Talks are downloaded in 1-hour chunks (equates to around 56MB at 128kbs or around 10MB at 24kbs) and there are probably around 200 hrs in total. http://www.archive.org/search.php?query=creator%3A%22Swami%20Para marthananda%22

Note that, if you do download or listen to these, there is an obligation in the tradition to help support the continued teaching (which is provided freely). You can send your donations to Swamiji at the following address (note that checks should be made payable to 'Mantra'. Please add a note to explain that you downloaded his lectures):

Swami Paramarthananda,
Sriram Apartments,
80, St. Mary's Road,
Abhiramapuram,
Chennai 600 018.

There is also a complete set of lectures by another one of Swami Dayananda's pupils - Swami Tadatmananda from the **arsha bodha center**. http://www.arshabodha.org/bhagavadgita.html

The **Gita Supersite** has various translations and commentaries available, including the English version of Shankara's commentary. http://www.gitasupersite.iitk.ac.in/

Swami Krishnananda's translation, with summaries of each chapter and extensive commentary may be downloaded at http://www.swami-krish-nananda.org/gita_00.html

A modern translation by **Ramanand Prasad** may be downloaded at http://eawc.evansville.edu/anthology/gita.htm

The dvaita commentaries of **Swami Prabhupada** can be read at http://www.bhagavad-gita.us/netscape.html and chanting of the complete Gita may be purchased on CDs.

The **International Gita Society** has a comprehensive site with study lessons, stories and other scriptures. http://www.gita-society.com/

A suite of hyperlinked study notes may be downloaded from the UK Branch of the Chinmayananda Foundation. These contain the complete text of **Swami Chinmayananda's commentary** and also show the Devanagari script for each verse. The package downloads as a zip file whose contents include an executable that sets up the files and installs the font. Excellent! http://www.chinmayauk.org/Resources/Downloads.htm

The Chinmaya Mission Chicago has a '**Guidance through Bhagavad**

Gita' consisting of a large number of short essays, sorted by topic (e.g. Meditation, Perfect Man, Spiritual Growth). Each essay is based upon one or more verses from the Gita and these are presented with Devanagari, transliteration and translation. http://www.chinmaya-chicago.org/guide.htm

Acharya has a multilingual on-line Gita and a Sanskrit word list containing all words in the Gita with a reference to the verse(s) in which they occur. There are also 12 on-line lessons in real-audio format. http://acharya.iitm.ac.in/sanskrit/gita/gita_ref.php

The 'pocket edition' of the translation by **Swami Tapasyananda** is available at http://sss.vn.ua/bh_g_eng.htm

The Bhagavad Gita provides **Sowmya's** 'Essence of the Bhagavad Gita' (written or audio) as well as discourses, summaries and many links. http://www.gitaaonline.com/

Wikipedia has links to many more translations and other resources. http://en.wikipedia.org/wiki/Bhagavad_Gita

The Bhagavad Gita forms a part of the epic story '**The Mahabharata**'. A summary, stories, translations and articles may be found at http://www.mahabharataonline.com/ There is also an ongoing translation in simple English by M.V. Subrahmanyam at http://mahabharatinenglish.blogspot.com/

10. Sanskrit Resources

Sanskrit Documents is probably the main site for all Sanskrit-related information. Many documents may be downloaded in a variety of formats: PDF, PS, ITX, GIF, TXT, Sanskrit98, Sanskrit99, XDVNG. There are links to dictionaries and grammar-related tools and many exercises relating to conversational Sanskrit. Fonts etc. are available for download and links are provided to ITRANS and postscript tools. Finally, there are links to many other academic and personal Sanskrit-related projects around the world. There are even news broadcasts in Sanskrit, in Real Audio format. http://sanskrit.gde.to/

A regularly updated page of useful information and links is maintained at **Sanskrit Studies Links and Information**.

http://sanskritlinks. blogspot.com/

Dale Steinhauser has produced another large site of **Sanskrit Texts and Stotras**. Here is his own introduction to the site: "*Study Sanskrit, read Sanskrit texts, listen to Vedic pundits chant, or read Sanskrit humor. This site contains a wide variety of Sanskrit texts and stotras in the PDF format, which you can view or print for your personal use. Most of the texts are in Devanagari script, some with English translation. The Bhagavad-Gita, Devi Mahatmyam, all of the sahasranama stotras, and several other texts are also encoded in transliteration (by popular demand). A lot of attention has been put into formatting the texts for maximum aesthetic appeal and ease of use.*" http://sanskrit.safire.com/

Samskrita Bharati offers numerous publications to help in the learning of Sanskrit as well as some on-line audio. It has news about related events and details of how to help. http://www.samskrita-bharati.org/

If you want to learn Sanskrit, **Sanskrit & Sánscrito** produced by Gabriel Pradīpaka & Andrés Muni in Argentina is simply excellent. It takes you from the basics of learning to write and pronounce the letters up to a very comprehensive set of instructions and examples for combining letters (vowel, *visarga* and consonant *saMdhi*). Scriptures are translated and there are audio files of Patanjali's Yoga Sutras that may be listened to alongside the other material. A tremendous amount of effort is still going into this project and it shows. It is well presented and easy to read. http://www.sanskrit-sanscrito.com.ar/

Sudhir Kaicker has provided a freely downloadable tutor (nearly 38MB when I downloaded it) at **Sanskrita Pradipika**. This is aimed at providing adults who are learning on their own with a 'leisurely introduction'. It runs under Java run-time environment (so should be computer independent) in a small window that displays a small page of information at a time. It seems to do exactly what it claims. It is interactive to the extent that words may be constructed by typing at the keyboard. There is a very comprehensive set of declension tables for nouns and pronouns, with all of the various options displayed with just three clicks of the mouse. It can also sound out the letters but this facility is not included in the downloaded software to keep the size to a minimum. A CD can be mailed at the cost of the recipient. Later chapters explain *saMdhi*, declension and conjugation and sentence construction. Sudhir also now provides an 18 month course using Skype in addition to other tools. http://www.sanskrit-lamp.org/

A very comprehensive set of on-line lessons is produced by the **Systems Development Laboratory** at Chennai, India. Some of them may be downloaded for study off-line. There is also a free multilingual editor, for use in generating web pages containing Devanagari (and other) scripts. This is needed in order to be able to make full use of the lessons. http://acharya.iitm.ac.in/sanskrit/tutor.php

Chinmaya International Foundation (CIF), the Center for Sanskrit Research and Indology, has introduced the **Easy Sanskrit** Online Study Course. This course covers the salient aspects of Sanskrit Grammar and learning without unduly burdening the students with many details. The course lasts around 15 months at 3 hours per week, is accessible for all and costs $150 outside India. http://www.easysanskrit.chinfo.org/cif/

For the most serious students, a free downloadable, interactive version of *pANini's aShTAdyAyI* is available (for Windows 98/2000/XP) from **Ganakastadhyayi**. This classic work of around 4000 sutras explains the entire Sanskrit grammar in a very scientific manner and this computerized version by Dr Shivamurthy Swamiji provides a wealth of detail. http://www.taralabalu.org/panini/greetings.htm

The Sanskrit Heritage Site is maintained by Gérard Huet. Though the dictionary tools are aimed primarily at French speakers, most of the information is also in English. There is also an on-line tool whereby you can specify the stem of a noun (*prAtipadika* form), together with its gender and it will provide you with a tabular listing of all of the cases. There is also a '*saMdhi* analysis' utility that will attempt to break a sentence into words. http://sanskrit.inria.fr/

There is also an extensive page of categorised links. http://sanskrit.inria.fr/portal.html

Chitrapur Math is in the process of providing graded lessons in Sanskrit.

At the time of writing, this is up to month 17. Having had a quick look, they appear comprehensive and approachable. The later lessons have the student translating quite complex English sentences! http://www.chitrapurmath .net/sanskrit/step-by-step.htm

Wikipedia now has a good page of history, general information and links. http://en.wikipedia.org/wiki/Sanskrit

ITRANS is the transliteration scheme, developed by Avinash Chopde for writing Romanized Sanskrit, for transmission via the Internet. Full details of the scheme are given here. ITRANS itself is used with another tool called LaTeX. http://www.aczoom.com/itrans/

Since this is not at all straightforward, beginners or casual users are advised to use the web-interface (since its .ps and .pdf files are trans-portable for all platforms) or the special tool below. http://www.aczoom.com/itrans/online/

For easy ITRANS representation of Sanskrit, I recommend the use of the excellent software package '**Itranslator**', developed by the Sannyasis of Omkarananda Ashram Himalayas, Rishikesh, India. This program, compatible with the latest versions of Windows, is downloadable free of charge. Words can be typed in ITRANS and converted into Devanagari and Roman diacritical forms. These can then be copied and pasted into any Windows package. There is also a Unicode version, which will only run on systems supporting this (e.g. Windows XP). http://www.omkarananda-ashram.org/Sanskrit/Itranslt.html

If you only occasionally want to see the Devanagari representation, you can immediately translate an ITRANS word at the **giitaayan** site (which has a lyrics archive of Hindi songs on its homepage). There is also a table showing the ITRANS-Devanagari translations. http://www.giitaayan .com/x.htm

The ITRANS transliteration and Devanagari script for the alphabet may be viewed, and the correct pronunciation of each letter heard, at the **Sarasvati** site.http://members.tripod.com/sarasvati/devanagari/alphabet .html

Charles Wikner's excellent Sanskrit tutorial may be downloaded in its entirety or viewed chapter by chapter.http://www.danam.co.uk/Sanskrit/Sanskrit%20Introductory/Sanskrit%20Introductory.html

A downloadable pdf docment and an mp3 file teach you basic pronunciation at the **Devasthanam** site. This is the website of the Sanskrit Religions Institute. There is also a short list of Sanskrit terms and an essay on Sanskrit and the Hindu religion. Note that ITRANS is not used at this site. http://www.sanskrit.org/

umd_samskritam is a group established in 2005 in the US to promote the speaking of Sanskrit. The site aims to provide resources, act as a link for Sanskrit-related activities around the world and promote Sanskrit forums and blogs. Free weekend workshops are organized in the Washington-Maryland area. http://www.speaksanskrit.org/umd.shtml

A list of recommended books, divided up into 'Introductory Grammar and Readers', 'Reference Grammars', 'Dictionaries Sanskrit-English' and 'Dictionaries English-Sanskrit', is provided by the Columbia University's **'Inventory of Language Materials'**. http://www.realization.org/page/doc0/doc0078.htm

The dictionary that is essential if you are seriously interested in pursuing the language is that by **Monier-Williams**. It can be purchased in the West but is exorbitantly expensive (£120 or up to $300). If you are prepared to wait for it, you can obtain it much more cheaply from India.

The **University of Cologne** has done an incredible job of digitising much of the Monier-Williams Sanskrit to English dictionary. This may be used on-line and you can also enter a search word in English to find all of the Sanskrit words that may translate to this. Note that, as of summer 2008, there is a new and improved version –

http://www.sanskrit-lexicon.uni-koeln.de/monier/ – which allows entry of the search term in ITRANS format. Scanned images of each page in PDF format may be viewed also: http://www.sanskrit-lexicon.uni-koeln.de/scans/MWScan/index.php?sfx=pdf The dictionary may also be downloaded in its entirety (19Mb compressed to 7Mb) together with a superb utility for accessing the content. This facility has been provided by Louis Bontes at his site. http://members.chello.nl/l.bontes/

A CD version of the dictionary can be purchased for $2.95 from **Krishna.com** (the dictionary itself is freeware and occupies 421MB). It consists of TIF images of all of the pages together with a simple search tool to locate the relevant page. http://www.thekrishnastore.com/ Detail.bok?no=2295&bar

PDF versions of the Monier-Williams dictionary may be downloaded from the **Advaitin** website (thanks to Shri Prabhu) but note that the complete work is in excess of 400MB. The complete document is at http://www.advaitin.net/Sanskrit/MWComplete.pdf Volume 1 – http://www.advaitin.net/Sanskrit/MWVolume1.pdf and Volume 2 – http://www.advaitin.net/Sanskrit/MWVolume2.pdf

Apte's Sanskrit-English Dictionary may be searched on-line at the Middle Eastern Studies in Japan. http://www.aa.tufs.ac.jp/%7Etjun/sktdic/

There are 21 pages, (over 700 words at the time of writing) of the most frequently encountered Sanskrit **spiritually-related terms** at my own site. http://www.advaita.org.uk/discourses/definitions/definitions.htm

11. Teachers

Although I have previously included links in this section, I have decided to omit them this time for various reasons. There are lots of these (my spreadsheet list has over 240 and I have not been keeping it up to date) and it is obviously not possible for me to know whether or not all can be recommended. Sites are coming and going all the time and I would not wish to be accused of including or omitting specific ones. Also, it will be clear to the reader of this book that I would recommend that any seeker endeavor to find a *traditional* teacher and commit to attending their courses on a regular basis. As readers of my book 'Enlightenment: the Path through the Jungle' will know, I have condemned occasional satsang attendance, whether or not with the same teacher, as a pursuit most unlikely to lead to enlightenment. Many reasons for this view are presented in that book.

However, for those readers wishing to browse in this category, my site has pages relating to the following:

- Direct Path teachers
- Satsang teachers (4 pages of these)
- Neo-advaitin teachers
- Links to other 'databases' of teachers
- Lineage charts of all of the principal 'organizations' or Sages – Sivananda, Ramakrishna, Ramana Maharshi, Navnath (Nisargadatta), Osho, Krishna Menon, Adyashanti, Narayana Gurukula and 'Independent' teachers
- Links to diaries for upcoming satsangs

(Note that links relating to traditional teachers such as Swami Chinmayananda and Dayananda have been included in Section A.)

The links to all of these may be reached from

http://www.advaita.org.uk/teachers/teachers.htm

Appendix 2 – Recommended reading

This appendix is a cut-down, and updated version of that incorporated in 'Back to the Truth', my more advanced presentation on Advaita. I have included those books that should be considered as a comprehensive introduction to the subject and omitted some important but more difficult works.

Buying these books: There are direct links from my website (www.advaita.org.uk) to purchase these books from Amazon in both the US and the UK. (If you use these, you will reward me with a little commission!) Often, the books are only available from other sources such as direct from publishers in India, in which case links to those are provided instead.

A. Traditional

There are traditionally three 'types' of scriptures referenced by this philosophy. They are called the *prasthAna-traya* (*prasthAna* means 'system' or 'course' in the sense of a journey; *traya* just means 'threefold'). The first of these is *shruti*, which refers to the Vedas, incorporating the Upanishads. *shruti* literally means 'hearing' and refers to the belief that the books contain orally transmitted, sacred wisdom from the dawn of time. The second is *smRRiti* and refers to material 'remembered' and subsequently written down. In practice, it refers to books of law, in the sense of guidance for living, which were written and based upon the knowledge in the Vedas. Most often it is used to refer to just one of these books – the Bhagavad Gita. Finally, there is *nyAya prasthAna*, which refers to logical and inferential material based upon the Vedas, of which the best known is the Brahmasutra of Vyasa. This work was extensively commented on by Shankara in the *brahmasUtra bhAShya*, which analyzes the theory and arguments behind Advaita and counters all of the objections that might be posed to that mode of interpretation.

Although you need to be aware of all of these and should certainly look at them and maybe buy a few, they were written up to several thousand years ago, so you should not expect them to be either readable or immediately comprehensible! Ideally, they would be read to you and explained by a teacher who is thoroughly familiar with them.

1. Upanishads

There are very many translations and commentaries on these, either singly or in groups. There are not very many versions of the 'Complete' Upanishads, if it could be agreed what this means exactly, since there are certainly more than 100 separate ones. Upanishads such as the *bRRihadAraNyaka* or *ChAndogya* can run to as many as 1000 pages, including commentary, while some like the *tejabindu* are only a few pages. Because there are so many, it is difficult to recommend specific ones. The best thing to do is to visit a specialized bookshop and browse. See Section D on 'Buying Books'.

There are a number of collected works of the major Upanishads:

A version, with no Sanskrit, no literal translation and no commentary is **The Ten Principal Upanishads** put into English by Shree Purohit Swami and W. B. Yeats. (Ref. 5) This can definitely be recommended but should be read as poetry rather than as an aid to finding out about Advaita.

The best value for money I have discovered is a little book **Four Upanishads** by Swami Paramananda. (Ref. 9) It covers four of the principal Upanishads – Isha, Katha, Kena and Mundaka. There is no Sanskrit and not all verses are commented but the commentary that is provided goes straight to the heart of the matter.

The definitive version of eight of the major Upanishads is probably that translated by Swami Gambhirananda and with the commentary by Shankara, entitled unsurprisingly **Eight Upanishads** (Ref. 100). It comes in two volumes and does not include the two biggest Upanishads, which are also very important ones – the Brihadaranyaka and Chandogya.

If you want to look at individual Upanishads, the major ones are the

Kena, Katha, Isha or Ishavasya, Mundaka, Mandukya, Prashna, Taittiriya, Aitareya, Chandogya and Brihadaranyaka. Of these, I would recommend the first three to begin with. The Mandukya is possibly the most important, with its commentary (*kArikA*) by Gaudapada, but it is quite difficult so should not be attempted straight away.

For the **Kenopanishad** (Kena), I would recommend the one with commentary by Swami Muni Narayana Prasad (Ref. 57). It is not examined verse by verse as most treatments are. Instead there are many topics, such as 'What is Mind?,' 'The Unknowability of Truth,' and the meaning of the text is unfolded in a wider context. Although the correct Sanskrit terminology is used, it is a more modern interpretation.

Swami Chinmayananda has commentaries on most of the Upanishads, and all can be recommended as reliable, traditionally presented resources. Quoted in this book are extracts from the **Katha** (Ref. 103), **Mundaka** (Ref. 101), **Kena** (Ref. 102), **Isha** (Ref. 104) and **Mandukya** (Ref 8). The books are usually transcriptions of his discourses but are authoritative and fairly readable, with Devanagari and word by word translations followed by extensive interpretation.

The **Mandukya** and its *kArikA* by Gaudapada are essential if you want to learn about OM, states of consciousness or the *ajAti* theory of creation. Ref. 4 has Shankara's commentary and is translated and commented by Swami Nikhilananda. It is very good but really only for the serious student. If you wanted to read only one book to discover the 'bottom line' on Advaita philosophy, this would probably be it. A much more approachable version is the one commented by Swami Chinmayananda (Ref. 8). The book **Dispelling Illusion** by Douglas Fox (Ref. 58) is a more general (Westerner's) look at Gaudapada and his ideas as presented in the *kArikA*. Best of all, however, you should wait for my own book: 'OM: Key to the Universe', which will (endeavor to) explain these without the reader having to have considerable prior understanding of Advaita. This should be published by the end of 2012. It will draw heavily on Swami Paramarthananda's brilliant 80+ hours of talks unfolding this Upanishad and take into account all of the published commentaries (that I am aware of and have been able to purchase).

2. Bhagavad Gita

There are many different translations and commentaries on this classic work, where 'many' = tens if not hundreds. Some merely translate the Sanskrit, with varying degrees of accuracy and artistic license. Others provide several pages of commentary on each verse. I have only 12 different versions so it is perfectly possible that many of those I have not seen are excellent.

The most authoritative version is probably one that includes all of Shankara's commentaries and, of the two I am aware of, the better one is that translated by **Swami Gambhirananda** (Ref. 105). But, although I would unhesitatingly recommend it to serious students, beginners would almost certainly prefer one of those below.

Swami Dayananda has written **The teaching of the Bhagavad Gita** (Ref. 59). This is really using the Gita to present an overview of Advaita and it gives verses as illustrations rather than covering the entire book, verse by verse. It is, nevertheless, a very good book and I can thoroughly recommend it. (Indeed, *anything* by Swami Dayananda can be recommended.) He also provides a study course on the Gita, using extensive notes, which are excellent (available from http://www.arshavidya.org/).

The version by **Winthrop Sargeant** (Ref. 106) must be mentioned since this is the only one of which I am aware that has both original and Romanized Sanskrit, together with the meaning and grammar for each word. There is no commentary however. Nevertheless, if you want to study the Gita in depth, this is probably an essential buy.

Swami Chinmayananda has a voluminous edition published by Chinmaya Publications (Ref. 11). It is very good, albeit possibly a little verbose. It does suffer from a slight drawback in not having the original Sanskrit presentation of each verse. A free, electronic version of this may be downloaded however, (see below) and this does include the Sanskrit.

A supremely readable commentary for the modern reader is **The Living Gita** by Sri Swami Satchidananda (Ref. 107). Strictly speaking, this is Yoga rather than Advaita but that really does not matter – it is full of clearly expressed wisdom.

The version by **Swami Chidbhavananda** (Ref. 12) renders each verse in Devanagari, followed by Romanized Sanskrit and then a word for word translation. A full commentary is then given, often using excellent metaphors. Frequently, relevant quotations from Sri Ramakrishna are then presented. This is possibly the best to be recommended for the beginner, with the slight reservation that explanations may not always be in accord with traditional Advaita. (It is a long time since I read this, before I became aware of the divergence of neo-Vedanta, so I cannot make any confident statement about this.)

3. Brahma Sutra bhAShya

You will need a specialist bookstore to locate this if you are not buying it on-line. Note that, since you will presumably only be interested in the Advaitic interpretation, you will want the one with the *bhAShya* by Shankara. I have not removed this section, since the work is so important for Advaita but I really would not recommend attempting this until you have read everything else in this Appendix! It is really a work for removing any final doubts after you have thoroughly understood all the essential teaching. And, rather than attempting to read either of these books, I would really recommend that you listen to the lectures by Swami Paramarthananda (390 hours of them!)

The most popular version is probably the one with commentary by Swami Gambhirananda (Ref. 21). It is an exceedingly difficult book to read and, containing some of the most profound philosophical analysis, it is certainly not for the beginner.

Rather than a direct translation, this version is paraphrased by the Advaita scholar V. H. Date (Ref. 108) and is much more readable. Unless you really want the most accurate rendition, this is probably the best choice, though you may have difficulty finding a copy.

4. Other Classics of Advaita

Astavakra Gita (*aShTAvakra gIta* or *aShTAvakra saMhitA*) Not *shruti* and not really *smRRiti* either but a classic nonetheless. It is not known when, or by whom, the original work was written. It is named after the mythical Sage who appears in the Mahabharata and the Vishnu Purana, both very old scriptures. It is thought, however, that it was probably written more recently, either around the 8th Century or even as late as the 14th, by a follower of Shankara.

I would recommend the version translated and commented by Swami Nityaswarupananda (Ref. 13). A relatively small, thin and cheap version, easily fitting into the pocket, this can be carried around and is a source of the most wonderful uncompromising statements on pure Advaita. Complete with Devanagari Sanskrit and word for word translations.

Again, Swami Chinmayananda has a commentary (Ref. 14). A much weightier tome, this version may be easier to find.

There is a modern translation by Dr. Thomas Byrom (Ref. 117) with simple yet luminous prose. (This version may also be found on the Internet.)

The *Atmabodha* (Knowledge of Self) is one of the classic works on Advaita attributed to Shankara. Shankara is the nominal author of a number of books that are considered classics, almost of value comparable to those in the *prasthAna traya*.

Highly recommended, though only available from the Author's organization 'Vedanta Life Institute,' Sri Parthasarathy provides original Sanskrit with word for word translation (Ref. 17). The book is also liberally sprinkled with excellent metaphors and stories. The nature of the Real Self is dealt with at length.

The version by Raphael (Ref. 118) is short, with a good, clear, modern translation and commentary. It lacks Devanagari but has Romanized Sanskrit and uses Sanskrit terms throughout. There is an extensive glossary.

The *vivekachUDAmaNi* (Crest-jewel of discrimination). This is possibly the most famous of the books attributed to Shankara.

A simple but useful book that is not exactly a commentary, since no actual verses are presented, is that by Swami Prabhavananda and Christopher Isherwood (Ref. 18). It is eminently readable and presents the material with great clarity. Suitable for those new to Advaita.

Swami Dayananda Saraswati – **Vivekacudamani: Talks on 108 Selected Verses** (Ref. 99). This is the book that I would recommend to all those who think that they already understand Advaita. I have possibly learned more from this book than any other that I have read. The explanations are crystal clear, often entertaining and presented with the deep wisdom of probably the greatest living sage. There is only one possible problem in that there is a lot of Sanskrit and no glossary, so you have to note carefully as each new word is introduced. (Many of the terms used are in the Glossary of this book and most should be at my website.)

A somewhat more obscure book, also attributed to Shankara, is worth looking out for. It is very small, easily carried around in one's pocket, yet merits re-reading and study. Its title cannot even be written satisfactorily in the Roman alphabet, so here it is in ITRANS: *dRRigdRRishya viveka*, translated as 'an inquiry into the nature of the seer and the seen.' It addresses the topics of the illusory self, the universe, *mAyA* and *samAdhi*. The version translated and annotated by Swami Nikhilananda (Ref. 56) is the version with which I am familiar and can highly recommend. It is available from the Vedanta Society of Northern California for a mere $1.75.

The **Yoga Sutras of Patanjali**, recommended in the translation by Swami Satchidananda (Ref. 33). The '*yoga*' here refers to Raja Yoga (*rAja* = royal), also called *aShTA~Nga* (eightfold) Yoga, defined as 'the system of concentration and meditation based on ethical discipline.' Note that this is not Advaita (*yoga* is a dualistic philosophy) but there is much overlap in the area of mental preparation and the readable style of Swami Satchidananda, with many stories and metaphors, is able to communicate the ideas very clearly. Each sutra is given in Sanskrit, with word by word translation, followed by extensive commentary where necessary to bring out the meaning. There is much of practical value in this book as well as clarity of theory.

5. Philosophical Treatments

There are many books which address specific philosophical aspects of Advaita in an academic manner. Most of these are probably only attractive to those actually studying the subject at university but some are so well written and approachable and contain so much useful background material that they are worth attempting by anyone wanting to understand Advaita.

Methods of Knowledge According to Advaita Vedanta by Swami Satprakashananda (Ref. 119). The cover description states: 'The book deals with an exposition of the six means of valid knowledge leading to Self-realization.'

This is excellent – not for absolute beginners but it is very readable, yet comprehensive and authoritative. I have not come across such lucid explanations of the most abstruse aspects of Advaita before. It also explains the differences between Advaita and other branches of Indian Philosophy. Everything is set out in point by point explanation. And it has probably the most comprehensive index of any book I have seen!

Advaita Vedanta: A Philosophical Reconstruction by Eliot Deutsch (Ref. 2).

This reads like an academic Western Philosophical text and presents Advaita from an objective analytical viewpoint. This might tend to put off many potential readers but should not necessarily do so. Whilst it may seem dry at times and does require some effort to read, it presents some difficult concepts in a very clear manner and is an essential addition if you are building a library of key texts on the philosophy.

B. Modern and Neo-Advaita

These cover the now classic dialogues of sages such as Nisargadatta Maharaj and Ramana Maharshi and selections from the growing numbers of books written by present day satsang teachers, including the more radical, absolutist neo-Advaitins. Ideally, there would be (at least) two sections here, since some teachers would not wish to be associated with the other 'camp,' so to speak. But the dividing lines seem to be becoming increasingly hazy these days with some teachers, who might have been considered generally traditional, making statements more usually attributed to neo-Advaitins. Accordingly, I have grouped them all together and hope that I don't upset anyone!

1. Books by recent Sages

The main works of the Sage Atmananda **Krishna Menon**, who influenced both Jean Klein and Francis Lucille, are **Atma Darshan** (Ref. 60) and **Atma Nirvriti** (Ref. 61). Both are very short, originally in verse form in the Malayalam language, and translated by the author. So simple, straightforward and logically presented, yet presenting all of the key issues of Direct Path Advaita. Excellent!

I Am by **Jean Klein** (Ref. 30). There are a number of books available by Jean Klein, all in the form of short questions followed by longer answers on topics typically raised by those seeking answers to spiritual questions. Most are available in at least English, French and Spanish. His teaching is very much Direct Path and attempts to provide answers that can give some satisfaction to the intellect. He often brings a refreshing lightness to the mind with its tendency to become mired in irresolvable logical analysis. This book in particular is full of insightful observations. Many of his books, including this one, have now been published by Non-Duality Press.

I am That – Discourses by Nisargadatta Maharaj (Ref. 26). This is probably the best known book by any modern day Sage and justly so. It consists of short dialogues that he had with visitors, who traveled from around the world to listen to his blunt and forceful answers to questions on a variety of topics of concern to those still trapped in the illusory world. There are many wonderful, direct and unambiguous statements from this illiterate seller of cigars in the back streets of Bombay. It is an essential buy.

Some will take exception to including Osho in a list of 'recent sages' but there is no denying that some of his recorded material is extraordinarily perceptive. He is also capable of transmitting it in a very clear manner, interlaced with many (often rude) jokes to keep one awake. There are so many books by him that it is very difficult to recommend just one or two (even assuming that you have read them all, which I haven't). They are principally transcriptions of the talks he gave over many years or of the question and answer sessions that he held with his disciples. Many are based around a particular classical work such as an Upanishad. Whilst the philosophy that he propounded was usually commensurate with that of

Advaita, he drew his inspiration from many other sources, including Buddhism, Sufism and Hassidism.

The Mustard Seed (Ref. 44) is based upon the Gospel according to St. Thomas, the Christian work discovered amongst the Dead Sea Scrolls. Although this document may not be universally accepted amongst Christians, he uses it to bring out very clearly the non-dual teachings of Christ. It is quite a long book – nearly 500 pages – but it is nevertheless amazing how many topics are covered. Always readable and provocative, it is often very funny too. Extremely good.

Also highly recommended are **Heartbeat of the Absolute**, Ref. 43 and **I Am That**, Ref. 120. Both are discourses on the Isha or Ishavasya Upanishad. The former is based on talks given in April 1971. The latter is published under Osho's previous pseudonym, Bhagwan Shree Rajneesh and is based upon talks in October 1980. If asked to choose between them, I would probably prefer 'Heartbeat' (although 'I am That' contains more jokes!).

Finally, **What is Meditation?** (Ref. 41) unlike most of his books, is very short. It consists of brief extracts from his other work, which are relevant to the subject of meditation, telling us what it is and what it isn't, how to deal with thoughts, the nature of silence and much more. He is a master of metaphor and example and, if you are learning to practice meditation, this is an ideal prompt for relevant issues.

Talks with Sri Ramana Maharshi (Ref. 24). This is the classic book of conversations recorded by Sri Munagala S. Venkataramiah over the period 1935 – 9. Previously published in three volumes, they are now available in a single book of over 600 pages, published by Sri Ramanasramam. Very readable, yet full of wisdom. It has a comprehensive index and glossary. Another essential buy! Also available for free download – see section III.

Be As You Are: The Teachings of Sri Ramana Maharshi, edited by David Godman (Ref. 69). Short, but full of the wonderfully clear teachings of probably the most important teacher of the past millennium. This can be recommended whole heartedly as one of the very best books on Advaita. David Godman researched many sources and combined the material so as to provide fuller answers to the various questions, which are sorted into topics.

The **Gospel of Sri Ramakrishna** by M (Ref. 22), translated and with an introduction by Swami Nikhilananda documents the teaching of this 19th Century Self-realized saint through his dialogues recorded during the last four years of his life. There is an extensive introduction providing biographical details. I have only read this abridged version (the full version is over 1000 pages) but can highly recommend it. His words are full of compassion and wisdom and many of his stories are used in modern Advaita teachings.

2. General Books on Advaita

Vedanta Treatise: The Eternities by A. Parthasarathy (Ref. 20). Swami Parthasarathy has written several books, including one on the Gita, one on Shankara's Atmabodha and a commentary on several of the Upanishads. The Vedanta Treatise was his attempt to summarize Vedanta from his readings of the classical texts and from his studies with his own guru, Swami Chinmayananda. A new edition was produced in 2004. He still travels the world giving lectures on the Gita and also runs a school in Bombay, which provides a three-year residential course on Vedanta. An excellent introductory book, it tends to be more practical than theoretical, emphasizing *bhakti* and *karma yoga* aspects more than those of *j~nAna*. This is in line with the quotation on all of his cassettes that 'The Bhagavad Gita is a technique, a skill for dynamic living, not a retirement plan.'

The Science of Enlightenment by Nitin Trasi (Ref. 35). This provides a comprehensive coverage of the subject in an informed manner. It reads like a school textbook on the subject (though this is in no way intended to be a criticism) and has, indeed, been selected by the Department of Education in India for university libraries. It quotes very extensively from the works of Ken Wilber. It is thus particularly useful if you wish to acquaint yourself with the latter's work but, like me, find him not particularly readable.

Introduction to Vedanta (Understanding the Fundamental Problem) by Swami Dayananda (Ref. 19). Exactly what it says – an introduction to some of the key concepts, explained in simple terms for the beginner. 'The fundamental problem,' 'The Informed Seeker' and 'Ignorance and Knowledge' form the core of this very clear exposition. It also uses all of the correct Sanskrit terms so that these will be understood when moving on to more general reading.

Two more general books on Advaita by Swami Dayananda, both highly recommended, are **Self-Knowledge**, Ref. 121, and **Dialogues with Swami Dayananda**, Ref. 94. The former is based on nine talks on *Atma vidyA* given in May 2003 while the latter is collected from various sources and was originally published in 1988. Both are very readable and suitable for any level of student. They are both short but contain key topics presented with original lucidity. Swami Dayananda is, in my view, the best living teacher of traditional Advaita and one of the few to teach in the west. (I would have to qualify this by saying that I refer to his *written* material, since I find his spoken teaching difficult to follow. His disciple, Swami Paramarthananda is my preferred teacher in this respect.) He is able to explain the most difficult aspects clearly, using modern language and often amusing metaphors.

Vedanta Sutras of Narayana Guru by Swami Muni Narayana Prasad (Ref. 34). Based upon twenty-four short sutras from Narayana Guru, Swami Muni has provided a commentary that is both lucid and informative. It is authoritative, yet eminently readable, covering many of the topics of this book. Despite its unpromising title, this is certainly one of the better books on Advaita, traditional or modern. Full references are provided and there is a comprehensive glossary of Sanskrit words.

Back to the Truth: 5000 Years of Advaita by Dennis Waite (Ref. 95). Someone pointed out that I was not recommending my own books in this section and that I really ought to be. Modesty aside, I obviously think that what is said here is worth reading or I wouldn't have written it. I will not try to write a subjective-objective review of it however and refer anyone interested to the section of my website devoted to extracts, endorsements etc. Suffice to say that it is a more detailed examination of the topics that have been introduced in this book. http://www.advaita.org.uk/discourses/backto_truth/backto_truth.htm.

How to Meet Yourself (and find true happiness) by Dennis Waite

(Ref. 71). This is effectively my introductory book on Advaita. Disguised as a 'self-help' book, it provides a very gradual introduction to Advaita without any overt philosophy and without any Sanskrit. It uses the findings of sociological surveys, evolutionary psychology and western philosophy to point towards the truth. Again, for details and extracts from the book, see the website.

http://www.advaita.org.uk/discourses/meet_yourself/meet_yourself.htm.

Enlightenment: the Path Through the Jungle by Dennis Waite (Ref. 80). This looks specifically at what enlightenment is (and isn't), pointing out all of the misunderstanding in many 'New Age' writings. It addresses the various ways in which teachers speak about this, contrasting traditional, direct path, satsang and neo-advaita 'methods' and presenting arguments as to why some succeed while others are most unlikely to do. http://www.advaita.org.uk/discourses/enlightenment/enlightenment.htm.

3. Books by Modern (satsang) Teachers and writers

There are quite a number of western teachers holding satsangs regularly around the world and many of these are selling the recorded material subsequently on CD or even DVD as well as transcribed into book form. Dialogues in books may or may not be edited and, consequently, the quality of questions and answers is variable.

Given that a good teacher will be addressing responses directly to a specific seeker at his or her level of understanding, it necessarily follows that these may not be suitable for any particular reader and the context may also be lacking. Accordingly, 'satsang dialogue' books are intrinsically not a good medium for teaching Advaita.

The redeeming facts are that there are many basic questions that repeatedly arise in satsang and such answers are generally understood by all. Also, some teachers are very good at explaining even difficult topics so that their material is usually worthwhile regardless. The books recommended in this section are not all of this type but, where they are, they do not suffer too much from these drawbacks.

Living Reality: My Extraordinary Summer with **'Sailor' Bob Adamson** by James Braha (Ref. 122). This book does contain dialogue but is superior to most of them on at least four counts. Firstly, the teacher is 'Sailor' Bob Adamson, one of the clearest satsang teachers. Secondly, instead of questions from many different seekers, those here are mainly from a single person, the author, and hence are much more coherent and focused. Thirdly, James Braha has provided valuable commentaries between sections, in which he is able to summarize and express his own extensive understanding of the topics under discussion. Finally – and this is the factor that especially recommends it – the whole book is presented as a real-life adventure, in which we share the excitement of a prolonged visit by an enlightened teacher. Sailor Bob spent a full five weeks in the author's home giving private and public talks, and we get an intimate and fascinating account of the entire experience.

Eternity Now – Dialogues on Awareness by Francis Lucille (Ref. 36). This contains transcriptions from some of his audiocassette discussions with David Jennings (who utilizes the teachings of Advaita in his psychotherapy practice) together with additional material, such as answers to email questions (including my own). As noted earlier, his approach is direct path and, as such, there is nothing of the traditional *bhakti* or *karma* methods here. The questions are answered in an incisive and uncompromising way that will appeal to those who feel that they have to use their minds and intellects to analyze everything.

Acceptance of What Is – A Book About Nothing by Wayne Liquorman (Ref. 28). This book presents much of the material that you will hear if you attend one of his talks and in the same style – humorous yet uncompromising. It is possibly the best book to read for an entertaining introduction to the key principles of Advaita as taught by Ramesh Balsekar, with its emphasis on 'non-doership.'

Awakening to the Dream by Leo Hartong (Ref. 74). Leo's teaching is usually regarded as neo-Advaita, influenced as he has been by both Tony Parsons and Nathan Gill. Nevertheless, it retains some of the best traditional metaphors and styles. It is a marvelous exposition of non-dual teachings, straight from the heart. Though drawing on quotations from a wide variety of sources (not just Advaita), it is principally a crystal clear presentation from the author's own experience. Highly recommended!

Tony Parsons is possibly the most widely recognized of the modern neo-Advaita teachers (though this term is not one which they themselves use). His first book was **The Open Secret** (Ref. 32), a short book relating the experiences of the author in a candid and unpretentious manner. It is a refreshing antidote to the tendency of many books to over-intellectualize the topic. It is repeatedly made clear that there is 'no separate identity.'

The Texture of Being by Roy Whenary (Ref. 123). A practical guide to living the spirit of non-duality amidst the vicissitudes of the apparent world. Roy appeals from the heart directly to the heart for us to recognize our true nature and abandon once and for all the traditional pursuits of pleasure, prestige and prosperity, which can never lead to happiness. Instead we should open ourselves up to the silence and clarity, there to discover the beauty and fulfillment of the reality that is already here and now.

The Teachers of One Living Advaita: Conversations on the Nature of Non-Duality by Paula Marvelly (Ref. 124). All seekers will empathize with this sincere and beautifully written, personal search for the truth of the Self, as the author traverses the world to interview a number of modern teachers of Advaita . There is much to learn about their personal backgrounds, teaching styles and content and gems of wisdom are elicited by the penetrating questions. But for me it was the interludes between these, where the author writes about her own feelings and reactions that make this book special. The reader shares her moments of confusion, loneliness and yearning as well as those of peace, understanding and acceptance, culminating in a samAdhi experience in Ramana's Virupaksha cave at Arunachala. Wonderful!

The Wisdom of Balsekar (Ref. 125) is a compilation of extracts from Ramesh's other books, themed by topic (e.g. action, bondage, death, desire, effort, ego etc.). A wonderful selection presenting an overview of his clear and logical approach to the teaching. Edited by Alan Jacobs, president of the Ramana Maharshi Foundation UK and approved by Ramesh.

Silence of the Heart: Dialogues with Robert Adams (Ref. 70). Robert Adams did not write books or give lectures. Towards the end of his life he attracted a small group of students who would come to him for satsang.

After Robert's death in 1997, some of these students transcribed some tapes of Robert's talks, and this book consists of these transcriptions. The style is simple and direct. Robert, like Ramana, advocated self-inquiry.

A Natural Awakening by Philip Mistlberger (Ref. 126). Many students of Advaita think that to become enlightened is to attain a permanent state of peace and happiness in which they no longer have any worries or fears.

It seems that many teachers attempt to subvert the traditional teachings by diluting them with ideas from western psychology in order that they may satisfy this need. If they can make the person feel good (instead of undermining their idea that there actually is a person), they claim to have succeeded. This completely misses the point and invariably the student ends up confused and dissatisfied. The reason that this can happen is that the teacher is usually poorly trained in psychology and has not correctly understood the philosophy himself (irrespective of whether or not he is himself 'enlightened').

In order to address the perceived needs of these western students, what seems to be needed is a teacher who fully understands both. He will then be able to address the psychological issues authoritatively in their own context whilst at the same time expanding the students' awareness into being able to see the truth behind their seeming problems.

In my own studies and research, I have read many books on Advaita from all traditions and I have never encountered anyone with the ability to teach in this way – until now. I invariably pencil in notes in the margins of books whenever I encounter particularly useful explanations or helpful metaphors so that a very good indicator of the value of a book can be gained by the number of such annotations. Based upon this, I can state categorically that this is a very good book indeed!

Awakening to the Natural State by John Wheeler (Ref. 127). This is not drawn from satsang material but from emails and from personal discussion of the author with 'Sailor' Bob Adams. Additional comments and clarification has been added and the quality is generally high so that this book can definitely be recommended.

Perfect Brilliant Stillness by David Carse (Ref. 128). The Self cannot be described but David Carse makes a very good effort. Quoting from Sufi and Taoist sages as well as Advaitin ones, he helps uncover the non-dual truth that is the essence of the phenomenal appearance. The language he uses is direct and carries the conviction of experience. In many books on Advaita there is the distinct feeling that what is said is in the realm of theory or based upon what has been read elsewhere; one is left in no doubt that this is not the case here. Although nothing new is being said, the material comes across so clearly, simply and self-evidently. And I think this is the key to why the book succeeds. The words carry the understanding to those seeking the explanations but they cannot prevent the heart-felt, mind-less, direct 'knowing' from shining through and piercing the merely intel-lectual.

Although much is said about the inadequacy and ultimate failure of language to speak of reality, David's writing is very good. I have said in my own books that it is not possible to talk clearly about this subject without using the correct Sanskrit terminology but this book seems to give the lie to that statement. There are some very original metaphors and many brilliant, quotable observations. Sometimes, every other paragraph seems to contain a new profundity.

David is not a teacher of Advaita and specifically states that he does not teach. Beginners will probably not benefit and should perhaps look elsewhere to begin with. But, if you think you know it all already yet feel that 'it' has still not clicked, this is definitely for you. It is the book for those who want to differentiate between intellectual understanding and realization. I have also noted that it seems to receive praise from both tradi-tional and neo-Advaitins – and that is praise indeed!

I have mentioned earlier that I always pencil in the margins of any Advaita books that I read these days. Positive comments are marked: 'good', '!' and Q (for 'quote'); things that I don't understand are marked '?' or, if I disagree, 'x'. There are very few '?', only a couple of x's and many Q's and good's. What more can I say? The only adverse comment that I would make – and it is a warning for potential readers as much as anything else – is that the early chapters do go on a bit! So, if you find that, don't be put off and give up; keep reading – it just gets better... and better!

Two books published since the first edition of this book deserve special mention because they deal with Direct Path teaching. The first of these is by Greg Goode, who has been mentioned a number of times – **Standing as Awareness: The Direct Path** (Ref. 136). I wrote the foreword to the first (electronic) edition of the book, so can highly recommend it . (At the time of writing, I have not yet seen the published version so have not reviewed it.)

The second book is **The Transparency of Things: Contemplating the Nature of Experience** (Ref. 137) by Rupert Spira. I have written a very long review (which you may read at my website) of this book but the conclusion was as follows: *"I suggest that this book is going to be of most interest to seasoned seekers, who may find new and insightful views into some of the familiar topics in advaita. I fear that those who are not already used to the manner of speaking about non-duality will quickly discard the book - it will simply be too difficult for them. It requires both serious interest and genuine commitment to stay with it. But, for those who are prepared to make the effort there is much to savor and I recommend it highly to them. I personally found it to be a delight and a frustration (in equal measure!) and, on that basis, perhaps I ought not to award more than 4*. But there is so much good stuff in here, and it towers above most other modern books on the subject, that I have few qualms about awarding 5*."*

4. Books which are not strictly Advaita

The Book (on the taboo against knowing who you are) by Alan Watts – (Ref. 39). This is a very readable book, written by the man who started out as a Christian in England and became a popular speaker and writer on most Eastern philosophies, especially Zen, during the 1960's. The teaching espoused by this particular book is predominantly Advaita and it is advertised as the book that you give to your children when they set out to make their own way in life, answering all of the questions that they will ask about meaning and purpose. A large number of his talks are available on CDs, videos and audiocassette, mostly from his son's website at http://www.alanwatts.com. There are also a number of Internet 'radio stations' that broadcast these talks on a regular basis.

Another highly recommended book by Alan Watts is **The Wisdom of**

Insecurity (Ref. 40), subtitled 'a message for an age of anxiety.' Not just about the impossibility of finding certainty or security in our lives but about the meaninglessness of past and future, memory and desire.

With respect to meditation, the most widely known and practiced method in the west is that brought over by Maharishi Mahesh Yogi in the 1960's. The movement still flourishes though we may hear less about it these days and the method remains a simple and readily accessible one. It can be used simply to reduce stress or as part of a more structured spiritual 'path'. **The TM Technique**: An Introduction to Transcendental Meditation and the Teaching Method of Maharishi Mahesh Yogi by Peter Russell (Ref. 129) is an excellent presentation of the topic, its history, practice and benefits.

C. Free Books

There are an increasing number of books being made available for free download on the Internet and some of these are excellent. Most are in Adobe's PDF format, which is clear and readable on a good computer monitor and, of course, printable if you prefer to read in bed or whilst eating your lunch. An outstanding example is the 'Notes' of Atmananda Krishna Menon (Ref. 13), long unavailable but a second edition may be download at my website. (It may also be published by the time you read this book.) Books by Swamis Sivananda and Krishnananda have long been available but Sri Ramanasramam have recently made books on the conversations of Ramana Maharshi available. Also, some modern western teachers make edited satsang material available in this way – Nirmala is a notable example. Below are listed some of the best that I am aware of, together with link information. (Again, it should be noted that there is a section at my website containing details of all these together with links.)

1. Traditional

From The Upanishads by Ananda Wood (Ref. 130) – This is a free translation of selected passages from a number of the Upanishads into blank verse, along with some occasional prose. Divided up according to clear topic headings. An original adaptation to make them more accessible to the modern reader. www.advaita.org.uk/discourses/ananda_wood/ananda_wood.htm.

Interpreting The Upanishads by Ananda Wood (Ref. 131) – This focuses on particular ideas from the Upanishads, and explains how these ideas can be interpreted. For each idea, selected passages are translated and placed for comparison beside much freer retellings that have been taken from the first book. The Sanskrit is often referenced with explanation of alternative translations. www.advaita.org.uk/discourses/ananda_wood/ananda_wood.htm.

Swami Chinmayananda's commentary on the **Bhagavad Gita** (Ref. 11) is available as an excellent html-based package, containing the complete text. It is available for download from http://www.chinmayauk.org/Geeta_download.shtml. This does contain the Sanskrit (unlike the book version) as well as additional study notes.

At http://www.swami-krishnananda.org, you can download complete books by **Swami Krishnananda** on the Upanishads (including the Chandogya and Brihadaranyaka) and the Panchadashi. Swami Sivananda's book on the Brahma Sutras may also be downloaded in its entirety. The hardcopy versions may also be ordered from the same website.

A translation of the *aShTAvakra gIta* by John Richards (Ref. 132) is available at http://www.realization.org/page/doc0/doc0004.htm.

The commentary on the *aShTAvakra saMhitA* (a different name for the same work) by V. Subrahmanya Iyer may be downloaded from http://www.wisdomsgoldenrod.org/publications/.

'**Self Realization** (*brahmAnubhava*): The Advaitic Perspective of Shankara: Indian Philosophical Studies IV' by Vensus A. George covers the work of Shankara in considerable depth. It is written in a scholarly manner with detailed references but is nevertheless very readable. It is. It may be purchased but is also available for free download for personal study from http://www.crvp.org/pubs.htm.

Most of the Upanishads, works by Shankara and a large number of other classics are available electronically at http://www.celextel.org/. Only the English translation (i.e. no Sanskrit), without commentary, is provided but this is a tremendous resource.

2. Books by Recent Sages

Notes on Spiritual Discourses of Shri Atmananda, taken by Nitya Tripta (Ref. 98). This is Krishna Menon's magnum opus on Direct Path teaching. Long unavailable, because a weighty tome originally published only in small numbers, the copyright has now been transferred and the new holder wishes to make this wonderful document available to all seekers, as easily as possible. It consists of 1,450 notes of varying length, covering a wide range of subjects in his unique pithy and logical style. There is also a detailed biography. A version of the second edition may now be downloaded from www.Advaita.org.uk/discourses/downloads/notes _pdf.zip. Most of the proofing and scholarly checking has been done in the latest version. The file has been zipped for minimum size (1.7Mb), 500+ pages including a comprehensive index with hyperlinked page numbers.

Maha Yoga by 'Who' (Ref. 25). This is essentially a book about Advaita as taught by Ramana Maharshi who bridges the gap between traditional and direct path methods. The author, only identified as 'Who' on the title page, was Sri K. Laksmana Sarma, who studied for over twenty years with Ramana. He defines Maha Yoga as 'the Direct Method of finding the Truth of Ourselves.' The key topics addressed are happiness, ignorance, world, soul, god, the nature of the Self and the means for realizing this, and the role of the Sage and devotion. Some difficult concepts are explained with transparent clarity and the entire book is readable and authoritative yet written with obvious humility. Highly recommended. It may be downloaded from http://sriramanamaharshi.org/Allpub_demo.html.

Talks with Sri Ramana Maharshi (Ref. 24). This is the classic book of conversations recorded by Sri Munagala S. Venkataramiah over the period 1935 – 9. Very readable, yet full of wisdom. It has a comprehensive index and glossary. It is downloadable as a 'zipped' file at http://www.sriramanamaharshi.org/downloads/talks_full.zip.

Other classic collections of material by or about Ramana Maharshi are available from the same site – http://www.sriramanamaharshi.org/bookstall /downloadbooks.html – including **The Collected Works,** edited by Arthur

Osborne (Ref. 133) and **Day by Day with Bhagavan.** (Ref. 84).

All (?) books by **Osho** are available at http://oshoworld.com/. They are downloadable as PDF documents, although you must send an email request for each book first in order to obtain the download address. This is automatically provided by return email. Another site which offers PDF files of the books (without the email request) is http://www.messagefrommasters. com/Ebooks/Osho_Books.htm.

The Way of the Bird: Commentaries on the Teachings of **Sri Ranjit Maharaj** by **Andrew Vernon** (Ref. 134). Ranjit Maharaj was the less well-known disciple of Siddharameshwar Maharaj, along with the famous Nisargadatta Maharaj. This book consists of his terse words on a wide range of topics but, fortunately, these are elaborated and explained by Andrew Vernon in an exceptionally lucid manner making the whole book a mine of valuable knowledge. Available from http://www.wayofthebird.com/.

3. Others

A retired philosophy lecturer and author, **Jonathon Bennett**, is in the process of performing the most tremendous service to lovers of philosophy everywhere – that of rendering a number of classics of western philosophy into comprehensible, modern language (without changing the essence). He has already 'translated' works by Berkeley, Descartes, Hobbes, Hume, Kant, Leibnitz, Locke and Spinoza. These may be downloaded from http://www.earlymoderntexts.com/ as PDF files for private use or for teaching purposes.

D. Buying Books

The Internet is an excellent resource for buying books on Advaita simply because bookstores that stock these books are so difficult to find unless you live in India. You will be fortunate indeed if you happen to have such a store within easy access of your home. Buying off the Internet using a credit card is very easy and, providing that the web site has a secure facility, also very safe.

Large organizations such as Amazon are excellent in that they have huge stocks and a very efficient service. Prices are also often lower than you will find elsewhere. Because Advaita is such a specialist subject however, and many books are printed without ISBN by small Ashrams, you will not always find the books listed at Amazon or other large on-line sellers. In this case it is often necessary to buy direct from the publisher.

Buying books from India is very easy. The quality of the printing and binding is not always as good as you would expect from western publishers and books usually have a unique smell (which you will grow to love!). Delivery often takes a long time too (over a month is not unusual). The very big point in favor of this route, however, assuming there is any choice, is that books are usually extremely cheap compared to buying in the west. As an example, the Bhagavad Gita with Shankara's commentary translated by Swami Gambhirananda was $20 from Amazon.com in Aug. 2005 and Rs110 = $2.51 from Motilal Banarsidass. (Of course, you do also have to take account of the postage charge.)

1. In the UK and Europe

Watkins Books is the bookshop that I like to visit whenever I travel to London in the UK. It has a large section downstairs devoted to Advaita, both traditional and modern. It is in the process of building an on-line purchase facility and this may well be available by the time that you read this. http://www.watkinsbooks.com/

Non-Duality Press publishes books in the categories of satsang and neo-Advaita and, more recently, Direct Path. http://www.non-dualitypress.com/

InnerQuest in Paris, France sell videos, DVDs, CDs and books on non-dual teachings. There are numerous ones by Ramana Maharshi and the elusive 'Atma Darshan' and 'Atma Nirvritti' by Atmananda Krishna Menon. http://www.inner-quest.org/

2. In the US

Chinmaya Publications are able to supply all the books by Swami

Chinmayananda that are currently in print. http://www.chinmayapublica-
tions.org/

Arsha Vidya Gurukulam has already been mentioned in the Organizations
section but must have another mention here since it is the principal
(sometimes only) source for the excellent books by Swami Dayananda.
http://www.arshavidya.org/

Inner Directions publish a number of books, videos and audiotapes on
non-duality. Books and DVDs are principally of Ramana Maharshi,
Nisargadatta and Tony Parsons. http://www.innerdirections.org/

Nataraj Books at Springfield, Virginia have an extensive collection of
books from India (over 5,000 titles) on various subjects, including some
that are difficult to obtain elsewhere. There is a facility to order online.
https://www.natarajbooks.com/main.aspx

The **Vedanta Press** of Southern California has a huge selection and on-line
ordering providing that you live in the US. http://www.vedanta.com/

3. In India

Vedicbooks.net has a huge collection of books and an excellent website to
sell them on-line. Purchases may be made in $ or £ and paid for by credit
card or, for maximum convenience, versatility and safety by Paypal. Since
books are very much cheaper in India and often only available there, this is
an easy way to buy. (The additional reference in the link below is to gain
me a small commission if you use it!) http://www.vedicbooks.net/index.
php?ref=109&affiliate_banner_id=8

Vedams Books are good for buying books on Vedanta (or anything else to
do with India). There is a detailed description of nearly every book so you
can check whether it sounds like what you are looking for before you order.
http://www.vedamsbooks.com/

Motilal Banarsidass publishes many books on Advaita, both traditional and modern and it is surprisingly cheap to buy these for export to the UK or US, much cheaper than buying the equivalent books from your local bookstore. They have a detailed on-line catalogue and you can purchase books using credit cards. Instead of doing this on-line, you print out a form, fill in the details and fax this. Alternatively the form is emailed after completion. http://www.mlbd.com/

Sundeep Prakashan also publishes a wide range of material relating to India, including a good selection of books on Advaita. Books may be purchased on line via credit cards and prices are quoted in US $. They also publish my book 'An Essential Guide to Sanskrit' (Ref. 143). http://www.sundeepbooks.com/

Samata Books publish the complete works of Shankara as well as his commentary on the Bhagavad Gita. http://www.samatabooks.com/

Indian Books Centre are publishers of Indological Books. Books may be ordered on-line but there are, as yet, no credit card facilities. http://indian-bookscentre.com

Exotic India sell everything related to Indian art - paintings, sculptures. jewelry, beads and textiles - but they also hold a huge stock of books on Philosophy (over 1000 titles). There are full details of each book; prices are quoted in your currency and include very fast, air-mail postage. You can pay by Paypal as well as credit cards and the service is excellent. http://www.exoticindiaart.com/

Saujanya Books have a large number of relevant books with prices, including airmail, in US $ and payment by Visa or Mastercard. http://www.saujanyabooks.com/index.htm

Eastern Book Corporation also sell books on many different subjects (with around 800 on aspects of Hinduism). Books are sold at the Indian cover price, which makes them substantially cheaper than many Indian exporters Credit cards are accepted. http://www.easternbookcorporation.com/

Some books published by Ashrams can only be purchased from them directly and, in the case of some books, this is very worthwhile. The **Advaita Ashrama** at http://www.advaitaashrama.org/ is one such example, publishing such books as Swami Nikhilananda's translation of the Mandukya Upanishad. **Sri Ramakrishna Math** at http://www.sriramakrishnamath.org/ is another specialist publisher, of the recommended Upadesha Sahasri by Shankara, for example.

Appendix 3 – Introduction to Sanskrit and ITRANS

Introduction

Hopefully everyone will have realized that the Sanskrit words I have been using so far do not really look the way I have written them in the language itself. Sanskrit uses an alphabet quite unlike ours. For a start, it contains nearly twice as many letters (more than three times the number of vowels) and these letters can look quite different depending upon where they appear in a word and which other letters are adjacent. The language is also written in 'Devanagari' script, which is quite unreadable without a lot of study and practice.

Now I have no intention of attempting to teach you all of this. It is most likely that you are not really interested (I certainly wasn't to begin with), in which case I would be wasting my time. If you actually are interested, then you will probably be looking elsewhere. Apart from this, I know little more than how to look up words in the dictionary myself, so would be unable to teach you very much anyway.

ITRANS transliteration

All that this appendix will attempt to do is to explain to you how to pronounce the Sanskrit words used in this book. They have been written (italicized in brackets after what is usually a poor attempt to render the word phonetically in English) in what is called transliterated form, using the ITRANS scheme. Avinash Chopde devised this scheme for use on the Internet. His software, and details about the system, may be downloaded from his website, http://www.aczone.com/itrans/. There already existed at least one widely used scheme for rendering Sanskrit letters in a 'Romanized' way. However, since this used symbols called macrons (lines above letters) and dots above and below letters, it was quite unsuitable for computer keyboards with basic letters and the normal fonts provided with word processors. Accordingly, this scheme uses only the usual letters of our alphabet, together with the occasional special character such as the tilde ~.

General

Sanskrit it is an extremely interesting language. It is amazingly logical. There are lots of rules but, once you have learnt them, there are none of the tiresome exceptions found in most languages. Also, once you have learned how to pronounce a letter, it is *always* pronounced in that way. Unfortunately, simply learning the letters is not sufficient to enable you to look up words in the dictionary. Letter combinations can look quite different from the same letters on their own. Also words found in the scriptures usually consist of combinations of many separate words and, when words join, they often change. An example that you will have seen in the book is *sachchidAnanda*. If you did not know this word, you would have to know the rules of these combinations in order to be able to work out that the separate words of which this consists – *sat*, *chit* and *Ananda* – in order to be able to look them up. You can see that, when a word ending in t combines with one beginning with ch, the t also changes to a ch. And the t at the end of chit becomes a d. Accordingly, you will not find this word in the dictionary under 'sach' but just after 'sat'. This particular word is present in its complete form because it is in such common usage but infrequent combinations will not themselves be listed and you have to break them down into the individual words to find out the meaning. (This is known as euphony or *saMdhi*.)

Finally, it is interesting to note in passing that there is a close parallel between the structure of the language and the Advaita-related myth of the creation. Indeed, some schools of thought, notably in the North of India and Kashmir, believe that the universe was 'spoken' into existence. Though this 'primordial' language is beyond ordinary sound, Sanskrit is its earthly manifestation as it were and embodies many of the 'universal principles'. The language itself is believed to embody the truth of the unity of the Self. Since pure Advaita tells us that there is effectively no such thing as creation, the value of discussing these ideas is ultimately academic. Such studies can help prepare the mind to acknowledge those truths that remain forever beyond its grasp but they can also prove a hindrance. They have more appeal to those whose nature is inclined towards *bhakti yoga* rather than *j~nAna*.

The entire language evolves in an almost mathematical way from a fundamental sound. The laws governing the way that words are constructed, and the grammar used to join them, are strict. It is amazing that the language, though the most ancient known and no longer in general use, remains true to its original form and someone learning it now would be able to communicate perfectly well with someone speaking the language thousands of years ago.

The five basic vowels

The first letter of the alphabet forms the fundamental sound from which all others are derived simply by moving the tongue and lips. It is made by opening the mouth wide and letting the vocal chords operate. The sound which emerges sounds like a cross between the short 'a' in cat and 'u' in but. It is written as '*a*' in ITRANS but the correct letter in the proper script, called *devanAgarI* (meaning city of the gods), is: -

अ *a*

This is the first letter of the alphabet and the first vowel or, to use its correct term, *svara*, meaning sound. I will not show the Devanagari for any of the other letters for the reasons already discussed above.

If the back of the tongue is now raised slightly towards the back of the roof of the mouth, keeping the front of the tongue down against the back of the lower teeth, and the same short movement of the vocal cord is made, a slightly different sound emerges. This sounds a bit like the short 'i' in bit. It is written as *i* in ITRANS.

The next two vowels seem strange to Westerners but follow the logic of the development. The underlying sound for both of these is the *i* sound just covered but the tip of the tongue is first moved further forward in the mouth. If you raise the tip of the tongue until it is almost touching the roof of the mouth and then, make the 'i' sound as before, the next vowel sound emerges. Modern students often actually flick the tongue downwards as the sound is made so that the result sounds something like 'ri' in the word rip, though the rolling 'r' beginning is not clearly enunciated because the tongue never actually touched the roof of the mouth. However, strictly speaking this is not correct. It is written *RRi* in ITRANS (or, in old releases,

R^i).

This procedure is repeated but now the tip of the tongue moves further forward still, to just behind the front teeth, before the 'i' is sounded. Again, modern speakers often flick the tongue up towards the roof and down so that the sound that actually comes out is 'lri'. Again, not strictly correct but it hardly matters since there is only one word in the language that uses this letter! It is written *LLi* in ITRANS (or, in old releases, *L^i*).

Continuing the development, the emphasis finally shifts to the lips (labial position), having begun in the throat (guttural position), moved to at the back of the mouth (palatal), then to the roof of the mouth (cerebral) and then the teeth (dental). If a circle is formed of the lips but without any tension and the basic sound is made, a short 'oo' sound comes out as in soot or cut. This is the last of the simple vowels, written *u*.

These five vowels with their characteristic mouth positions effectively head up the five main groups of consonants. Consonants all effectively still sound the basic 'a' but 'stop' it from coming out in that simple way by varying the position of the tongue and lips in the way dictated by the vowel at the head of the group.

The long vowels

The basic five vowels above are all *short* vowels – *hrasva*. This means that, when pronounced, the sound is made as short as possible whilst still being distinguishable – really quite short! Each of these vowels *can* be sounded long. The length is actually very precise. If the short form is treated as one measure, then the long form should be two measures. The long form is called *dIrgha*. In ITRANS, the vowel is shown as long either by putting two of them, as with the *ii* in *diirgha* or by capitalizing it thus: – *dIrgha*. The latter form has been used as standard in this book.

When the vowels become long, the pronunciation naturally changes slightly, too. Thus, the short *a* becomes *aa* or *A* and sounds like the 'a' in calm. The short *i* becomes *ii* or *I* and sounds like the double 'ee' sound in words like sleep. The short *RRi* becomes *RRI* (or *R^I* in old releases of ITRANS). Here there is no option of having two small i's. The *dIrgha* vowel is sounded as for the *hrasva* form but with the ending 'ee' instead of 'i'. Similarly, the short *LLi* becomes *LLI* (or *L^I* in the old releases of ITRANS) but, since there are no words at all known to contain it, this hardly seems to matter! Finally, short *u* becomes long *uu* or *U* and sounds like the double 'oo' in root.

The vowels can be sounded for longer than two measures, in which case they are called *pluta* – prolonged. In this case they are written with a number '3' below and just to the right of the letter, both in *devanAgarI* and in the Romanized version. This form cannot be represented in ITRANS.

The compound vowels

Now, if the sound *a* is made and continues to sound while the mouth is slowly closed, the sound made before the lips come together is *u*. If these two sounds are made together or, more practically speaking, if the sound corresponding to the mid-point between these two is made, the sound that emerges is *o* (as in 'boat'). This new letter is called a compound vowel. Similarly, when *a* combines with *i*, it forms the compound vowel *e*. If you sound a prolonged a_3, and then raise the back of the tongue towards the *i* position, but stop before you get there, you should hear the *e* sound. It's a bit like the 'a' in 'hate' but not as open as we would pronounce this. If, after making the above sound for *e*, you relax the tongue back towards the *a* position but again stop before you get there, there is another sound formed as a compound between *a* and *e* which sounds like the 'ie' in 'die'. It is written *ai*.

In a similar way to that described above, if the mouth moves from the *a* (open-mouthed) position to the *o* (partially closed) position but stops half-way, there is a sound similar to 'ow' in 'brown'. This is written *au* in ITRANS.

These, then are the fourteen vowels but there are two final letters to be added to complete the group of sixteen, so-called *mAtRRikA*. They are not really part of the alphabet but act as modifications to a preceding vowel. (Note that, because of this, if they are sounded as letters in their own right, they assume an 'a' before rather than after.)

The first of these is called an *anusvAra*. It is written as *M* and causes the preceding vowel to be sounded through the nose. The precise nasal sound is determined by the consonant that follows it, in that it uses the mouth position corresponding to that for the consonant so that the effect is something like the nasal consonant (*anunAsika*) described below.

The other special letter, not really part of the alphabet, also modifies the sound of the preceding vowel, is written *H* and it has the effect of adding a brief, breathing out, 'unvoiced' sound after the vowel. It is as though there were a word beginning with 'h' immediately following and you start to sound it as soon as you finish the preceding letter (i.e. without changing the mouth position) but then realize your mistake and stop before the word itself starts to sound. It is called a *visarga*.

So, to recap, the 16 vowels, or *mAtRRikA*, are as follows: -

a A i I u U RRi RRI LLi LLI e o ai au aM aH

The first group of consonants (guttural)

The Sanskrit term for consonants is *vya~njana*, meaning a 'decoration' (of the basic vowel sound). Twenty-five of these are grouped in five sets of five 'underneath' the five basic vowels described above. They are formed by positioning the mouth (tongue or lips) in such a way as to 'stop' the sound of the vowel in some way. The first group uses the mouth position of the *a* sound for decorating. This all takes place at the back of the mouth where it becomes the throat – the 'guttural' position.

Strictly speaking it is not possible to pronounce a consonant on its own. It is in itself only a positioning of the mouth to 'stop' the sound made by a vowel. Accordingly, when speaking the alphabet, the sound of *a* is used by default after each letter. The first consonant of this group is written *k*, sounded (with *a*) 'ka' as in cat.

When talking about the letter on its own, the sound 'a' is automatically assumed after it, since it cannot be sounded on its own without a vowel. Clearly it could occur at the end of the word (as 'k' in 'rack' for example). In this case it would have an additional mark under the letter, called a 'halant', which means 'don't make any vowel sound after this'. This used to be written *k.h* – *.h* after any consonant in ITRANS means that it is followed by a halant and 'a' is not sounded after it. In fact, it is no longer necessary in ITRANS to do this – if the letter is written on its own, a halant is inserted automatically.

The second consonant in the guttural group is written *kh*. Its pronunciation is much like the preceding one but with the addition of a slight breathy sound caused by actually letting out some air immediately following the 'k' sound. It is often sounded as though it were 'k-h' in an imaginary word 'k-hat' but there is much too much emphasis in this – it is really more subtle. Consonants such as *k* are said to be 'with little breath' (*alpaprANa*) while ones like *kh* are 'with much breath' (*mahAprANa*).

The third in this group is written *g*, sounded 'g' as in gap (*alpaprANa*). The fourth is written *gh* and, like 'kh' is *mahAprANa* and sounds like 'gh' in doghouse.

The final consonant in this group is the first of the type mentioned briefly above – *anunAsika*, meaning that the sound is made through the nose. It is written ~*N*. There are four n-related sounds; hence the need for the tilde and capitalization. It has the sound of 'ng' made at the back of the throat and sounding through the nose, like 'sing' but with the ending further back in the throat like someone being strangled rather than singing!

The second group of consonants (palatal)

This second group forms the sounds in the back part of the mouth but not the throat. Based on the *i* vowel, these use the back of the tongue and the rear of the mouth; they are called 'palatal'. They follow the same pattern as the previous group (as do all five of these groups of consonants, you will be pleased to know!) in that the first and third members are *alpaprANa*, the second and fourth are *mahAprANa*, and the fifth is *anunAsika*. The first, then is written *ch* and is sounded like the 'cha' in chap but, whereas English pronounces this by using the *front* of the tongue near the *front* of the roof of the mouth, Sanskrit uses the *rear* parts.

The second character is written *Ch* (or *chh* in older versions). Since I have already said that the pattern of the first group is repeated in the others, you might guess that this is sounded pretty much like *ch* but with some added breath – and you would be right! Just remember not to make it too pronounced so that it comes out like 'ch-ha' and it should be fine.

The third is written *j* and pronounced more or less as would expect, like the 'ja' in 'jam' spoken as far back in the mouth as you can without injuring yourself. It uses minimum breath again as for all in this third 'row' of the main consonants. The fourth is written *jh* and you can work out now how it should sound – like 'j-ha' but not too much so.

The final letter in this group the second of the *anunAsika* characters (the 'n' type sounds made through the nose). It is written ~*n* and has a sort of 'ny' sound, as in canyon. However, whereas the latter is made by the front of the tongue at the front of the mouth, you have to try to make this sound with the back of the tongue at the rear of the mouth.

The third group of consonants (cerebral)

This third group has now moved the mouth position another step forward so that the tip of the tongue is used, pointing up to the roof of the mouth. To construct the main consonants, the tongue actually touches the roof. It is called the cerebral position. The first is written *T.* All of this third, (middle) group are written as capital letters to differentiate them from the fourth group. (In the Romanized transliteration, the letters have a dot beneath them.). *T* is pronounced as the 't' in tub but instead of having the tongue forward of the roof of the mouth, put it right up to the roof as you say it. That should have been spoken 'with only a small breath' as usual (*alpaprANa*). The second letter is the same but with more breath as you make the sound (*mahAprANa*), a bit like 'po-th-ole' (pothole). It is written *Th.*

The next is written *D* and pronounced like 'd' in dot but, as before, with the tip of the tongue right up in the roof of the mouth. The fourth letter sounds the same as the third but with more breath (e.g. go-dh-ead) and is written *Dh.* The last in the group is another 'na' sound but with the tongue in the roof of the mouth. Written, as you already know, *N.*

The fourth group of consonants (dental)

This group of consonants are sounded just behind the teeth and called, unsurprisingly, dental. The first is *t.* It is sounded just like our t, as in 'tip'. Then comes the equivalent letter, but with more breath (*mahAprANa*), *th*, as in 'butthead'. Next is *d* as in 'dog' and the breathy equivalent *dh*, as in 'redhead'. Finally, in this group, is the one sounded through the nose (*anunAsika*) *n*, as in ...er 'nose'.

The fifth group of consonants (labial)
And so, at last, the final group of the main consonants sounded at the lips and called labial. The first is *p* just like our p, as in 'put'. Then comes the corresponding breathy *ph*, as in uphill. Next is *b*, as in 'bad' and the *mahAprANa bh,* as in 'clubhouse'. And finally the *anunAsika* in this group is *m*, as in 'man'.

Table of basic consonants
The table of the five groups of consonants, with the corresponding vowel shown in Column 1 for reference, is as shown below: -

Guttural	*a*	*k*	*kh*	*g*	*gh*	*~N*
Palatal	*i*	*ch*	*Ch*	*j*	*jh*	*~n*
Cerebral	*RRi*	*T*	*Th*	*D*	*Dh*	*N*
Dental	*LLi*	*t*	*th*	*d*	*dh*	*n*
Labial	*u*	*p*	*ph*	*b*	*bh*	*m*

The semi-vowels
There are two small groups of letters left. The first of these is the group of four so-called 'semi-vowels'. They are formed by combining the four main vowels other than 'a' with 'a'. Thus, if you sound *i* and then immediately move to the *a* sound, what emerges sounds like 'ya' and this is the first semi-vowel or *antaHsthA*: – *y* as in 'yap'. If you sound *RRi* and move to *a*, you get *r* as in 'rap'. If you sound *LLi* and move to *a*, you get *l* as in 'lap'. Finally, if you sound *u* and move to *a*, you get *v* as in 'wag'. Note that Americans seem to prefer to ignore this logical derivation and pronounce it as 'va' in 'van'. Since it is somewhat illogical to write it as beginning with a 'v' while sounding it as a 'w', I suppose both sides of the Atlantic have a case.

The sibilants

Almost last of all, there are three sibilants or sss-sounds. (A sibilant is called *UShman* in Sanskrit.) These are in the palatal, cerebral and dental positions. (In theory there are also ones in the other two positions but these are so rare that they are usually ignored.). In the palatal position, there is *sh* sounded by making a shh sound in that mouth position; it comes out like the ending of a soft German 'ich' with the default *a* ending of course. The second, in the cerebral position, is *Sh* (or *shh* in older releases) made by sounding 'sha' with the tongue up to the roof of the mouth. Finally is the dental *s*, sounding like the normal 's' in 'sand'.

h

This leaves the last letter in the alphabet, *h*, sounding, as you would expect, as 'h' in 'hat'. It is sometimes considered to be another sibilant and is also called *UShman*, which literally means 'heated'.

The complete alphabet

The order of the alphabet, if you want to look up a word in the dictionary, is pretty much the order used here in introducing the letters. The 16 *mAtRRikA* are at the beginning, followed by the basic consonants – guttural, palatal, cerebral, dental and labial. Then come the 4 semi-vowels (*antaHsthA*) and the three sibilants and finally *h*.

Further study

As you will certainly have realized by now, in order to learn how to sound these correctly, you really need to listen to someone who knows. Since it is unlikely that you will be sufficiently interested to go into it this deeply, however, just follow the instructions and don't worry about how it feels. We are unused to making full use of our mouth and tongue in speaking and, since Sanskrit makes almost scientific use, we will find much of it peculiar and initially uncomfortable. If you want a more thorough introduction, with little in the way of expense or commitment, there is a truly excellent one available off the Internet. You can download this free of charge and the only cost is the subsequent printing. It is called 'A Practical Sanskrit

Introductory' and was produced by Charles Wikner. You can access it from: http://www.danam.co.uk/Sanskrit/Sanskrit%20Introductory/Sanskrit%20I ntroductory.html . As well as describing the alphabet in much more detail and teaching the Devanagari script, this introduces the grammar and some vocabulary. Finally, if you are really serious, an excellent book – '*devavANIpraveshikA* – An Introduction to the Sanskrit Language' (Ref. 144) may be purchased.

Conclusion

If you read through this a few times and refer to it when in doubt, you should be able to make a creditable attempt to pronounce any of the words in this book. Of course, such a brief introduction cannot give you any real idea of the language, which is extremely beautiful in more ways than one. Here is what the Vedic prayer, given in the Introduction, actually looks like in the original Sanskrit: -

असतामा सद्गमय ।   - *asatomA sadgamAyA* |
तमसोमा ज्योतिर्गमय ।   - *tamasomA jyotirgamAyA* |
मृत्योर्मा अमृतं गमय ॥   - *mRRityormA amRRitaMgamAyA* ||

Lead me from the unreal to the real,
Lead me from darkness into light,
Lead me from death to immortality.

BIBLIOGRAPHY

1. Consciousness in Advaita Vedanta. William M. Indich. Motilal Banarsidass Publishers, Delhi 1995. ISBN 81-208-1251-9.

2. Advaita Vedanta – A Philosophical Reconstruction. Eliot Deutsch. University of Hawaii Press, Honolulu 1973. ISBN 0-8248-0271-3.

3. The Chandogya Upanishad. Commentary by Swami Krishnananda. The Divine Life Society, Himalyas, India 1984. No ISBN.

4. The Mandukya Upanishad with Gaudapada's Karika and Shankara's Commentary. Translated by Swami Nikhilananda. Advaita Ashrama, Himalayas, India 1987. No ISBN.

5. The Ten Principal Upanishads. Put into English by Shree Purohit Swami and W. B. Yeats. Faber and Faber Limited, London 1970. ISBN 0-571-09363-9.

6. The Self and it's States. Andrew O. Fort. Motilal Banarsidass Publishers Pvt. Ltd., Delhi 1990. ISBN 81-208-0633-6.

7. The Brihadaranyaka Upanishad. Swami Krishnananda. The Divine Life Trust Society 1984. No ISBN.

8. Discourses on Mandukya Upanishad. Swami Chinmayananda. Central Chinmaya Mission Trust, Bombay, 1990. No ISBN.

9. Four Upanishads. Swami Paramananda. Sri Ramakrishna Math, Madras, 1974. ISBN 81-7120-233-0.

10. The Bhagavad Gita, with the Commentary of Sri Shankaracharya. Samata Books, Madras, 1977. No ISBN.

11. The Holy Geeta: Commentary by Swami Chinmayananda. Central Chinmaya Mission Trust, 1996. No ISBN.

12. The Bhagavad Gita: Commentary by Swami Chidbhavananda. Sri Ramakrishna Tapovanam, 1986. No ISBN.

13. Astavakra Samhita: Translation and Commentary by Swami Nityaswarupananda. Advaita Ashrama, 1990. No ISBN.

14. Astavakra Gita: Commentary by Swami Chinmayananda. Central Chinmaya Mission Trust, 1997. No ISBN.

15. Pancadasi of Sri Vidyaranya Swami. English Translation by Swami

Swahananda. Sri Ramakrishna Math, Madras, 1980. No ISBN.

16. Sri Shankaracharya's Bhaja Govindam. Swami Chinmayananda. Central Chinmaya Mission Trust, 1991. No ISBN.

17. Atmabodha, Knowledge of Self. Commentary by A. Parthasarathy. Vedanta Life Institute, Bombay, 1990. No ISBN.

18. Shankara's Crest-Jewel of Discrimination (Vivekachudamani). Translated by Swami Prabhavananda and Christopher Isherwood. Vedanta Press, 1978. ISBN 0-87481-038-8.

19. Introduction to Vedanta. Understanding the Fundamental Problem. Swami Dayananda. Vision Books, New Delhi, 1989. ISBN 81-7094-037-0.

20. Vedanta Treatise: The Eternities, A. Parthasarathy, 2004. ISBN 8187111577.

21. Brahma Sutra bhashya of Shankaracharya. Translated by Swami Gambhirananda. Advaita Ashrama, 1996. ISBN 81-7505-105-1.

22. The Gospel of Sri Ramakrishna, Abridged Edition. Translated into English with an Introduction by Swami Nikhilananda. Ramakrishna-Vivekananda Center, 1958. ISBN 0-911206-02-7.

23. The Essential Teachings of Hinduism. Edited by Kerry Brown. Arrow Books Limited, London, 1990. ISBN 0-09-978530-7.

24. Talks with Sri Ramana Maharshi. Sri Ramanashramam, Tiruvannamalai, 1994. No ISBN.

25. Maha Yoga of Bhagavan Sri Ramana. "Who". Sri Ramanashramam, Tiruvannamalai, 1984. No ISBN.

26. I am That. Sri Nisargadatta Maharaj. Chetana (P) Ltd., Bombay, 1981. ISBN 085655-406-5.

27. Pointers From Nisargadatta Maharaj. Ramesh S. Balsekar. Chetana (P) Ltd., Bombay, 1982. ISBN 81-85300-19-4.

28. Acceptance of What Is – a Book About Nothing. Wayne Liquorman. Advaita Fellowship, 2000. ISBN 0-929448-19-7.

29. Be Who You Are. Jean Klein. Element, 1989. ISBN 1-85230-103-1.

30. I Am. Jean Klein. Third Millennium Publications, 1989. ISBN 1-877769-19-3.

31. The Truth Is. Sri H. W. L. Poonja. Yudhishtara, 1995. No ISBN.

32. The Open Secret. Tony Parsons. The Connections, 1995. ISBN 0-9533032-0-9.

33. The Yoga Sutras of Patanjali. Translation and Commentary by Sri Swami Satchidananada. Integral Yoga Publications, 1990. ISBN 0-932040-38-1.

34. Vedanta Sutras of Narayana Guru. Swami Muni Narayana Prasad. D. K. Printworld (P) Ltd., New Delhi, 1997. ISBN 81-246-0085-6.

35. The Science of Enlightenment. Nitin Trasi. D. K. Printworld (P) Ltd., New Delhi, 1997. ISBN 81-246-0130-5.

36. Eternity Now, Francis Lucille, Non-Duality Press, 2008. ISBN 978-0955829086.

37. Clarity. Nathan Gill. GOB Publications, 2000. No ISBN.

38. Self Enquiry. Tri-Annual Review of the Ramana Maharshi Foundation, U.K. ISSN 1357-0935.

39. The Book. On the Taboo Against Knowing Who You Are. Alan Watts. Vintage Books, 1966. ISBN 0-679-72300-5.

40. The Wisdom of Insecurity. A Message for an Age of Anxiety. Alan Watts. Rider, 1994. ISBN 0-7126-9588-5.

41. What is Meditation? Osho. Element, 1995. ISBN 1-85230-726-9.

42. I Am That. Discourses on the Isa Upanishad. Bhagwan Shree Rajneesh. Rajneesh Foundation International, 1984. ISBN 0-88050-580-X.

43. Heartbeat of the Absolute. Commentaries on the Ishavasya Upanishad. Osho. Element, 1980. ISBN 1-85230-490-1.

44. The Mustard Seed. Discourses on the Sayings of Jesus from the Gospel According to Thomas. Osho. Element, 1975. ISBN 1-85230-498-7.

45. The Penguin Krishnamurti Reader. Edited by Mary Lutyens. Penguin Books Ltd., 1954, 1963, 1964. No ISBN.

46. Atmananda Tattwa Samhita. The Direct Approach to Truth as Expounded by Sri Atmananda. Compiled by K. Padmanabha Menon. Advaita Publishers, 1973. No ISBN.

47. Think. A Compelling Introduction to Philosophy. Simon Blackburn. Oxford University Press, 1999. ISBN 0-19-210024-6.

48. Confessions of a Philosopher. Bryan Magee. Weidenfeld & Nicholson, 1997. ISBN 0-297-81959-3.

49. Four Quartets. T. S. Eliot. Faber & Faber, 1944, 1979. ISBN 0-571-04994-X.

50. A Sanskrit English Dictionary. M. Monier-Williams. Motilal Banarsidass Publishers Private Limited, Delhi, 1899. ISBN 81-208-0065-6.

51. Comparative Philosophy. Original Live Recordings. Alan Watts. Electronic University. ISBN 1-882435-05-2.

52. A Guide for the Perplexed. E. F. Schumacher. Abacus, 1977. ISBN 0-349-13130-9.

53. Mechanism of Mind. Edward de Bono. Viking, 1969. ISBN 0-140-21445-3.

54. The Farther Reaches of Human Nature. Abr*aham* Maslow. Viking, 1971. ISBN 0-140-21645-6.

55. The Man Who Mistook His Wife for a Hat. Oliver Sacks. Picador, 1986. ISBN 0-330-29491-1.

56. dRRigdRRiShaya viveka. An inquiry into the nature of the seer and the seen. With Commentary by Swami Nikhilananda. Sri Ramakrishna Ashrama, Mysore, 1976. ISBN 0-902-47927-X.

57. Kena Upanishad. Swami Muni Narayana Prasad. D. K. Printworld (P) Ltd., New Delhi 1995. ISBN 81-246-0034-1.

58. Dispelling Illusion, Gaudapada's Alatashanti. Translated and Introduction Douglas A. Fox. State University of New York Press, 1993. ISBN 0-7914-1502-3.

59. The teaching of the Bhagavad Gita. Swami Dayananda. Vision Books Pvt. Ltd., 1989. ISBN 81-7094-032-X.

60. Atma Darshan (At the Ultimate). Sri Atmananda (Krishna Menon). Advaita Publishers, 1989. ISBN 0-914793-16-0.

61. Atma Nirvriti (Freedom and Felicity in the Self). Sri Atmananda (Krishna Menon). Advaita Publishers, 1989. ISBN 0-914793-05-5.

62. Chandogya Upanishad. Swami Swahananda. Sri Ramakrishna Math, Madras, 1980. No ISBN.

63. Sayings of Sri Ramakrishna – An Exhaustive Collection. Sri

Ramakrishna Math, Madras, 1987. No ISBN.

64. The Problems of Philosophy. Bertrand Russell. Oxford University Press, 1971. ISBN 0-19-888018-9.

65. Sight Unseen. Bryan Magee and Martin Milligan. Phoenix Paperback, 1995. ISBN 0-75380-503-0.

66. A History of the Mind. Nicholas Humphrey. Vintage Books, 1993. ISBN 0-09-922311-2.

67. No Mind I am the Self. David Godman. Bhanumathy Ramanadham Sri Rakshmana Ashram. No ISBN. (Out of Print)

68. Upadesha Sahasri. Sri Shankaracharya. Sri Ramakrishna Math, Mylapore, Madras, 1989. ISBN 81-7120-059-1.

69. Be As You Are. The Teachings of Sri Ramana Maharshi. Edited by David Godman. Arkana, 1985. ISBN 0-14-019062-7.

70. Silence of the Heart, Robert Adams, Acropolis Books, 1999. ISBN 1-889051-53-5.

71. How to Meet Yourself (and find true happiness), Dennis Waite, O Books, 2007. ISBN 1-84694-041-9.

72. Dialog 'The Boss', from Newsletter of the Ramana Maharshi Foundation UK, August 2002. No ISBN.

73. From an interview with *shraddhA*, given at a satsang in Lucknow, India, 26th August 1994, recorded at http://www.firehorse.com.au/philos/papaji/ .

74. Awakening to the Dream: The gift of lucid living, Leo Hartong, Trafford, 2001. ISBN 1-4120-0425-X.

75. Doing Nothing: Coming to the End of the Spiritual Search, Steven Harrison, Jeremy P. Tarcher/Putnam, 1997. ISBN 1-58542-172-3.

76. A Collection: Talks and essays of Swami Dayananda, Sri Gangadhareswar Trust, 1999. No ISBN.

77. Realization of the Absolute (The naiShkarmya siddhi of shrI sureshvara), translated by A. J. Alston, Shanti Sadan, 1959. ISBN 0-85424-021-7.

78. Spiritual Enlightenment: The Damndest Thing, Jed McKenna, Wisefool Press, 2002. ISBN 0-9714352-3-5.

79. A Tradition of Teachers: Shankara and the Jagadgurus Today. William

Cenkner, Motilal Banarsidass, 1983. ISBN 81-208-1763-x.

80. Enlightenment: The Path Through The Jungle, Dennis Waite, O Books, 2008. ISBN 978 1 84694 118 4.

81. Blueprints for Awakening, Premananda, Open Sky Press Ltd, 2008. ISBN 978-0-9555730-4-0.

82. Extract from a talk given in Amsterdam on 27th July 2002, recorded at http://www.theopensecret.com/.

83. As It is: The Open Secret to Living an Awakened Life, Inner Directions Foundation, ISBN 1878019104.

84. Day by Day With Bhagavan, A. Devararaja Mudaliar, Sri Ramanasramam, 2002. ISBN 8188018821. Electronically available from http://sriramanamaharshi.org/Allpub_demo.html.

85. Who Am I? (Nan Yar?): The Teachings of Bhagavan Sri Ramana Maharshi, Translation by Dr. T. M. P. Mahadevan, Sri Ramanashramam, 1982. No ISBN.

86. Ellam Ondre, Vijai R. Subramaniyam . Written in Tamil in the nineteenth century, translated by 'Who' as 'All is One' in 1950, and highly recommended by Ramana Maharshi. Downloaded from http://www.realization.org/.

87. DirectApproach E-Group, 14th Nov. 2002.

88. Absolute Consciousness. Bhagavan Ramana's Centenary of Enlightenment Publication as selected by Grace J. Mc Martin published by Ramana Maharshi Centre for Learning, Bangalore , second edition, 1997. ISBN : 81-85378-54-1.

89. 'Remarks on Enlightenment' by José le Roy , published in 'Noumenon' newsletter, Winter 1996, Vol. 2 Number 2, Noumenon Press, PO Box 1280, Wandsbeck, 3631 South Africa.

90. Quoted from an interview with Jan Kersschot, downloaded from the Internet, but contained, along with many others in the book 'Coming Home – An Invitation to Rediscover our True Nature', Inspiration, 2001. ISBN 9080250341.

91. 'Guru's Grace and Self-knowledge' by A. R. Natarajan from Jan. 99 Issue of Ramana Way.

92. Extracted from article:168067 of Elist soc.culture.indian,

Organization: Penn State University, Date: Tue, 1 Mar 1994, Dinesh
Agrawal.

93. The Power of Now: A Guide to Spiritual Enlightenment, Eckhart
Tolle, Hodder and Stoughton, 2001. ISBN 0 340 733500.

94. Dialogues with Swami Dayananda, Sri Gangadhareswar Trust, 1988.
No ISBN.

95. Back to the Truth, Dennis Waite, O Books, 2007, ISBN 1905047614.

96. Passionate Presence: Experiencing the Seven Qualities of Awakened
Awareness by Catherine Ingram (Gotham Books, Penguin/Putnam)
Copyright (c) Catherine Ingram, 2003.

97. Introduction to Vedanta, Dr. K. Sadananda, Advaitin Egroup Jan.
2007.

98. Notes on Spiritual Discourses of Shri Atmananda taken by Nitya
Tripta, 2nd Issue not yet published. Electronically available from
http://www.advaita.org.uk/.

99. vivekachUDAmaNi – Talks on 108 Selected Verses, Swami
Dayananda Saraswati, Sri Gangadharesvar Trust, 1997. No ISBN.

100. Eight upaniShad-s with the Commentary of shaMkarAchArya,
Volume 1, translated by swAmI gambhIrAnanda, Advaita Ashrama,
1957. ISBN 81-7505-016-0.

101. Mundakopanishad, Swami Chinmayananda, Central Chinmaya
Mission Trust, 1988. No ISBN.

102. Discourse on Kenopanishad, Swami Chinmayananda, Central
Chinmaya Mission Trust, 1952. No ISBN.

103. Kathopanishad, Swami Chinmayananda, Central Chinmaya Mission
Trust, 1994. No ISBN.

104. Discourse on Isavasya Upanishad, Swami Chinmayananda, Central
Chinmaya Mission Trust, 1980. No ISBN.

105. Bhagavad Gita, with the commentary of Shankaracharya, translated
by Swami Gambhirananda, Advaita Ashrama, sixth impression 2003.
ISBN 81-7505-041-1.

106. The Bhagavad Gita, Winthrop Sargeant, State University of New
York, 1994. ISBN 0-87395-830-6.

107. The Living Gita: A Commentary for Modern Readers, Sri Swami

Satchidananda, Integral Yoga Publications, 1988. ISBN 0-932040-27-6.

108. Vedanta Explained: Shankara's Commentary on the Brahma-sutras, V. H. Date, Munshiram Manoharlal Publishers Pvt. Ltd., 1973. No ISBN.

109. Not-so Total Recall, John McCrone, New Scientist 13th May 2003.

110. Insights Into Vedanta – Tattvabodha, Swami Sunirmalananda, Sri Ramakrishna Math, 2005. ISBN 81-7823-229-4.

111. The Brihadaranyaka Upanishad, with the Commentary of Shankaracharya, Translated by Swami Madhavananda, Advaita Ashrama, eleventh impression 2008, ISBN 81-7505-102-7.

112. Ten Upanishads of Four Vedas, Researched and Edited by Ram K. Piparaiya, Bharatiya Vidya Bhavan, 2003. ISBN 81-7276-298-4.

113. The Principal Upanishads, S. Radhakrishnan, HarperCollins Publishers India, 1994. ISBN 81-7223-124-5.

114. The Twelve Principal Upanishads Vol. 1, Dr. E. Röer, D. K. Printworld (P) Ltd., 1906. ISBN 81-246-0167-4.

115. Choice Upanishads, A. Parthasarathy, A. Parthasarathy, 2001. No ISBN.

116. Mandukya Upanishad (with Gaudapada's Karika), Translated and with notes based in Shankara's commentary by Swami Lokeswarananada, Ramakrishna Mission Institute of Culture, 1995. ISBN 81-85843-71-6.

117. The Heart of Awareness : A Translation of the Ashtavakra Gita, Thomas Byrom, Shambhala, 2001. ISBN 1570628971.

118. Atmabodha (Self Knowledge), Translated and commentary by Raphael, Aurea Vidya Foundation, Inc. 2003. ISBN 1-931406-06-5.

119. Methods of Knowledge according to Advaita Vedanta, Swami Satprakashananda, Advaita Ashrama, 1965. ISBN 81-7505-065-9.

120. I Am That: Discourses on the Isa Upanishad, Bhagwan Shree Rajneesh, Rajneesh Foundation International (Now Osho International Foundation), 1984. ISBN 0-88050-580X.

121. Self-Knowledge, Swami Dayananda Saraswati, Arsha Vidya Gurukulam, 2003. ISBN 0-9748000-0-7.

122. Living Reality: My Extraordinary Summer with "Sailor" Bob Adamson, James Braha, Hermetician Press, 2006. ISBN 0935895-10-8.

123. The Texture of Being, Roy Whenary, Lotus Harmony Publishing, 2002. ISBN 0-9543100-0-4.

124. The Teachers of One. Living Advaita. Conversations on the Nature of Non-duality, Paula Marvelly, Watkins Publishing, 2002. ISBN 1 84293 028 1.

125. The Wisdom of Balsekar, Edited by Alan Jacobs, Watkins Publishing, 2004. ISBN 1 84293 079 6.

126. A Natural Awakening: Realizing the True Self in Everyday Life, P. T. Mistlberger, TigerFyre Publishing, 2005. ISBN 0-9733419-0-4.

127. Awakening to The Natural State, John Wheeler, Non-Duality Press, 2004. ISBN 0-9547792-3-1.

128. Perfect Brilliant Stillness, David Carse, Non-Duality Press, 2005. ISBN 0954779282.

129. The TM Technique: An Introduction to Transcendental Meditation and the Teaching Method of Maharishi Mahesh Yogi, Peter Russell, Routledge & Kegan Paul, 1976. ISBN 0 7100 0068 5.

130. From the Upanishads, Ananda Wood, Full Circle Publishing Ltd, 2003. ISBN 8176210005. Electronically available from www.advaita.org.uk.

131. Interpreting the Upanishads, Ananda Wood, Full Circle Publishing Ltd., 2003. ISBN 8176210013. Electronically available from www.advaita.org.uk.

132. Astavakra Gita, Translation by John Richards, Electronically available from http://www.realization.org/home.htm.

133. The Collected Works of Ramana Maharshi, edited by Arthur Osborne, Weiser Books, 1997. ISBN 0877289077.

134. The Way of the Bird – Commentaries on the Teaching of Sri Ranjit Maharaj, Andrew Vernon, 2003. Electronically available from http://www.wayofthebird.com/.

135. Nothing Personal: Seeing Beyond the Illusion of a Separate Self, Nirmala, Endless Satsang Press, 2001. No ISBN. Electronically

Available from http://www.enlightenedbeings.com/nirmala.html.

136. Standing as Awareness: The Direct Path, Greg Goode, Non-Duality Press, 2009. ISBN 978-0956309150.

137. The Transparency of Things: Contemplating the Nature of Experience, Rupert Spira, Non-Duality Press, 2008. ISBN 978-0955829055.

138. The Concise Yoga Vasistha, Swami Venkatesananda, State University of New York Press, 1984. ISBN 978-0873959544.

139. Eight upaniShad-s with the Commentary of shaMkarAchArya, Volume 2, translated by swAmI gambhIrAnanda, Advaita Ashrama, 1957. ISBN 81-7505-017-9.

140. An Advaita Vedanta Perspective on Language, John Grimes, Sri Satguru Publications, 1991. ISBN 81-7030-250-1.

141. Critique of Pure Reason, Immanuel Kant, Translated by Norman Kemp Smith, Bedford Books, 1969. ISBN 978-0312450106.

142. The Will to Power – Is 'Free Will' All in Your Head?, Christof Koch, Scientific American Mind, November 2009.

143. An Essential Guide to Sanskrit (For Spiritual Seekers), Dennis Waite, Black & White, 2005. ISBN 818932000-9.

144. *devavANIpraveshikA* – An Introduction to the Sanskrit Language, Robert P. Goldman and Sally J. Sutherland, Center for South and Southeast Asia Studies, University of California, Berkeley, 1987. No ISBN.

INDEX

Note: Page Number in **bold** = Main Entry; Page Number in *italic* = Definition.

75, 82, 95, 141, 236

chitta, 103

Christianity, 82

Chuang Tzu, 41

Churchill, Winston, 51

cinema, crying at - indicating
attachment, 104

clouds
metaphor for activity, 206
metaphor for good and evil, 79
metaphor for ignorance, 247

coffee making, no 'doing', 128

coin attached to forehead, story of,
263

Coleridge Samuel Taylor, 42

company, good, **136**

concentration, 98

confusion of levels (of reality), 171

conscience, 79, 224

Consciousness, 33, 152, **224**, **241**
original meaning, *224*

contradiction in Advaita, **221**

creation, 175, **186**

creativity, 42

cycling uphill, example of not
'doing', 204

dama, *98*

dancer - metphor for *Ishvara*, 87

day and night - metaphor for
appearance and reality, 265

Dayananda, Swami, 56, 63, 107,
109, 120, 131, 192

day-dreaming, 43, 69

de Bono, Edward, 38

death, **236**, 242

decision making, 45

deep sleep state, 225, **232**
ego disappears, 248

depression, 195

Descartes, René, 26, 160, 228, 245

desire, **61**, 200
caused by a perceived lack, 63
insatiable, 200

destiny, 105

detachment, 98

determinism, **207**
fifty-mile painting metaphor,
218
vs fatalism, 209

dharma, 83, **107**

Dick, Philip K., 164

ding an sich, 164

Direct Path, **279**

disappointment, 199

disciplines required for Self-
realisation, 94

discrimination, 66, 98, **132**

Disraeli, Benjamin, 17

dissatisfaction, 195

doer, no such thing, 222

doing - you are not the doer, 128

dream - metaphor for appearance
vs reality, 150

dream and waking state similarity,
229

dream lion, 272

dream of marriage - metaphor for

BOOKS

O is a symbol of the world, of oneness and unity. In different cultures it also means the "eye," symbolizing knowledge and insight. We aim to publish books that are accessible, constructive and that challenge accepted opinion, both that of academia and the "moral majority."

Our books are available in all good English language bookstores worldwide. If you don't see the book on the shelves ask the bookstore to order it for you, quoting the ISBN number and title. Alternatively you can order online (all major online retail sites carry our titles) or contact the distributor in the relevant country, listed on the copyright page.

See our website **www.o-books.net** for a full list of over 500 titles, growing by 100 a year.

And tune in to myspiritradio.com for our book review radio show, hosted by June-Elleni Laine, where you can listen to the authors discussing their books.

MySpiritRadio